LEGAL RESEARCH

IN A NUTSHELL

EIGHTH EDITION

By

MORRIS L. COHEN

Librarian (Retired) and Emeritus Professor of Law
Yale Law School

KENT C. OLSON

Director of Reference, Research and Instruction
University of Virginia Law Library

Mat #40154093

Nutshell Series, In a Nutshell, the Nutshell Logo and West Group are trademarks registered in the U.S. Patent and Trademark Office.

COPYRIGHT © 1968, 1971, 1978, 1985, 1992, 1996 WEST PUBLISHING CO.
COPYRIGHT © 2000 By West, a Thomson business

> 610 Opperman Drive
> P.O. Box 64526
> St. Paul, MN 55164–0526
> 1–800–328–9352

Printed in the United States of America

ISBN 0–314–14707–1

PREFACE

Legal Research in a Nutshell has seen considerable change since it was first published in 1968. Each edition has focused increasingly on electronic methods of research. Lexis and Westlaw were first introduced in the 1978 edition, followed by CD-ROM in 1992. The 1996 edition added the first references to the Internet, although web addresses were not included until 2000. This eighth edition finds a wide variety of Internet resources integrated into a discussion once dominated by books and commercial databases.

Yet in some respects the *Nutshell* of 1968 is not so distant. We continue to devote considerable attention to printed, or "traditional," legal resources. While electronic methods are essential in today's legal research, they have not fully supplanted the sophisticated editorial tools that form the basis of our legal literature. Many online sources are based on printed works and thus incorporate their structure and logic. An understanding of these works is required for effective research, whether in print or electronic media. Successful research also requires an appreciation for the computer's ability to execute searches which are impossible with print materials, and for its power to retrieve information unavailable on a local library's shelves. An integrated approach to print and electronic sources pervades most of this text and shapes the actual practice of modern legal research.

We present legal materials in the order in which they are often consulted by beginning researchers. The first five chapters provide an introductory overview and cover essential secondary and primary sources in American law. General background sources such as legal encyclopedias

and law review articles are discussed at the outset, just as they are usually the first sources consulted in research. Case law sources and research methods are discussed next, in keeping with the central place of court decisions in the American legal system and in legal education, followed by a discussion of constitutional and statutory law. The next five chapters cover sources such as legislative history, administrative regulations, court rules, looseleaf services, and directories. While these issues are somewhat more specialized than the basic case law and statutory sources, they are no less important in many research situations. The final two chapters provide a brief introduction to research in international and foreign law. These topics may be beyond the scope of many introductory courses in legal research, but we feel that no consideration of legal resources is quite complete without recognizing the place of the United States in a larger community. Our discussion of international and foreign law resources reflects their increased role in practice and in scholarship.

In addition to printed resources and numerous Westlaw and LexisNexis databases, we discuss a wide range of government and commercial Internet sites. The Internet is notoriously fluid, of course, and yesterday's valuable site may be today's dead link. All addresses listed were still valid as of May 2003, but we are also maintaining a regularly updated set of links online <www.law.virginia.edu/nutshell>. This should cut down both on frustration caused by obsolete references and on the time wasted in carefully typing lengthy URLs.

This book is designed to serve both as a reference work and as a practical teaching tool, for use by individuals or in legal research courses. In either case, simply reading its text will not make you an effective researcher. Skill in legal research can only be achieved by combining knowledge

with experience. Reading in the *Nutshell* should be accompanied by practice. Ruth McKinney's *Legal Research: A Practical Guide and Self-Instructional Workbook* (4th ed. 2003) can be used as a companion volume to this work and contains extensive cross-references to relevant sections of Legal Research in a Nutshell.

The authors wish to thank law library colleagues at Yale and the University of Virginia for supporting the preparation of this edition. We owe a particular debt of gratitude to Elizabeth Lambert, reference librarian at Harvard Law School, who assisted us throughout the composition and editing process. Her keen eye and unflagging enthusiasm have been essential in making this a Nutshell that we hope is more durable and at the same time easier to crack.

Morris L. Cohen
Kent C. Olson

New Haven, Connecticut
Charlottesville, Virginia
May 2003

TABLE OF CONTENTS

CHAPTER 5. CONSTITUTIONS AND STATUTES ... 138

CHAPTER 6. LEGISLATIVE INFORMATION 183

CHAPTER 1
THE RESEARCH PROCESS

■   ■   ■   ■   ■   ■   ■   ■   ■   ■

§1-1. INTRODUCTION

Legal research is an essential component of the practice of law. It is the process of identifying the law that governs an activity and finding materials that explain or analyze that law. These resources give lawyers the knowledge with which to provide accurate and insightful advice, to draft effective documents, or to defend their clients' rights in court. Ineffective research wastes time, and inaccurate research leads to malpractice.

Determining what law applies to a particular situation is a skill requiring expertise in legal analysis. Lawyers must be able to analyze factual situations, determine the relevant fields of legal doctrine, and apply rules developed by courts, legislatures, and administrative agencies. Finding these rules is a skill requiring expertise in legal research, or the effective use of the law library's extensive array of online and printed resources. Successful research provides the information and knowledge necessary for confidence in one's legal analysis.

Legal research involves the use of a variety of resources, some created by lawmaking bodies such as courts and leg-islatures, and others by scholars and practicing lawyers. Legal research demands an understanding of which resources to consult in each situation. Experienced researchers know which sources are authoritative or useful for what purposes, and how to use these sources most effectively. Versatility and flexibility are needed, as no single approach can work every time.

§1-2. THE SOURCES OF THE LAW

The law consists of those recorded rules that society will enforce and the procedures by which they implemented. These rules and procedures are created in various ways. Statutes are enacted by elected representatives, for exam-

ple, while common law doctrines are shaped over the course of many years in court decisions. These are just two of many sources of the law, but the distinction between statutory and common law is one of several dichotomies and classifications that characterize the legal system.

The law has numerous sources, from the United States Constitution to the pronouncements of municipal agencies. Both the federal government and the states have lawmaking powers, and in each case three branches —legislative, executive, and judicial—share in this responsibility. As the elected voice of the citizens, the legislature raises and spends money, defines crimes, regulates commerce, and generally determines public policy by enacting statutes. Some of these statutes are broadly worded statements of public policy, while others regulate activity in minute detail.

The executive branch is charged with enforcing the law, but in doing so it too creates legally binding rules. The president and most governors can issue executive orders, and administrative agencies provide detailed regulations governing activity within their areas of expertise. Agencies also act in a "quasi-judicial" capacity by conducting hearings and issuing decisions to resolve particular disputes. These *administrative law* sources are less familiar to law students and the public than statutes and court decisions, but they may be just as important in determining legal rights and responsibilities. Attorneys in heavily regulated areas such as environmental law or telecommunications may work more closely with agency pronouncements than with congressional enactments.

The judicial branch plays a complex role in this system. Judges apply the language of constitutions and statutes to court cases, often involving circumstances that could not have been foreseen when the laws were enacted. In most

instances, these judicial interpretations become as important as the text of the provisions they interpret. The courts have determined, for example, that sexual harassment is a form of employment discrimination under the Civil Rights Act of 1964 even though those words never appear in the statute. Through the power of *judicial review,* asserted by Chief Justice Marshall in *Marbury v. Madison,* the courts also determine the constitutionality of acts of the legislative and executive branches.

Judges also create and shape the *common law.* In a common law system such as ours, the law is expressed in an evolving body of doctrine determined by judges in specific cases, rather than in a group of prescribed abstract principles. As established rules are tested and adapted to meet new situations, the common law grows and changes over time.

An essential element of the common law is the doctrine of precedent, or *stare decisis* ("let the decision stand"). Under this doctrine, courts are bound to follow earlier decisions. These provide guidance to later courts faced with similar cases, and aid in preventing further disputes. People can study earlier cases, evaluate the legal impact of planned conduct, and modify their behavior to conform to existing rules. Although the law changes with time, precedent is designed to provide both fairness and stability. It is the importance of judicial decisions as precedent that gives them such a vital place in American legal research.

The first year law school curriculum sorts legal issues another way, into distinct areas of doctrine such as contract, tort, and property. In doing so, it provides law students with a framework for analyzing legal situations and applying a particular body of rules. Real life does not divide so neatly into issues of contract or tort, but legal materials generally follow this paradigm. A lawyer with a

case involving injury from a defective product, for example, may need to research breach of warranty issues in texts and articles on contracts as well as strict liability and negligence issues in the tort literature.

Other distinctions that pervade legal thinking include *civil* and *criminal law, substance* and *procedure,* and *state* and *federal jurisdiction.* Law students must learn how legal issues fit into these dichotomies, not only to solve problems but to know where to look for answers. It is necessary, however, to learn how to classify a question without pigeonholing the situation too narrowly. Analysis within a particular doctrinal area can clarify a specific issue, but most situations contain issues from a number of areas. A lawyer who does thorough research on causation issues but forgets about the statute of limitations or service of process is a losing lawyer.

§1-3. THE FORMS OF LEGAL INFORMATION

Effective legal research requires more than knowledge of the nature of the legal system. An understanding of the ways in which legal information is disseminated is also needed. Several characteristics have affected the research process. Laws are published chronologically, requiring tools to provide access by subject. Legal literature comprises both official, primary statements of the law and an extensive body of unofficial secondary writings. Information is accessible both in print and electronically, creating a wide range of choices in research.

A. ACCESS TO CHRONOLOGICAL PUBLICATIONS

The legal system is created over the course of time, and the law in force today is a combination of old and new enactments and decisions. The United States Constitution has been in force for more than 200 years, and many judi-

cial doctrines can be traced back even farther. Other laws are just days or weeks old, as legislatures, courts, and executive agencies address issues of current concern.

These laws have been published as they were issued, whether in volumes of legislative acts or court reports, or through electronic dissemination. They retain their force and effect until they are expressly repealed or overruled. To determine the law that governs a particular situation, the researcher may need access to all of these sources, no matter how old or how new they may be.

This has led to the creation of a complex collection of resources designed to provide topical access to this vast body of material. Today the most widely used approach is keyword searching in databases containing the full text of thousands of court decisions or other documents. More traditional means of access to court opinions include digests classifying summaries of points from cases; texts and reference works summarizing and comparing similar cases; and citators allowing researchers to trace doctrines forward in time. For access to statutes and regulations, laws in force are arranged by subject in codes which are accessible by extensive indexes. Mastering these various means of access to the law is a necessary part of any legal research.

It is just as important for lawyers and others interested in the legal system to keep up with new developments, and an extensive body of resources exists to provide current information. New statutes, regulations, and court decisions are issued by the government and by commercial publishers, both in print and through electronic means. Newsletters, looseleaf services and websites provide notice of and analyze these new developments. In addition, the codes and texts lawyers use are updated regularly to reflect changes. One of the most common forms of updating print publications is the *pocket part,* a supplement

which fits inside the back cover of a bound volume. Many publications are issued in looseleaf binders so that they can be updated with supplementary inserts or replacement pages. Electronic updating is even faster and more efficient, as new documents can be added to a database within minutes of their release.

B. Primary and Secondary Sources

Legal sources differ in the relative weight they are accorded. Some are binding authority; some are only persuasive in varying degrees; and some are useful only as tools for finding other material. Each source must be used with a sense of its place in the hierarchy of authority. A decision from one's state supreme court has more authority than a scholarly article, but an influential article may have more persuasive force than rulings of courts in other jurisdictions.

The most important distinction is between *primary* and *secondary sources.* Primary sources are the official pronouncements of the governmental lawmakers: the court decisions, statutes, and regulations that form the basis of the legal doctrine. Not all primary sources have the same force for all purposes. A decision from a state supreme court is mandatory authority in its jurisdiction and must be followed by the lower state courts. A state statute also must be followed within the state. Other primary sources are only persuasive authority; a court in one state may be influenced by decisions in other states faced with similar issues, but it is free to make up its own mind. A statute or regulation from one state is not even persuasive authority in another state.

Works which are not themselves the law, but which discuss or analyze legal doctrine, are considered secondary sources. These include treatises, hornbooks, restatements, and practice manuals. Much of the most influential legal

writing is found in the academic journals known as *law reviews*. Secondary sources serve a number of important functions in legal research. Scholarly commentaries can have a persuasive influence on the law-making process by pointing out flaws in current legal doctrine or suggesting solutions. More often, they serve to clarify the sometimes bewildering array of statutes and court decisions, or provide current awareness about developing legal doctrines. Finally, their footnotes provide extensive references to primary sources and to other secondary material.

Some materials, such as digests or citators, are simply finding tools and have no secondary authority at all. Their purpose is not to persuade but to facilitate access to other sources, which must be examined to determine their applicability to a particular situation.

c. Print and Electronic Resources

Most of the resources to be discussed in this text first appeared in printed form, and developed as print publications over several decades or even centuries. Detailed editorial systems such as digests, citators, and annotated codes were created to make sense of the jumble of primary sources. In recent years, of course, more and more material has become available electronically. The computer has not completely replaced the book, however, and the astute researcher knows how to take advantage of both media.

Electronic research has significantly affected the process of legal research. The computer can integrate a variety of tasks that are conducted with separate print sources, such as finding cases, checking the current validity of their holdings, and tracking down secondary commentary. The ability to search the full text of documents for specific combinations of words has freed researchers from relying solely on the choices of editors who create indexes and digests. Each

research situation presents a unique set of factual and legal issues, and the computer makes it possible to find documents which address this specific confluence of issues.

Yet editors have hardly been put out of work. Researchers forced to work only with an uncontrolled mass of electronic data can quickly find themselves drowning in unsorted information. Tools such as digests and indexes continue to provide the invaluable service of sorting material by subject and presenting it in a comprehensible fashion.

Computerized research has also blurred the distinctions among different types of information and broadened the scope of legal inquiry. Research in case law, for example, was traditionally a process quite distinct from research in secondary commentary or social sciences. Using electronic databases, it is much more convenient and natural to switch from one source to another and back again, bringing to legal research more empirical experience and a wider range of scholarly commentary. Hypertext links between documents make it possible to pursue various leads and ideas as they arise, rather than following one linear research path.

Two major commercial database systems, LexisNexis and Westlaw, are widely used in law schools and in legal practice as comprehensive legal research tools. Originally designed for access through proprietary software, both of these systems are now used primarily through the World Wide Web (<www.lexis.com> and <www.westlaw.com>). These websites, however, are available only to subscribers and other paying customers. Law students generally have access through their school's subscriptions, but for other researchers these can be expensive tools. (Much, but not all, of the information on lexis.com is available to university faculty and students through LexisNexis Academic <web.lexis-nexis.com/universe/>.)

A growing number of other commercial online research systems provide lower-cost alternatives to LexisNexis and Westlaw for access to primary sources. These systems generally provide reliable access to case law and statutes, but offer a smaller range of secondary sources and other features. Some of these, such as Loislaw <www.loislaw.com> and VersusLaw <www.versuslaw.com>, are available free to law students.

Free Internet sites can also be valuable sources of legal information. Some provide access to statutes and recent case law, but the Internet is more important as a source of legislative documents and administrative agency materials. It also provides an invaluable means of linking scholars and researchers through websites, discussion groups, and electronic mail.

§1-4. LEGAL LANGUAGE

One of the tasks facing law students is mastering a new way of speaking and writing. The law has developed its own means of expression over the centuries. Latin words and phrases are still prevalent, from the familiar writs of *certiorari* or *habeas corpus* to doctrines such as *res ipsa loquitur,* and even everyday words such as *instrument* or *intent* may have specialized meanings in legal documents.

A good law dictionary is needed to understand the language of the law. The leading work, *Black's Law Dictionary* (7th ed. 1999), edited by Bryan A. Garner, provides definitions for nearly 25,000 terms, and includes pronunciations and more than 2,000 quotations from scholarly works. It can be used to find new legal terminology and to define older terms found in historical documents. Black's is also available in a somewhat shorter abridged edition (2000), and a considerably smaller pocket edition (2d ed. 2001), and it can also be searched on Westlaw.

Some lawyers continue to use *Ballentine's Law Dictionary* (3d ed. 1969), which is also available online through LexisNexis. *Ballentine's* was once the major competitor to *Black's*, but it is now considerably out of date and lacks many modern legal terms and usages. Several other, shorter dictionaries can also be found in law libraries and bookstores. Among the best are Steven H. Gifis, *Law Dictionary* (4th ed. 1996), and Daniel Oran, *Oran's Dictionary of the Law* (3d ed. 2000). *Merriam-Webster's Dictionary of Law* (1996) is available both in print and as a free Internet resource <dictionary.lp.findlaw.com>.

Bryan A. Garner, editor of *Black's Law Dictionary,* is also author of *A Dictionary of Modern Legal Usage* (2d ed. 1995), which focuses on the way words are used in legal contexts. It is an entertaining guide to legal language's complexities and nuances, with definitions and essays providing articulate advocacy for clear and simple writing, and is available on LexisNexis. *Mellinkoff's Dictionary of Legal Usage* (1992) is a complementary work providing examples of usage and distinctions among related terms.

A variety of other language reference works exist. William C. Burton, *Burton's Legal Thesaurus* (3d ed. 1998) helps writers choose correct terms, and can aid researchers in identifying and choosing words when searching in indexes or preparing online searches. Fred R. Shapiro, *Oxford Dictionary of American Legal Quotations* (1993) is the most scholarly of several sources providing access to the most memorable uses of legal language. It is arranged topically, with precise citations to original sources and indexes by keyword and author.

§1-5. LEGAL CITATIONS

A second hurdle in understanding legal literature is understanding the telegraphic citation form used in most sources. Before reading *Tarasoff v. Regents of the University of*

California, a researcher must be able to decipher "551 P.2d 334 (Cal. 1976)" and understand that "551" is the volume number, "334" the page number, and "P.2d." the abbreviation for the Pacific Reporter, Second Series, a source for California Supreme Court opinions. This form may seem obscure at first, but in a very succinct manner it provides the information necessary to find the source and to recognize the scope of its precedential value.

This citation form is centuries old, but the standard guide to its present use is *The Bluebook: A Uniform System of Citation* (17th ed. 2000), published by the Harvard Law Review Association. The Bluebook establishes rules both for proper abbreviations and usage of signals such as "cf." and "But see." A few journals follow the somewhat simpler rules in the *University of Chicago Manual of Legal Citation* (1989), known as the *Maroonbook.* The Association of Legal Writing Directors' *ALWD Citation Manual* (2d ed. 2003) is used in numerous law schools and by several journals as a more straightforward and easier-to-learn alternative to the *Bluebook.* Cornell Law School's Legal Information Institute publishes an online *Introduction to Basic Legal Citation* <www.law.cornell.edu/citation/>, a handy, concise guide that incorporates both *Bluebook* and *ALWD* rules.

Recent years have seen a trend towards citations to legal authorities that do not depend on reference to a particular volume and page number, and that thus can be used whether documents are retrieved in printed volumes, through subscription databases, or from free Internet sites. A *public domain citation* system assigns official numbers to documents such as court decisions sequentially as they are issued, and also numbers each paragraph to allow references to specific portions of the text. This approach has been endorsed by the American Bar Association, and public domain citations are now required by the *Bluebook.* Only a few jurisdictions, however, have adopted rules requiring

paragraph numbers or other public domain citation features. The American Association of Law Libraries (AALL) has issued a *Universal Citation Guide* (1999) providing rules and examples of these formats. An AALL website <www.aallnet.org/committee/citation/> provides access to the guide and updated information.

No matter what citation rules are followed, part of the puzzle is simply deciphering the abbreviations used. Reference sources such as *Black's Law Dictionary* and the *Bluebook* contain tables listing the major abbreviations found in legal literature, but these are hardly comprehensive. Cases and law review articles contain numerous abbreviations and citations that are cryptic even to experienced researchers. Two specialized abbreviations sources, Mary Miles Prince, *Bieber's Dictionary of Legal Abbreviations* (5th ed. 2001) and Donald Raistrick, *Index to Legal Citations and Abbreviations* (2d ed. 1993) provide extensive coverage of both common and obscure abbreviations. *Bieber's Dictionary* is also available electronically on LexisNexis.

§1-6. Beginning A Research Project

Often the hardest part of the research process is finding the first piece of relevant information. Once one document is found, it usually can lead to a number of other sources. Cases cite earlier cases as authority; a statute's notes provide useful leads to decisions, legislative history documents, and secondary sources; and law review articles cite a wide variety of sources. Finding the first piece of the puzzle, though, can be a challenge.

Where does a researcher begin when working on a new problem? To some extent, this is a matter of personal preference and familiarity with particular tools. It makes sense to start with material which you can use most effectively. There are, however, some guidelines that can make for better choices.

Before looking anywhere, step back and study the problem carefully. If possible, determine whether the jurisdictional focus is federal or state. Be sure you understand the terms in which the problem is stated; if not, consult a good dictionary or other reference source. Formulate tentative issues, but be prepared to revise your statement of the issues as research progresses and you learn more about the legal background.

It is generally best to begin research by going to a trustworthy secondary source–a legal treatise or a law review article. The mass of primary sources retrieved by keyword searching can be overwhelming, and using a subject index or digest to find cases or statutes on point is often frustrating. Primary sources can be confusing, ambiguously worded documents. Access to secondary materials, on the other hand, is usually easier and more straightforward. These materials try to explain and analyze the law. They summarize the basic rules and the leading primary sources and place them in context, allowing the researcher to select the most promising primary sources to pursue.

The choice of the appropriate starting point should be influenced by the nature of the problem. When researching a new or developing area of law, start by looking for a recent periodical article. A law review article can provide an overview of the field, references to important cases and statutes, and a relatively current perspective. Articles from more than six hundred journals are available in online full-text databases, and the periodical indexes are among the easiest tools for subject access to legal literature.

When researching an issue that fits within a traditional area of legal doctrine, begin by consulting a subject treatise or hornbook in the area. A good treatise explains the major issues and terminology, and provides a context in which

related matters are raised or considered. The names of some of the most famous treatises, such as *Corbin on Contracts* or Wright & Miller's *Federal Practice and Procedure,* are familiar to any law student. Treatises in other areas can be found by using a law library's online catalog or asking a reference librarian.

If no treatise is available, a legal encyclopedia such as *American Jurisprudence 2d* or *Corpus Juris Secundum* can be a useful first step. These works attempt to cover the entire field of legal doctrine, so their focus is rather diffuse. They do, however, outline the basic rules in each area and provide extensive references to court decisions.

There are times when the first research step will be the major case-finding tools to be discussed in this book, such as digests and annotations. These tools are specifically designed to gather together cases with similar facts or issues, and they can be great resources for finding relevant court decisions. Because the appropriate place to look is not always obvious, however, it is often easier to use digests or annotations once a few cases have been found by other means. These cases will then provide easy leads into the digest system or annotated reports.

When it is apparent that the issue to be researched is statutory in nature, it may be most efficient to begin with an annotated code. This is particularly the case in areas with substantial governmental regulation, such as antitrust, banking, labor, or taxation. The statutory language may not provide a clear overview of the field, but an annotated code leads directly to most of the other relevant primary sources and may provide references to secondary sources as well. Looseleaf services often combine the statutory text with editorial explanatory notes.

Resources such as treatises and encyclopedias are usually easier to understand in print, as it is simpler to scan headings, get an overview of an area, and learn about related issues. At times, though, the computer databases of LexisNexis or Westlaw may be more effective starting points. If you are generally familiar with an area of law and are researching a narrow question or a particular combination of issues, an online search may be the best way to focus your research. It is still necessary to choose an appropriate database from the array of cases, statutes, law review articles, and other resources.

Free Internet sites are not comprehensive, but they can provide places to start if more thorough resources are not readily available. Several websites provide directories organizing legal material by jurisdiction and topic. Among the most popular are the commercial site FindLaw <www.findlaw.com> and Cornell Law School's Legal Information Institute <www.law.cornell.edu>. These sites provide links to primary sources, directories, journals, and numerous other sources. Google <www.google.com> and other Internet search engines can also find relevant sites, although it may be difficult to evaluate results and weed out superficial or misleading information. Search engines limited to legal sites, such as FindLaw's LawCrawler <lawcrawler.findlaw.com>, may yield more focused results.

Finally, sometimes the first step of research does not involve using either books or databases. Instead it may be more efficient to send an e-mail or make a telephone call. Government agencies and professional associations are staffed with experts who can answer questions, provide invaluable references, or send essential documents. It's usually best to do one's homework first, and to make sure that the information isn't posted on the agency's or organi-

zation's website. Numerous directories are available to identify contact persons at legislative offices, administrative agencies, and nongovernmental organizations.

These various options are the sorts of choices one must make in any research process. It is important to remember that professional help may be available to guide you in the choice of the first resource. Law librarians are trained to provide just this sort of assistance. While they are not permitted to interpret the law or provide legal advice to library users, librarians can assist patrons in determining how best to track down the relevant sources.

§1-7. COMPLETING A RESEARCH PROJECT

Knowing when to stop researching can be just as difficult as knowing where to begin. To every research situation, however, comes a time when it is necessary to synthesize the information found and produce the required memorandum, brief, or opinion letter.

Sometimes the limits to research are set by the nature of the project. An assignment may be limited to a specified number of hours or a certain amount of money. If so, the ability to find information quickly and accurately is essential.

A more difficult decision must be made when there is no clear limit to the amount of research to be done. In such cases you must do enough research to be confident that your work is based on information that is complete and accurate. The surest way to achieve this confidence is to try several different approaches to the research problem. If a review of the secondary literature, a digest search, and online queries produce different conclusions, more research is necessary. When these various approaches lead

to the same primary sources and a single conclusion, chances are better that a key piece of information has not eluded you.

No matter what criteria are used in determining when to stop researching, it is essential to verify that sources to be relied upon are still in force and "good law." No research is complete if the latest supplements haven't been checked, current-awareness sources haven't been searched for new developments, and the status of cases to be relied upon hasn't been determined.

Confidence in your research results is more likely when you have confidence generally in your research skills. Familiarity with legal resources and experience in their use will produce the assurance that your research is complete and accurate.

§1-8. Conclusion

As we will see in the following chapters, the law has a voluminous literature and a wide range of highly developed research tools. Many of these are unfamiliar even to experienced scholars in other disciplines. Learning to use these tools requires patience and effort, but in time you should become aware of the different functions they serve, their strengths and weaknesses, and the ways they fit together.

Too many practitioners of legal research understand little about the tools they use. As a result, they spin their wheels and overlook aids and shortcuts designed to help them. If you learn how legal resources work as you encounter them, and hone your skills through practice, this mastery will save you valuable time and effort.

CHAPTER 2
BACKGROUND AND ANALYSIS

■ ■ ■ ■ ■ ■ ■ ■ ■ ■

§ 2-1. INTRODUCTION

While it is the primary sources of law—the constitutional provisions, legislative enactments, and judicial decisions—that determine legal rights and govern procedures, these primary sources can be notoriously difficult places in which to find answers. Certainly they are not the easiest places to begin a research project. The prudent researcher looks first for an explanation and analysis of the governing legal doctrines.

One of the most important purposes of the sources discussed in this chapter is to set forth and analyze established legal doctrine, explaining its nuances and leading researchers to understand how a problem fits into this doctrinal structure. They provide the context necessary to see how a particular issue relates to other concerns. They can also serve as an introduction to a new area of law or refresh a reader's recollection of a familiar area.

Some secondary sources, particularly treatises and law review articles, contain influential insights that can shape law reform or stimulate new legislation. Others are more practical, providing a straightforward overview of the law without advocating changes. Some sources are written primarily for law students and spell out basic doctrines, while others are designed for practicing lawyers and provide guidelines and forms to simplify common procedures.

One function that most secondary sources share is that they provide references to the primary sources which are the next step in research. Most texts and articles discuss the leading cases and major statutes, and contain extensive footnotes leading directly to these and numerous other sources. For the reader these footnote references may be among the more mundane aspects of a secondary source, but for the researcher they can be invaluable.

§ 2-2. OVERVIEWS

Even basic resources such as legal encyclopedias can be daunting to someone new to legal literature. For a start in understanding a legal problem, it may be helpful to begin with resources written for a more general audience.

Several works explain the nature of the American legal system and provide a broad outline of basic institutions and doctrines. Two of the most respected of these are Alan B. Morrison, ed., *Fundamentals of American Law* (1996), and E. Allan Farnsworth, *An Introduction to the Legal System of the United States* (3d ed. 1996). They explain common legal concepts and procedures, survey doctrinal areas such as contract law, corporations, and labor law, and provide references to major cases and other sources. Farnsworth's book is quite short, but it includes "Suggested Readings" of basic texts in each area it discusses.

Several encyclopedias provide basic coverage of legal issues. One of the broadest and most accessible for general readers is *West's Encyclopedia of American Law* (12 vols. 1998, supplemented by an annual *American Law Yearbook*). *West's Encyclopedia* has more than 4,000 entries, including articles on basic legal doctrines and terminology, major court decisions, government agencies, and influential jurists and lawyers. Its articles are a mix of legal theory, history, and politics. Volume 3, for example, includes biographies of Marcia Clark and Eldridge Cleaver as well as overviews of Constitutional Law and Contracts.

Other reference works cover more specific topics in greater depth. Some, such as Joshua Dressler, ed., *Encyclopedia of Crime and Justice* (4 vols., 2d ed. 2002), or Leonard W. Levy & Kenneth L. Karst, eds., *Encyclopedia of the American Constitution* (6 vols., 2d ed. 2000), are well-respected interdisciplinary treatments with contributions from legal scholars as well as historians and political

scientists. Kermit L. Hall, ed., *Oxford Companion to American Law* (2002) is a one-volume work covering a broad range of major legal concepts, institutions, cases, and historical figures, with most articles accompanied by references for further reading. David M. Walker's *Oxford Companion to Law* (1980) focuses on British institutions and legal history, but it also covers American topics and contains a great deal of useful information on our common law heritage.

Works such as these provide a broad perspective on legal issues, and can place these issues in the context of other political or societal concerns. They generally will not, however, answer more specific questions about particular legal situations, and they contain references to relatively few primary sources. For more detailed coverage, we must turn to works designed specifically for lawyers and law students.

§ 2-3. LEGAL ENCYCLOPEDIAS

Legal encyclopedias are not simply general encyclopedias about legal topics, but works that attempt to describe systematically the entire body of legal doctrine. Articles are arranged alphabetically, and most cover very broad areas such as constitutional law or criminal law.

Encyclopedias are relatively easy to use and provide straightforward summaries of the law, and thus they are among the first law library resources consulted by many students. In most instances, however, their perspective is quite limited. Legal encyclopedias tend to emphasize case law and neglect statutes and regulations, and they rarely examine the historical or societal aspects of the rules they discuss. Encyclopedias are relatively slow to reflect subtle changes in the law or to cover significant trends in developing areas. Unlike law review articles or scholarly treatis-

es, they simply summarize legal doctrine without criticism or suggestions for improvement. They are generally not viewed as persuasive secondary authority, but rather as introductory surveys and as tools for case finding. Their extensive citations to judicial decisions give encyclopedias their major value in legal research.

A. AMERICAN JURISPRUDENCE 2D AND CORPUS JURIS SECUNDUM

Two national legal encyclopedias were once competing works but are now both published by Thomson West: *American Jurisprudence 2d (Am. Jur. 2d)* and *Corpus Juris Secundum (C.J.S.)*. Each of these sets contains more than 130 volumes, with articles on more than 400 broad legal topics. Some articles, such as "Cemeteries" or "Dead Bodies," are narrowly defined and cover just a few dozen pages, but more extensive articles such as "Corporations" or "Evidence" can occupy two or three volumes. Each article begins with a topical outline of its contents and an explanation of its scope. This is followed by an exhaustive text divided into numbered sections, explaining concepts and providing references to cases and other sources.

While *Am. Jur. 2d* and *C.J.S.* are quite similar, there are differences between these two works. Exhibits 1 and 2 show pages from the *Am. Jur.* Weapons and Firearms article and the *C.J.S.* Weapons article, discussing the potential liability of gun manufacturers. Note that they approach the same issue from somewhat different perspectives. *Am. Jur. 2d* says that firearm manufacturers generally "will not be held liable on a strict products liability theory," while *C.J.S.* states that "products liability may . . . provide a cause of action." While both encyclopedias list numerous cases to support their text, there is very little overlap in the cases they choose to cite.

third person, he and his employer, if any, can be found liable for the result-ing injuries.[2] So long as he acts as a reasonably prudent man would act in a similar situation, he is not liable.[3]

§ 43 Liability of manufacturer or seller of firearm or ammunition

Research References

West's Key Number Digest, Weapons ⬦18(.5) to (2)

Products Liability: Firearms, Ammunition, and Chemical Weapons, 96 A.L.R. 5th 239

Firearm or ammunition manufacturer or seller's liability for injuries caused to another by use of gun in committing crime, 88 A.L.R. 5th 1

Liability of one who provides, by sale or otherwise, firearm or ammunition to adult who shoots another, 39 A.L.R. 4th 517

Products liability: air guns and BB guns, 94 A.L.R. 3d 291

Manufacturer's duty to test or inspect as affecting his liability for product-caused injury, 6 A.L.R. 3d 91

Privity of contract as essential to recovery in negligence action against manufacturer or seller of product alleged to have caused injury, 74 A.L.R. 2d 1111

Complaint, petition, or declaration—Injury due to negligent manufacture of ammunition or firearm, 25 Am. Jur. Pleading and Practice Forms, Weapons and Firearms § 5

Gun manufacturers are under no legal duty to protect citizens from the de-liberate and unlawful use of their products.[1] The "ultra hazardous activity doctrine" does not apply to the manufacture or sale of firearms, as opposed to their use, and thus manufacturers and dealers cannot be held strictly liable under that doctrine for damages resulting from the use of those firearms.[2] Handgun manufacturers are held to the most exacting duty of care in the design of their product.[3] A manufacturer's negligence may arise from the fail-ure to test and inspect its product.[4] Generally, firearm manufacturers and sellers will not be held liable on a strict products liability theory when sued by victims of firearms incidents, usually because the plaintiffs cannot estab-lish that there was a defect in the weapon.[5]

---

[2]Cerri v. U.S., 80 F. Supp. 831 (N.D. Cal. 1948); Giant Food, Inc. v. Scherry, 51 Md. App. 586, 444 A.2d 483, 29 A.L.R.4th 134 (1982); Atchison v. Procise, 24 S.W.2d 187 (Mo. Ct. App. 1930); Cook v. Hunt, 1936 OK 672, 178 Okla. 477, 63 P.2d 693 (1936); Goo-drich v. Morgan, 40 Tenn. App. 342, 291 S.W.2d 610 (1956).

[3]Shaw v. Lord, 1914 OK 32, 41 Okla. 347, 137 P. 885 (1914); Hatfield v. Gracen, 279 Or. 303, 567 P.2d 546 (1977); Goodrich v. Morgan, 40 Tenn. App. 342, 291 S.W.2d 610 (1956).

[Section 43]
[1]City of Philadelphia v. Beretta U.S.A. Corp., 277 F.3d 415 (3d Cir. 2002) (applying Pennsylvania law).

[2]Penelas v. Arms Technology, Inc., 778 So. 2d 1042 (Fla. Dist. Ct. App. 3d Dist. 2001), review denied, 799 So. 2d 218 (Fla. 2001).

[3]Endresen v. Scheels Hardware and Sports Shop, Inc., 1997 ND 38, 560 N.W.2d 225 (N.D. 1997).

[4]Herman v. Markham Air Rifle Co., 258 F. 475 (E.D. Mich. 1918); Sears, Roebuck & Co. v. Davis, 234 So. 2d 695 (Fla. Dist. Ct. App. 3d Dist. 1970); McLain v. Hodge, 474 S.W.2d 772 (Tex. Civ. App. Waco 1971), writ refused n.r.e., (Apr. 19, 1972).

[5]Merrill v. Navegar, Inc., 26 Cal. 4th 465, 110 Cal. Rptr. 2d 370, 28 P.3d 116 (2001); Penelas v. Arms Technology, Inc., 778 So. 2d 1042 (Fla. Dist. Ct. App. 3d Dist. 2001),

Exhibit 1.   79 AM. JUR. 2D *Weapons and Firearms* § 43 (2002).

misuse of the firearm or the injury inflicted, since a firearm is an inherently dangerous instrumentality.[16] However, negligent entrustment is available as a theory of liability only where the defendant had unrestricted control over the firearm.[17]

Theft.

Although the owner of a dangerous instrumentality such as a firearm is required to exercise a high degree of care when using a firearm or authorizing its use,[18] a firearm liability may not generally be imposed against the owner of a firearm for criminal use of firearm following theft, either based on negligence,[19] or on the theory of strict liability.[20]

§ 61 Manufacture and sale

> The manufacturer and the seller of a weapon may be liable to one injured as the result of negligence. Strict or products liability may also provide a cause of action against such persons.

Research References

West's Key Number Digest: Weapons ⬤1

A firearm, in the use for which it is intended, is a dangerous instrument within the scope of the principle that, under the ordinary rules of negligence, a manufacturer of such an instrument is liable in damages for an injury resulting from the negligent use of defective materials or from want of proper care and skill in either design[1] or the manufacturing process.[2] The most that is required, however, is the production of a weapon suitable for use under the conditions existing at the time it is put on the market,[3] and the manufacturer is not liable where the weapon is not used in an ordinary and reasonably foreseeable manner.[4] Under general rules, the complaint, declaration, or petition must be sufficient to state a cause of action,[5] and a want of proper care and skill in the manufacture must be alleged and proved[6] by sufficient evidence.[7] The mere bursting of a firearm does not alone suffice to make the manufacturer liable.[8]

Manufacturers have been held strictly liable for some injuries caused by firearms on a product liability basis,[9] though there is authority to the effect that the manufacture of fire-

[16]Ohio.—Byers v. Hubbard, 107 Ohio App. 3d 677, 669 N.E.2d 320 (8th Dist. Cuyahoga County 1995).

[17]Colo.—Payberg v. Harris, 931 P.2d 544 (Colo. Ct. App. 1996).

[18]Mich.—Resteiner v. Sturm, Ruger & Co., Inc., 223 Mich. App. 374, 566 N.W.2d 53, Prod. Liab. Rep. (CCH) ¶ 14945 (1997).

[19]Md.—Valentine v. On Target, Inc., 112 Md. App. 679, 686 A.2d 636 (1996), cert. granted, 344 Md. 719, 690 A.2d 525 (1997) and judgment aff'd, 353 Md. 544, 727 A.2d 947 (1999).

Wash.—McGrane v. Cline, 94 Wash. App. 925, 973 P.2d 1092 (Div. 1 1999), review denied, 138 Wash. 2d 1018, 989 P.2d 1141 (1999).

Negligent entrustment

Father's estate was not liable for negligently entrusting juvenile with dangerous instrument, based upon juvenile's theft of pistol from father, where father was not aware that juvenile possessed pistol and therefore had no opportunity to prevent or control juvenile's use of it.

N.Y.—Brahm v. Hatch, 203 A.D.2d 640, 609 N.Y.S.2d 956 (3d Dep't 1994).

[20]Mich.—Resteiner v. Sturm, Ruger & Co., Inc., 223 Mich. App. 374, 566 N.W.2d 53, Prod. Liab. Rep. (CCH) ¶ 14945 (1997).

[Section 61]

[1]U.S.—Rodriguez v. Glock, Inc., 28 F. Supp. 2d 1064 (N.D. Ill. 1998).

La.—Cappo v. Savage Industries, Inc., 691 So. 2d 876, Prod. Liab. Rep. (CCH) ¶ 15042 (La. Ct. App. 2d Cir. 1997), writ denied, 700 So. 2d 509 (La. 1997).

N.D.—Endresen v. Scheels Hardware and Sports Shop, Inc., 1997 ND 38, 560 N.W.2d 225, Prod. Liab. Rep. (CCH) ¶ 14902 (N.D. 1997).

[2]N.Y.—Favo v. Remington Arms Co., 67 A.D. 414, 73 N.Y.S. 788 (3d Dep't 1901).

[3]N.Y.—Favo v. Remington Arms Co., 67 A.D. 414, 73 N.Y.S. 788 (3d Dep't 1901).

[4]N.Y.—Favo v. Remington Arms Co., 67 A.D. 414, 73 N.Y.S. 788 (3d Dep't 1901).

[5]**Pleading held insufficient**

Pa.—Scurfield v. Federal Laboratories, 335 Pa. 145, 6 A.2d 559 (1939).

[6]Ill.—Miller v. Sears, Roebuck & Co. of Illinois, 250 Ill. App. 340, 1928 WL 4151 (1st Dist. 1928), cert. denied.

N.Y.—Favo v. Remington Arms Co., 67 A.D. 414, 73 N.Y.S. 788 (3d Dep't 1901).

[7]Conn.—Welshausen v. Charles Parker Co., 83 Conn. 231, 76 A. 271 (1910).

[8]Conn.—Welshausen v. Charles Parker Co., 83 Conn. 231, 76 A. 271 (1910).

[9]U.S.—Bell v. Glock, Inc. (USA), 92 F. Supp. 2d 1067 (D. Mont. 2000).

Pa.—DiFrancesco v. Excam, Inc., 434 Pa. Super. 173, 642 A.2d 529 (1994), appeal granted, 540 Pa. 599, 655 A.2d 988 (1995) and appeal dismissed as improvidently granted, 543 Pa. 627, 674 A.2d 214 (1996).

Exhibit 2.   94 C.J.S. *Weapons* § 61 (2001).

In *C.J.S.,* but not *Am. Jur. 2d,* each section or subsection begins with a concise statement of the general legal principle. This "black letter" summary is followed by text elaborating on the topic. Generally, the discussion in *Am. Jur. 2d* tends to focus a bit more on federal law, while *C.J.S.* seeks to provide an overall synthesis of state law. Until the 1980s, in fact, it claimed to restate "the entire American law as developed by all reported cases"; recently published volumes are more selective.

Am. Jur. 2d and *C.J.S.* contain references to other case finding materials. Both encyclopedias provide relevant key numbers, classifications that can be used to find cases in West digests. *Am. Jur. 2d* also includes references to *American Law Reports (ALR)* annotations, which describe and analyze cases on specific topics. Digests and *ALR* will be discussed in Chapter 4 with other case-finding tools.

While the discussion in both works is accompanied by copious footnotes to court decisions, neither work cites any state statutes. The case references provide citations, but only very recent volumes (*Am. Jur. 2d* volumes published since 1997 and *C.J.S.* since 1998) include the dates of decisions in citations.

Volumes in both sets are updated annually with pocket part supplements providing notes of new developments, and each encyclopedia publishes several revised volumes each year. In the instance of Exhibits 1 and 2, the *Am. Jur. 2d* volume was published in 2002 while the *C.J.S.* volume dates from 2001. Some volumes are much older than these, and researchers may need to be careful not to rely on obsolete information. An older encyclopedia volume may neglect recent trends or cite cases that are no longer good law.

The basic means of access to the encyclopedias are the multivolume softcover indexes published annually for each set. It might be possible to browse through an article

outline and find a relevant issue, but legal encyclopedias articles are very lengthy and cover extensive areas of legal doctrine. A pinpoint reference from the index usually saves considerable time. The indexes are very detailed and extensive, but finding the right section may require patience and flexibility. It may be necessary to rethink the terms used or to follow leads in cross-references. Some of these cross-references even refer to separate indexes in the volumes containing specific articles. Each encyclopedia also includes a tables volume listing the federal statutes, regulations, court rules, and uniform laws discussed in the set, and *C.J.S.* has a multivolume table of cases it cites.

Westlaw provides access to both encyclopedias, while *Am. Jur. 2d* is also available through LexisNexis and on CD-ROM. The online versions include tables of contents, making it easier to see how a particular section fits in a broader context. Because neither system includes the encyclopedias' indexes, however, it might be best to limit a keyword search to terms used in section headings. A natural language search, which shows the most relevant document first rather than the most recent, is particularly effective with resources such as encyclopedias. Every document, or section, is the same age so there is no concern that new developments might be missed.

Am. Jur. 2d is often shelved with several related publications. The *Am. Jur. Deskbook* provides a variety of reference information about the legal system, including outlines of government structure, standards of the legal profession, financial tables, and demographic data of legal interest. There are also several multivolume adjunct sets to *Am. Jur. 2d*, some focusing on trial preparation and practice *(Am. Jur. Trials* and *Am. Jur. Proof of Facts)* and others providing legal forms *(Am. Jur. Legal Forms 2d and Am. Jur. Pleading and Practice Forms)*. These sets are all also available on Westlaw and CD-ROM.

B. JURISDICTIONAL ENCYCLOPEDIAS

Several states have multivolume encyclopedias specifically focusing on the law of those jurisdictions. These state encyclopedias often do a better job of tying together statutory and case law than the national encyclopedias. While not generally viewed as authoritative, they can provide both a good general overview of state law and extensive footnotes to primary sources. Like the national encyclopedias, these sets are updated by annual supplements.

Fewer than half of the states have their own legal encyclopedias, but these include the eight most populous jurisdictions (California, Florida, Illinois, Michigan, New York, Ohio, Pennsylvania, and Texas). Several of these sets are available through LexisNexis or Westlaw, as well as in print. Many states have other reference works that provide extensive coverage of their law, although not necessarily made up of alphabetically arranged articles like the national encyclopedias. Sets such as *Kentucky Jurisprudence* and *New Jersey Practice,* for example, contain separate volumes for doctrinal areas such as criminal procedure, domestic relations, and evidence. They may not cover all legal topics comprehensively, but they do address most major areas.

West Group also publishes an encyclopedia focusing specifically on federal law, *Federal Procedure, Lawyers' Edition.* It emphasizes procedural issues in civil, criminal and administrative proceedings, but many of its eighty chapters also discuss matters of substantive federal law. Because it deals exclusively with federal law rather than attempting to generalize about fifty state jurisdictions, it is often more precise and useful than *C.J.S.* or *Am. Jur. 2d* and includes helpful pointers for federal practice.

§2-4. TEXTS AND TREATISES

Thousands of texts and treatises written by legal scholars and practitioners address topics of substantive and procedural law. These range from multivolume specialized treatises and detailed surveys to short monographs on specific issues or limited aspects of practice in particular jurisdictions.

For centuries, legal treatises have played a vital role in legal research. They analyze the developing common law and contribute their own influence to this development. By synthesizing decisions and statutes, texts and treatises help to impose order on the chaos of individual precedents. Although they lack legal authority and effect, some are written by scholars of outstanding reputation and are well respected by the courts. Other texts offer convenient guides by which practitioners can familiarize themselves with specialized fields of law. Often these texts contain practice checklists and sample forms.

Several distinct types of legal texts are published:

• Multivolume scholarly surveys of particular fields in depth (e.g., *Moore's Federal Practice, Wigmore on Evidence*) provide exhaustive coverage of specific subjects. Many of the original multivolume treatises were written by leading scholars (such as James William Moore or John H. Wigmore), but a number of titles are now produced by editorial staffs at publishing companies. While these are not accorded the same level of deference as the work of a respected scholar, they nonetheless provide extensive commentaries and numerous references to primary sources.

• Hornbooks and law school texts (e.g., *McCormick on Evidence* or Thomson West's Nutshell Series) are written primarily for a student audience but can also be of value to

anyone seeking an overview of a doctrinal area. They vary widely in the extent of citations they provide to cases and other sources. These are distinct from the *casebooks* designed as teaching tools, which reprint cases for discussion and tend to provide a less straightforward summary of legal doctrine.

• Practitioners' handbooks and manuals, many published by groups such as the American Law Institute-American Bar Association (ALI-ABA) Joint Committee on Continuing Legal Education or the Practising Law Institute (PLI), are less useful for students but can be invaluable in real life. They tend to address practical concerns, and many provide useful features designed to simplify routine aspects of law practice. Works focusing on the law of a specific state may be particularly useful for quickly determining the laws in force and finding relevant primary sources.

• Scholarly monographs on relatively narrow topics, such as Lawrence Lessig's *The Future of Ideas: The Fate of the Commons in a Connected World* (2001) or Philip Hamburger's *Separation of Church and State* (2002) can help provide an understanding of the history or policy background of a particular area. They are often published by university presses and are similar to scholarly works in other disciplines. Because they are generally not exhaustive in their coverage of doctrinal issues and are rarely updated on a regular basis, such works are usually not the best sources for current research leads.

• Self-help publications, such as those published by Nolo Press (e.g., *Patent It Yourself* and *Your Rights in the Workplace*), can be useful starting points and often provide clear introductions to areas of law. They may oversimplify complex issues, however, and they tend to provide fewer leads to primary sources than works designed specifically for lawyers.

For any of these publications to be reliable for coverage of current legal issues, it must reflect changes in the law promptly and accurately. Some form of updating, whether by looseleaf inserts, pocket parts or periodic revision, is usually essential to preserve a treatise or text's value. An outdated text may be of historical or intellectual interest, but it cannot be relied upon as a statement of today's law.

Although printed texts remain the norm, an increasing number are available electronically. Westlaw provides access to more than 200 treatises, including major works such as *Couch on Insurance*, LaFave & Scott's *Substantive Criminal Law, McCarthy on Trademarks and Unfair Competition,* Rotunda & Nowak's *Treatise on Constitutional Law,* and Wright & Miller's *Federal Practice and Procedure.* LexisNexis has a number of Matthew Bender treatises, including *Chisum on Patents, Collier on Bankruptcy,* Grad's *Treatise on Environmental Law, Immigration Law and Procedure,* and *Nimmer on Copyright.* A number of treatises are also available in CD-ROM products focusing in specialized areas of practice. Electronic texts are not necessarily more up to date than their print counterparts, but full-text searching allows means of access beyond browsing and subject indexes.

Exhibit 3 shows a page from a two-volume products liability treatise by Professor Marshall S. Shapo of the Northwestern University School of Law. Shapo goes into much greater detail than the encyclopedias on the development of litigation against gun manufacturers and possible theories of recovery. Like many other treatises, this work is available on CD and through Internet subscription as well as in print.

4056

compensation through the price of the product. Sensitive to our common vulnerability, that outcome would teach that in some circumstances, good luck occasionally imposes small obligations on the lucky to the unlucky.

[6] Handguns

Another vexing problem, which partakes of concepts of strict liability, intervening cause, "obviousness," and causation in fact, is that of the handgun that is employed by its purchaser, or another, to shoot a third party. Most courts that have ruled on the subject have refused to impose strict liability on handgun manufacturers, but the reasoning has left something to be desired as a matter of legal categorization and has led to some raging arguments about judicial policy making. A brief treatment of the subject by a Louisiana appellate court is symbolic of some of these difficulties. Affirming a defendants' judgment, the court found "quite persuasive" the reasoning of the Fifth Circuit in a case presenting the "identical issue." The Louisiana court quoted the Fifth Circuit's reference to the fact that its handgun plaintiffs had "not alleged that there was anything functionally wrong with" the weapons that caused their injuries and also the federal court's judgment that the plaintiffs could not recover as a matter of law "[b]ecause the guns functioned precisely as they were designed, and because the dangers of handguns are obvious and well-known to all members of the consuming public."[160] There is a hint of

---

[160] Strickland v. Fowler, 499 So. 2d 199, 201-202 (La. Ct. App. 1986) (quoting Perkins v. F.I.E. Corp., 762 F.2d 1250, 1275 (5th Cir. 1985)), cert. denied, 500 So. 2d 411 (La. 1986). See also King v. R.G. Indus., Inc., 182 Mich. App. 343, 346, 451 N.W.2d 874, 875 (1990) (noting that plaintiffs had not alleged "that the gun was functioning improperly at the time of its discharge"). Cf. Treadway v. Smith & Wesson Corp., 950 F. Supp. 1326 (E.D. Mich. 1996), in which a teenager accidentally fatally shot his friend with a revolver that had no manual safety guard and lacked a warning that a user could fire the weapon from the so-called "hang-up position." Granting summary judgment to the defendant, the court summarizes Michigan and Sixth Circuit precedents as holding "that the open and obvious danger rule applies to both design defect and failure to warn claims sounding in negligence where the product at issue is a simple tool," a locution frequently used in Michigan case law,

see, e.g., ¶ 19.11[1][a] infra, text accompanying notes 346.1-346.3.

A Wisconsin appellate court applied the same logic in a case in which the defendant was a manufacturer of bullets, which were loaded in a weapon whose firing appeared to have been accidental, rather than deliberate. In this case, the plaintiff's friend had cocked a pistol and pulled the hammer. Hearing a noise coming from downstairs, he tried to put the cocked weapon on a cabinet so he could turn down his stereo. The weapon fired as the owner put it down, and the bullet struck the plaintiff's decedent in the brain. In affirming a summary judgment for the defendant on both strict liability and negligence counts, the court not only used the language of "patent, open and obvious," but observed that "[t]he fired bullet was designed to and did exactly what any reasonable person would expect it to do." Schilling v. Blount, Inc., 152 Wis.2d 608, 620, 449 N.W.2d 56, 61 (App. 1989). Paralleling

¶8.05[6]

Exhibit 3.　1 Marshall S. Shapo, Law of Products Liability 4056 (4th ed. 2001).

There are several ways to find relevant and useful texts and treatises. Usually the basic starting place is a law library's online catalog. A subject or title keyword search may turn up a large number of publications, but most catalogs allow searches to be limited to recent publications or to books kept in a reserve collection. (Online catalogs from other libraries can also be helpful in identifying what resources are available for purchase or interlibrary loan. Union catalogs and other more extensive bibliographic sources will be discussed in Chapter 10, at pages 312-323.)

Following research leads provided by other sources is usually a reliable way to find useful works. Treatises are often cited in cases and law review articles, and such references are likely to lead to works which are considered well-reasoned and reputable. Recommendations from professors or reference librarians may also be effective in identifying the most reliable and influential sources.

Several printed guides list legal publications by subject. Most, unfortunately, do not differentiate between major treatises and obscure monographs, and few are updated regularly. The most extensive and current guide is found in Kendall Svengalis's annual *Legal Information Buyer's Guide and Reference Manual*. A 250-page chapter on treatises provides annotated listings in about sixty subject areas. Its annotations are more descriptive than critical, but they provide useful information about the scope and expense of the treatises works listed. Most state legal research guides (listed in Appendix B at page 404) describe or list the treatises and practice materials focusing on the law of particular jurisdictions.

It may be difficult to evaluate texts without extensive use and expertise in the subject area, but several considerations may aid in deciding whether a particular work would be of value in research. Questions to ask may include:

- a text's purpose and intended audience;
- its organization and scope;
- the reputation of the author and publisher, based on such factors as the value of their previous publications;
- the clarity, comprehensiveness and usefulness of its scholarly apparatus (footnotes, tables, index, bibliography, etc.); and
- the adequacy and timeliness of supplementation.

With growing familiarity in a particular area of law comes a sense of which sources are useful for providing background information, for working through a complicated legal issue, or for providing references to further research sources.

§2-5. RESTATEMENTS OF THE LAW

Some of the most important commentaries on American law are found in the series called *Restatements of the Law.* These American Law Institute (ALI) texts attempt to organize and articulate the rules in selected subject fields. The reporters and advisors who have drafted *Restatements* are well-known scholars and jurists, and their work is perhaps more persuasive in the courts than any other secondary material. The *Restatements* provide excellent summaries of basic doctrines, useful both for students learning an area of law and for lawyers seeking to apply the law to novel issues arising in practice.

Each *Restatement* covers a distinct area of law. The first series of nine *Restatements (Agency, Conflict of Laws, Contracts, Judgments, Property, Restitution, Security, Torts, and Trusts)* was published between 1932 and 1946, and after several years a second series (of all the original topics except restitution and security, as well as *Foreign Relations Law*) was issued to reflect new developments or later thinking. Several components of the *Restatement of the Law* (Third) have been published: *Foreign Relations Law* (1987),

Trusts—Prudent Investor Rule (1992), *Unfair Competition (1995), Suretyship and Guaranty* (1996), *Property —Mortgages (1997), Torts—Products Liability* (1998), volume one of *Property—Wills and Other Donative Transfers* (1999), *The Law Governing Lawyers* (2000), *Property—Servitudes* (2000), and *Torts—Apportionment of Liability* (2000). The ALI has also published two works as *Principles* (rather than *Restatements*): *Principles of Corporate Governance: Analysis and Recommendations* (1994), and *Principles of the Law of Family Dissolution: Analysis and Recommendations* (2002).

The process of drafting a *Restatement* or *Principles* is a long one, usually involving the publication of several preliminary and tentative drafts. Projects at the tentative draft stage include *Restatements Third* covering *Agency; Restitution and Unjust Enrichment; Torts—Liability for Physical Harm (Basic Principles);* and *Trusts.*

The *Restatements* are divided into sections, each of which contains a concise "black letter" statement of law, followed by explanatory comments and illustrations of particular examples and variations on the general proposition. Exhibit 4 shows a page from the recent *Restatement* on products liability and its use of black letter rule, comment, and illustration.

The comments and illustrations are followed in recent *Restatements* by Reporter's Notes providing background information on the development of the section. In the three earliest *Restatements* in the second series *(Agency, Torts, and Trusts)*, the Reporter's Notes are not printed after each section but appear in separate appendix volumes. The appendices for these and the other *Restatements* in the second and third series also contain annotations of court decisions which have applied or interpreted each section. Cases and law review articles citing *Restatements* can also be found in *Shepard's Restatement of the Law Citations.*

§ 11. Liability of Commercial Product Seller or Distributor for Harm Caused by Post–Sale Failure to Recall Product

One engaged in the business of selling or otherwise distributing products is subject to liability for harm to persons or property caused by the seller's failure to recall a product after the time of sale or distribution if:

(a)(1) a governmental directive issued pursuant to a statute or administrative regulation specifically requires the seller or distributor to recall the product; or

(2) the seller or distributor, in the absence of a recall requirement under Subsection (a)(1), undertakes to recall the product; and

(b) the seller or distributor fails to act as a reasonable person in recalling the product.

Comment:

a. Rationale. Duties to recall products impose significant burdens on manufacturers. Many product lines are periodically redesigned so that they become safer over time. If every improvement in product safety were to trigger a common-law duty to recall, manufacturers would face incalculable costs every time they sought to make their product lines better and safer. Moreover, even when a product is defective within the meaning of § 2, § 3, or § 4, an involuntary duty to recall should be imposed on the seller only by a governmental directive issued pursuant to statute or regulation. Issues relating to product recalls are best evaluated by governmental agencies capable of gathering adequate data regarding the ramifications of such undertakings. The duty to recall or repair should be distinguished from a post-sale duty to warn about product hazards discovered after sale. See §§ 10 and 13.

Illustration:

1. MNO Corp. has manufactured and distributed washing machines for five years. MNO develops an improved model that includes a safety device that reduces the risk of harm to users. The washing machines sold previously conformed to the best technology available at time of sale and were not defective when sold. MNO is under no common-law obligation to recall previously-distributed machines in order to retrofit them with the new safety device.

b. Failure to recall when recall is specifically required by a governmental directive issued pursuant to statute or other governmental regulation. When a product recall is specifically required by a governmental directive issued pursuant to a statute or regulation, failure reasonably to comply with the relevant directive subjects the seller or other distributor to liability for harm caused by such failure. For the product seller or other distributor to be subject to liability

Exhibit 4. RESTATEMENT (THIRD) OF TORTS —PRODUCTS LIABILITY § 11 (1998).

There has been no general index to the *Restatements* since the first series, but each *Restatement* includes its own index. The current editions of all *Restatements* are also accessible online through both Westlaw and LexisNexis. The American Law Institute website <www.ali.org> has information on publications and pending projects, but not the full text.

§2-6. LAW REVIEWS

Some of the most important scholarly commentary in American law appears in the academic legal journals known as law reviews. A number of influential articles have led directly to major changes in legal doctrine. Because thousands of law review articles are published every year, however, effective research requires learning several means of access and evaluating articles carefully.

The law review is a form of scholarly publication unknown to most disciplines. It is usually edited by law students rather than established scholars, and serves as an educational tool for its editors as well as a forum for discussion of legal developments and theories. Most reviews follow a fairly standard format, containing lengthy *articles* and shorter *essays* by professors and lawyers, as well as *comments* or *notes* by students. Articles and essays by established scholars are more influential, but the student contributions may also be very useful in research. Like the articles, they are usually accompanied by extensive footnotes citing to primary sources and other secondary sources. These footnotes help to make law reviews an invaluable part of the research process.

Exhibit 5 shows a page from a student comment in a recent law review issue, on the same topic as the encyclopedia and treatise pages shown earlier in this chapter. Note that one footnote quotes from the *Restatement (Second) of*

86   *WEST VIRGINIA LAW REVIEW*   [Vol. 103:81

easily sold and used to commit acts of violence,[35] and (3) that handgun manufacturers' negligent marketing and distribution practices make it easy for criminals to obtain illegal handguns.[36]

A.   The "Ultrahazardous Activity" Doctrine

The ultrahazardous activity doctrine originated from England in the famous nineteenth century case *Rylands v. Fletcher.*[37] The *Rylands* court held that "a defendant will be liable when he damages another by a thing or activity unduly dangerous and inappropriate to the place where it is maintained."[38] Most courts, however, including the Western District of New York, have adopted the standard illuminated in the Restatement (Second) of Torts Section 519 that provides:

> (1) One who carries on an **abnormally dangerous activity** is subject to liability for harm to the person, land, or chattels of another resulting from the activity, although he has exercised the utmost care to prevent the harm . . . (2) This strict liability is limited to the kinds of harm, the possibility of which makes the activity abnormally dangerous.[39]

The idea that the marketing and distribution of handguns is ultrahazardous is premised upon two extremely flawed theories: (1) that the distribution and marketing, rather than the *use*, of handguns is an abnormally dangerous activity, and (2) that the potential risk of criminal handgun misuse outweighs any value that handguns may have in the community.[40] Although many courts would agree that a

---

U. L. REV. 149, 151 (1986). *See also* RESTATEMENT (SECOND) OF TORTS §§ 519, 520 (1966). For a more in depth exposition on the legal history and elements of strict liability see Paul R. Bonney, *Manufacturer's Strict Liability for Handgun Injuries: An Economic Analysis,* 73 GEO. L.J. 1437, 1438 (1985).

[35]   *See* H. Todd Iveson, *Manufacturers' Liability to Victims of Handgun Crime: A Common Law Approach,* 51 FORDHAM L. REV. 771, 780-81 (1983).

[36]   *See id.* at 771-72.

[37]   159 Eng. Rep. 737 (1865), rev'd L.R. 1 Ex. 265 (1866), *aff'd as* Rylands v. Fletcher, L.R. 3 H.L. 330 (1868).

[38]   Andrew O. Smith, *The Manufacture and Distribution of Handguns as an Abnormally Dangerous Activity,* 54 U. CHI. L. REV. 369, 381 (1987)(paraphrasing the holding of *Rylands*).

[39]   RESTATEMENT (SECOND) OF TORTS § 519 (1966). The Restatement (Second) of Torts § 520 (1966) outlines specific factors that courts should take into account when determining whether handgun distribution is an "abnormally dangerous activity" such as:

The existence of a high degree of risk of some harm to the person, land or chattels of others; the likelihood that the harm that results from it will be great; the extent to which the activity is not a matter of common usage; the inappropriateness of the activity to the place where it is carried on; and the extent to which its value to the community is outweighed by its dangerous attributes.
See id.

[40]   Andrew J. McClurg, *The Tortious Marketing of Handguns: Strict Liability is Dead, Long Live Negligence,* 19 SETON HALL LEGIS. J. 777, 788 (1995).

Exhibit 5.   Colin K. Kelly, Note, Hamilton v. Accu-Tek:
*Collective Liability for Handgun Manufacturers
in the Criminal Misuse of Handguns,* 103 W. VA.
L. REV. 81, 86 (2000).

Torts, and that others provide references to a leading nineteenth century English case and to several other law review articles.

In addition to general law reviews, an ever growing number of specialized academic journals are published on topics from agricultural law to telecommunications. Some law schools publish a dozen or more general and specialized journals. Most specialized journals are student-edited, but a few, such as *Florida Tax Review* and *Supreme Court Review,* are edited by law school faculty members.

Articles in periodicals and journals can be found through a variety of means. For many students, the most frequently used approach is the full-text databases available through LexisNexis and Westlaw. Another full-text source described below, HeinOnline, is particularly useful for historical research. In addition, indexes available online and in print can expand retrieval and focus it more specifically on a topic in question. Other means of finding articles are based on particular cases or statutes under discussion, and use tools to be discussed in later chapters. Resources such as *Shepard's Citations* or KeyCite (Chapter 4) and annotated codes (Chapter 5) provide references to articles citing cases, statutes, or other documents.

Both Westlaw and LexisNexis have databases containing the text of thousands of articles, from several hundred law reviews, with coverage for some reviews extending back to the early 1980s and many more beginning in the 1990s. It is possible to search in a specific law review or in databases combining the hundreds of available titles. LexisNexis law review coverage is available both through lexis.com (for most legal professionals and law students) and through LexisNexis Academic <web.lexis-nexis.com/universe/> (for university faculty and students).

Both major search methods, natural language and Boolean, can be useful in searching for law reviews. A natural language search finds articles that discuss search concepts at greatest length and are therefore most likely to be relevant. A Boolean keyword search can be used to find any article using any particular combination of words, including phrases, case names, or titles of other articles or books. Even if an article retrieved is not directly on point, its footnotes may provide references to other, more relevant sources—including treatises or journal volumes that are not themselves in the online database.

Another electronic service, HeinOnline <www.heinonline.org>, began in 2000 with a somewhat different approach. Like the general-interest database JSTOR, it provides digitized page images from the printed journals, allowing desktop access to be the equivalent of going to the library shelves. Unlike Westlaw or LexisNexis, its coverage extends back to the very first volumes of the journals in its database, making it particularly valuable in legal history research. It includes nearly 300 law reviews, and for most titles its coverage extends nearly (but not quite) to the most recent issues. Its search mechanism is not as flexible or convenient as those offered by Westlaw or LexisNexis, so it is best used for historical research or for retrieval of known documents.

Free Internet sites provide some access to recent law review literature. Some law review websites feature only tables of contents or abstracts, but a growing number make the full text of recent articles available. A few law reviews, such as *Tribal Law Journal* <tlj.unm.edu>, are published only electronically. The University of Southern California Law Library provides a convenient list of links to law review websites <lawweb.usc.edu/library/resources/journals.html>, noting which sites provide the full text of articles.

Full-text searching is a powerful tool, but it does have limitations. Searching for particular terms can retrieve too many extraneous articles that only mention these terms in passing, not just those that focus specifically on a particular subject. In addition, thousands of law review articles are not available electronically and might never be found through online searches. For these reasons, periodical indexes remain valuable resources.

Two general indexes to English-language legal periodical literature are published. Both are issued in printed volumes with monthly updating pamphlets and on CD-ROM, but the most convenient form of access for most researchers is online. *Index to Legal Periodicals and Books (ILP)* is available through WilsonWeb, and to some subscribers through LexisNexis, Westlaw and other database systems. *LegalTrac* is available as part of the Gale Group's *InfoTrac* system, and is known as *Legal Resource Index (LRI)* on Westlaw and LexisNexis.

Each of these indexes covers more than 800 law reviews and periodicals, with more than two decades of online coverage. They offer both keyword and natural language searching, with results displayed newest to oldest or ranked by relevance. Their most valuable feature is the extensive subject indexing, allowing one easily to find articles on related topics. *LegalTrac* uses detailed Library of Congress subject headings with extensive subheadings and cross-references, while *ILP* generally has fewer, broader headings. Articles on gun manufacturer liability, for example, might be indexed under "Firearms industry - Cases" in *LegalTrac* and "Weapons" in *ILP*.

Depending on the means of access, the indexes may also offer direct links to the full text of articles indexed. This method combines the best of both research worlds: expert indexing to ensure that relevant articles aren't missed, and immediate online access to the relevant texts.

Exhibit 6 shows records for several articles found by searching for "firearms industry" and "products liability" in *LegalTrac.* Note that links to the full text of two of the articles are included below their citations. The full record for each article includes links to lists of articles assigned to its subject headings, making it easy to use one relevant work to find others.

Index to Legal Periodicals and Books (ILP) is the older of the two indexes, and began publication in 1908. (Earlier articles are covered by the Jones-Chipman *Index to Legal Periodical Literature,* with indexing back to 1770.) Its printed version indexes articles by subject and author, with a book review section and tables listing cases and statutes that are the focus of articles. The printed counterpart to LegalTrac, known as the *Current Law Index (CLI),* has been published since 1980. It has separate subject and author indexes, as well as case and statute tables. *LegalTrac* and *LRI* are somewhat broader in scope than CLI, with citations to several legal newspapers and to relevant articles in non-law periodicals.

Law reviews are but one of several types of legal periodicals. More specialized and practice-oriented sources such as bar magazines, legal newspapers, and newsletters, as well as tools providing notice of newly published articles, are considered in Chapter 9.

§2-7. CONCLUSION

This brief survey of major secondary sources focuses on general resources that are likely to be of the most assistance to beginning researchers. Encyclopedias, texts, *Restatements,* and law review articles are essential tools for someone starting out in analyzing a legal problem. They provide a broad introductory overview of legal doctrine and references to the primary sources that must be examined.

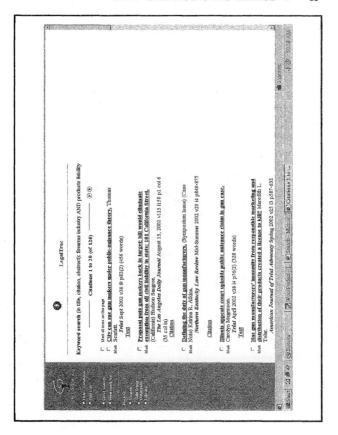

Exhibit 6.   LegalTrac search results list.

Secondary legal literature is much more extensive than these few materials, and additional resources will be discussed in later chapters. These general tools, however, can provide a solid basis for successful research of most legal issues.

CHAPTER 3
CASE LAW SOURCES

■   ■   ■   ■   ■   ■   ■   ■   ■   ■

§3-1. INTRODUCTION

Reports of judicial decisions are among the most important sources of legal authority in the common law system. Over the course of time, judges shape legal doctrines to address the complex issues of changing society. Legislative enactments now cover an ever broader range of issues, but case law continues to retain its vitality. Even a statute that may appear straightforward must be read in light of the court decisions which construe and apply its provisions.

Court reports are the subject of this chapter and Chapter 4. This chapter describes the court reports and online databases in which cases are found, while the following chapter discusses ways to use these resources to find relevant cases. Together, the two chapters provide an introduction to case law research.

To use court reports effectively, it is necessary to understand the hierarchical structure of the American judicial system. Litigation usually begins in a *trial court*. The jurisdiction of these courts may be based on geography (the U.S. District Courts in the federal system, or county courts in many states) or subject (the U.S. Tax Court, or state family courts and probate courts). In the trial court, *issues of fact* (such as which of two cars entered an intersection first) are decided by the fact finder, either the judge or a jury. These findings are binding on the parties and cannot be appealed. *Issues of law* (such as whether a witness's statement is admissible at trial) are decided by the judge, and a party who disagrees with these rulings can appeal them to a higher court.

Appeals from the decisions of trial courts are generally taken to an *intermediate appellate court* (the U.S. Courts of Appeals and similar state tribunals). An appellate court usually consists of a panel of three or more judges, who typically confer and vote on the issues after considering

written briefs and oral argument for each side. One of the judges writes an opinion summarizing the question and stating the court's holding. Dissenting judges may write separate opinions outlining their views.

The *court of last resort* in each jurisdiction (called the Supreme Court in the federal system and in most states) usually reviews cases from the intermediate appellate courts, but may take appeals directly from trial courts. Unlike other appellate courts, most courts of last resort have discretion in deciding which cases they will hear. Their role in the judicial system is not to resolve every individual dispute, but rather to establish rules, review legislative and administrative acts, and resolve differences among intermediate appellate courts. A court of last resort's decisions on issues of law are binding on all courts within its jurisdiction.

Numerous works provide more extensive discussions of the role of judges in deciding cases and creating legal doctrine. Daniel John Meador's *American Courts* (2d. ed. 2000) is one of the more concise introductory works.

Most court reports consist of the decisions of courts of last resort and intermediate appellate courts on issues of law. Very few trial court decisions are published. Trial court decisions on issues of fact have no precedential effect and usually do not even result in written judicial opinions. A jury verdict at the end of a trial, for example, produces no published decision unless the judge must rule on a motion challenging the verdict on legal grounds. Some trial court decisions on issues of law are published, but they are generally less important than appellate court decisions. Selected intermediate appellate court decisions and nearly all decisions from courts of last resort are published both in printed volumes and electronically.

A bit of history may help in understanding court reports. The American colonies inherited the English legal system and its common law tradition. Colonial lawyers and judges relied on English precedents, as no decisions of American courts were published until *Kirby's Reports*, in Connecticut, in 1789. Reports from other states and from the new federal courts soon followed. *Official* series of court reports (published pursuant to statutory direction or court authorization) began in several states in the early 1800s. Many of these early reports were cited by the names of their reporters and are known as *nominative reports.*

As the country grew in the 19th century, the number of reported decisions increased dramatically and official reporting systems began to lag further and further behind. The need for timely access to cases was met by commercial publishers. In 1876, John B. West began publishing selected decisions of the Minnesota Supreme Court in a weekly leaflet, the *Syllabi*. Three years later he launched the *North Western Reporter*, covering five surrounding states as well as Minnesota. By 1887 West published cases from every state and the federal system, in what became known as the National Reporter System. These reporters continue to be widely used today. Exhibit 7 shows the beginning of a case in *West's Pacific Reporter*.

In recent years the major development in access to court decisions has been electronic dissemination, through a variety of computerized means. New decisions are now available electronically much earlier than they are published in print form. The most widespread electronic resources are the commercial databases Westlaw and LexisNexis, but a number of smaller companies and numerous government and law school websites also provide access to court decisions.

ingly, that conviction and sentence are affirmed.

¶ 50 WE CONCUR: RUSSELL W. BENCH, Judge, and JAMES Z. DAVIS, Judge.

2002 UT App 229

STATE of Utah, Plaintiff and Appellee.

v.

Wade WILLIS, Defendant and Appellant.

No. 20010495-CA.

Court of Appeals of Utah.

July 5, 2002.

Defendant was convicted in Fourth District Court, Provo Department, Gary D. Stott, J., of possession of a firearm by a restricted person. Defendant appealed. The Court of Appeals, Jackson, P.J., held that Weapons Restriction Statute was not unconstitutional.

Affirmed.

1. Criminal Law ⟨⟩134(3)

A constitutional challenge to a statute presents a question of law, which is reviewed for correctness.

2. Constitutional Law ⟨⟩48(1, 3)

When addressing a constitutional challenge to a statute, the reviewing court presumes that the statute is valid, and resolves any reasonable doubts in favor of constitutionality.

3. Weapons ⟨⟩1, 4

Weapons Restrictions Statute that prohibited defendant from possessing a firearm was a valid exercise of State police power and did not violate Second Amendment, where statute restricted the right under very limited circumstances such as felony indictment or conviction. U.S.C.A. Const.Amend. 2; Const. Art., 1, § 6, U.C.A. 1953, 76-10-503(2)(a).

Margaret P. Lindsay, Provo, for Appellant.

Mark L. Shurtleff and Brett J. DelPorto, Salt Lake City, for Appellee.

Before Judges JACKSON, DAVIS, and THORNE.

OPINION

JACKSON, Presiding Judge:

¶ 1 Defendant appeals his conviction subsequent to a conditional guilty plea to possession of a firearm by a restricted person, a second-degree felony, in violation of Utah Code Ann. § 76-10-503(2)(a) (Supp.2001) (Weapons Restrictions Statute).[1] We affirm.

[1, 2] ¶ 2 Defendant challenges the statute under which he was convicted as being unconstitutional on its face. " 'A constitutional challenge to a statute presents a question of law, which we review for correctness. . . . When addressing such a challenge

---

with the factual premise of Perez's complaints, but points out that the trial court also rushed and interrupted the prosecuting attorney and objected, sua sponte, to prosecution questions as well, albeit with less frequency than befell Perez's counsel. The State also points out that many of these problems were rectified with the jury instructions, including instructions recognizing the jury as sole judge of the evidence and Perez's right to remain silent. See generally State v. Harmon, 956 P.2d 262, 273-77 (Utah 1998).

It is enough for purposes of this appeal to observe that Perez has failed to demonstrate that these actions, most of which were not objected to at the time, so tainted his trial that, but for those

events, he likely would have been acquitted. See State v. Litherland, 2000 UT 76, ¶ 31, 12 P.3d 92 ("To demonstrate plain error, [an appellant] must show an error occurred that should have been obvious to the trial court and that prejudiced the outcome of his trial.") (emphasis added).

1. This section provides in pertinent part: "(a) Category I restricted person who purchases, transfers, possesses, uses, or has under his custody or control . . . (a) any firearm is guilty of a second degree felony." Utah Code Ann. § 76-10-503(2)(a) (Supp.2001)

Exhibit 7.   State v. Willis, 52 P.3d 461 (Utah Ct. App. 2002).

The first print appearance of a new decision is the official *slip opinion* issued by the court itself, usually an individually paginated copy of a single decision. Slip opinions provide the text of new cases and are often available free from official court websites, but they have two major drawbacks for research purposes. They rarely provide editorial enhancements summarizing the court's decision and facilitating the research process, and because their page numbering is not final they must be cited by docket number and date rather than to a permanent published source. Several jurisdictions have ameliorated this second problem by assigning public domain citations to their recent cases. Such opinions are numbered sequentially as they are issued, and each paragraph is numbered so that a particular point in an opinion can be identified. The public domain citation for the case in Exhibit 7, *State v. Willis*, is 2002 UT App 229, indicating that this is the 229th decision delivered in 2002 by the Court of Appeals of Utah. The page shown includes the first two numbered paragraphs of the court's opinion.

The next form of printed court reports provides the editorial summaries and page citations lacking in slip opinions. Cases usually appear first in weekly or biweekly pamphlets known as *advance sheets*, containing a number of decisions paginated in a continuous sequence, and then in bound volumes. The volumes consolidate the contents of several advance sheets, and most contain alphabetical tables of the cases reported as well as subject indexes or digests. They are numbered consecutively, often in more than one successive series. When the volumes of a reporter reach an arbitrary number (such as 100 or 300), publishers frequently start over with volume 1, second series. Some reporters are now in their third or fourth series. If a reporter is in a second or later series, that must be indicated in its citation in order to distinguish it from the same volume number in the first series. The case in Exhibit 7, for

example, is on page 461 of volume 52 of the third series of the *Pacific Reporter*. It is cited as *State v. Willis*, 52 P.3d 461 (Utah App. 2002). Even though many researchers find and read cases online instead of in printed reports, cases are still identified by citations to the published volumes. Generally, only cases unavailable in print are cited to electronic sources.

Most court reports include editorial features which make it easier to find and understand the decisions. In West's National Reporter System series, each case is prefaced with a one-paragraph summary of its holding, called a *synopsis*, and with numbered editorial abstracts, or *headnotes*, of the specific legal issues. Each headnote is assigned a legal topic and a number indicating a particular subdivision of that topic. This classification plan, known as the *key number system*, consists of over four hundred broad topics and tens of thousands of subtopics. The headnotes are reprinted by subject in *digests*, which allow uniform subject access to the cases of different jurisdictions and will be discussed in Chapter 4. *State v. Willis* in Exhibit 7 has three numbered headnotes, in the Criminal Law, Constitutional Law, and Weapons topics. The first two headnotes represent points addressed in the last paragraph on the page, as is indicated by the bracketed [1, 2] that precedes the paragraph.

Exhibit 7 includes several other standard features of court reports. The docket number, located immediately below the names of the parties, is useful for tracking down briefs and other information. In the middle of the right column is a list of the lawyers representing the parties. Below this are the names of the judges who heard the case, and that of the judge writing the majority opinion.

LexisNexis adds its own editorial material, including a case summary outlining the procedural posture, overview and outcome, as well as computer-generated core terms

and "core concept" headnotes. Exhibit 8 shows the LexisNexis version of *State v. Willis*, including these editorial features. LexisNexis also provides the names of the attorneys and judges, but not on the screen shown in this exhibit.

§3-2. SUPREME COURT OF THE UNITED STATES

The Supreme Court of the United States stands at the head of the judicial branch of government, and provides the definitive interpretation of the Constitution and federal statutes. Its decisions are studied not only by lawyers but by political scientists, historians, and citizens interested in the development of social and legal policy.

The Supreme Court is the court of last resort in the federal system. It also has the final word on federal issues raised in state courts, and it hears cases arising between states. The Court exercises a tight control over its docket and has wide discretion to decline review, or to *deny a writ of certiorari* as it is called in almost all cases. The Supreme Court usually accepts for consideration only those cases that raise significant policy issues. In recent years it has issued opinions in fewer than ninety cases during its annual term, which begins on the first Monday of October and ends in late June or early July.

Numerous reference works explain the history and role of the Supreme Court in the American political and legal system. Two of the more highly esteemed are Leonard W. Levy et al., eds., *Encyclopedia of the American Constitution* (6 vols., 2d ed. 2000), and Kermit L. Hall, ed., *Oxford Companion to the Supreme Court* (1992), which both provide encyclopedic coverage of the Court and include articles on major cases, doctrinal areas, and individual justices. Hall's *Oxford Guide to United States Supreme Court Decisions* (1999) is an abridged but updated work with entries only for cases. Joan Biskupic & Elder Witt, *Guide to the U.S.*

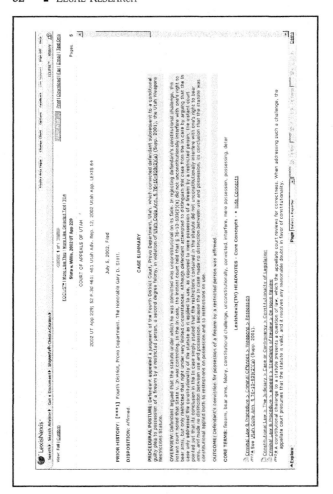

Print | Download | Fax | Email | Text Only

◁ ◁ 1 of 1 ▷ ▷
FOCUS™ | More Like This | More Like Selected Text | TOA

State v. Willis, 2002 UT App 229

COURT OF APPEALS OF UTAH

2002 UT App 229; 52 P.3d 461; 451 Utah Adv. Rep. 12; 2002 Utah App. LEXIS 64

July 5, 2002, Filed

PRIOR HISTORY: [***1] Fourth District, Provo Department. The Honorable Gary D. Stott.

DISPOSITION: Affirmed.

CASE SUMMARY

PROCEDURAL POSTURE: Defendant appealed a judgment of the Fourth District Court, Provo Department, Utah, which convicted defendant subsequent to a conditional guilty plea to possession of a firearm by a restricted person, a second degree felony, in violation of Utah Code Ann. § 76-10-503(2)(a) (Supp. 2001), the Utah Weapons Restrictions statute.

OVERVIEW: Defendant argued that the statute under which he was convicted was unconstitutional on its face. In rejecting defendant's constitutional challenge, the instant court noted that State v. Iv was controlling. In the in case, the instant court held that § 76-10-503(2)(a) did not unconstitutionally interfere with one's right to bear arms, but only restricted that right under very limited circumstances, although defendant attempted to distinguish that case from the in case by arguing that the in case only addressed the constitutionality of the statute as it applied to use, as opposed to mere possession of a firearm by a restricted person, the instant court pointed out that in its conclusion in the in case simply stated that the restrictions contained in the statute did not unconstitutionally interfere with one's right to bear arms, and made no distinction between use and possession. Because the in case made no distinction between use and possession, its conclusion that the statute was constitutional applied both to restrictions on possession and to restrictions on use.

OUTCOME: Defendant's conviction for possession of a firearm by a restricted person was affirmed.

CORE TERMS: firearm, bear arms, felony, constitutional challenge, unconstitutionally, convicted, interfere, mere possession, possessing, deter

LexisNexis(TM) HEADNOTES - Core Concepts - + Hide Concepts

☐ Criminal Law & Procedure > Criminal Offenses > Weapons > Possession
HN1✦ See Utah Code Ann. § 76-10-503(2)(a) (Supp. 2001).

☐ Constitutional Law > The Judiciary > Case or Controversy > Constitutionality of Legislation
☐ Criminal Law & Procedure > Appeals > Standards of Review > De Novo Review
HN2✦ A constitutional challenge to a statute presents a question of law, which the appellate court reviews for correctness. When addressing such a challenge, the appellate court presumes that the statute is valid, and it resolves any reasonable doubts in favor of constitutionality.

Page [Select a Reporter ▾]

◀ Explore

Supreme Court (2 vols., 3d ed. 1996) is arranged thematically rather than alphabetically, but it too explains major doctrines and provides historical background. The major practical guide for lawyers bringing a case before the Court is Robert L. Stern et al., *Supreme Court Practice* (8th ed. 2002).

Of websites providing background information on the Court, one of the most useful is from the Supreme Court Historical Society <www.supremecourthistory.org>. It includes sections on the Court's history and how it works, as well as a guide to researching various Supreme Court topics. The Court's own website <www.supremecourtus.gov> also includes a variety of information in its "About the Supreme Court" section.

Reference sources are useful for historical and general background, but they cannot cover the latest developments and they are no substitute for reading the opinions of the Supreme Court. The Court makes law through its decisions in individual cases. These decisions are available in a variety of printed and electronic means. They are published in three permanent bound reporters and in a weekly newsletter providing access to new decisions, and they can be searched and retrieved through several commercial databases and free Internet sites.

A. THE UNITED STATES REPORTS

Begun in 1790 as a private venture, the *United States Reports* (cited as U.S.) became official in 1817 and continues today as the official edition of United States Supreme Court decisions. Several volumes of *U.S. Reports* are published every year. The decisions appear first in slip opinion form, followed by an official advance sheet (called the "preliminary print"), and finally the bound *U.S. Reports* volume. Unfortunately, as with many government publications, the *U.S. Reports* tends to be published rather slowly.

More than six months pass before a decision appears in the preliminary print, and another year before its inclusion in a bound volume. (In contrast, the decisions are available electronically within minutes of their issuance.)

The early volumes of Supreme Court decisions are now numbered sequentially as part of the *U.S. Reports* series, but for many years they were cited only by the names of the individual reporters. *Bluebook* citations to these early cases include a parenthetical reference to the nominative reporter volume, as in *Marbury v. Madison*, 5 U.S. (1 Cranch) 137 (1803), while *ALWD* rules use the *U.S. Reports* citation only. Some Supreme Court Justices, on the other hand, continue the practice of citing only the nominative reports. A familiarity with the following reporters' names and their periods of coverage will make it easier to read and understand older citations:

Nominative Reports			**U.S. Reports**
Dallas	1-4	(1790-1800)	1-4
Cranch	1-9	(1801-1815)	5-13
Wheaton	1-12	(1816-1827)	14-25
Peters	1-16	(1828-1842)	26-41
Howard	1-24	(1843-1861)	42-65
Black	1-2	(1861-1863)	66-67
Wallace	1-23	(1863-1875)	68-90

Beginning with volume 91 (October Term 1875), *U.S. Reports* volumes are cited only by number and not by the name of the reporter. Thus the official citation of the Supreme Court's decision in *Muscarello v. United States* is 524 U.S. 125 (1998), meaning the case beginning on page 125 of volume 524 of the *U.S. Reports*. The opening pages

of the official report of *Muscarello* appear in Exhibits 9 and 10. This version does not include numbered headnotes, but the Court's reporter of decisions prefaces the text of each decision with a *syllabus* summarizing the case and the Court's holding. Following the syllabus, Exhibit 10 identifies the attorneys in the case and shows the beginning of the majority opinion by Justice Breyer.

B. SUPREME COURT REPORTER AND LAWYERS' EDITION

Because the *U.S. Reports* are published so slowly, the need for more timely publication is met by several commercial versions. Two of these publications, Thomson West's *Supreme Court Reporter* (cited as S. Ct.) and LexisNexis's *United States Supreme Court Reports, Lawyers' Edition* (known simply as *Lawyers' Edition*, and cited as L. Ed.) are published in advance sheets within a few weeks of decision, and later in bound volumes with editorial research aids not in the official edition.

The *Supreme Court Reporter* began in 1882, with cases from volume 106 of the *U.S. Reports*. As a component of West's National Reporter System, it includes the publisher's editorial synopses and headnotes. Each headnote is designated by topic and assigned to a classified key number within the topic. Subject access to the headnotes is provided in the *United States Supreme Court Digest*, a companion set to the reporter. Since the same key number system is used for court decisions throughout the country, the same point of law can also be researched in digests covering other federal courts and state courts. The opening page of *Muscarello v. United States* as it appears in the *Supreme Court Reporter* at 118 S. Ct. 1911 is shown in Exhibit 11, including the synopsis and first West headnote.

Syllabus

MUSCARELLO v. UNITED STATES

CERTIORARI TO THE UNITED STATES COURT OF APPEALS FOR THE FIFTH CIRCUIT

No. 96-1654. Argued March 23. 1998—Decided June 8, 1998*

A person who "uses or carries a firearm" "during and in relation to" a "drug trafficking crime" is subject to a 5-year mandatory prison term. 18 U. S. C. § 924(c)(1). In the first case, police officers found a handgun locked in the glove compartment of petitioner Muscarello's truck, which he was using to transport marijuana for sale. In the second case, federal agents at a drug-sale point found drugs and guns in the trunk of petitioners' car. In both cases, the Courts of Appeals found that petitioners had carried firearms in violation of § 924(c)(1).

Held: The phrase "carries a firearm" applies to a person who knowingly possesses and conveys firearms in a vehicle, including in the locked glove compartment or trunk of a car, which the person accompanies. Pp. 127–139.

    (a) As a matter of ordinary English, one can "carry firearms" in a wagon, car, truck, or other vehicle which one accompanies. The word's first, or basic, meaning in dictionaries and the word's origin make clear that "carry" includes conveying in a vehicle. The greatest of writers have used "carry" with this meaning, as has the modern press. Contrary to the arguments of petitioners and the dissent, there is no linguistic reason to think that Congress intended to limit the word to its secondary meaning, which suggests support rather than movement or transportation, as when, for example, a column "carries" the weight of an arch. Given the word's ordinary meaning, it is not surprising that the Federal Courts of Appeals have unanimously concluded that "carry" is not limited to the carrying of weapons directly on the person but can include their carriage in a car. Pp. 127–132.

    (b) Neither the statute's basic purpose—to combat the "dangerous combination" of "drugs and guns," *Smith* v. *United States*, 508 U. S. 223, 240—nor its legislative history supports circumscribing the scope of the word "carry" by applying an "on the person" limitation. Pp. 132–134.

    (c) Petitioners' remaining arguments to the contrary—that the definition adopted here obliterates the statutory distinction between "carry" and "transport," a word used in other provisions of the "fire-

---

*Together with No. 96-8837, *Cleveland et al.* v. *United States*, on certiorari to the United States Court of Appeals for the First Circuit.

Exhibit 9.   Muscarello v. United States, 524 U.S. 125 (1998).

126 MUSCARELLO *v.* UNITED STATES

Opinion of the Court

arms" section of the United States Code; that it would be anomalous to construe "carry" broadly when the related phrase "uses . . . a firearm," 18 U. S. C. § 924(c)(1), has been construed narrowly to include only the "active employment" of a firearm, *Bailey* v. *United States*, 516 U. S. 137, 144; that this Court's reading of the statute would extend its coverage to passengers on buses, trains, or ships, who have placed a firearm, say, in checked luggage; and that the "rule of lenity" should apply because of statutory ambiguity—are unconvincing. Pp. 134–139.

No. 96–1654, 106 F. 3d 636, and No. 96–8837, 106 F. 3d 1056, affirmed.

BREYER, J., delivered the opinion of the Court, in which STEVENS, O'CONNOR, KENNEDY, and THOMAS, JJ., joined. GINSBURG, J., filed a dissenting opinion, in which REHNQUIST, C. J., and SCALIA and SOUTER, JJ., joined, *post*, p. 139.

Robert H. Klonoff argued the cause for petitioner in No. 96–1654. With him on the briefs were *Gregory A. Castanias, Paul R. Reichert,* and *Ron S. Macaluso. Norman S. Zalkind,* by appointment of the Court, 522 U. S. 1074, argued the cause for petitioners in No. 96–8837. With him on the briefs were *Elizabeth A. Lunt, David Duncan,* and *John H. Cunha, Jr.,* by appointment of the Court, 522 U. S. 1074.

James A. Feldman argued the cause for the United States in both cases. With him on the brief were *Solicitor General Waxman, Acting Assistant Attorney General Keeney,* and *Deputy Solicitor General Dreeben.*†

JUSTICE BREYER delivered the opinion of the Court.

A provision in the firearms chapter of the federal criminal code imposes a 5-year mandatory prison term upon a person who "uses or carries a firearm" "during and in relation to" a "drug trafficking crime." 18 U. S. C. § 924(c)(1). The question before us is whether the phrase "carries a firearm" is limited to the carrying of firearms on the person. We hold that it is not so limited. Rather, it also applies to a person

---

†*Daniel Kanstroom, David Porter,* and *Kyle O'Dowd* filed a brief for the National Association of Criminal Defense Lawyers et al. as *amici curiae* urging reversal.

Exhibit 10. Muscarello, 524 U.S. at 126.

Arg. 9.

* * *

[8] When Congress makes Indian reservation land freely alienable, it manifests an unmistakably clear intent to render such land subject to state and local taxation. The repurchase of such land by an Indian tribe does not cause the land to reassume tax-exempt status. The eight parcels at issue here were therefore taxable unless and until they were restored to federal trust protection under § 465. The judgment of the Court of Appeals with respect to those lands is reversed.

It is so ordered.

524 U.S. 125, 141 L.Ed.2d 111

ᴸ₁₂₅Frank J. MUSCARELLO, Petitioner,

v.

UNITED STATES.

Donald E. CLEVELAND and Enrique Gray–Santana, Petitioners,

v.

UNITED STATES.
Nos. 96–1654, 96–8837.

Argued March 23, 1998.

Decided June 8, 1998.

The United States District Court for the Eastern District of Louisiana, Marcel Livaudais, Jr., J., granted motion to quash defendant's conviction of carrying firearm during and in relation to drug trafficking crime in light of intervening case law. The Fifth Circuit Court of Appeals, 106 F.3d 636, reversed and remanded. In second case, defendant was convicted of same firearms offense following jury trial before the United States District Court for the District of Massachusetts, Robert E. Keeton, J. The First Circuit Court of Appeals, 106 F.3d 1056, affirmed. Both defendants petitioned for certiorari. The Supreme Court, Justice Breyer, held that: (1) phrase "carries a firearm" is not limited to carrying of firearms on person, but also applies to person who knowingly possesses and conveys firearms in a vehicle, which person accompanies, and (2) both carrying drugs and weapons in truck of vehicle to drug-sale location and carrying firearm in locked glove compartment of vehicle while transporting drugs were "carrying firearm" within statute.

Affirmed.

Justice Ginsburg filed dissenting opinion, in which Chief Justice Rehnquist, and Justices Scalia and Souter joined.

1. Weapons ⬥10

Phrase "carries a firearm" as used in statute imposing mandatory prison term upon person who uses or carries firearm during and in relation to drug trafficking crime, is not limited to carrying of firearms on person, but also applies to person who knowingly possesses and conveys firearms in a vehicle, including in the locked glove compartment or trunk of a car, which the person accompanies. 18 U.S.C.A. § 924(c)(1).

See publication Words and Phrases for other judicial constructions and definitions.

Exhibit 11.   Muscarello v. United States, 118 S. Ct. 1911 (1998).

Lawyers' Edition contains all Supreme Court decisions since the Court's inception in 1790. It is now in a second series, and its version of *Muscarello* is cited as 141 L. Ed. 2d 111 (1998). Like the *Supreme Court Reporter*, *Lawyers' Edition* contains editorial summaries and headnotes for each case.

Its headnotes are reprinted, arranged by topic, in *United States Supreme Court Digest, Lawyers' Edition*. The *Lawyers' Edition* classification system, however, does not appear in other reports, so it is useful only for Supreme Court research. The headnotes are followed by "Research References," providing citations to relevant coverage in legal encyclopedias, digests, annotations, and the *United States Code*.

At the back of each *Lawyers' Edition* volume are two features not found in the *U.S. Reports* or the *Supreme Court Reporter*: annotations (legal analyses on issues arising in about four decisions per volume), and short summaries of selected briefs submitted by the lawyers who argued the cases. Another useful *Lawyers' Edition* feature is the "Citator Service," with summaries of later Supreme Court cases citing a particular decision. These summaries are found in annual pocket parts for each volume since 32 L. Ed. 2d (1972), and in a separate *Citator Service* pamphlet covering 1 to 31 L. Ed. 2d (1956-72).

Both the *Supreme Court Reporter* and *Lawyers' Edition* are published first in biweekly advance sheets, several months before the official preliminary print is available. At the end of the annual term they are then published in "interim edition" bound volumes. The permanent bound volumes are not published until the cases appear in the *U.S. Reports* volumes, so that the commercial editions can include *star paging* with references to the official *U.S. Reports* page numbers. Star paging allows the researcher to use the commercial volumes while citing directly to the official text. This feature is shown right before the petitioner's name at the beginning of *Muscarello* in Exhibit 11.

Even for researchers without access to online databases, it is usually quite easy to find a case in either the *Supreme Court Reporter* or *Lawyers' Edition* if one has the official *U.S.*

Reports citation. Each of the commercial volumes indicates on the spine which *U.S. Reports* volumes it covers, and tables in the beginning of the volumes match up the starting pages of particular cases. For researchers with the name of a decision, but not its citation, the digests accompanying both reporters include extensive case tables listing Supreme Court cases by name. *Lawyers' Edition* is also accompanied by a *Quick Case Table with Annotation References*, a paperback volume listing opinions alphabetically and providing references to the U.S., L. Ed. and S. Ct. citations. This table may be more manageable than others, because it is limited to cases with opinions and omits the thousands in which the Supreme Court has simply denied review.

c. UNITED STATES LAW WEEK

While *Supreme Court Reporter* and *Lawyers' Edition* are published much sooner than the official *U.S. Reports*, there is still a lag of several weeks while their synopses and headnotes are prepared. Another publication provides access to Supreme Court cases much sooner in a newsletter format, reproducing the official slip opinions and mailing them to subscribers the same week they are announced. This service, *The United States Law Week* (cited as U.S.L.W.), published by the Bureau of National Affairs, is the preferred citation for very recent Supreme Court decisions.

U.S. Law Week also provides information about the Supreme Court's docket, arguments, and other developments, making it a comprehensive source of current information about the Court's activities. Using its Topical Index and Table of Cases to find out about cases on the Court's docket can be confusing at first, because page references are provided only if an opinion has been issued. Other entries (for cases pending on the docket or those in which review has been denied) simply provide a docket number;

to find more information it is necessary to turn to a Case
Status Report table for page references. These index features are indicated in Exhibit 12, showing entries referring
to *Muscarello v. United States* in the 1997-98 *U.S. Law Week*
volume.

U.S. Law Week also provides weekly coverage of other
legal developments in a separate *General Law* binder. The
Case Alert section of this binder summarizes major new
decisions from federal and state courts, and the Legal
News section notes legislative and administrative actions
and includes various special reports and analyses. Two
Legal News features are of particular interest to law
students. A monthly Circuit Split Roundup summarizes
conflicts among Courts of Appeals with opposite decisions
on a particular issue. This may suggest paper or note
topics. Announcements of new judicial nominations and
confirmations can provide leads for students seeking clerkships.

U.S. Law Week is also available online as a subscription-
based Internet service <www.bna.com/products/lit/
uslw.htm>. The *Supreme Court Today* section of the site
provides several ways to track Supreme Court cases and is
continuously updated with new decisions, filings, and
other developments.

d. Electronic Resources

The Supreme Court's official website
<www.supremecourtus.gov> has new opinions as soon as
they are announced. They appear in Adobe Acrobat's PDF
format, reproducing the appearance of the printed slip
opinions. The site has slip opinions since March 2000, as
well as much larger PDF files containing the contents of
U.S. Reports volumes back to 1991. It also provides

Firearms and other weapons

Drug offenses, gun use in relation to
—Guilty pleas, subsequent ruling decriminalizing facts upon which plea based, defendant may collaterally attack conviction if able to overcome procedural default by showing actual innocence, 96-8516; ▶ 4346; no ruling in companion cases, 96-1440; 97-1721
—Locked glove compartment or trunk is "carrying," 96-1654; 96-8837; ▶ 4459
—Pickup bed, truck driven by trafficker, "carrying," 97-1623

Murphy; Lynn v., 97-1049
Murphy v. Sofamor Danek Group Inc., 97-1265
Murphy v. United Parcel Service Inc., 97-1992
Murphy Bros. Inc. v. Michetti Pipe Stringing Inc., 97-1909
Murr v. U.S., 97-11
Murray; Lawson v., 97-1790
Murray v. Trans Union Corp., 97-51
Muscarello v. U.S., 96-1654; ▶ 66:4459
Musco Corp. v. Qualite Inc., 96-1889
Muskogee, Okla. v. Allen, 97-978

96-1652	filed (04/14/97) 65:3728, Rule 46 dism (06/24/97) 66:3001
96-1653	filed (4/17/97) 66:3026, sum 66:3054, rev den (10/06/97) 66:3254
96-1654	filed (4/18/97) 66:3026, sum 66:3045, rev grant (12/12/97) 66:3416, interim order (03/09/98) 66:3590, oral arg (03/23/98) 66:3673, dec (06/08/98) ▶ 66:4459
96-1661	filed (4/15/97) 66:3026, sum 66:3064, rev den (10/06/97) 66:3254
96-1680	filed (4/21/97) 66:3026, sum 66:3047, judg aff (10/06/97) 66:3253
96-1693	filed (4/23/97) 66:3026, sum 66:3045, rev grant (09/29/97) 66:3203, interim

Exhibit 12. Excerpts from THE UNITED STATES LAW WEEK Supreme Court Index, Table of Cases, and Case Status Report (1997-98).

information on cases pending on the docket, schedules of oral arguments, court rules, selected documents, and general information on the Court.

New opinions are also transmitted to several other organizations, including Westlaw and LexisNexis. In addition to speedy access to the latest opinions, these databases provide complete historical coverage of the Supreme Court since 1790, so that every Supreme Court case since its inception can be searched by keyword, parties' names, or names of justices. For cases since 1980, Westlaw provides the option to view and print a PDF file of the version in the printed *Supreme Court Reporter* volumes.

Researchers without Westlaw or LexisNexis access can also find older Supreme Court opinions at several free Internet sites. LexisNexis's website for small law firms, lexisONE <www.lexisone.com>, provides free access to the entire retrospective Supreme Court collection back to 1790. FindLaw <www.findlaw.com/casecode/supreme.html> has all opinions since 1893, with hypertext links between cases, and USSC+ <www.usscplus.com/> has free coverage back to 1885. USSC+ provides recent opinions in PDF, matching the official slip opinions, and offers a free e-mail digest service when new Supreme Court decisions are announced.

Cornell Law School's Legal Information Institute <supct.law.cornell.edu/supct/> is a major source for recent opinions, with all opinions since 1990 and several hundred selected older decisions. Cornell also has a notification service for new decisions, providing the official syllabus by e-mail with links to the full text. Another free e-mail service, at Willamette University College of Law <www.willamette.edu/wucl/wlo/us-supreme/>, provides same-day summaries of certiorari granted, oral arguments, and decisions.

Subscription sites such as Loislaw <www.loislaw.com> and VersusLaw <www.versuslaw.com> also have more than a century of older decisions. These are just two of several commercial legal research sites providing access to court decisions. A number of publishers offer CD-ROM vesions of Supreme Court opinions; some of these include only recent cases, while others provide complete coverage since 1790.

§3-3. LOWER FEDERAL COURTS

The federal court system has grown extensively from the thirteen District Courts and three Circuit Courts created by the Judiciary Act of 1789. The intermediate appellate courts in the federal system, the United States Courts of Appeals, are divided into thirteen circuits, consisting of the First through Eleventh Circuits (each covering several states), the District of Columbia Circuit, and the Federal Circuit. The map in Exhibit 13 shows the jurisdiction of these circuits. The general trial courts, the United States District Courts, are divided into ninety-four districts, with one or more in each state. In addition, there are several specialized trial courts, such as the Bankruptcy Courts, the Court of Federal Claims, and the Court of International Trade.

There is no counterpart to the *U.S. Reports* for the decisions of the U.S. Courts of Appeals and District Courts. The only officially published sources are the individual slip decisions issued by the courts themselves. Many federal court decisions are available, however, in commercially published reports and electronic sources.

The only comprehensive printed sources for lower federal court decisions are reporters published by Thomson West. In 1880 West's *Federal Reporter* began covering decisions of both the district and circuit courts. More than 1,600 volumes later it is now in its third series (cited as F.3d). In 1932, with the increasing volume of litigation in the federal

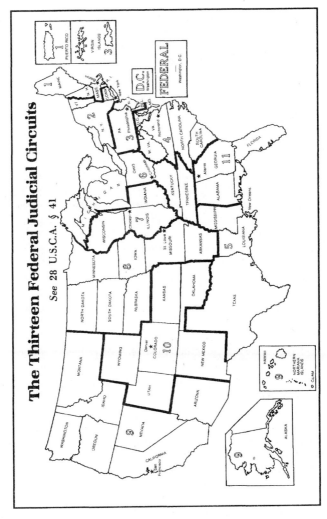

Exhibit 13. Map of United States Court of Appeals circuits.

courts, West began another series called *Federal Supplement* (F. Supp.) for selected U.S. District Court decisions, leaving the *Federal Reporter* to cover the decisions of the U.S. Courts of Appeals. *Federal Supplement* is now in its second series (F. Supp. 2d), and also includes decisions of the U.S. Court of International Trade and rulings from the Judicial Panel on Multidistrict Litigation. Like the *Supreme Court Reporter*, both of these reporters contain editorial synopses and headnotes with key numbers, allowing researchers to find cases through West's series of digest publications.

Because the *U.S. Reports* is limited to Supreme Court decisions, any citation to *U.S.* clearly indicates the deciding court. Citations to the *Federal Reporter* or *Federal Supplement* must identify the specific circuit or district in parentheses, as in *United States v. Muscarello*, 106 F.3d 636 (5th Cir. 1997). This is vital information in evaluating the scope and precedential value of a decision, but it is often omitted by beginning researchers.

The *Federal Reporter* and *Federal Supplement* publish thousands of new decisions each year. Unlike Supreme Court decisions, however, not every case considered by the lower federal courts is represented by a decision published in one of these reporter series. Some matters are settled or tried to a jury verdict and do not result in any written opinions. Decisions in many cases are issued as slip opinions but are not published in the reporters. In an attempt to limit the proliferation of reported cases, each circuit has local court rules establishing criteria to determine whether decisions are published (e.g., establishing a new rule of law, resolving a conflict in the law, or involving issues of continuing public interest) and restricting the citation of "unpublished" decisions. These vary from circuit to circuit, but some courts prohibit citation of such decisions; some allow citation, but with restrictions; and some limit their precedential value.

Some "unpublished" decisions are available in printed sources. In 2001 West began a new reporter series, *Federal Appendix*, limited to Court of Appeals decisions "not selected for publication in the *Federal Reporter*." These decisions, from every circuit but the Fifth and Eleventh, are published with headnotes and are indexed in West's digests, but it is up to the researcher to determine to what extent they can be cited as precedent. More unreported decisions can be found online from Westlaw, LexisNexis, and court websites. For some decisions, particularly in older cases, it may be necessary to contact the clerk of the court.

Cases from the lower federal courts before 1880 are found in a separate thirty-volume West series called *Federal Cases*. Before the inception of the *Federal Reporter*, federal court decisions were issued in more than 100 different series of nominative reports. *Federal Cases*, published between 1894 and 1897, reports over 20,000 of these decisions. This set incorporated virtually all available lower federal court decisions from 1789 to 1880, arranged in alphabetical sequence by case name.

Another West series, *Federal Rules Decisions* (F.R.D.), began publication in 1940 and contains a limited number of U.S. District Court decisions dealing with procedural issues under the Federal Rules of Civil Procedure and the Federal Rules of Criminal Procedure. *Federal Rules Decisions* also includes proceedings of judicial conferences and occasional speeches or articles dealing with procedural law in the federal courts.

Thomson West also issues a number of other reporters in specialized subject fields of federal law. These selective reporters include: *Military Justice Reporter* (1978-date), containing decisions of the U.S. Court of Appeals for the Armed Forces (formerly the U.S. Court of Military Appeals), as well as selected decisions of the Court of

Criminal Appeals for each branch of the military;
Bankruptcy Reporter (1980-date), containing decsions of the
U.S. Bankruptcy Courts and bankruptcy decisions from the
U.S. District Courts; *Federal Claims Reporter* (1982-date),
containing decisions of the U.S. Court of Federal Claims
(formerly U.S. Claims Court); and *Veterans Appeals Reporter*
(1991-date), containing decisions of the U.S. Court of
Veterans Appeals. These last three reporters also reprint
decisions from the Courts of Appeals and Supreme Court
in their subject areas.

West's National Reporter System does not include deci-
sions from the U.S. Tax Court, which are published by the
government, in *Reports of the United States Tax Court* (1942-
date), and by the major commercial tax publishers.
Also published by the government are the reports of
various specialized federal courts such as *U.S. Court of
International Trade Reports* (formerly *U.S. Custom Court
Reports*) (1938-date); *Cases Decided in the U. S. Court of
Appeals for the Federal Circuit* (1982-date); and *U. S. Court of
Claims Reports* (1863-1982), covering decisions of the former
U.S. Court of Claims.

Federal court decisions are also printed in a variety of
other sources, including commercial topical reporters
designed for practitioners in specialized subject areas.
Some cases appearing in these sources are not available in
the *Federal Reporter* or *Federal Supplement*, although there is
extensive duplication. In addition to *Federal Rules Decisions*,
West publishes two more series of cases on procedural
issues which are *not* part of its National Reporter System,
Federal Rules Service (1939-date) and *Federal Rules of
Evidence Service* (1979-date). Other reporters in specialized
areas include *American Maritime Cases* (1923-date),
Environment Reporter Cases (1970-date), and *U.S. Patents
Quarterly* (1929-date). Several topical reporters, such as

BNA's *Fair Employment Practice Cases* (1969-date) and CCH's *Trade Cases* (1948-date), are published as adjuncts to looseleaf services on those topics.

Westlaw and LexisNexis are major sources of lower federal court decisions. They provide full-text coverage of all federal court cases that appear in print in the various West reporters, back to the earliest decisions in *Federal Cases,* and new decisions are available online well before they are published in the *Federal Reporter* or *Federal Supplement.* Once the final printed version of a case is published in a bound reporter volume, Westlaw makes the page images available online. In addition, the electronic services also provide access to many decisions which never appear in the reporters, making them the most comprehensive sources for current decisions. Both services include in their databases thousands of decisions not available in any other form, except as slip opinions. As a result many case citations are to the online databases. Exhibit 14 shows a case available on Westlaw but not in print, *NAACP v. Acusport Corp.,* 2001 WL 282923 (E.D.N.Y. Mar. 16, 2001). The same case is available from LexisNexis, where its citation is 2001 U.S. Dist. LEXIS 3218.

Recent decisions from the Courts of Appeals are also available from free Internet sites. LexisONE provides five years of free coverage, and in most instances sites for individual circuits have opinions going back to about 1995. Cases can generally be retrieved by party name, date, docket number, or keyword. Quick access to the sites for specific circuits is provided by sites such as the Federal Courts Finder <www.law.emory.edu/FEDCTS/> or the U.S. Courts homepage <www.uscourts.gov/links.html>.

District and bankruptcy courts are also represented on the Internet, but most of these sites focus on local rules and procedures rather than the text of decisions. The U.S.

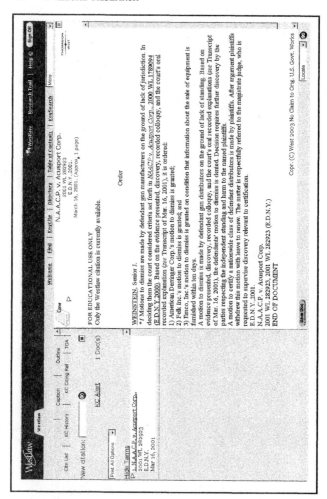

Exhibit 14.   NAACP v. Acusport Corp., 2001 WL 282923
(E.D.N.Y. Mar. 16, 2001).

Courts homepage provides links to each court's site, and FindLaw has a list of websites <www.findlaw.com/ 10fedgov/judicial/district_courts.html> with brief descriptions of their contents.

More extensive Internet access to Court of Appeals decisions is available through commercial services such as Loislaw and VersusLaw. Loislaw coverage generally begins in 1924, while VersusLaw has coverage from 1930 for most circuits. Both services only very recently began to include district court opinions. Lower federal court decisions are published on CD-ROM as well, in most instances in separate products for individual circuits.

§3-4. State Courts

Although federal law governs an increasingly wide range of activities, state courts have a vital lawmaking role on many issues, including important areas such as family law, contracts, insurance, and substantive criminal law. A state's court of last resort has the final say in interpreting the state's constitution and statutes.

The structure of most state court systems roughly follows the federal paradigm, with various trial courts, intermediate appellate courts, and a court of last resort. There are, however, wide variations. A few states have no intermediate appellate courts, with appeals going directly from the trial court to the state supreme court. Other states have more complicated systems, with more than one appellate court for different subject areas. Some states even have separate courts of last resort for civil and criminal matters.

A good way to develop a quick familiarity with a state court system is to examine a chart of its structure, such as those found in the U.S. Bureau of Justice Statistics publication *State Court Organization 1998* or the National Center

for State Courts' annual *State Court Caseload Statistics*. Both organizations have these publications online in PDF (<www.ojp.usdoj.gov/bjs/pub/pdf/sco9808.pdf> and </www.ncsconline.org/D_Research/csp/CSP_Main_Page. html>). The tables are reprinted in several other sources, such as *BNA's Directory of State and Federal Courts, Judges, and Clerks* (biennial), *Legal Researcher's Desk Reference* (biennial), and *WANT's Federal-State Court Directory* (annual).

Just as Supreme Court decisions are published both in the official *U.S. Reports* and in commercial reporters, so decisions from state appellate courts are traditionally published both in official reports, issued by or under the auspices of the courts themselves, and in West's series of National Reporter System volumes. LexisNexis and Westlaw provide comprehensive coverage of state appellate cases, and recent decisions are available on the Internet. Every state has at least one CD-ROM version of its cases, and some cases appear in topical reporters with specialized subject coverage.

A. Official Reports

Like the *U.S. Reports*, state official reports are the authoritative version of a court's decisions and must be cited in briefs before that court. In many instances they are less used than commercial reporters, which are usually published more quickly with superior research aids. In fact, twenty-one states have ceased publishing official reports series and have designated a commercial reporter as the authoritative source of state case law. Appendix A of this book, on page 380, gives information on the current status of the published reports in each state.

Forms of publication vary from state to state. Some states publish just one series of reports, containing decisions of the state supreme court and in some instances of intermediate appellate courts as well. More than a dozen states

issue two or more series of reports, with separate series for decisions of the supreme court, for intermediate appellate decisions, and in a few states for selected trial court decisions. New York, for example, has three official series: *New York Reports*, covering the Court of Appeals, the state's court of last resort; *Appellate Division Reports*, covering the Appellate Divisions of the Supreme Court; and *Miscellaneous Reports*, with decisions of various lower courts. Official slip decisions and advance sheets are published for the courts of some states, but not for every state. Exhibit 15 shows the first page of *Commonwealth v. Wilkerson*, an opinion of the Supreme Judicial Court of Massachusetts, in *Massachusetts Reports*. Instead of numbered headnotes, note that it simply has an introductory paragraph summarizing the decision.

Even though official reports do not generally include links to a comprehensive digest system like West's, they can still provide a valuable perspective on the decisions of a state's appellate courts. If the summaries or headnotes are written by court staff or by lawyers practicing in that state, they may be more attuned to local judicial developments than headnotes written by commercial editors. Some official reports include research leads not mentioned in the West reporters, and others provide their own classification and digest systems. Although official reports are less widely used than West's, in some jurisdictions they maintain an important research role.

As with the early *U.S. Reports* volumes, the early reports of several of the older states were once cited only by the names of their reporters. Many of these volumes have now been incorporated into the numbered series, but it may still be necessary to use an abbreviations dictionary or other reference work to understand some case citations. Westlaw and LexisNexis generally recognize the nominative reporter citations, so there may be no need to decipher the citation before retrieving a case online.

COMMONWEALTH vs. RON P. WILKERSON.

Barnstable. January 10, 2002. - February 25, 2002.

Present: MARSHALL, C.J., GREANEY, IRELAND, SPINA, COWIN, SOSMAN, & CORDY, JJ.

Probable Cause. Arrest. Search and Seizure, Arrest, Probable cause. *Constitutional Law,* Search and seizure, Probable cause. *Registrar of Motor Vehicles,* Records.

On a criminal defendant's motion to suppress certain physical evidence on the ground that his arrest was constitutionally invalid because probable cause was based on what was later disclosed to be erroneous information provided to the arresting officer by the registry of motor vehicles about the status of the defendant's license. the motion was properly denied, where, since the arresting officer relied ⟨n records of an independent State agency rather than police records to make the otherwise proper arrest, there was no unlawful conduct to be deterred by exclusion of the evidence, and nothing to encourage the police to maintain current and accurate computer records. [139-143]

An issue whether Miranda warnings were necessary at the time of a criminal defendant's arrest was not present, where no contention as to the need for, and lack of, the warnings was raised at the hearing on the defendant's motion to suppress evidence or at trial, and where nothing was raised at the trial to require the judge to inquire sua sponte into the voluntariness of the defendant's postarrest statements. [143]

COMPLAINT received and sworn to in the Barnstable Division of the District Court Department on May 15, 2000.

A pretrial motion to suppress evidence was heard by *Joan E. Lynch,* J., and the case was tried before her.

The Supreme Judicial Court on its own initiative transferred the case from the Appeals Court.

Harris Krinsky for the defendant.

Julia K. Holler, Assistant District Attorney, for the Commonwealth.

GREANEY, J. A jury in the District Court convicted the defendant of possession of a firearm (a rifle) without a firearms identification card, G. L. c. 269, § 10G. The defendant argues

Exhibit 15.   Commonwealth v. Wilkerson, 436 Mass. 137 (2002).

B. National Reporter System

West's National Reporter System includes a series of *regional reporters* publishing the decisions of the appellate courts of the fifty states and the District of Columbia. The National Reporter System divides the country into seven regions, and publishes the decisions of the appellate courts of the states in each region together in one series of volumes. Five of these sets are now in their second series (*Atlantic* (A.2d), *North Eastern* (N.E.2d), *North Western* (N.W.2d), *South Eastern* (S.E.2d), *Southern* (So. 2d in the *Bluebook*, or S.2d in the *ALWD Citation Manual*)); and two have started their third series (*Pacific* (P.3d) and *South Western* (S.W.3d)). These sets are supplemented by separate reporters for the two most populous states, also in their second series: *California Reporter* (Cal. Rptr. 2d) and *New York Supplement* (N.Y.S.2d). (Cases from the highest courts of California and New York appear in both the regional and the state reporter, while lower court cases are not published in the *Pacific* or *North Eastern Reporter*.) These nine reporters, together with West's federal court reporters, comprise a uniform system tied together by the key number headnote and digest scheme. The map in Exhibit 16 shows which states are included in each region of the reporter system. Appendix A, on page 380, indicates the scope of coverage for each state appellate court in the regional reporters.

West also publishes individual reporters for over thirty additional states. Unlike the *California Reporter* and *New York Supplement*, however, most of these other series simply reprint a state's cases from its regional reporter, including the original regional reporter pagination. These "offprint" reporters are published for practitioners who need their own state courts' decisions but not cases from other states.

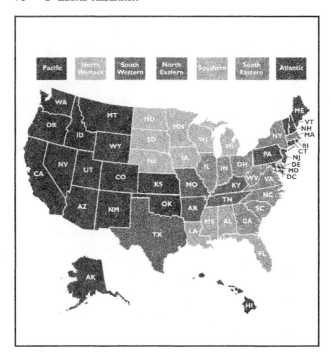

Exhibit 16. Map of West National Reporter System.

Exhibit 17 shows the first page of the Massachusetts Supreme Judicial Court decision in *Commonwealth v. Wilkerson,* as printed in West's *North Eastern Reporter.* Note that this version includes an introductory synopsis and three numbered headnotes. In addition, the *North Eastern Reporter* version includes star paging indicating the exact page breaks in the official *Massachusetts Reports.*

436 Mass. 137

COMMONWEALTH

v.

Ron P. WILKERSON.

Supreme Judicial Court of Massachusetts,
Barnstable.

Submitted Jan. 10, 2002.

Decided Feb. 25, 2002.

Defendant was convicted, in the District Court Department, Barnstable Division, Joan E. Lynch, J., of possession of a firearm without a firearms identification card. Defendant appealed, and the appeal was transferred. The Supreme Judicial Court, Greaney, J., held that erroneous information from registry of motor vehicles provided probable cause for defendant's arrest.

Affirmed.

1. Automobiles ⚖=349(4)

Information furnished to police officer by registry of motor vehicles, that motorist's license to drive had been suspended, provided probable cause to arrest motorist for operating a vehicle after license suspension, though the information was later determined to be erroneous, where the police were not responsible for the error; the error was in the records of the registry of motor vehicles, and the registry of motor vehicles was an independent State agency. U.S.C.A. Const.Amend. 4; M.G.L.A. Const. Pt. 1, Art. 14; M.G.L.A. c. 16, § 9; c. 90, §§ 8, 22, 30.

2. Arrest ⚖=63.4(4)

Probable cause to arrest is not vitiated when the basis on which the police officer acted is shown after the fact to have been erroneous, because the existence of probable cause is determined at the moment of arrest, not in light of subsequent events. M.G.L.A. Const. Pt. 1, Art. 14.

3. Criminal Law ⚖=394.4(4)

The interest in deterring unlawful police conduct, which is the foundation of the exclusionary rule, is not implicated where police rely on erroneous records of an independent State agency to make an otherwise proper arrest. U.S.C.A. Const. Amend. 4; M.G.L.A. Const. Pt. 1, Art. 14.

Harris Krinsky, Boston, for the defendant.

Julia K. Holler, Assistant District Attorney, for the Commonwealth.

Present: MARSHALL, C.J.,
GREANEY, IRELAND, SPINA, COWIN,
SOSMAN, & CORDY, JJ.

GREANEY, J.

A jury in the District Court convicted the defendant of possession of a firearm (a rifle) without a firearms identification card, G.L. c. 269, § 10G. The defendant argues that his pretrial motion to suppress the rifle (seized from the trunk of the automobile he was driving after the arrest and the impoundment of the vehicle) should have been granted. He asserts that his arrest for operating the automobile after his license had been suspended was constitutionally invalid because, in making the arrest, the police officer relied on erroneous information furnished by the registry of motor vehicles (registry) regarding the status of the defendant's driver's license. The defendant also argues that his statements made to the police after his arrest should have been suppressed because he was not afforded the Miranda warnings. Finally, the defendant claims that the trial

Exhibit 17. Commonwealth v. Wilkerson, 763 N.E.2d 508
(Mass. 2002).

In most states, cases appear in both official and National Reporter System editions. Cases are traditionally cited to both of these sources, with the official reports cited first. Note in Exhibit 17 that the official citation is printed above the name of the case. The two citations for the same decision are known as *parallel citations*. In *Commonwealth v. Wilkerson*, 436 Mass. 137, 763 N.E.2d 508 (2002), for example, the citation to the official *Massachusetts Reports* precedes the unofficial *North Eastern Reporter*.

The *Bluebook* and *ALWD Citation Manual* require parallel citations *only* for cases cited in documents submitted to that state's courts; in other documents such as law review articles and memoranda, only the National Reporter System citation is used. (If Massachusetts had a public domain citation system like Utah's, that citation would be included along with the West citation.) If the cited reporter does not clearly identify the deciding court (e.g., *Massachusetts Reports*), remember to include this information in parentheses with the date: *Commonwealth v. Wilkerson*, 763 N.E.2d 508 (Mass. 2002).

Frequently a researcher has a citation to only one report of a case and needs to find the other, either to complete the citation in a brief or to examine the other version. The parallel citation is not always printed at the beginning of the case, as it is in Exhibit 17. Many state reports are not published quickly enough for their citations to be included in the regional reporters. But parallel citations can be found in a variety of sources.

One of the simplest printed sources for finding parallel citations is a West publication called the *National Reporter Blue Book*, which is updated annually and lists the starting page of each case in the official reports and provides cross-references to National Reporter System citations. For some states, West also publishes a *Blue and White Book*,

which also provides references from the regional reporter back to the official reports. Easy access to parallel citations is provided online whenever a case is retrieved, and by *Shepard's Citations* and KeyCite, resources to be discussed in the following chapter.

Not all cases have parallel citations. Only the official reports exist for older state cases, before West's National Reporter System was created in the 1880s. In the twenty-one states that have discontinued their official reports, on the other hand, recent cases have only West reporter citations.

c. Electronic Resources

The computer systems of LexisNexis and Westlaw are virtually comprehensive sources for state court decisions, lacking only a very few early nominative reports from some states. New decisions from all state appellate courts are added to the databases before they are available in published form. The online systems include some opinions not printed in the official reports and commercial reporters, but coverage is generally limited to the same courts for which reports are published. Very few state trial court decisions are available either in print or in online case databases.

Other commercial online databases also provide access to state court decisions; Loislaw, for example, has at least fifty years of case law for every state. Numerous state CD-ROM publications are available as well, many combining court decisions with current statutory codes and other materials.

Free Internet sites provide convenient access to court decisions beginning in the mid- to late-1990s, although some states maintain only the most recent three months of decisions on their official websites. A few states lead the

way with much more extensive databases; the Oklahoma State Courts Network <www.oscn.net> has the entire history of the state's appellate courts, back to 1890. As it does with the U.S. Courts of Appeals, lexisONE provides a five-year collection of state appellate decisions.

The easiest way to find websites for state court decisions is through a general legal resources site such as FindLaw. Its State Resources page <www.findlaw.com/11stategov/> provides links to official and commercial sites under "Primary Materials" for each state. Several law school sites, including Cornell's Legal Information Institute <www.law.cornell.edu/opinions.html>, have similar links, and the National Center for State Courts has a "Court Web Sites" list <www.ncsconline.org/D_KIS/ info_court_web_sites.html> with links to state judiciary systems and individual courts.

§3-5. CONCLUSION

This chapter has introduced case law as it is published in the United States today, both in print and through a variety of electronic means. While publication methods have changed dramatically in recent years, the structure of court systems and the inherent nature of judicial decisions remain relatively constant. This chapter's focus has been on the cases themselves, leaving to subsequent chapters the methods of finding case law relevant to a research problem. Chapter 4 will discuss several of the most important means of case research.

In addition to their value as legal precedent and their importance in legal research, court reports constitute a literary form with other values as well. They describe human problems and predicaments—domestic crises, moral failings, economic troubles. They reflect the larger social, polit-

ical and economic trends and conditions of life in particular periods and places. And they frequently have a unique literary quality which adds to the tone and substance of the prose of their time. Judicial decisions have always been an influential part of our literature.

CHAPTER 4
CASE LAW RESEARCH

■ ■ ■ ■ ■ ■ ■ ■ ■ ■

§4-1. Introduction

For the doctrine of precedent to operate effectively, lawyers must be able to find cases which control or influence a court's decisionmaking. This requires locating "cases on point," earlier decisions with factual and legal issues similar to a dispute at hand. It is then necessary to determine that these decisions are valid law and have not been reversed, overruled, or otherwise discredited. Judicial decisions, however, are published in chronological order, rather than by subject, and court reports are generally not updated once they are published. Other resources are therefore needed to provide subject access to decisions and to verify their current status.

This chapter discusses several major tools which perform these functions, but it is not exhaustive. Several resources discussed in other chapters—such as legal encyclopedias, law reviews, annotated codes, and looseleaf services—are also valuable in case research. Much of legal research revolves around finding cases, a pursuit that is not confined to the methods introduced in this one chapter.

We start with an overview of online research methods. Although many law students begin by using print materials, electronic case research is the approach most widely used in legal practice today. Our survey of online research methods is brief, but more in-depth knowledge comes from experience, training classes, and guides prepared for specific tools. It is easy to learn the basics of online research, but the expertise gained from practice and study will dramatically improve search effectiveness. Anyone can run an online search, but only a competent researcher can be confident that the results are accurate and complete.

The printed tools introduced in this chapter, West digests, *ALR* annotations, and *Shepard's Citations,* are complex resources unlike research materials in most other disci-

plines. At first they may seem more confusing than helpful, but skill in their use can yield more thorough, accurate results than online research alone. The assistance of editors who have analyzed and classified related cases can lead to insights that a searcher using only full-text databases might never reach.

§4-2. ELECTRONIC RESEARCH

Electronic resources are powerful and effective tools in legal research. Full-text databases allow researchers to determine their own criteria for each search, freeing them from reliance on publishers' indexing decisions, and hypertext links permit them to move effortlessly from one document or service to another and back again.

This discussion focuses primarily on the online databases Westlaw and LexisNexis, the most powerful and comprehensive electronic resources. Whether to use Westlaw or LexisNexis for particular research (if a choice is available) is a decision based in part on personal preference and in part on the features and materials they offer. Each has advantages, and familiarity with both will make for more successful research. Law schools generally have subscriptions allowing their students unlimited use of both databases, and most larger law firms subscribe to at least one of these services.

For other researchers, however, these commercial online systems may be unavailable or prohibitively expensive. Other options are available. Many college and university libraries subscribe to LexisNexis Academic, with many of LexisNexis's features, and other commercial services such as Loislaw and VersusLaw provide case research at relatively low cost. Some researchers may have access to their state's case law on CD-ROM rather than online. Generally

these services and products provide access in ways similar to Westlaw and LexisNexis, although their interfaces and search engines may be less flexible and sophisticated.

Free Internet sites may be a starting point in case research, but they rarely provide a complete answer. They may offer a searchable database of a particular court's opinions, but most are limited in coverage to the past few years (or months), and opportunities to search multiple jurisdictions are limited. (A notable exception is lexisONE.com, which permits searching the most recent five years of cases from all state courts or all federal courts.) Although free sites are most useful for obtaining copies of new decisions and monitoring recent developments, they may provide one or two cases that can lead to other documents. It is essential, however, not to overlook important precedent just because it is too old for a limited database.

Westlaw and LexisNexis have much more than case law, of course. Chapter 2 has discussed their coverage of secondary sources. They also have important resources in statutory and administrative research, and provide a wealth of business and news databases. This section provides a general overview of how to use these systems, with a focus on their case law databases.

A. Westlaw

One of the first choices confronting an online researcher is the selection of an appropriate database. Westlaw has a wide selection of case law databases, some limited to particular jurisdictions or specific subject areas and others combining cases from the entire federal court system, from every state, or from all available federal and state courts. Whether to limit research to a particular jurisdiction or topical area depends upon a variety of factors, including cost

(searches in large databases are generally more expensive), the purpose of the research, and the value of precedent from other jurisdictions or in other subjects. Often the only relevant cases for a research issue are those from a particular state or within a narrow doctrinal area. For some research questions, however, other cases may be persuasive authority or may provide useful analogies. Exhibit 18 shows part of Westlaw's online directory, indicating some of its federal case law databases. The *i* icon after the name of each database leads to an explanation of its scope of coverage. The directory is also available as the IDEN database, which can be searched to find databases containing specific publications or with particular terms in their descriptions.

Westlaw offers two basic methods of searching: natural language, and terms and connectors (or Boolean). Each of these search methods has its strengths. A natural language search allows the researcher to enter a phrase, or a combination of words (e.g., *Are handgun manufacturers liable for injuries to shooting victims?* or simply *handgun manufacturer liability*). The computer assigns relative weights to the terms in a query, depending on how often they appear in the database. It then retrieves a specified number of documents which appear most closely to match the query, giving greater weight to the less common terms. Not all terms will necessarily appear in every document retrieved, but one can specify "control concepts" that *must* appear in all documents.

A terms and connectors search can provide greater precision in retrieval, but it does require learning a structured search syntax. Specific terms or phrases are joined by logical connectors such as *and*, or by proximity connectors specifying the maximum number of words that can separate the search terms (e.g., /10) or specifying that the words appear in the same sentence (/s) or the same paragraph

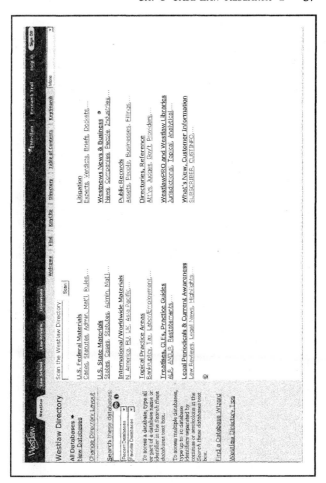

Exhibit 18. Westlaw directory screen.

(/p). In Westlaw, an *or* connector is understood between two adjacent terms. The search *handgun firearm*, for example, searches for documents containing either the word *handgun* or the word *firearm*. To search for a phrase such as "products liability," it is necessary to place the phrase in quotation marks. A terms and connectors search screen is shown in Exhibit 19.

Another aspect of terms and connectors searching is the use of the truncation symbols *!* and ***. An exclamation point is used to find any word beginning with the specified letters. *Manufactur!*, for example, will find *manufacturer, manufactured*, and *manufacturing*. Without the truncation symbol, only the word itself and its plural form are retrieved. *Manufacturer* will retrieve *manufacturers*, but not *manufactured* or *manufacturing*. The asterisk is less frequently used, but represents a particular character or a limited number of characters. *Legali*e* will retrieve either the American *legalize* or the British *legalise*, and *hand*** will retrieve *hand, handy* or *handle* but not *handgun*.

Whether natural language or terms and connectors searching is used, the terms entered will determine what cases are retrieved. Since more than one term can usually be used to denote a particular concept, it is important to enter synonyms or related terms. One decision may use the word *ambiguous*, another *vague*, and a third *unclear*. Whether searching with terms and connectors or natural language, it is important to use synonyms and related concepts. Westlaw provides help in identifying additional terms with an online thesaurus. For *handgun*, for example, it provides such terms as *firearm, pistol*, and *weapon*. In a terms and connector search, these alternates are simply typed one after the other, as in *handgun firearm weapon /p manufacturer*; in a natural language search, alternate terms are included in parentheses after the term to which they relate, as in *handgun (firearm weapon) manufacturer liability*.

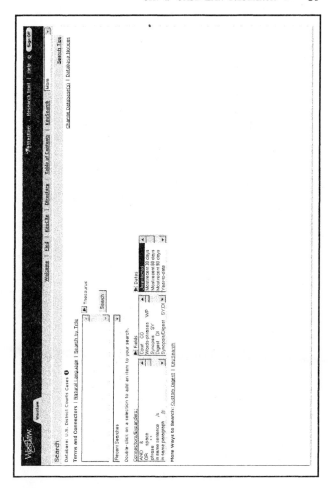

Exhibit 19. Westlaw search screen.

One major difference between the two types of searching is that a natural language search always retrieves the same number of cases, unless it includes control concepts. The initial display shows twenty documents, but up to one hundred can be retrieved by clicking on a right arrow. A terms and connectors search, on the other hand, can retrieve anywhere from nothing to thousands of cases, depending on how well the search is prepared and how often the terms appear in the database. The number of retrieved cases can be a useful indication of whether an appropriate search was performed. In a natural language search, the first few cases may be right on point but the degree of relevance can drop off precipitously. It is important to recognize when relevance declines, and to be aware that reading every case retrieved will usually be a waste of time. The effectiveness of a search depends on the quality of the resulting cases, not their quantity.

Researchers generally develop a preference for natural language or terms and connectors search methods, but they are best suited for different purposes. Because natural language searching retrieves documents based on how frequently search terms appear, it is ideal for finding documents on issues revolving around frequently used terms such as "summary judgment." Many cases mention the standards for summary judgment, but the few decisions focusing on it in depth would be retrieved first as most relevant. Terms and connectors searches require documents to match a request exactly, so this approach is generally preferable when searching for a particular phrase or a precise combination of terms. It is often fruitful to perform similar searches using both methods.

An important feature of Westlaw searching is the use of document fields. These are specific parts of a case, such as the names of the parties, the judge writing the opinion, or the date of decision. Limiting a search to a particular field

can produce a much more specific result. A search for *bell* retrieves any cases mentioning a person named Bell or simply using the word *bell* anywhere in the opinion. A title search, *ti(bell)*, retrieves only those cases where one of the parties is named Bell.

Some fields allow research that is virtually impossible by other means. It would be a lengthy and tedious process manually to find all opinions written by a particular judge, but online databases can easily retrieve a complete list of a judge's opinions with searches such as *ju(molloy)*. The researcher can examine a judge's decisions on a particular topic by combining this request with other search terms.

In Westlaw, one can use the *synopsis* and *digest* fields to search only for words in the introductory summary and headnotes that precede opinions in West reporters. Limiting the search to words important enough to be mentioned in the synopsis or headnotes retrieves a smaller body of cases more precisely on point. West's digest topics and key numbers (which will be discussed below in § 4-3) can also be used in Westlaw searches, either alone or in combination with other search terms.

The entire list of available fields is shown in a drop-down box on the terms and connectors search screen, as shown in Exhibit 19. In natural language searching, the only fields that can be applied are court (CO), attorney (AT), and judge (JU), listed on the search screen as "restrictions."

Once a search is entered, Westlaw displays a list of retrieved cases on the left and the text of the first case on the right. A "standard list" displays simply the names and citations of the cases retrieved, while an "enhanced list" includes the appearance of the search terms. Case displays include the synopsis and headnotes from West reporters, providing a quick guide to a case's relevance to a research

issue. Buttons at the bottom of the screen allow the researcher to go to that part of the opinion with terms matching the search query or to the next document. Natural language search results also include a *Best* button to focus on that part of the document that most closely matches the query. Exhibit 20 shows an "enhanced list" display for a query about handgun manufacturer liability, including the text of the U.S. District Court case *Bell v. Glock, Inc.*

As part of the screen display of a case, Westlaw provides citations to published versions, whether in official reports, West's National Reporter System, or looseleaf topical reporters. It also provides star paging references showing the exact reporter page on which particular text is printed, so that a quotation or reference can be cited to the appropriate page.

If a completed search retrieves too many cases, you can narrow the focus of inquiry by using the *Locate* feature. This allows you to examine the retrieved set of documents for specific terms, whether or not they were included in the initial request. Instead of identifying a new set of cases replacing the original search result, *Locate* searches for and highlights particular terms among the retrieved documents. This feature is particularly valuable if each new search costs money, because it does not incur an additional search charge.

It is also possible, of course, to edit a query by adding new terms or to pursue new topics, perhaps in another database. Clicking on "edit query" provides a new search screen, including a "change database(s)" link to specify other courts to check.

Most judicial opinions cite extensively to other cases, as well as to statutes and other documents, and it is often important or helpful to examine these other sources.

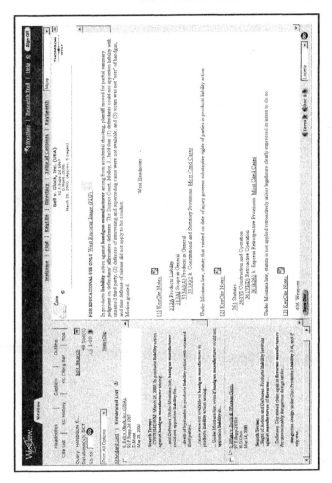

Exhibit 20.   Bell v. Glock, Inc., 92 F. Supp. 2d 1067
(D. Mont. 2000) (Westlaw).

Westlaw case displays include hypertext links to these other sources if they are available online. A researcher using book sources would have to make notes for possible future reference, but a Westlaw researcher can follow these leads as they arise. Clicking on a hyperlink opens up a new "link viewer" window, making it easy to return to the original citing document.

Westlaw's KeyCite feature is an integral part of case display. It shows whether a case is still good law, and provides a convenient way to find cases on related topics. KeyCite performs several valuable functions in the research process, but it will be discussed later in the chapter with other citators, in § 4-5 beginning on page 125.

One valuable Westlaw feature which many students overlook is the ability to save a search and have the system automatically run it to check for new material on a daily or weekly basis. This feature can be accessed by clicking on the WestClip link on the top left part of the screen, and provides for notification by e-mail or when you sign onto Westlaw. WestClip provides a very convenient way to stay abreast of developments in a specific case or in an area of interest. Another time- and money-saving feature is Research Trail, which saves searches for two weeks and allows you to return to earlier searches without additional charges.

This has been only a cursory summary of major Westlaw features. Much more detail, with extensive illustrations and search examples, is provided in the booklet *Discovering Westlaw* and in other Westlaw research aids.

B. LEXISNEXIS

Using LexisNexis is quite similar to using Westlaw, with just enough differences to make either a challenge for someone familiar only with one system. The first step in

using LexisNexis is to choose an appropriate database
from the menu on the screen. Exhibit 21 shows the
LexisNexis display of federal court databases, with "i"
icons linking to information about the scope of each database .

For years a major distinction between Westlaw and
LexisNexis was that Westlaw included editorial summaries
of cases while LexisNexis had only the court opinions. This
has changed dramatically, as LexisNexis has now added
summaries to most of the cases in its databases. These
summaries have made LexisNexis much more useful in
case research, where determining a case's holding is usually more important than simply finding relevant terms. The
summary is followed by computer-generated core terms
and headnotes containing "core concepts." Exhibit 8 in the
previous chapter, on page 52, shows these features as part
of a case display.

LexisNexis offers both natural language and terms and
connectors searching. Natural language searching is similar
to Westlaw's. The researcher can specify the number of
documents retrieved, from as few as ten to as many as 250.
"Mandatory terms" that *must* appear in all documents can
be added and may produce a smaller result.

LexisNexis terminology for terms and connectors searching is slightly different than Westlaw's. Most connectors
are similar, although the word *or* must be included
between synonyms or related terms. Because an *or* is not
understood between adjacent words, phrases in LexisNexis
do not have to be entered in quotations. Proximity connectors begin with *w/* (as in *w/10*, *w/s*, or *w/p*), although each
system is forgiving enough to understand the other's format. Like Westlaw, LexisNexis uses the *!* and *** characters
to truncate terms and find word variations. Exhibit 22
shows a basic terms and connectors search screen.

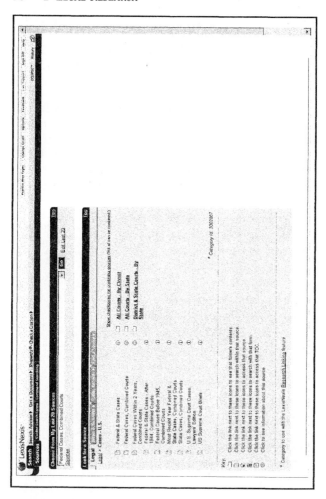

Exhibit 21. LexisNexis directory screen.

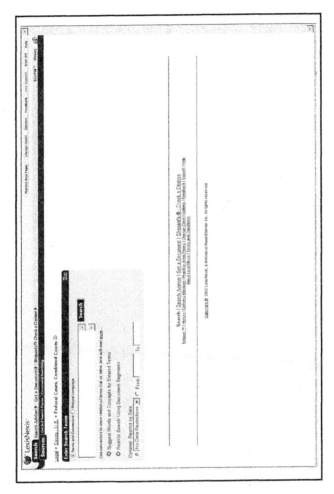

Exhibit 22. LexisNexis search screen.

LexisNexis includes a "suggest words or concepts for entered terms" feature that is broader than a thesaurus. It lists not only synonyms and related concepts but terms that regularly appear in close proximity to the term. *Handgun*, for example, leads to such terms as *arrest, possession, probable cause, search warrant*, and *victim*. These may suggest further search terms or other lines of inquiry.

The LexisNexis counterpart to Westlaw's *fields* are called *segments*. Among the most useful segments are *name* for a particular party and *opinionby* for a particular judge. (Although they accept each other's proximity connectors, LexisNexis and Westlaw generally do *not* recognize searches using the other system's field or segment names.) Each of LexisNexis's introductory editorial features can be used as a document segment, making it possible to search for terms appearing only in the overview or the headnotes. Segments are added to a terms and connectors search by clicking on "Restrict search using document segments," and to a natural language search as "mandatory terms."

LexisNexis has three basic display formats. *Cite* provides a list of citations, including the overview and core terms; the researcher can choose *Show hits* to display the search terms as well. *Full* displays an entire document, and *KWIC*, short for "key words in context," shows an individual case with a window of 25 words around the occurrence of the search terms. For natural language search results, *SuperKWIC* shows the part of the document that most closely matches the query. Exhibit 23 shows the SuperKWIC display for *Bell v. Glock, Inc.*, retrieved with a query about handgun manufacturer liability.

LexisNexis includes star paging references to official reports, West's National Reporter System, and looseleaf topical reporters; the "[*1068]" at the beginning of the opinion text in Exhibit 23 indicates the *Federal Supplement*

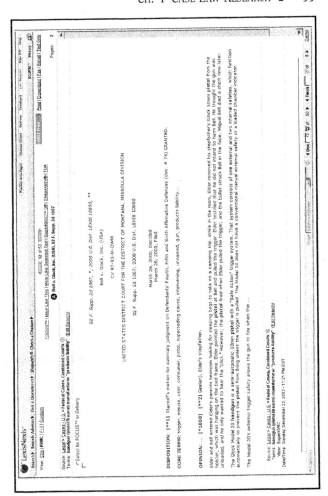

Exhibit 23.   Bell v. Glock, Inc., 2000 U.S. Dist. LEXIS 10850
(D. Mont. Mar. 28, 2000).

page on which this excerpt appears. It also provides hyperlinks to cases, statutes, law review articles, and other documents available in its databases. Like Westlaw's *Locate*, the *Focus* feature provides a way to examine a retrieved set of documents for specific terms without incurring additional charges.

Two LexisNexis features providing other ways to focus or expand research are *More like this* and *More like selected text*. *More like this* finds either cases that cite the same authorities (*core cites*) or cases that use similar terms (*core terms*). Choosing this feature when viewing the *Bell* case, for example, leads to options to retrieve documents citing the same cases *Bell* cites or to find similar cases by selecting from a list of core terms in *Bell* (including *affirmative defense*, *misuse*, *products liability*, and *superseding cause*).

A feature that may be useful when beginning a research project is *Search Advisor*. This provides a way to explore legal topics (such as Torts—Strict Liability—Abnormally Dangerous Activities), and then to search for cases within this specific subject area.

LexisNexis offers a service, *Eclipse*, that automatically runs a search on a daily or weekly basis to monitor new developments. Along with *Focus*, *More like this*, and *More like selected text*, *Save as Eclipse* is listed above the title on a case display. (Another choice listed, *Shepardize*, will be discussed separately in § 4-5.) These searches can be retrieved by clicking on the *Eclipse* heading at the top right of the screen. To the right of *Eclipse*, the *History* link allows you to return to any search performed earlier the same day without incurring additional search costs.

Further information about LexisNexis is available in its annual *Understanding LexisNexis* publication. Like this discussion, it focuses on features available to lawyers and law

students through the lexis.com website. Some, but not all,
of these features are also available to users of LexisNexis
Academic and lexisONE. These sources use terms and connectors searching only, not natural language, but proximity
connectors and document segments can be used.
LexisNexis Academic display options include an expanded
list showing hits, KWIC, and full; while lexisONE provides
only a basic list and full text. Neither Academic nor
lexisONE includes the case summaries or other editorial
additions provided by lexis.com, and neither includes
hypertext links to other documents cited in retrieved cases.

§4-3. West Digests

Digests, which reprint in a subject arrangement the headnotes from court reports, are among the most powerful
methods of case-finding. Despite the ease and flexibility
of keyword access, electronic searching may miss relevant
cases that can be found in the digests. Editorial analysis in
organizing and classifying cases may lead to analogous
cases that use different words from those that might occur
to a researcher. Similar legal issues may arise, for example,
in cases involving handgun manufacturers and cigarette
companies, but it may not occur to a researcher to explore
both tobacco and firearms.

Several digest systems are published; those focusing on
specific subject areas will be discussed briefly in Chapter 9.
The most comprehensive digest system is Thomson West's
key number system, covering every case in the publisher's
National Reporter System. The West digest system consists
of over 400 topics, arranged alphabetically from
Abandoned and Lost Property to Zoning and Planning.
Each topic is divided into numbered sections designating
specific points of law for that topic. These individual sections are called *key numbers*. Some narrow topics like Party

Walls employ relatively few key numbers, while broader ones such as Taxation or Trade Regulation may have thousands.

The entries in West's digests come directly from the headnotes in National Reporter System volumes. Each headnote is classified by topic and key number to designate its subject. Exhibit 24 shows the first page of the U.S. District Court decision in *Bell v. Glock, Inc.*, 92 F. Supp. 2d 1067 (D. Mont. 2000), with headnotes assigned to the topics Products Liability, Statutes, and Weapons.

All headnotes for cases in an advance sheet or reporter volume are reprinted in a Key Number Digest in the front of the advance sheet or at the back of the bound reporter volume. These digests serve as subject indexes to the cases in the advance sheet or volume. Exhibit 25 shows the digest from the *Federal Supplement* volume containing the *Bell* decision, including the first *Bell* headnote under Products Liability West key number 2, "Products in general: Constitutional and statutory provisions." Only a small percentage of the key numbers are used in this volume's decisions, but West then reprints these headnotes, arranged by key number, in multivolume digest series to provide subject access to the cases in hundreds of reporter volumes.

Although digests are valuable case-finders, they do have several shortcomings. They consist simply of case abstracts, with no explanatory text, and the researcher must often wade through many irrelevant entries to find citations to significant authorities. Digest entries may reflect dicta and may even misstate points of law in the cases they abstract. The digests don't indicate that a case may no longer be good law, unless it has been directly reversed or modified. It is essential to locate and read the cases themselves in order to find those which are actually pertinent, and then to verify their status through other means.

BELL v. GLOCK, INC. (USA) **1067**
Cite as 92 F.Supp.2d 1067 (D.Mont 2000)

Diana L. BELL, both personally and as
Personal Representative of the Estate
of Miguel A. Bell, deceased, Plaintiff,

v.

GLOCK, INC., (USA), and Glock
Gies.m.b.H, (Austria)
Defendants.

No. CV 9783MDWM.

United States District Court,
D. Montana,
Missoula Division

March 28, 2000.

In products liability action against
handgun manufacturer arising from accidental shooting, plaintiff moved for partial
summary judgment on defendants' affirmative defenses. The District Court, Molloy, J., held that: (1) defendants could not
apportion liability with unnamed third party; (2) defenses of intervening and superseding cause were not available; and (3)
victim was not "user" of handgun, and thus
defense of misuse did not apply to his
conduct.

Motion granted.

1. Products Liability ⚖2

Under Montana law, statute that existed on date of injury governs substantive
rights of parties in products liability action.

2. Statutes ⚖262

Under Montana law, statute is not
applied retroactively unless legislature
clearly expressed its intent to do so.

3. Weapons ⚖18(1)

Under Montana law, handgun manufacturer could not apportion liability for
death of bystander in products liability
action with unnamed third parties. MCA
27-1-703.

4. Weapons ⚖18(1)

Under Montana law, defenses of intervening and superseding cause were not
available to handgun manufacturer in
products liability action arising from acci-

dental shooting; victim did not assume risk
of accident, and gun was being misused in
foreseeable manner by unnamed third party. MCA 27-1-719.

5. Weapons ⚖18(2)

Under Montana law, even if handgun
manufacturer could not apportion liability
in products liability action with unnamed
third party, manufacturer could introduce
evidence of conduct of victim and third
party as it related to what happened in
incident, background facts leading to incident, or to rebut claim that one or more
alleged defects was substantial factor in
victim's death.

6. Weapons ⚖18(1)

Under Montana law, shooting victim
was not "user" of handgun, and thus did
not assume risk associated with product,
absent evidence that victim invited shooter
to point gun at him and fire. MCA 27-1-
719(5)(a).

See publication Words and Phrases for other judicial constructions
and definitions.

7. Weapons ⚖18(1)

Under Montana law, shooting victim
was not "user" of handgun, and thus defense of misuse did not apply to his conduct. MCA 27-1-719(5)(b).

Alan J. Lerner, Law Offices of Alan J.
Lerner, Kalispell, MT; Edward P. Moriarity, Spence Moriarity & Schuster, Jackson,
WY; Evan F. Danno, Law Offices of Evan
F. Danno, Kalispell, MT; Michael A. Viscomi, Viscomi Law Office, Kalispell, MT;
Sleandor S. Badaruddin, Badaruddin Law
Office, Atlanta, GA, for Diana L. Bell, both
personally, and as Personal Representative
of the Estate of Miguel A. Bell, deceased,
plaintiffs.

John F. Renzulli, Christopher P. Orlan-
do, Renzulli & Rutherford, New York, NY,
William E. Jones, Peter J. Stokstad, Gar-
lington, Lohn & Robinson, PLLP, Missoula, MT, for Glock, Inc. (USA), Glock Gies.
M.B.H (Austria), defendants.

Exhibit 24.   Bell v. Glock, Inc., 92 F. Supp. 2d 1067
(D. Mont. 2000).

PRISONS

☞4(5). Particular rights, privileges, and restrictions.

S.D.N.Y. 2000. Provisions of Individuals with Disabilities in Education Act (IDEA) requiring school districts to proactively attempt to identify all youngsters with disabilities and, for each child, develop an individualized education plan (IEP), apply where child is incarcerated. Individuals with Disabilities Education Act, § 614, as amended, 20 U.S.C.A. § 1414.—Handberry v. Thompson, 92 F.Supp.2d 244.

☞13(5). Segregation and solitary confinement; classification.

N.D.Ind. 2000. Three years of prison disciplinary segregation did not present violation of a liberty interest subject to due process protection. U.S.C.A. Const.Amend. 14.—Dabney v. Anderson, 92 F.Supp.2d 801.

Any placement in administrative segregation after the duration of prison disciplinary segregation was not a violation of a liberty interest since prisoner was not in custody pursuant to his finding of guilt. U.S.C.A. Const.Amend. 14.—Id.

☞13(9). —— Counsel and witnesses.

N.D.Ind. 2000. Prisoner did not have a right to either retained or appointed counsel in prison disciplinary hearing. U.S.C.A. Const.Amend. 6.—Dabney v. Anderson, 92 F.Supp.2d 801.

☞15(5). Forfeiture before release.

N.D.Ind. 2000. Loss of good time credit was a liberty interest subject to due process protection. U.S.C.A. Const.Amend. 14.—Dabney v. Anderson, 92 F.Supp.2d 801.

PRODUCTS LIABILITY

I. SCOPE IN GENERAL.

(A) PRODUCTS IN GENERAL.

☞2. Constitutional and statutory provisions.

D.Mont. 2000. Under Montana law, statute that existed on date of injury governs substantive rights of parties in products liability action.—Bell v. Glock, Inc. (USA), 92 F.Supp.2d 1067.

☞11. Design.

N.D.N.Y. 2000. Under New York law, manufacturer will be strictly liable for a design defect if: (1) the product is defective because it is not reasonably safe as marketed; (2) the product was used for a normal purpose; (3) the defect was a substantial factor in causing the plaintiff's injuries; (4) the plaintiff by the exercise of reasonable care would not have both discovered the defect and apprehended its danger; (5) the plaintiff would not have otherwise avoided the injury by the exercise of ordinary care.—Tompkins v. R.J. Reynolds Tobacco Co., 92 F.Supp.2d 70.

To establish a prima facie case under New York law for strict liability based on design defect, a plaintiff must show that the manufacturer breached its duty to market safe products when it marketed a product designed so that it was not reasonably safe and that the defective design was a substantial factor in causing plaintiff's injury.—Id.

Standard applied in New York in deciding whether a product is not reasonably safe is whether it is a product which, if the design defect were known at the time of manufacture, a reasonable person would conclude that the utility of the prod-

uct did not outweigh the risk inherent in marketing a product designed in that manner.—Id.

In New York, burden of proving that product is not reasonably safe rests with plaintiffs, who are under an obligation to present evidence that the product, as designed, was not reasonably safe because there was a substantial likelihood of harm and it was feasible to design the product in a safer manner.—Id.

Manufacturer whose product is claimed to be not reasonably safe under New York law may produce evidence showing that utility outweighed risk; factors considered in the utility/risk balancing test, are: (1) the utility of the product to the public as a whole, (2) the utility of the product to the individual user, (3) the likelihood that the product will cause injury, (4) the availability of a safer design, (5) the potential for designing and manufacturing the product so that it is safer but remains functional and reasonably priced, (6) the degree of awareness of the product's potential danger that can be reasonably attributed to the plaintiff, and (7) the manufacturer's ability to spread the cost of any safety-related design changes.—Id.

A negligent design claim under New York law must establish that a feasible alternate design could have been used.—Id.

☞14. Warning or instructions.

N.D.N.Y. 2000. Under New York law, manufacturer has a duty to warn the appropriate audience of all potential dangers of which it, through the exercise of reasonable care, knows or should know. —Tompkins v. R.J. Reynolds Tobacco Co., 92 F.Supp.2d 70.

There is no duty under New York law to warn consumers of obvious risks and dangers, which is defined to mean those risks and dangers which could have been or should have been appreciated by the user or that can be recognized as a matter of common sense.—Id.

Under New York law, a negligence claim for failure to warn and a strict liability claim for failure to warn are considered to be equivalent.—Id.

☞15. Proximate cause and foreseeable injury; intended or foreseeable use.

W.D.Mo. 2000. Under Missouri law, plaintiff in products liability action is not required to exclude every causative factor, save that for which the defendant is liable; plaintiff is not required to "prove an absolutely positive causal connection," instead, a submissible case on causation is made where the evidence is susceptible to a reasonable inference that injuries to plaintiff resulted from defendant's product.—Nelson v. American Home Products Corp., 92 F.Supp.2d 954.

N.D.N.Y. 2000. To establish a prima facie case under New York law for strict liability based on design defect, a plaintiff must show that the manufacturer breached its duty to market safe products when it marketed a product designed so that it was not reasonably safe and that the defective design was a substantial factor in causing plaintiff's injury.—Tompkins v. R.J. Reynolds Tobacco Co., 92 F.Supp.2d 70.

(B) PARTICULAR PRODUCTS, APPLICATION TO.

☞59. Tobacco products.

N.D.N.Y. 2000. Claim that tobacco company actively concealed research results demonstrating the health risks associated with smoking was preempted with respect to events that occurred

(83)

Exhibit 25. Key Number Digest, 127 F.3d app. at 83 (2000).

A. FINDING CASES IN DIGESTS

To use a digest, you must identify a topic and key number relevant to the problem. Digest topics and key numbers can be found in several ways: (1) by using a Descriptive-Word Index after analyzing the factual and legal issues involved in a problem; (2) by surveying the outline of a relevant legal topic; or (3) from the headnotes of a case known to be on point. In addition, digests provide alphabetical tables of cases so that researchers can use names of known cases to find their citations and the topics and key numbers to which their headnotes have been assigned. The case tables in newer digest volumes include entries under both parties' names, while older volumes have separate defendant-plaintiff tables providing just citations and cross-references to the main tables.

Descriptive-Word Method. To find the appropriate key number under which relevant cases are digested, it is usually most productive to begin with a Descriptive-Word Index. These indexes, which list thousands of factual and legal terms, accompany each digest set.

You can approach a Descriptive-Word Index either by looking up legal issues, such as causes of action, defenses, or relief sought; or, usually more efficiently, by looking up factual elements in an action, such as parties, places, or objects involved. For example, in a products liability case involving handgun manufacturers, you might use the index to investigate some of the legal issues or facts involved in the case (weapons, strict liability, proximate cause, standing). Exhibit 26 shows a page from a Descriptive-Word Index, including a reference under the Weapons subheading "Civil liability, sale or use" to Weapons 18. Besides numerous references to the Weapons topic, entries on the page also lead to Aviation, Boundaries, Constitutional Law, and other topics throughout the digest.

WATERWAY

99B F P D 4th–528

References are to Digest Topics and Key Numbers

WATERWAY DISTRICTS

IMPROVEMENT of channels and streams, Nav Wat ⟳ 8.5

WATERWORKS

See heading **PUBLIC WATER SUPPLY**, generally.

WAVE LENGTHS

RADIO, Tel ⟳ 392

TELEVISION, Tel ⟳ 392

WAYS

BOUNDARIES, Bound ⟳ 19

EASEMENTS. See heading **EASEMENTS**, generally.

EMPLOYERS' liability, ways used in work, Emp Liab ⟳ 50

NECESSITY, ways of. See heading **EASEMENTS**, NECESSITY, ways of.

PRIVATE road. See heading **PRIVATE ROADS**, generally.

PUBLIC ways,
Highways. See heading **HIGHWAYS**, generally.
Streets. See heading **STREETS**, generally.

RIGHT-OF-WAY. See heading **RIGHT-OF-WAY**, generally.

WEALTH

Generally. See heading **PECUNIARY CONDITION**, generally.

EQUAL protection, status as suspect classification. Const Law ⟳ 213.1(1)

WEAPONS

ACTIONS for injuries, Weap ⟳ 18(2)

APPEAL and error in criminal proceedings. See heading **CRIMINAL APPEALS**, generally.

APPORTIONMENT of fault, Weap ⟳ 18(1)

ARMED robbery. See heading **ROBBERY**, ARMED robbery.

ASSAULT with dangerous or deadly weapon. See heading **ASSAULT AND BATTERY**, WEAPONS.

AVIATION,
Concealed weapons, Aviation ⟳ 16

WEAPONS—Cont'd

BEARING, right to,
Generally, Weap ⟳ 1
Ninth Amendment, Const Law ⟳ 82(6.1)
Second Amendment, incorporation through due process clause, Const Law ⟳ 274(2)

BOMBS,
Hoaxes,
Airports, Aviation ⟳ 16

BRANDISHING, Weap ⟳ 14

BURDEN of proof,
Civil proceedings, Weap ⟳ 18(2)
Criminal proceedings, Weap ⟳ 17(2)

CARRYING,
Generally, Weap ⟳ 5-13
Concealment, manner of, Weap ⟳ 10
Defenses in general, Weap ⟳ 12
See also heading **CRIMINAL LAW**, DEFENSES.
Elements in general, Weap ⟳ 6
Excuse or justification, Weap ⟳ 12
Intent or purpose, Weap ⟳ 7
Licenses, Weap ⟳ 12
Manner of carrying, Weap ⟳ 10
Necessity, defense of, Crim Law ⟳ 38
Occasions exempted from prohibition, Weap ⟳ 11
Permits, Weap ⟳ 12
Persons exempted from prohibition,
Generally, Weap ⟳ 11
Mail carriers, Weap ⟳ 11(3)
Officers, Weap ⟳ 11(1)
Travelers, Weap ⟳ 11(2)
Places within scope of prohibition, Weap ⟳ 9
Weapons within scope of prohibition, Weap ⟳ 8

CHILDREN and minors,
Civil liability for acts of minor, Weap ⟳ 18
Possession by minor, offense, Weap ⟳ 4
Sale or transfer to minor, offense, Weap ⟳ 4

CIVIL liability, sale or use, Weap ⟳ 18

COMMERCE power, regulation under, Commerce ⟳ 82.50

CONCEALMENT, Weap ⟳ 10

CONSTITUTIONAL law,
Generally, Weap ⟳ 3
Bearing, right to. See subheading BEARING, right to, under this heading.

Exhibit 26. Descriptive-Word Index, 99B FEDERAL PRACTICE DIGEST 4TH, at 528 (2002).

Finding appropriate key numbers in the index can sometimes be a simple step. A researcher using any legal index, however, should be prepared for some frustration. Even the most thorough index cannot list every possible approach to a legal or factual issue. It is often necessary to rethink issues, reframe questions, check synonyms and alternate terms, and follow leads in cross-references.

When turning from the index to the volume of digest abstracts, it is often helpful to look first at the outline of the topic to verify that the legal context is indeed appropriate. A researcher looking for cases on substantive negligence issues, for example, may find that a reference leads instead to a key number dealing with the standard of review for summary judgment. Exhibit 27 contains the outline for the Weapons topic, showing how key number 18 fits with other issues involving the regulation and use of firearms.

Topic Approach. An alternative approach used by some researchers bypasses the Descriptive-Word Index and goes directly to the West digest topic that seems most relevant to the problem. Each topic begins with a scope note, indicating which subjects it includes and which are covered in related topics. The Weapons topic, for example, covers issues such as the right to bear arms and offenses involving concealed weapons, but it does not incorporate matters such as the regulation of militias (covered in the Militia topic) or specific crimes committed using weapons (covered in topics such as Homicide or Assault and Battery).

Once the correct topic is found, analyze the outline of key numbers to select the appropriate key number for a specific issue. An advantage of this method is that it provides the context of the individual key numbers; reading through the outline may help clarify issues or raise concerns the researcher had not yet considered. This can be a very time-consuming approach, however, and beginning

53 11th D Pt 1—827

WEAPONS

SUBJECTS INCLUDED

Right to bear arms in self-defense or in defense of the state

Regulation of manufacture, dealing in, and use of weapons

Liabilities for injuries therefrom caused by negligence

Offenses of having or carrying weapons concealed or in any other manner prohibited, pointing or shooting firearms, etc., not constituting any other distinct offense

SUBJECTS EXCLUDED AND COVERED BY OTHER TOPICS

Militia, matters relating to, see MILITIA

Specific injuries or crimes committed by use of weapons, see ASSAULT AND BATTERY, HOMICIDE, and other specific topics

For detailed references to other topics, see Descriptive-Word Index

Analysis

⊂➤1. Right to bear arms.
2. Power to make regulations.
3. Constitutional and statutory provisions.
4. Manufacture, sale, gift, loan, possession, or use.
5. Carrying weapons.
5.1. —— In general.
6. —— Nature and elements of offenses in general.
7. —— Intent or purpose.
8. —— Weapons prohibited.
9. —— Places prohibited.
10. —— Manner of carrying or concealment.
11. —— Persons and occasions exempted or privileged.
   (.5). In general.
   (1). Officers and persons aiding them.
   (2). Travelers.
   (3). Mail carriers.
12. —— Licenses or permits.
13. —— Justification or excuse.

14. Pointing or exhibiting weapon.
15. Shooting firearms.
16. Penalties and forfeitures.
17. Criminal prosecutions.
   (.5). In general.
   (1). Indictment and information.
   (2). Presumptions and burden of proof.
   (3). Admissibility of evidence.
   (4). Weight and sufficiency of evidence.
   (5). Questions for jury.
   (6). Instructions.
   (7). Appeal and error.
   (8). Sentence and punishment.
18. Liabilities for injuries from illegal or negligent manufacture, sale, or use.
   (.5). In general.
   (1). Right of action and defenses.
   (2). Procedure.

For detailed references to other topics, see Descriptive-Word Index

Exhibit 27.   Weapons, 53 11th Decennial Digest Part 1, at 827 (2002).

researchers may not have the legal background to choose the right topic and determine the appropriate issues. In most instances, the index is a faster and more reliable starting point.

Case Headnotes. The easiest and most foolproof way to use the digest is to begin with the headnotes of a case on point. When you already know of a relevant case, you can find it in the National Reporter System volume or on Westlaw, scan its headnotes for relevant issues, and then use the key numbers accompanying these headnotes in

searching the digest. This eliminates the need to search through indexes or to analyze the digest's classification system, and reduces the likelihood of turning to the wrong issue or getting stuck in a dead end. This method, of course, requires that at least one initial case be found through other means, but several other case-finding resources—from legal encyclopedias to online full-text searches—have already been discussed.

B. DECENNIAL AND GENERAL DIGESTS

West digests are available for the entire country, for some regions, for individual states, and for a few specific subjects. Choosing the right digest depends on the scope of the inquiry. For some research you may want to find cases from only one jurisdiction, but for other projects you may be interested in developments throughout the country. A more focused digest obviously covers fewer cases but is usually easier to use.

The most comprehensive series of digests is known as the American Digest System. Its most current component, the *General Digest*, collects and publishes headnotes from all West advance sheets. The *General Digest* is published about every three weeks, with each volume covering the entire range of more than 400 digest topics. One *General Digest* volume gathers entries from about twenty reporter volumes from federal and state courts.

The entries in the *General Digest* do not cumulate, so one may have to look through several dozen volumes to search for recent cases. This search is eased somewhat by tables listing the key numbers found in each volume. These tables cumulate every tenth volume. If 27 *General Digest* volumes have been published, for example, it would be necessary to check the tables in volumes 10, 20, and 27. An excerpt from one of these tables is shown in Exhibit 28.

WEAPONS
☞
1—21, 23, 25, 26, 27
3—21, 22, 23, 24, 25, 26, 27
4—21, 22, 23, 24, 25, 26, 27
5.1—21, 23, 25
6—24, 25, 26, 27
7—27
8—23, 24, 25, 26
9—22, 23, 24
10—21, 25, 27
11(0.5)—22
11(2)—21
12—22, 23, 24, 26, 27
13—23, 25
14—25
15—21, 27
16—24, 25, 27
17(1)—21, 22, 23, 25, 26, 27
17(2)—21, 22, 24, 25, 27
17(3)—26
17(4)—21, 22, 23, 24, 25, 26, 27
17(5)—21, 22, 26
17(6)—23, 24, 25, 26
17(8)—21, 27
18(1)—21, 23, 27
18(2)—23

Exhibit 28.   Table of Key Numbers, 27 General Digest 1419
(2002).

After five years, West recompiles the headnotes from the
General Digest and publishes them in a multivolume set
called a *Decennial Digest*. The name *Decennial* comes from
the fact that these sets used to be published every ten
years. The *Eighth Decennial*, for example, covers cases
decided between 1966 and 1976. Due to the increased volume of case law, West now compiles these digests every
five years. The *Eleventh Decennial Digest, Part 1* is the most
recent set, covering 1996-2001.

The first unit of the American Digest System, called the *Century Digest*, covers the long period from 1658 to 1896. It was followed by a *First Decennial Digest* for 1897 to 1906, and subsequent Decennials for each decade since. The topics and key numbers used for points of law are generally the same in each unit of the digest system, from the most recent back to the *First Decennial*. The *Century Digest* employs a slightly different system, but the *First Decennial* provides cross-references between the two units. Thus research using a digest key number can turn up cases from the seventeenth century to the present.

The law, of course, has not remained static over these centuries. West attempts to reflect new developments by revising and expanding old topics and by establishing new topics. When they are introduced, new or revised topics are accompanied by tables converting older topics and key numbers into those newly adopted and vice versa. In 2001, for example, the new topics Child Custody and Child Support were created, with subject matter formerly found in Divorce, Parent and Child, and other topics. The new topics include conversion tables so that researchers can find related cases whether they are using the older *Decennials* or the newest *General Digest* volumes.

The digest changes slowly, however, and it may take several years for new areas of legal doctrine to be recognized and to receive adequate coverage. The Weapons key numbers assigned to the *Bell* headnotes, for example, deal with liability for illegal or negligent manufacture of firearms, not with more specific issues such as manufacturers' liability to shooting victims or municipal lawsuits based on public nuisance theories. Because cases in newly developing areas of the law are often assigned to general key numbers, digest research may not be the best way to find cases in these areas.

C. JURISDICTIONAL AND REGIONAL DIGESTS

The American Digest System covers cases in all of West's reporters, and is therefore a massive, sometimes unwieldy finding tool. West also publishes digests covering the decisions of smaller geographical or jurisdictional units. There are digests for four of the regional reporter series (*Atlantic*, *North Western*, *Pacific*, and *South Eastern*), and for every state but Delaware, Nevada and Utah. The state digests include references to all the cases West publishes from the state's courts, as well as federal cases arising from the U.S. District Courts in that state. (Federal courts often interpret and apply state law, sometimes addressing issues with which the state courts have not yet dealt.)

One advantage of using a state digest instead of the American Digest System is that a single volume can contain all relevant headnotes from a century or more. (For about a dozen states, the current digest only provides coverage of cases back to 1930 or later, and an earlier digest must be consulted for complete retrospective coverage to the earliest court decisions. Most research, however, requires consulting only the current set for cases on point.) Instead of being issued in ten-year installments, state digests cumulate and are kept up to date by annual pocket parts in the back of each volume, by quarterly pamphlets between annual supplements, and by occasional replacement volumes incorporating the newer material.

Another significant advantage to state digests arises when classifications change, as happened with the Child Custody and Child Support topics in 2001. As part of the process West editors reclassified the headnotes in thousands of older relevant cases, but this change is reflected only on Westlaw and in newly recompiled state digest volumes. *Decennial Digests* are closed sets, and conversion tables are needed to find relevant cases under the older classifications.

West also publishes a separate series of digests for federal court decisions, containing headnotes reprinted from the *Supreme Court Reporter, Federal Reporter, Federal Appendix, Federal Supplement, Federal Rules Decisions,* and the reporters for specialized federal courts. The current set is known as the *Federal Practice Digest 4th.* Its volumes are supplemented by annual pocket parts, and the entire set is further updated with bimonthly pamphlets. Earlier cases are covered by four previous sets, the *Federal Digest* (1754-1939), *Modern Federal Practice Digest* (1939-61), *Federal Practice Digest 2d* (1961-75), and *Federal Practice Digest 3d* (1975 to mid-1980s).

The decisions of the Supreme Court of the United States are also covered by a West digest devoted solely to its decisions, the *United States Supreme Court Digest.* (Note that *Lawyers' Edition* is also accompanied by its own digest, *United States Supreme Court Digest, Lawyers' Edition,* which uses a different classification system.) Other digests for specialized federal courts include *West's Bankruptcy Digest, Military Justice Digest, Federal Claims Digest,* and *Veterans Appeals Digest.*

Regional and jurisdictional digests include Tables of Cases which can be used to find decisions by name. These tables are usually more convenient than the *Decennial Digest* tables since they cover longer time periods and are updated by pocket parts. If the jurisdiction of a case is not known, of course, it may be necessary to consult the tables in the *Decennial* or *General Digests.*

d. Words and Phrases

West reprints some headnote abstracts in a separate multivolume set, *Words and Phrases.* Headnotes are included in *Words and Phrases* if the court is defining or interpreting a legally significant term, and they are arranged alphabeti-

cally rather than by key number. *Words and Phrases* can be a useful tool when the meaning of a specific term is in issue. Most of the current *Words and Phrases* volumes were published more than 25 years ago, so here it is usually most productive to *begin* research in the pocket part.

The *Words and Phrases* set covers the entire National Reporter System. Shorter Words and Phrases lists also appear in many West digests and in West reporter volumes and advance sheets. Earlier lists simply give the names and citations for the defining cases, but digest Words and Phrases volumes published since 1999 now include the text of the relevant headnotes. Exhibit 29 shows a page from the Words and Phrases section of the *Federal Practice Digest 4th,* including a headnote from *Bell v. Glock, Inc.* interpreting the meaning of the term "user." (Note in Exhibit 24 that headnote 6 of *Bell* is followed by a reference to Words and Phrases as a source for other judicial constructions and definitions.)

E. DIGESTS AND KEY NUMBERS ON WESTLAW

Westlaw researchers can take full advantage of West's digest system. In addition to limiting a search to the headnote or digest field, as noted earlier, you can also incorporate key numbers into a search. For use in Westlaw, each of the topics has been assigned a number between 1 and 414. Weapons is topic 406, for example, and a search for Weapons 18 is 406k18. This key number can used in combination with other terms to create a very precise and effective search.

Key number searching is powerful, but it is not intuitive. To make key number use more accessible, Westlaw has a feature it calls Keysearch. To use Keysearch, you scan a list of 45 broad topics and numerous more detailed subtopics until you reach the specific focus of your inquiry. Clicking on this term leads to a search screen on which you can

USE OF MONEY

bills. 41 P.S. § 502.—Pollice v. National Tax Funding, L.P., 225 F.3d 379.—Usury 27.

USE OF PHYSICAL FORCE

C.A.7 (Ill.) 2002. Defendant's act of prying open the window of a locked vehicle qualified as a "use of physical force" against the property of another, and thus, his state burglary conviction arising out of that act was a "crime of violence" as would make the burglary conviction an "aggravated felony" for purpose of federal sentencing guideline for unlawfully entering or remaining in the United States. 18 U.S.C.A. § 16(a); U.S.S.G. § 2L1.2, 18 U.S.C.A.: S.H.A. 720 ILCS 5/19–1.—U.S. v. Alvarez-Martinez, 286 F.3d 470.—Crim Law 793.

USE OF THE MAILS

C.A.6 (Ohio) 1999. Defendant's receipt of mailed bank statements, in his capacity as attorney for charity fund, did not satisfy "use of the mails" requirement of mail fraud statute, even though charity's bank account was essential part of defendant's scheme to defraud via diversion of charity fund monies, and mailing of bank statements was incident to the maintenance of that account, absent any evidence that defendant actually used the bank statements in furtherance of or as a step in his scheme to defraud, such as use of statements to monitor account and to withdraw the balance. 18 U.S.C.A. § 1341.—U.S. v. Hartsel, 199 F.3d 812, 1999 Fed.App. 417P, certiorari denied 120 S.Ct. 1679, 529 U.S. 1070, 146 L.Ed.2d 487.—Postal 35(8).

USE OR MISUSE OF TANGIBLE PROPERTY

E.D.Tex. 1999. While information coming from use of "facilitated communication" (FC) equipment, under supervision and direction of state agency caseworkers, was not "tangible property" within meaning of Texas Tort Claims Act (TTCA), use of FC on student was "use or misuse of tangible property" within meaning of TTCA, where student was too young for FC and could not read, caseworkers never confirmed whether or not student could read, student did not have physical impairment, FC was not scientific tool to be used to confirm or deny abuse allegations and was inherently unreliable, and FC was used in violation of school district policy and federal law. V.T.C.A., Civil Practice & Remedies Code § 101.021.—Morris v. Dearborne, 69 F.Supp.2d 868.—States 112.2(1).

USE OR OPERATION

C.A.2 (N.Y.) 1999. Under New York Vehicle and Traffic Law, loading and unloading of a vehicle constitutes "use or operation" of vehicle, for negligent conduct in connection with which owner may be held liable. N.Y.McKinney's Vehicle and Traffic Law § 388, subd. 1.—Argentina v. Emery World Wide Delivery Corp., 188 F.3d 86.—Autos 192(1).

USER

D.Mont. 2000. Under Montana law, shooting victim was not "user" of handgun, and thus did not assume risk associated with product, absent evidence that victim invited shooter to point gun at him and fire. MCA 27–1–719(5)(a).—Bell v. Glock, Inc. (USA), 92 F.Supp.2d 1067.—Weap 18(1).

D.Mont. 2000. Under Montana law, shooting victim was not "user" of handgun, and thus defense of misuse did not apply to his conduct. MCA 27–1–719(5)(b).—Bell v. Glock, Inc. (USA), 92 F.Supp.2d 1067.—Weap 18(1).

S.D.Ohio 2000. Propane gas supplier was a "user" of consumer reports under the Fair Credit Reporting Act (FCRA) for purposes of residential propane gas consumers' class action against supplier, alleging supplier violated the FCRA by failing to comply with notice requirement before taking adverse action against consumers on basis of information contained in reports, where supplier routinely consulted credit scoring program when a potential customer first called it for propane service. Consumer Credit Protection Act, § 615, as amended. 15 U.S.C.A. § 1681m.—Mick v. Level Propane Gases Inc., 183 F.Supp.2d 1014.—Cred R A 1.

USER FEE

D.Hawai'i 2001. United States did not charge bicyclist an "admission price" or "user fee" for use of bike path, within meaning of the Hawai'i Recreational Use Statute (HRUS), although city imposed a general bicycle registration fee upon bicyclist and naval employees' use of bike path reduced Navy's need for parking spaces, where admission to bicycle path was not conditioned upon payment of a fee. HRS § 520–12.—Brown v. U.S., 180 F.Supp.2d 1132.—Autos 252.

Bkrtcy.E.D.Mich. 1999. Unlike tax, "user fee" is a charge designed as compensation for government-supplied services, facilities, or benefits.—In re Danny's Markets, Inc., 239 B.R. 342, subsequently reversed 266 F.3d 523.—Tax 1.

USER FEES

Bkrtcy.E.D.Mich. 1999. Unlike tax, "user fees" are intended to reimburse government for costs incurred in providing specific quantifiable services, and are not true revenue measures.—In re Danny's Markets, Inc., 239 B.R. 342, subsequently reversed 266 F.3d 523.—Tax 1.

USERS

S.D.N.Y. 2001. World Wide Web sites that employed intermediary to rent space to advertisers were "users" of electronic communications service, i.e. users of Internet access, within meaning of Electronic Communications Privacy Act (ECPA); thus, under ECPA exception for conduct authorized by user "with respect to a communication of or intended for that user," sites could authorize intermediary to intercept individual site visitors' communications with sites, e.g. searches, in order to gather information to use in selecting advertisements to display to visitors. 18 U.S.C.A. §§ 2510(13), 2701(a), (c)(2).—In re DoubleClick Inc. Privacy Litigation, 154 F.Supp.2d 497.—Tel 461.15.

Exhibit 29. Words and Phrases, 114 FEDERAL PRACTICE DIGEST 4TH, at 130 (1999).

specify a database and add additional search terms if you wish. Westlaw automatically creates a search to match the legal topic. Its search does not appear on the initial screen, but is revealed by clicking on *View/Edit Full Query.* For Products Liability—Particular Products—Weapons and Ammunition—Handguns, it creates the search *((406k18 /p hand-gun! pistol revolver) & sy,he(department design! discount distribut! manufacturer "product liability" retail! sale seller sold strict! wholesale!)).* (For cases without West headnotes, it prepares an even more extensive terms and connectors search.) This is a bit more elaborate than the search most users might draft on their own, and combines the relevant key number with numerous additional terms.

§4-4. AMERICAN LAW REPORTS ANNOTATIONS

At the same time that West was developing its National Reporter System in the late 19th century, other publishers were attempting a different approach to case reporting. They selected "leading cases" for full-text publication, and provided commentaries, or *annotations*, which surveyed the law on the subject of the selected case and in the process described other decisions with similar facts, holdings, or procedures. Selective publication was not a successful alternative to comprehensive reporting, but the annotations have proved to be valuable case research tools.

Among the early sets of annotated reporters were the "Trinity series" (*American Decisions, American Law Reports* and *American State Reports*) (1871-1911) and *Lawyers Reports Annotated (LRA)* (1888-1918). *LRA's* successor, *American Reports (ALR),* began in 1919 and is now published in two current series: *ALR5th* for general and state legal issues, and *ALR Federal* for issues of federal law. A few annotations limited to Supreme Court cases are also published in *United States Supreme Court Reports, Lawyers' Edition.*

Annotations summarize the cases on a specific topic and classify decisions that have reached conflicting results. The coverage of *ALR* is not encyclopedic, and not every research issue is covered by its annotations. An annotation directly on point, however, can save considerable research time. It does the initial time-consuming work of finding relevant cases, and arranges them according to specific fact patterns and holdings. Because it synthesizes the cases into a narrative discussion, rather than simply offering a collection of headnotes, an annotation is usually easier to use than a digest.

Annotations differ significantly from other narrative resources such as treatises and law review articles. Their main purpose is to organize the varied judicial decisions from around the country into a coherent body of law. They generally do not criticize these decisions or analyze legal problems, nor do they attempt to integrate case law into a broader view of society as the better secondary sources do. The work of the publisher's editorial staff rather than of leading legal scholars, they are best viewed as research tools rather than as secondary authority which may persuade a tribunal. If they are cited, it is as convenient compilations of prevailing judicial doctrine.

A. FORMAT AND CONTENTS

An *ALR* volume contains from ten to twenty annotations, each analyzing decisions on an issue raised in an illustrative recent case, which is printed in full either before the annotation or at the end of the volume. Each annotation begins with a table of contents, a detailed subject index, and a table listing the jurisdictions of the cases discussed. In volumes published since 1992 (the beginning of *ALR5th*), this introductory material has also included a Research References section providing leads to encyclopedias, practice aids, digests, and other sources, as well as sample electronic search queries and relevant West digest

key numbers. Exhibits 30 and 31 show pages from the beginning of an *ALR5th* annotation on the liability of firearm manufacturers for injuries caused by the use of guns in committing crimes. Exhibit 30 shows the table of contents, organizing the annotation's sections according to theories of liability and whether or not liability was established. Exhibit 31 shows parts of the index, listing specific fact situations and legal issues arising in the cases discussed, and the jurisdictional table, a state-by-state listing of the cases.

The first two sections of an annotation are "Introduction," describing its scope and listing related *ALR* annotations, and "Summary and Comment," providing a general overview and giving practice pointers. Exhibit 32 shows the list of related annotations in § 1[b] and the beginning of the § 2 summary of the firearm manufacturer annotation. The remaining sections of the annotation then summarize cases on point from throughout the country, arranged according to their facts and holdings.

The annotation in Exhibits 30-32 was published in 2001, but older annotations also provide references to recent case law through the use of annual supplements. Volumes in *ALR3d*, *ALR4th*, *ALR5th,* and *ALR Federal* are updated through annual pocket parts describing new cases, but *ALR1st* and *ALR2d* use other methods. These older annotations are not used as often as those in the newer series, but many remain current and continue to be updated. *ALR2d* volumes have no pocket parts, so new cases are instead summarized in a separate set of blue *Later Case Service* volumes, which *do* have annual pocket parts. Annotations in *ALR1st* are updated through a set called *ALR1st Blue Book of Supplemental Decisions,* which simply lists the citations of relevant new cases.

TABLE OF CONTENTS

Research References
Index
Jurisdictional Table of Cited Statutes and Cases

ARTICLE OUTLINE

Exhibit 30. George L. Blum, Annotation, *Firearm or Ammunition Manufacturer or Seller's Liability for Injuries Caused to Another by Use of Gun in Committing Crime,* 88 A.L.R.5TH 1, 2 (2001).

Strict products liability, §§ 3-5, 7, 8, 11, 12

Summary and comment, § 2

Tavern or bar, §§ 5, 6[b], 12

Theft of firearms, §§ 3, 6[b]

.357 Magnum ammunition, § 13[b]

Tobacco, compared, §§ 5, 6[a]

Training of employees, § 6[a]

21, sale of ammunition to person under age of, § 13[b]

.22 caliber pistol, ammunition used in, § 13[b]

Ultrahazardous activity, §§ 5, 8, 12

Underage person, sale of ammunition to, § 13[b]

Unreasonably dangerous, handguns as, § 3

Unreasonably unsafe design, Saturday night specials as by nature of, § 4[b]

Unsound mind, sale to person of, § 6[a]

Use and manufacturing distinguished, § 5

Victims or the like, actions brought by, §§ 3-6, 11-13

Warn of dangers of criminal misuse, duty to, § 4[b]

Whiskey, compared, § 4[b]

Wife, shooting of by husband, §§ 4[b], 5, 6[b]

Jurisdictional Table of Cited Statutes and Cases*

UNITED STATES

18 U.S.C.A. § 921. See §§ 4[a], 13[b]

18 U.S.C.A. § 922. See § 13[b]

18 U.S.C.A. § 922(b)(1). See § 13[a]

18 U.S.C.A. § 922(d)(1). See § 6[a]

18 U.S.C.A. § 922.b.1. See § 13[b]

Brown v. Wal-Mart Stores, Inc., 976 F. Supp. 729 (W.D. Tenn. 1997)—§ 2[b]

Delahanty v. Hinckley, 900 F.2d 368 (D.C. Cir. 1990)—§ 4[b]

Leslie v. U.S., 986 F. Supp. 900 (D.N.J. 1997)—§§ 2[b], 12

Martin v. Harrington and Richardson, Inc., 743 F.2d 1200 (7th Cir. 1984)—§§ 3, 5

McCarthy v. Olin Corp., 119 F.3d 148, Prod. Liab. Rep. (CCH) ¶ 15016 (2d Cir. 1997)—§§ 6[b], 11, 13[b]

Perkins v. F.I.E. Corp., 762 F.2d 1250 (5th Cir. 1985)—§ 3

ALASKA

Adkinson v. Rossi Arms Co., 659 P.2d 1236 (Alaska 1983)—§ 6[b]

* Statutes, rules, regulations, and constitutional provisions bearing on the subject of the annotation are included in this table only to the extent that they are reflected in the court opinions discussed in this annotation. The reader should consult the appropriate statutory or regulatory compilations to ascertain the current status of relevant statutes, rules, regulations, and constitutional provisions.

For federal cases involving state law, see state headings.

Exhibit 31. 88 A.L.R.5TH at 6.

[b] Related annotations

Validity, construction, and application of state or local law prohibiting manufacture, possession, or transfer of "assault weapon," 29 A.L.R.5th 664. 29 ALR5th 664.

Validity of state gun control legislation under state constitutional provisions securing the right to bear arms. 86 ALR4th 931.

Products liability: sufficiency of evidence to support product misuse defense in actions concerning weapons and ammunition. 59 ALR4th 102.

Liability of one who provides, by sale or otherwise, firearm or ammunition to adult who shoots another. 39 ALR4th 517.

Liability of private citizen or his employer for injury or damage to third person resulting from firing of shots at fleeing criminal. 29 ALR4th 144.

Products liability: blasting materials and supplies. 18 ALR4th 206.

Liability of one who sells gun to child for injury to third party. 4 ALR4th 331.

Products liability: air guns and BB guns. 94 ALR3d 291.

Liability for injury or death of minor or other, incompetent inflicted upon himself by gun made available by defendant. 75 ALR3d 825.

Right of member of Armed Forces to recover from manufacturer or seller for injury caused by defective military material, equipment, supplies, or components thereof. 38 ALR3d 1247.

Res ipsa loquitur doctrine with respect to firearms accident. 46 ALR2d 1216.

Liability of manufacturer or wholesaler for injury caused by third person's use of explosives or other dangerous article sold to retailer in violation of law. 11 ALR2d 1028.

§ 2. Summary and comment

[a] Generally

Some courts apply strict rules of accountability for injuries resulting from the discharge of a firearm. It has been held that one is liable civilly for damages for injuries inflicted by an unintentional discharge of a firearm unless one shows that the injury was unavoidable. In several cases courts held that the test of liability is not whether the injury was accidentally inflicted, but whether the defendant was free from all blame. According to the theory of these cases, it is no defense that the act occurred by misadventure, and without the wrongdoer's intending it. The defendant must show such circumstances as would appear to the court that the injury done to the plaintiff was inevitable, and the defendant was not chargeable

12

Exhibit 32.   88 A.L.R.5TH at 12.

If later cases substantially change the law on a subject covered by an annotation, a new annotation is written to supplement or to completely supersede the older annotation. The older volume's pocket part or other supplement alerts the researcher to the existence of the newer treatment (another good reason to *always* check the pocket part). Another way to determine whether an annotation has been superseded is to check the "Annotation History Table" in the back of each volume of the *ALR Index*, which lists all superseding and supplementing annotations.

B. Finding Annotations

The basic tool for subject access to *ALR* is the seven-volume *ALR Index*, which provides coverage of annotations in *ALR2d*, *ALR3d*, *ALR4th*, *ALR5th*, and *ALR Federal*, and is kept current by quarterly pocket parts. (The annotations in the first series of *ALR* are indexed in a separate *ALR First Series Quick Index*, and *Lawyers' Edition* annotations are listed in the *Quick Case Table with Annotation References*.) A less comprehensive *ALR Quick Index* covers only *ALR3d*, *ALR4th*, and *ALR5th*, and is published as an annual softcover volume; a separate *ALR Federal Quick Index* is limited to *ALR Federal* annotations. Exhibit 33 shows a page from the *ALR Index*, including references under "Weapons and Firearms" to the annotation illustrated and to other annotations on firearms manufacturing.

Remember that section 1[b] of almost all *ALR* annotations provides a list of other annotations on related topics. If a quick check of the index does not turn up an annotation directly on point but does lead to one on a related issue, the most productive next step may be to turn to that annotation and read through its list of related annotations. This list could lead to analogies or concepts you may not have thought to check in the index. The section 1[b] list shown in Exhibit 32, for example, includes a dozen cross-

references to annotations on topics such as the validity of "assault weapon" prohibitions and liability for selling guns to children.

Another means of access to annotations is through the *ALR Digest to 3d, 4th, 5th and Federal*, a multivolume set classifying *ALR*'s annotations and cases in a system similar to West's digests. Older digests cover *ALR1st* and *ALR2d*.

One can also find relevant annotations by using a particular cited case or statute. The two citators to be discussed in the next section, KeyCite and Shepard's Citations, both include coverage of annotations citing cases, and KeyCite also lists annotations citing statutes. In print, the *ALR Index* is accompanied by a volume listing the statutes, rules and regulations cited in *ALR2d* to *5th* and *ALR Federal*, and both *ALR5th* and *ALR Federal* have multivolume tables of cases listing the decisions cited in those series.

Many other sources, including some annotated codes and encyclopedias, provide references to relevant *ALR* annotations. Note, for example, the *ALR* references in *Am. Jur. 2d* in Exhibit 1, on page 24.

Annotations beginning with *ALR2d* are available online through Westlaw and LexisNexis, and beginning with *ALR3d* are also published on CD-ROM. (Westlaw even has new annotations that have not yet been released for publication in the print *ALR*.) In any of these versions, the full texts of the annotations are searchable by particular combinations of terms. Because annotations describe the facts of the cases discussed, including aspects unrelated to the subject of the annotation, it is often most productive to limit searches to words in annotation titles or to use natural language searches that rank documents by relevance.

ALR INDEX

WEAPONS AND FIREARMS—Cont'd
Labor and employment—Cont'd
forbidding carrying of weapons, as
to person on his own premises or at
his place of business, 57 ALR3d
938
Lesser offenses, propriety of lesser-
included-offense charge to jury in
federal prosecution for crime involving
property rights, 105 ALR Fed 669
Liability of one who provides firearm, 39
ALR4th 517
Licenses and permits
Ammunition (this index)
concealed weapons, who is entitled to
permit to carry concealed weapons,
51 ALR3d 504
dealers, validity, construction, and
application of provisions of Gun
Control Act of 1968 (18 U.S.C.A.
§ 922(m) and 923(g)) and
implementing regulations relating to
firearms registration and recording
requirements imposed upon federally licensed firearms dealers, 33
ALR Fed 824
engaging business under 18 U.S.C.A.
§ 923(a), providing that no person
shall engage in business as a firearms or ammunition importer,
manufacturer, or dealer without a
federal license, 53 ALR Fed 932
possession, see group Possession in
this topic
revocation or denial of application for
license to import, manufacture, or
deal in firearms or ammunition, 61
ALR Fed 511
transient nonresidents, application of
statute or regulation dealing with
registration or carrying of weapons
to transient nonresident, 68 ALR3d
1253
willfully, when has applicant for
license under Gun Control Act of
1968 willfully violated statute or
regulations within meaning of 18
U.S.C.A. § 923(d)(1)(C), 59 ALR
Fed 254
Mace (this index)

WEAPONS AND FIREARMS—Cont'd
Manufacturers and manufacturing
assault weapons: validity, construction,
and application of state or local law
prohibiting manufacture, possession,
or transfer of "assault weapon," 29
ALR5th 664
crime, firearm or ammunition
manufacturer or seller's liability for
injuries caused to another by use of
gun in committing crime, 88
ALR5th 1
engage in business under 18 U.S.C.A.
§ 923(a), providing that no person
shall engage in business as a firearms or ammunition importer,
manufacturer, or dealer without a
federal license, 53 ALR Fed 932
judicial review, under 18 U.S.C.A.
§ 923(f)(3), of revocation or denial
of application for license to import,
manufacture, or deal in firearms or
ammunition, 61 ALR Fed 511
products liability, firearms, ammunition, and chemical weapons, 15
ALR4th 909
Military equipment, right of member of
armed forces to recover from
manufacturer or seller for injury caused
by defective military material, equipment, supplies, or components thereof,
38 ALR3d 1247
Minors, see group Children in this topic
Misuse defense, sufficiency of evidence to
support, see group Products liability in
this topic
Motive, see group Intent or motive in this
topic
Motor vehicles, see group Automobiles
and highway traffic in this topic
Multiple offenses, receipt, possession, or
transportation of multiple firearms as
single or multiple offense under 18
U.S.C.A. App. 1 § 1202(a)(1), making it
federal offense for convicted felon to
receive, possess, or transport any
firearm, 62 ALR Fed 829
Multiple victims, single act affecting
multiple victims as constituting multiple
assaults or homicides, 8 ALR4th 960

Consult POCKET PART for Later Annotations
654

Exhibit 33. Weapons and Firearms, T-Z ALR INDEX 654
(2001).

§4-5. Citators

The body of published American case law is filled with decisions which have long since been overruled or limited to specific facts. Before relying on any case, an attorney must verify its current validity. This process of updating cases was traditionally performed by checking printed volumes known as *Shepard's Citations*, and as a result it is sometimes known as *Shepardizing*. Shepard's information is now available electronically on LexisNexis as well as in print, and Westlaw has a competing electronic resource, KeyCite, that provides a similar service.

Citators perform three major functions, whether they are used electronically or in print:

• Providing parallel citations for the decision and references to other proceedings in the same case, allowing researchers to trace a case's judicial history;

• Indicating if subsequent cases have overruled, limited, or otherwise diminished a case's precedent, providing the information needed to determine whether it is still good law; and

• Listing research leads to later citing cases, as well as periodical articles, attorney general opinions, *ALR* annotations, and other resources, enabling researchers to find related cases and to trace the development of a legal doctrine forward from a known case to the present.

KeyCite and Shepard's are invaluable resources not only because they validate research already done and ensure that cases are still "good law." They also serve as powerful links from one document to others on related issues, providing one of the most effective ways to find sources for further research.

One can update a case by searching full-text databases for its name or citation, and retrieving a list of all later documents which have cited it. The advantage of KeyCite and Shepard's is that they do more than simply list the citing cases. They analyze and sort these cases, providing information about their impact on the cited case and their relevance to a particular research issue.

A. KEYCITE

Westlaw's citator service, KeyCite, is incorporated fully into its case research system. Any case display on Westlaw provides several links to KeyCite information. Tabs on the left side of the screen include *KC History* (decisions which may bear a direct impact on a case's validity) and *KC Citing Ref* (the full list of citing documents). In addition, a small symbol at the top of the case display indicates what citator information is available. A red flag generally indicates that a case is not good law on some point, and a yellow flag that there is some negative history. If neither of these flags is applicable, a blue "H" indicates that there is some case history information available or a green "C" shows that there are citing references. Clicking on one of these symbols leads directly to the case's KeyCite display. KeyCite information can also be accessed by typing a citation into a form on Westlaw's initial welcome screen, or by clicking on the KeyCite link at the top of any Westlaw screen.

KeyCite History includes prior and subsequent cases in the same litigation, so that it can be traced through the appellate process, and negative indirect history cases, those in different litigation that may have an adverse impact on the precedential value of the cited case. Be aware, however, that "negative" history is broadly construed. A lower court decision that declines to extend a Supreme Court precedent to an unrelated area is listed as "distinguishing" its

holding. This is considered a negative citation, even though it has no impact on the precedential value of the Supreme Court decision.

KeyCite Citing References lists negative citing cases first, and then the remaining cases by the extent to which they discuss the cited case, with rankings from four stars (an extended discussion) to one star (mentioned in a list with other citations). KeyCite also indicates those cases that quote directly from the cited case, by adding quotation marks to the display. Secondary sources such as law review articles and *ALR* annotations are listed last, without rankings. Links provide access to the full text of any of these citing documents.

KeyCite provides several ways for researchers to focus their retrieval. *Limits* can be used to see only those references from specific jurisdictions, or those that cite the point of law in particular headnotes. KeyCite can also limit by depth of treatment (number of stars) or by type of citing document (cases, law review articles, treatises and encyclopedias). One of the most powerful KeyCite tools is the ability to use the *Locate* feature to run a keyword search within the citing documents. This can focus immediately on those documents applying a precedent to a particular set of facts.

Another way to move directly from a displayed case to a KeyCite result is to use the *KeyCite Notes* link preceding each headnote. This takes you directly to a screen on which you choose what type of citing documents you wish to see (or to a notice that there are no *KeyCite Notes* references for the headnote), and then to a list of KeyCite references limited to those discussing this particular legal issue.

Exhibit 34 shows KeyCite results for *First Commercial Trust Co. v. Lorcin Engineering, Inc.*, 900 S.W.2d 202 (Ark. 1995), one of the cases discussed in the *ALR* annotation

shown earlier in this chapter. The right part of the screen
shows the beginning of the case, including KeyCite Notes
links for the first two headnotes. Citing references are
shown on the lower left, limited for this exhibit to cases
from Arizona and New York, as well as the citing *ALR*
annotation. Note that the Arizona case has two stars (*cited*),
while the New York case gets just one star (*mentioned*). A
yellow flag to the left of the New York case name indicates
that it has some negative history of its own, perhaps
diminishing the value of its citation to our case. The *ALR*
citation, like other secondary sources, is not ranked for
depth of treatment.

In the same way that WestClip provides automatic notification of new cases matching a particular search, KeyCite
has a notification service that monitors developments in a
case's history or citing references. This service, KeyCite
Alert, can be set up to send notices for any case history
developments, for just negative history, or for any and all
citing references. It can also limit citing references by headnote, jurisdiction, KeyCite locate terms, or depth of treatment, providing an easy way to learn of new cases meeting
very specific citing criteria. One could, for example, receive
KeyCite Alert notifications of any Arkansas cases affecting
Lorcin Engineering's value as precedent on a particular
point.

B. SHEPARD'S CITATIONS ONLINE

Shepard's Citations is an integral part of LexisNexis case
research. One of the choices at the top of a case display is
"Shepardize," and in most instances a signal to the left of
the case name indicates the nature of citing documents. A
red stop sign indicates strong negative treatment (e.g., the
case has been reversed or overruled), while a yellow cau-
tion sign indicates possible negative treatment (e.g., its
holding has been criticized or limited). A green plus sign

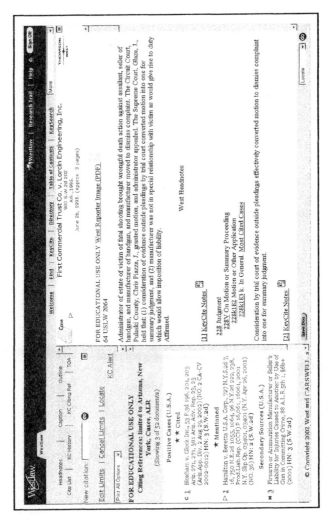

Exhibit 34. KeyCite display for First Commercial Trust Co. v. Lorcin Engineering, Inc., 900 S.W.2d 202 (Ark. 1995).

indicates positive history or treatment, and a blue circle indicates other citing references. Like KeyCite, Shepard's has a broad definition of "negative" treatment.

You can also choose *Shepard's—Check a Citation* from the menu at the top of the LexisNexis screen, and then type in a citation. When choosing this approach, you have the option of retrieving a list of decisions which may bear a direct impact on a case's validity ("Shepard's for Validation," limited to proceedings in the same litigation and any negative citing cases) or the full list of citing documents ("Shepard's for Research").

Shepard's does not rank documents as Westlaw does, but instead provides a broader range of treatment codes. Some, but not all, positive cases are given treatment codes such as "followed" or "explained" to indicate the nature of their citations. Citing cases are displayed by jurisdiction, beginning with cases from the home jurisdiction of the cited case. *Restrictions* on Shepard's can be used to see only those references with particular treatments (negative only, positive only, or your choice of specific codes), as well as cases from specific jurisdictions or those that cite the point of law in particular headnotes. It is also possible to run a "focus" search within the text of the citing cases to find specific fact patterns or terminology.

Exhibit 35 shows a Shepard's screen from LexisNexis, displaying the same result as the KeyCite exhibit above. In this instance neither of the citing cases shown has a treatment code, but the New York Court of Appeals citation is followed by a triangle indicating its own possible negative history. Links provide immediate access to the text of any of these documents.

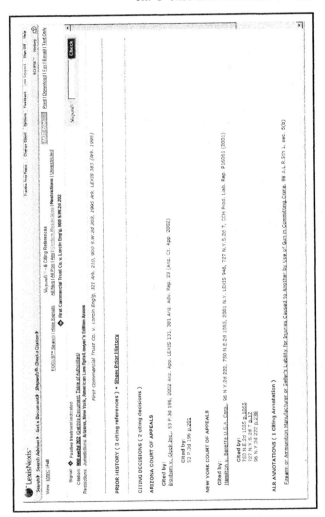

Exhibit 35. Shepard's display for First Commercial Trust Co. v. Lorcin Engineering, Inc., 900 S.W.2d 202 (Ark. 1995).

Although their editorial treatment and arrangement differ, KeyCite and Shepard's generally provide references to the same citing cases. Both include cases that are designated as unpublished but are available through the online databases, as well as cases published in the official reports, West reporters, and other topical reporters. Occasionally one service includes a reference to an unpublished decision available through its database but not the other, but the differences in case coverage are slight. Both provide thorough coverage and timely notice of new developments.

Coverage of secondary sources in the two services does differ. Both have references to *ALR* annotations and to law reviews available online. Shepard's also lists citing references in selected law reviews back as far as 1957, even though most of the earlier articles are not available online in full text. KeyCite is limited to materials available on Westlaw, but it generally provides more extensive coverage of recent law reviews as well as legal encyclopedias and treatises. For the *Lorcin Engineering* case, for example, Shepard's lists the *ALR* annotation and nineteen citing law review articles. KeyCite includes all of these and adds six additional articles not found in Shepard's as well as references in four treatises and encyclopedias.

It is important when using either KeyCite or Shepard's Citations to understand that their signals and editorial signposts are just tools for the researcher, not authoritative statements of the law. Relying on a red flag or a stop sign is no substitute for reading a citing document and determining for yourself its scope and effect. A case that has been overruled on one point may still be good law on other issues, but learning this requires reading the overruling case itself and then examining *its* subsequent history.

c. Shepard's Citations in Print

While the electronic versions of KeyCite and Shepard's compete for customers, *Shepard's Citations* is the choice for researchers using print resources. There is no print version of KeyCite, but sets of *Shepard's Citations* are published for the Supreme Court, the lower federal courts, every state, the District of Columbia, Puerto Rico, and each region of the National Reporter System.

In order to convey a large amount of information in a small space, the print versions of *Shepard's* use a system of one-letter symbols to indicate the treatment of citing cases. The letter *c*, for example, stands for *criticized*; *d* for *distinguished*; and *j* for *citing in dissenting opinion*. In addition, the abbreviations used to identify citing sources are usually shorter than the citations commonly used in the *Bluebook* and other sources. *California Reporter 2d* becomes *CaR2d* in a *Shepard's* volume. These symbols and abbreviations may be confusing at first, but they are listed in tables at the front of each volume.

Printed *Shepard's Citations* can never be quite as current as the electronic resources, but most sets are supplemented biweekly or monthly. Each contains one or more maroon bound volumes, and supplementary pamphlets of varying colors. To help researchers know which volumes or supplements they need to use, the cover of each supplement includes a list, "What Your Library Should Contain," of the current volumes and pamphlets for the set.

Exhibit 36 shows a page from *Shepard's Southwestern Reporter Citations*, indicating treatment of the *Lorcin Engineering* case at 900 S.W.2d 202. After the page number and the name and date of the case, the first citation is the parallel citation, 321 Ark. 210, listed in parentheses. This is followed by a related proceeding (indicated by the code *cc*), in this instance a criminal case arising from the same

shooting at issue in the *Lorcin* case. Other cases have more significant history citations; note that the case at 900 S.W.2d 67, near the top of the first column, was reversed (*r*).

Next are citations of later citing decisions in Arkansas courts, as printed in the *South Western Reporter*. These indicate the exact pages on which the Shepardized case is cited, rather than the first page of the citing decisions. At 914 S.W.2d 289, the citing court discussed a legal principle in the first *Lorcin* headnote, as indicated by the small raised "1" to the left of the page number for the citing case. Decisions from Arkansas courts are followed by citations to federal court decisions, arranged by circuit, and to decisions from other states. *Lorcin* has been *followed* (f) by an Eighth Circuit decision, and *distinguished* (d) by a California case. (This volume was published before the cases and annotation shown in Exhibits 34 and 35 were listed, but these are covered in later supplements.) An important treatment code can be found near the bottom of the last column, indicating that the case at 900 S.W.2d 227 has been *overruled* (o) and *overruled in part* (op) by later cases.

References to the *Lorcin* case in law review articles are noted in *Shepard's Arkansas Citations*, but not in *Shepard's Southwestern Reporter Citations*. On the other hand, citing cases from other states appear only in the regional series and not in the state *Shepard's*. Both state citators and regional citators list citing cases from the home jurisdiction and in federal courts, but neither provides a complete list of all citing documents.

Supplementary *Shepard's* pamphlets include one feature not found in the bound volumes. Recent citing cases, included before their reporter citations are available, are listed by Lexis citations. LexisNexis subscribers can use

Vol. 900 SOUTHWESTERN REPORTER, 2d SERIES

—60—
Watson v
Texas
1995
s 877SW826
909SW[1]263
913SW[4]732
928SW[5]258
958SW[1]836
958SW[2]837
958SW[3]837
961SW[1]352
986SW346
987SW[1]229
991SW[6]832
999SW[5]62
15SW615
—67—
Anderson v
Gilbert
1994
r 897SW783
—71—
Disco Mach. of
Liberal Co. v
Payton
1995
906SW[2]277
906SW[3]277
937SW487
—75—
Ankrom v
Dallas
Cowboys
Football Club,
Ltd.
1995
WD
913SW[2]648
934SW[5]405
934SW[6]405
988SW[4]189
—82—
Jim Sowell
Constr. Co., Inc.
v Dallas Cent.
Appraisal Dist.
1995
WD
948SW[8]15
948SW[9]15
d 948SW[11]17
—87—
Jones v Night-
ingale
1995
ER
923SW[3]704
928SW[3]132
928SW[8]133
934SW[8]410
966SW[5]752
999SW[6]614

Cir. 5
5FS2d[6]500
—90—
North Dallas
Diagnostic Ctr.
v Dewberry
1995
WD
j 930SW274
935SW[13]487
945SW[11]893
948SW[4]932
956SW[2]580
988SW[4]875
993SW[2]842
7SW233
7SW[5]234
—97—
Jefferson v
Texas
1995
939SW760
942SW[8]731
23SW203
—103—
Jones v Texas
1995
914SW[9]213
933SW[7]711
d 948SW[6]25
d 948SW[12]25
950SW[5]161
950SW[13]162
950SW[12]162
954SW[2]842
954SW[4]842
954SW[10]842
964SW[11]341
973SW[4]415
—108—
Blake v
Amoco Fed.
Credit Union
1995
942SW[7]27
—117—
Walls v First
State Bank
1995
WD
f 943SW927
964SW[6]81
983SW[10]837
997SW881
4SW[2]213
7SW[2]133
26SW708
Cir. 11
931FS863

—124—
Disco Mach. of
Liberal Co. v
Payton
1995
WD
985SW[1]616
—128—
Burns v Drew
Woods, Inc.
1995
WD
951SW297
—134—
Durst v Texas
1995
PDRR
~ 941SW[14]943
947SW[14]264
17SW[8]409
17SW[8]706
—142—
Peveto v
D'Entremont
1995
WD
—160—
Echols v
Echols
1995
WD
964SW[5]321
d 967SW491
973SW[1]426
993SW[1]301
993SW[2]301
j 993SW306
Wis
f 611NW267
—167—
Hillard v
Arkansas
1995
(321Ark39)
906SW[1]313
921SW[2]928
938SW[2]813
974SW[3]447
Haw
909P2d585
51Æ431n
68Æ353n
—170—
Elders v
Arkansas
1995
(321Ark60)
j 910SW662
f 973SW828
973SW[8]828
973SW[9]828

—175—
Arkansas v
Roberts
1995
(321Ark31)
j 902SW237
906SW[3]683
910SW[3]681
913SW[3]263
942SW[3]863
987SW[3]698
—177—
Neal v Wilson
1995
(321Ark70)
s 964SW199
s 16SW228
cc 112F3d351
905SW487
906SW[5]688
909SW[4]644
913SW773
954SW[4]233
f 989SW[4]914
—185—
Roetzel v
Brown
1995
(321Ark187)
981SW117
—187—
Wicoff v
Arkansas
1995
(321Ark97)
918SW694
d 924SW[2]236
d 924SW[2]245
j 924SW247
989SW[4]514
998SW[3]753
f 998SW755
—191—
Wacaser v
Insurance
Comm'r
1995
(321Ark143)
914SW298
945SW[1]361
946SW[1]651
946SW[2]651
j 984SW401
984SW404
12SW[1]660
W Va
490SE835
—195—
Marsh &
McLennan v
Herget
1995
(321Ark180)

909SW[1]647
911SW254
914SW[1]731
923SW[5]865
930SW[5]373
f 938SW[1]230
f 938SW[2]230
939SW283
j 940SW439
19SW[1]602
20SW433
f 33SW150
—200—
In re Estate
F.C.
1995
(321Ark191)
912SW[2]413
937SW[2]653
~ 6SW117
d 10SW[5]924
j 10SW925
27SW733
f 32SW26
Mo
950SW[3]517
950SW[5]517
—202—
First Commer-
cial Trust Co. v
Lorcin Eng'g.
Inc.
1995
(321Ark210)
cc 900SW523
913SW271
913SW296
913SW766
914SW[1]289
j 915SW261
922SW698
926SW431
j 947SW788
962SW787
971SW254
986SW840
Cir. 8
f 77F3d[3]1082
954FS[3]1329
978FS1231
Calif
d 89CaR2d182
j 89CaR2d203
—205—
Hamilton v
Pulaski County
Special Sch.
Dist.
1995
(321Ark261)
907SW138
948SW98
958SW530
964SW[7]386
966SW[2]880

—209—
Baker v Milam
1995
(321Ark234)
912SW[1]927
912SW[2]927
915SW689
918SW[1]149
918SW[2]149
920SW[1]485
920SW[2]485
921SW[1]946
921SW[2]946
923SW[1]863
923SW[2]863
924SW[1]806
924SW[2]806
f 955SW511
955SW[5]511
j 955SW514
—212—
Cook v Recov-
ery Corp.
1995
(50AkA49)
a 911SW581
—215—
Belcher v
Holiday Inn
1995
s 868SW87
s 896SW440
—216—
Morgan v
Clinton State
Bank
1995
(50AkA67)
—221—
Thurman v
Thurman
1995
(50AkA93)
953SW[5]68
954SW[3]953
984SW[3]44
—227—
Missouri v
McCrary
1995
916SW[4]348
931SW[3]841
o 2SW[1]864
op 8SW[4]79
—233—
Hedrick v
Chrysler Corp.
1995
945SW[1]684
957SW[1]514
994SW[1]591
19SW[1]701

1172

Exhibit 36. 2 (pt. 6) SHEPARD'S SOUTHWESTERN REPORTER CITATIONS 1172 (2001).

these citations to find the cases online, while other *Shepard's* users can learn the names of the cases by entering the citation in lexisONE or calling a toll-free customer service number.

Electronic citators have several advantages over printed *Shepard's Citations*. New cases are added within hours or days. Coverage is not divided into separate state and regional citators, with each displaying only some of the citing documents. Citing entries are compiled into a single online listing, eliminating the need to search through multiple volumes and pamphlets. Because page space is not a concern, case treatments and names of publications are spelled out rather than abbreviated. One can easily narrow retrieval to specific treatments or headnote numbers, without scanning a lengthy list of citations. Finally, hypertext links make it possible to go directly from the online citator to the text of citing cases. For many researchers, the printed version of *Shepard's Citations* nonetheless remains a useful means to verify the validity of decisions and to find research leads.

§4-6. CONCLUSION

This chapter has introduced both electronic and print resources for case research. Many students tend to rely very heavily on online resources, and only when they leave law school do they learn that computerized research can be very expensive. Yet financial constraints are only one reason not to rely exclusively on methods that depend on the researcher's ability to phrase an effective search request. If the language of a decision does not precisely match the request, it will remain undiscovered unless other research methods are also used. The database systems are most effective as part of a research strategy integrating a number of different approaches.

Often the author or editor's work in organizing and analyzing cases is indispensable. Treatises and law review articles analyze the leading cases in a subject area, while digests and annotations sort and index cases by precise facts or issues. Full-text searches may not identify the most important cases or distinguish easily between holding and dictum. There are times when printed tools can achieve results with greater speed and precision than online research.

No single case-finder is the best for all purposes. Selection of the most useful resource depends upon the nature of the problem at hand. Research involving the interpretation of a statute leads to an annotated code for case-finding, while a problem requiring general back ground knowledge of a topic suggests that researcher begin with a treatise. Each research problem must be analyzed separately, the available tools evaluated, and an appropriate approach chosen. Inevitably personal preference plays a part when two or more case-finding tools seem equally useful. Experimentation and the development of skill in using all of these approaches will enable you to make the most effective choices for each problem encountered.

CHAPTER 5
CONSTITUTIONS AND STATUTES

■　　■　　■　　■　　■　　■　　■　　■　　■　　■

§5-1. INTRODUCTION

The preceding chapters have focused on case law because of the importance of appellate decisions in the common law system and in American legal education. The legislature, not the judiciary, is the branch of government charged with making laws, however, and legislative enactments play just as vital a role as decisions in today's legal system. Most appellate court decisions, in fact, involve the application or interpretation of statutes rather than the consideration of common law principles.

This chapter considers constitutions, which establish the form and limitations of government power, as well as legislation. These forms of law are discussed in one chapter because they are often published together, and because research methods are similar. In considering constitutional provisions or statutes, it is important to find not only the relevant text but also court decisions that interpret this text and define its terms. The most common research sources for both constitutions and statutes are *annotated codes,* which provide the text of the law in force accompanied by notes of court decisions.

The nature of legal authority assigned to constitutions and legislation is different from that of case law. These sources have binding or mandatory authority within their own jurisdiction, but in other jurisdictions they have no effect and are not even persuasive authority. One state's laws may influence another state's legislature considering similar legislation, and judicial decisions applying or construing a statute may persuade other courts confronting similar issues, but the statutory language itself carries no authority outside its own jurisdiction.

Determining early in the research process whether a problem involves constitutional or statutory provisions can save considerable time, as this significantly affects the

direction of your research. Experienced researchers develop a sense of which issues are likely to be governed by constitution or statute, and whether these issues are matters of federal or state law. Substantive criminal law, for example, is generally defined by the enactments of a state legislature, while defendants' procedural rights are determined by both federal and state constitutional law. As legislatures continue to enact statutes to govern traditional common law areas such as contract and tort, more and more questions involve some statutory research. Secondary sources and cases generally provide references to the relevant provisions, so it should soon become apparent from your introductory research whether statutory research is warranted.

§5-2. The U.S. Constitution

The United States Constitution is the basic law of the country, defining political relationships, enumerating the rights and liberties of citizens, and creating the framework of national government. Unlike statutes, which are often written in extreme detail and specificity, the Constitution contains concise statements of broad principles. It entered into force in March 1789, and it has only been amended 27 times in more than two centuries. Among the most important of these amendments are the Bill of Rights, guaranteeing personal liberties, and the Fourteenth Amendment, applying these protections to the states.

Although its text has changed little, the Constitution has been applied by the courts to numerous situations which its drafters could not have foreseen. In interpreting constitutional provisions, it is particularly important to examine relevant decisions of the Supreme Court and of the lower federal courts. Judicial interpretations of constitutional principles are no less important in legal research than the language of the Constitution.

The text of the Constitution appears in numerous publications ranging from simple pamphlets to standard reference works such as *Black's Law Dictionary*. It is included in online and CD-ROM collections of federal statutes and is available at dozens of government and private Internet sites. The Constitution Society provides an annotated listing of several online sources
<www.constitution.org/cs_found.htm>.

The Constitution is also printed at the beginning of the *United States Code*, the official publication of federal statutes. However, two annotated statutory publications, *United States Code Annotated (USCA) and United States Code Service (USCS)*, are more useful in legal research. These publications provide much more than just the text of the Constitution. Each clause is accompanied by abstracts of cases, arranged by subject and thoroughly indexed. Some major provisions have thousands of case abstracts in several hundred subject divisions. The Constitution is so heavily annotated that it occupies ten volumes in *USCA* and eight volumes in *USCS*. The annotations are regularly updated in annual pocket parts for each volume and interim pamphlets throughout the year. These exhaustive annotations make the annotated codes essential resources in determining how the Constitution's broad principles have been applied to specific circumstances.

Of the many commentaries on the Constitution, one of the most extensive and authoritative is *The Constitution of the United States of America: Analysis and Interpretation*, published every ten years by the Congressional Research Service of the Library of Congress. This text is a useful starting point for constitutional research, with a thorough analysis of Supreme Court decisions applying each provision of the Constitution. The current version, edited by Johnny H. Killian and George A. Costello, was published in 1996 and covers cases through June 1992. The volume is

updated by a biennial pocket part, the coverage of which generally lags a couple of years behind current developments. This edition of the Constitution is available on the Internet at two sites. GPO Access <www.gpoaccess.gov/constitution/> provides both text and PDF versions (the latter matching the look of the printed pages), and FindLaw <www.findlaw.com/casecode/constitution/> includes hypertext links to footnotes and to Supreme Court cases discussed. Both websites include full-text search capabilities. Exhibit 37 shows the beginning of this work's discussion of the Second Amendment, with footnotes citing several scholarly monographs, law review articles, and Supreme Court decisions.

Another helpful background source is Leonard W. Levy et al., eds., *Encyclopedia of the American Constitution* (6 vols., 2d ed. 2000), which includes articles on constitutional doctrines as well as on specific court decisions, people, and historical periods. Shorter works providing similar treatment of constitutional issues include Kermit L. Hall, ed., *The Oxford Companion to the Supreme Court* (1992), and Jethro K. Lieberman, *A Practical Companion to the Constitution* (1999). Of numerous scholarly works on the Supreme Court's constitutional jurisprudence, the most extensive is the multivolume Oliver Wendell Holmes Devise *History of the Supreme Court of the United States* (1971-date).

For further historical research, one can turn to the documents prepared by those who drafted, adopted, and ratified the Constitution. There was no official record of the debates in the constitutional convention, but Max Farrand's *The Records of the Federal Convention of 1787* (4 vols. 1937 & supp. 1987) is considered the most authoritative source. The traditional source for the state ratification debates is Jonathan Elliot, *The Debates in the Several State*

BEARING ARMS

SECOND AMENDMENT

A well regulated Militia being necessary to the security of a free State, the right of the people to keep and bear Arms shall not be infringed.

In spite of extensive recent discussion and much legislative action with respect to regulation of the purchase, possession, and transportation of firearms, as well as proposals to substantially curtail ownership of firearms, there is no definitive resolution by the courts of just what right the Second Amendment protects. The opposing theories, perhaps oversimplified, are an "individual rights" thesis whereby individuals are protected in ownership, possession, and transportation, and a "states' rights" thesis whereby it is said the purpose of the clause is to protect the States in their authority to maintain formal, organized militia units.[1] Whatever the Amendment may mean, it is a bar only to federal action, not extending to state[2] or private[3] restraints. The Supreme Court has given effect to the dependent clause of the Amendment in the only case in which it has tested a congressional enactment against the constitutional prohibition, seeming to affirm individual protection but only in the context of the maintenance of a militia or other such public force.

In *United States v. Miller*,[4] the Court sustained a statute requiring registration under the National Firearms Act of sawed-off

---

[1] A sampling of the diverse literature in which the same historical, linguistic, and case law background is the basis for strikingly different conclusions is: STAFF OF SUBCOM. ON THE CONSTITUTION, SENATE COMMITTEE ON THE JUDICIARY, 97TH CONGRESS, 2D SESS., THE RIGHT TO KEEP AND BEAR ARMS (Comm. Print 1982); Don B. Kates, HANDGUN PROHIBITION AND THE ORIGINAL MEANING OF THE SECOND AMENDMENT (1984); GUN CONTROL AND THE CONSTITUTION: SOURCES AND EXPLORATIONS ON THE SECOND AMENDMENT (Robert J. Cottrol, ed. 1993); STEPHEN P. HALBROOK, THAT EVERY MAN BE ARMED: THE EVOLUTION OF A CONSTITUTIONAL RIGHT (1984); Symposium, *Gun Control*, 49 LAW & CONTEMP. PROBS. 1 (1986); Sanford Levinson, *The Embarrassing Second Amendment*, 99 YALE L.J. 637 (1989).

[2] Presser v. Illinois, 116 U.S. 252, 265 (1886). See also Miller v. Texas, 153 U.S. 535 (1894); Robertson v. Baldwin, 165 U.S. 275, 281–282 (1897). The non-application of the Second Amendment to the States is good law today. Quilici v. Village of Morton Grove, 695 F. 2d 261 (7th Cir. 1982), cert. denied, 464 U.S. 863 (1983).

[3] United States v. Cruikshank, 92 U.S. 542 (1875).

[4] 307 U.S. 174 (1939). The defendants had been released on the basis of the trial court determination that prosecution would violate the Second Amendment and no briefs or other appearances were filed on their behalf; the Court acted on the basis of the Government's representations.

Exhibit 37. CONSTITUTION OF THE UNITED STATES OF AMERICA: ANALYSIS AND INTERPRETATION 1193 (Johnny H. Killian & George A. Costello eds., 1996).

Conventions on the Adoption of the Federal Constitution (2d
ed., 5 vols. 1836-45). A much more comprehensive modern
treatment originally edited by Merrill Jensen and now by
John P. Kaminski and Gaspare J. Saladino, *The Documentary
History of the Ratification of the Constitution* (16 vols. to date,
1976-date), is still in the process of publication and contains debates, commentaries and other documents. The
Library of Congress website provides full-text access to
both Farrand's *Records* and Elliot's *Debates*
<lcweb2.loc.gov/ammem/amlaw/>. Philip B. Kurland &
Ralph Lerner, eds., *The Founders' Constitution* (5 vols. 1987),
and Neil H. Cogan, ed., *The Complete Bill of Rights: The
Drafts, Debates, Sources, and Origins* (1997) are useful collections of excerpts from source documents arranged by the
constitutional provision to which they apply.

§5-3. STATE CONSTITUTIONS

Each state in governed by its own constitution, which
establishes the structure of government and guarantees
fundamental rights. While state constitutions are roughly
comparable to their federal counterpart, they tend to be
much more detailed and generally are amended far more
frequently. Some states have revised and replaced their
constitutions several times.

State constitutions can be important sources in cases
involving individual rights. While a state cannot deprive
citizens of federal constitutional rights, its constitution can
guarantee rights beyond those provided under the U.S.
Constitution. Just as the U.S. Supreme Court is the arbiter
of the scope of protections offered by the federal constitution, the state court of last resort determines the scope of
its constitution.

The best source for a state constitution is usually the
annotated state code, which provides both the latest text
and notes of court decisions interpreting and construing

constitutional provisions. Pamphlet texts are also published in many states, and state constitutions are available through the online databases, as part of state CD-ROM products, and on the Internet from state government sites. Of several sites providing multistate access to primary sources, the most convenient for the text of constitutions may be FindLaw's listing <www.findlaw.com/11stategov/indexconst.html>.

Current state constitutions are compiled in *Constitutions of the United States: National and State* (7 vols., 2d ed. 1974-date). William F. Swindler, ed., *Sources and Documents of United States Constitutions* (11 vols., 1973-79) also includes superseded state constitutions and other historical documents, with background notes, editorial comments, and a selected bibliography for each state. Swindler's work is based in part on the classic compilation edited by Benjamin Perley Poore, *The Federal and State Constitutions, Colonial Charters, and Other Organic Laws of the United States* (2 vols., 2d ed. 1878), still available in many libraries.

For research into a particular state's constitution, one of the best starting places may be a volume in the series *Reference Guides to the State Constitutions of the United States.* This monograph series began with Robert F. Williams, *The New Jersey State Constitution: A Reference Guide* (1990), and now covers almost forty states. Each volume includes a summary of the state's constitutional history, a detailed section-by-section analysis of the constitution with background information and discussion of judicial interpretations, and a brief bibliographical essay providing references for further research.

Journals and proceedings of state constitutional conventions can provide insight into framers' intent, although the lack of indexing in many older volumes can make for difficult research. These documents are available on microfiche

in *State Constitutional Conventions, Commissions, and Amendments,* covering all fifty states from 1776 through 1988, and are listed in a series of bibliographies beginning with Cynthia E. Browne's *State Constitutional Conventions from Independence to the Completion of the Present Union, 1776-1959: A Bibliography* (1973).

§5-4. PUBLICATION OF STATUTES

American statutes are published in three forms. The first printed version of a newly enacted statute is the *slip law.* Each law is issued by itself on a single sheet or as a pamphlet with separate pagination. Neither federal nor state slip laws are widely distributed, and their texts reach the public largely through electronic services and commercial publications.

Next are the *session laws.* The statutes are arranged by date of passage and published in separate volumes for each term of the legislature. Official session laws are generally published only in bound volumes after a session has ended, but commercial *advance session law services* provide the texts of new laws in pamphlet form on a more timely basis. Session law volumes are generally indexed, but these indexes rarely cumulate and subject access to more than one session can be difficult.

In most jurisdictions, the session laws constitute the *positive law* form of legislation, i.e., the authoritative, binding text of the laws. Other forms (such as codes) are only *prima facie* evidence of the statutory language, unless they have been designated as positive law by the legislature.

Although the chronologically arranged session laws contain the official text of legislative enactments, their use as research tools is limited. Researchers usually need the laws currently in force, rather than the laws passed during a specific legislative term. They also need convenient access

to amendments and related legislation. Statutory compilations, known generally as *codes,* collect current statutes of general and permanent application and arrange them by subject. The statutes are grouped into broad subject topics, usually called *titles,* and within each title they are divided into chapters and then numbered sections. The parts of a single legislative act may be printed together or may be scattered by subject through several different titles. A detailed index for the entire code provides access to the sections dealing with particular problems or topics.

Some jurisdictions have official code publications containing the text of the statutes in force. If an official edition is published, it is usually the authoritative text and should be cited in briefs and pleadings. However, most official codes are *unannotated;* that is, they do not include references to judicial decisions which have applied or construed the statutes. Finding relevant cases is such an important part of statutory research that the most useful sources are commercially published annotated codes which contain these notes of decisions. Most annotated codes also provide historical comments and cross references to legal encyclopedias and other publications.

Codes, whether annotated or unannotated, must be updated regularly to include the numerous statutory changes which occur every time a legislature meets. An outdated code is virtually useless for current research. Some official codes are updated only by the publication of revised volumes every few years. Most annotated codes, on the other hand, are supplemented by annual pocket parts and quarterly pamphlets.

Printed resources are particularly well suited for statutory research, because code volumes make it easy to find related provisions and to place a section in its context. To understand the scope of the language in a specific section,

it's often necessary to see an entire code chapter or title. A wide range of electronic resources, however, is available. The official website for almost every jurisdiction provides access to the text of its code. Most of these can be searched by keyword, but very few include notes of court decisions or other research references. More extensive annotated codes are available through the commercial online databases and on CD-ROM.

§5-5. FEDERAL STATUTES

The United States Congress meets in two-year terms, consisting of two annual sessions, and enacts several hundred statutes each term. These statutes range from simple designations of commemorative days to complex environmental or tax legislation spanning hundreds of pages. Each act is designated as either a *public law* or a *private law,* and assigned a number indicating the order in which it was passed. Pub. L. 108-1, for example, is the first public law passed during the 108th Congress (2003-04).

Public laws are designed to affect the general public, while private laws are passed to meet special needs of an individual or small group. The distinction between the two is sometimes blurred, as when a special interest group promotes "public" legislation that actually affects very few people. Both types are passed in the same way and both appear in the session laws, but in separate numerical series. Only public laws, however, become part of the statutory code.

A. SLIP LAWS AND SESSION LAWS

The slip law, an individually paginated pamphlet, is the first official text of a new statute and is available from Congress itself or from the U.S. Government Printing Office. Beginning with the 104th Congress in 1995, the

Government Printing Office's GPO Access provides PDF files of public laws through the Internet <www.gpoaccess.gov/plaws/>. For current legislation this is one of the quickest and most effective sources, with new laws online within a few days or weeks of enactment. For the very latest laws, it may be necessary to check a legislative site such as THOMAS <thomas.loc.gov> for the *enrolled bill*, or the version that was passed by both houses and sent to the President. THOMAS has enrolled bills back to the 101st Congress (1989-90).

After the end of each session of Congress, the public and private slip laws are cumulated, corrected, and issued in bound volumes as the official *United States Statutes at Large* for the session. These are cited by volume and page number. The Brady Handgun Violence Prevention Act, Pub. L. 103-159, 107 Stat. 1536 (1993), shown in Exhibit 38, begins on page 1536 of volume 107 of the *Statutes at Large.* Each annual volume, which may actually consist of several separate parts, contains an index.

There is a lengthy delay of two years or more before *Statutes at Large* volumes are published. Commercial and electronic resources provide the texts of federal enactments much more quickly. Two of the leading printed sources are monthly services accompanying *United States Code Annotated* and *United States Code Service.* These services, West Group's *United States Code Congressional and Administrative News* (USCCAN) and LexisNexis's *USCS Advance,* both provide the official pagination that will eventually appear in the *Statutes at Large.* Both services also include other materials such as new court rules, presidential documents, and selected administrative regulations. Neither *USCCAN* nor *USCS Advance* includes private laws, which are published only as slip laws and in the official *Statutes at Large.*

---

107 STAT. 1536   PUBLIC LAW 103-159—NOV. 30, 1993

Public Law 103-159
103d Congress

An Act

Nov. 30, 1993
[H.R. 1025]

To provide for a waiting period before the purchase of a handgun, and for the establishment of a national instant criminal background check system to be contacted by firearms dealers before the transfer of any firearm.

Be it enacted by the Senate and House of Representatives of the United States of America in Congress assembled,

Brady Handgun
Violence
Prevention
Act.
Inter-
governmental
relations.
Law
enforcement
and crime.
18 USC 921 note.

Effective date.
Termination
date.

TITLE I—BRADY HANDGUN CONTROL

SEC. 101. SHORT TITLE.

This title may be cited as the "Brady Handgun Violence Prevention Act".

SEC. 102. FEDERAL FIREARMS LICENSEE REQUIRED TO CONDUCT CRIMINAL BACKGROUND CHECK BEFORE TRANSFER OF FIREARM TO NON-LICENSEE.

(a) INTERIM PROVISION.—

(1) IN GENERAL.—Section 922 of title 18, United States Code, is amended by adding at the end the following:

"(s)(1) Beginning on the date that is 90 days after the date of enactment of this subsection and ending on the day before the date that is 60 months after such date of enactment, it shall be unlawful for any licensed importer, licensed manufacturer, or licensed dealer to sell, deliver, or transfer a handgun to an individual who is not licensed under section 923, unless—

"(A) after the most recent proposal of such transfer by the transferee—

"(i) the transferor has—

"(I) received from the transferee a statement of the transferee containing the information described in paragraph (3);

"(II) verified the identity of the transferee by examining the identification document presented;

"(III) within 1 day after the transferee furnishes the statement, provided notice of the contents of the statement to the chief law enforcement officer of the place of residence of the transferee; and

"(IV) within 1 day after the transferee furnishes the statement, transmitted a copy of the statement

---

Exhibit 38.   Brady Handgun Violence Prevention Act, Pub.
L. No. 103-159, tit. I, 107 Stat. 1536 (1993).

USCCAN has two additional features. It reprints selected congressional committee reports (usually considered the most important sources of legislative history, as will be discussed in Chapter 6), and it is recompiled into bound volumes at the end of each session. It provides a permanent source for federal session laws back to 1941, although it did not follow the official *Statutes at Large* pagination until 1975.

Other sources may be even more current than *USCCAN* or *USCS Advance* in printing new legislation. Looseleaf services in fields such as tax or trade regulation provide very current coverage of congressional action in their subject areas, and are usually supplemented on a weekly basis.

New public laws are also available rapidly online through Westlaw and LexisNexis, with searchable backfiles extending to the late 1980s. Potomac Publishing has comprehensive retrospective coverage of the *Statutes at Large* back to 1789 by subscription, in both CD-ROM and Internet <www.potomacpub.com> versions. The Library of Congress provides free access to the first seventeen volumes of the *Statutes at Large,* through 1873 <lcweb2.loc.gov/ammem/amlaw/lwsl.html>.

Although the *Statutes at Large* is not the most convenient source for federal legislation, it maintains a vital role in legal research. In most instances it is the official statement of the law, and it is a necessary source for determining the specific language Congress enacted at any given time. This is important for lawyers as well as historians. It is often necessary to determine when a particular provision took effect or was repealed, or to reconstruct the precise text as it was enacted. Sections of a public law may be distributed among several titles in the code, but the *Statutes at Large* provides each act of Congress in its entirety.

B. The United States Code

The first official subject compilations of federal legislation were the *Revised Statutes of the United States* of 1873, and its second edition of 1878. Congress enacted the first edition of the *Revised Statutes* as positive law in its entirety, expressly repealing the original *Statutes at Large* versions of its contents. It is therefore the authoritative text for most laws enacted before 1873, and is still needed occasionally in modern research.

Although the *Revised Statutes* rapidly became outdated, no other official compilation was prepared for almost fifty years. Finally, in 1926, the first edition of the *United States Code* was published, arranging the laws by subject into fifty titles. The *U.S. Code* is published in a completely revised edition of about 35 volumes every six years, with an annual supplement of one or more bound volumes. These supplements are cumulative, so it is necessary only to consult the main set and its latest supplement. Nearly half of the *U.S. Code* titles have been reenacted as positive law, and for them the code has become the authoritative text. For the others, the *Statutes at Large* is authoritative and the *U.S. Code* is *prima facie* evidence of the law. A list of all code titles, indicating which titles have been reenacted, appears in the front of each *U.S. Code* volume and is reproduced here as Exhibit 39.

Unlike citations to the *Statutes at Large* or to cases, citations to the *U.S. Code* refer to title and section rather than to volume and page. For example, 18 U.S.C. § 925A (2000), shown in Exhibit 40, is the citation for section 925A of Title 18 (Crimes and Criminal Procedure). This provision was added to the *U.S. Code* as part of the Brady Act, as shown by the parenthetical reference following its text to Pub. L. No. 103-119, title I, § 104(a).

In addition to the text of statutes, the *U.S. Code* also includes historical notes, cross references, and other research aids. Parenthetical references indicate the *Statutes at Large* or *Revised Statutes* sources of each section, including any amendments. These references lead to the version that may be the authoritative text, and from there to legislative history documents relating to the law's enactment. In Exhibit 40, note that § 926 was originally enacted in 1968 and was then amended later the same year and again in 1986 and 1994. The "Amendments" note following the section indicates the precise nature of each of these changes.

TITLES OF UNITED STATES CODE

*1. General Provisions.

2. The Congress.

*3. The President.

*4. Flag and Seal, Seat of Government, and the States.

*5. Government Organization and Employees; and Appendix.

†6. [Surety Bonds.]

7. Agriculture.

8. Aliens and Nationality.

*9. Arbitration.

*10. Armed Forces; and Appendix.

*11. Bankruptcy; and Appendix.

12. Banks and Banking.

*13. Census.

*14. Coast Guard.

15. Commerce and Trade.

16. Conservation.

*17. Copyrights.

*18. Crimes and Criminal Procedure; and Appendix.

19. Customs Duties.

20. Education.

21. Food and Drugs.

22. Foreign Relations and Intercourse.

*23. Highways.

24. Hospitals and Asylums.

25. Indians.

26. Internal Revenue Code; and Appendix.

27. Intoxicating Liquors.

*28. Judiciary and Judicial Procedure; and Appendix.

29. Labor.

30. Mineral Lands and Mining.

*31. Money and Finance.

*32. National Guard.

33. Navigation and Navigable Waters.

‡34. [Navy.]

*35. Patents.

*36. Patriotic and National Observances, Ceremonies, and Organizations.

*37. Pay and Allowances of the Uniformed Services.

*38. Veterans' Benefits; and Appendix.

*39. Postal Service.

40. Public Buildings, Property, and Works; and Appendix.

41. Public Contracts.

42. The Public Health and Welfare.

43. Public Lands.

*44. Public Printing and Documents.

45. Railroads.

*46. Shipping; and Appendix.

47. Telegraphs, Telephones, and Radiotelegraphs.

48. Territories and Insular Possessions.

*49. Transportation.

50. War and National Defense; and Appendix.

*This title has been enacted as positive law. However, any Appendix to this title has not been enacted as positive law.
†This title was repealed by the enactment of Title 31.
‡This title was eliminated by the enactment of Title 10.

Page III

Exhibit 39. Titles of United States Code, 1 UNITED STATES CODE iii (2000).

Even when discussing statutes currently in force, decisions and other documents sometimes refer to provisions by session law citation rather than by code section. It is then necessary to determine where a law is codified, as well as whether it is still in force. One of the simplest ways

in par. (4), and authorized the Secretary to permit the importation of ammunition for examination and testing in text following par. (4).

EFFECTIVE DATE OF 1996 AMENDMENT

Amendment by Pub. L. 104–106 effective on the earlier of the date on which the Secretary of the Army submits a certification in accordance with section 5523 of [former] Title 36, Patriotic Societies and Observances, or Oct. 1, 1996, see section 1624(c) of Pub. L. 104–106, set out as a note under section 4316 of Title 10, Armed Forces

EFFECTIVE DATE OF 1988 AMENDMENT; SUNSET PROVISION

Amendment by section 2(c) of Pub. L. 100–649 effective 30th day beginning after Nov. 10, 1988, and amendment by section 2(f)(2)(C), (E) effective 15 years after such effective date, see section 2(f) of Pub. L. 100–649, as amended, set out as a note under section 922 of this title.

EFFECTIVE DATE OF 1986 AMENDMENT

Amendment by Pub. L. 99–308 applicable to any action, petition, or appellate proceeding pending on May 19, 1986, see section 110(b) of Pub. L. 99–308, set out as a note under section 921 of this title.

EFFECTIVE DATE OF 1984 AMENDMENT

Amendment by Pub. L. 98–573 effective 15th day after Oct. 30, 1984, see section 214(a), (b) of Pub. L. 98–573, set out as a note under section 1304 of Title 19, Customs Duties.

EFFECTIVE DATE OF 1968 AMENDMENT

Amendment by Pub. L. 90–618 effective Dec. 16, 1968, except subsecs. (a)(1) and (d) effective Oct. 22, 1968, see section 105 of Pub. L. 90–618, set out as a note under section 901 of this title.

SECTION REFERRED TO IN OTHER SECTIONS

This section is referred to in section 922 of this title; title 22 section 2778.

§ 925A. Remedy for erroneous denial of firearms

Any person denied a firearm pursuant to subsection (s) or (t) of section 922—

(1) due to the provision of erroneous information relating to the person by any State or political subdivision thereof, or by the national instant criminal background check system established under section 103 of the Brady Handgun Violence Prevention Act; or

(2) who was not prohibited from receipt of a firearm pursuant to subsection (g) or (n) of section 922,

may bring an action against the State or political subdivision responsible for providing the erroneous information, or responsible for denying the transfer, or against the United States, as the case may be, for an order directing that the erroneous information be corrected or that the transfer be approved, as the case may be. In any action under this section, the court, in its discretion, may allow the prevailing party a reasonable attorney's fee as part of the costs.

(Added Pub. L. 103–159, title I, § 104(a), Nov. 30, 1993, 107 Stat. 1543.)

REFERENCES IN TEXT

Section 103 of the Brady Handgun Violence Prevention Act, referred to in par. (1), is section 103 of Pub. L. 103–159, which is set out as a note under section 922 of this title.

§ 926. Rules and regulations

(a) The Secretary may prescribe only such rules and regulations as are necessary to carry out the provisions of this chapter, including—

(1) regulations providing that a person licensed under this chapter, when dealing with another person so licensed, shall provide such other licensed person a certified copy of this license;

(2) regulations providing for the issuance, at a reasonable cost, to a person licensed under this chapter, of certified copies of his license for use as provided under regulations issued under paragraph (1) of this subsection; and

(3) regulations providing for effective receipt and secure storage of firearms relinquished by or seized from persons described in subsection (d)(8) or (g)(8) of section 922.

No such rule or regulation prescribed after the date of the enactment of the Firearms Owners' Protection Act may require that records required to be maintained under this chapter or any portion of the contents of such records, be recorded at or transferred to a facility owned, managed, or controlled by the United States or any State or any political subdivision thereof, nor that any system of registration of firearms, firearms owners, or firearms transactions or dispositions be established. Nothing in this section expands or restricts the Secretary's authority to inquire into the disposition of any firearm in the course of a criminal investigation.

(b) The Secretary shall give not less than ninety days public notice, and shall afford interested parties opportunity for hearing, before prescribing such rules and regulations.

(c) The Secretary shall not prescribe rules or regulations that require purchasers of black powder under the exemption in section 845(a)(5) of this title to complete affidavits or forms attesting to that exemption.

(Added Pub. L. 90–351, title IV, § 902, June 19, 1968, 82 Stat. 234; amended Pub. L. 90–618, title I, § 102, Oct. 22, 1968, 82 Stat. 1226; Pub. L. 99–308, § 106, May 19, 1986, 100 Stat. 459; Pub. L. 103–322, title XI, § 110401(d), Sept. 13, 1994, 108 Stat. 2015.)

REFERENCES IN TEXT

The date of the enactment of the Firearms Owners' Protection Act, referred to in subsec. (a), is the date of enactment of Pub. L. 99–308, which was approved May 19, 1986.

AMENDMENTS

1994—Subsec. (a)(3). Pub. L. 103–322 added par. (3).

1986—Subsec. (a). Pub. L. 99–308, § 106(1)–(4), designated existing provision as subsec. (a), and in subsec. (a) as so designated, in provision preceding par. (1) substituted "may prescribe only" for "may prescribe" and "as are" for "as he deems reasonably", and in closing provision substituted provision that no rule or regulation prescribed after May 19, 1986, require that records required under this chapter be recorded at or transferred to a facility owned, managed, or controlled by the United States or any State or political subdivision thereof, nor any system of registration of firearms, firearms owners, or firearms transactions or dispositions be established and that nothing in this section expand or restrict the authority of the Secretary to inquire into the disposition of any firearm in the course of a criminal investigation for provision that the Secretary give reasonable public notice, and afford an op-

Exhibit 40.   18 U.S.C. §§ 925A-926 (2000).

to do this is to use a *parallel reference table* found in three volumes at the end of the *U.S. Code.* The example shown in Exhibit 41 provides *U.S. Code* references for laws enacted in 1993, including the Brady Act shown in Exhibit 38. Note that it is possible to work from the year (1993), the term of Congress (103d), or *Statutes at Large* volume (107); and that some sections listed under Pub. L. 103-160 in this exhibit are not in the current *U.S. Code* because they have been repealed (Rep.). Other parallel reference tables provide access from the former numbering of revised titles to current section numbers, and from the *Revised Statutes* to the *U.S. Code.*

Another table, "Acts Cited by Popular Name," can be used to find an act if its citation is not known. This table lists laws alphabetically under either short titles assigned by Congress or names by which they have become commonly known, and provides citations to the laws in both the *Statutes at Large* and the *U.S. Code.* Exhibit 42 shows a page from this table in the 2000 *U.S. Code,* with a reference under the heading "Brady Handgun Violence Prevention Act." Note that this law is listed under its official name, rather than under "Brady Act" or "Brady Bill," by which it may be more commonly known. "Popular names" are not necessarily the ones that appear in newspapers and on television.

Without a reference to a specific statute, the place to begin research in the *U.S. Code* is its general index. This basic tool for finding federal statutes by subject consists of several volumes, and it is updated in each annual supplement. Exhibit 43 shows a page from the index providing references to a variety of provisions under the heading "Weapons," including numerous references under "Manufacturers and manufacturing" and other subheadings to federal firearms provisions in 18 U.S.C. §§ 921-930. Statutory indexes are often full of cross-references (such as

Page 605 — TABLE III—STATUTES AT LARGE

| 103d Cong. | | | | U.S.C. | | |
107 Stat.	Pub. L.	Section	Page	Title	Section	Status
1993—Nov.	30	103-39	102(c)	1541	18	924	
			103	1541	18	922 nt
			104(a)	1543	18	925A
			104(b)	1543	18	prec. 921
			105	1543	18	921 nt
			106(a)	1543	42	3759
			106(b)	1544	18	922 nt
			201	1544	18	923
			301	1545	18	921 nt
			302(a)-(c)	1545	18	922
			302(d)	1545	18	924
			303	1545	18	923
		103-160	107(c)	1564	50	1521
			126	1567	10	2401 nt
			152(b)	1578	10	2281 nt
			155(b)	1579	50	1521 nt
			156(a)-(1)	1581	10	4543
			156(a)-(2)	1582	10	prec. 4531
			158(b)	1582	10	2208
			158(c)	1582	10	4543 nt
			214(a)	1586	10	2370a
			214(b)	1586	10	prec. 2351
			232, 234	1583, 1595	10	2431 nt	Rep.
			235	1598	10	2431 nt
			240, 242(a)-(e)	1603-1605	10	2431 nt+a	Rep.
			242(f)(1)	1605	10	2609	Rep.
			242(f)(2)	1605	10	prec. 2601
			243	1605	10	2431 nt

Exhibit 41. Table III-Statutes at Large, 29 UNITED STATES CODE 605 (2000).

the "Juvenile Delinquents and Dependents" entry in Exhibit 43) and long lists of subheadings and sub-subheadings. Indexes can be unwieldy and confusing, but they remain essential resources in statutory research. Statutes are often easier to find through indexes than through full-text keyword searches, which may yield too many irrelevant results.

Electronic sources for the *United States Code* include commercial databases, CD-ROM, and free Internet sites. The Westlaw and LexisNexis versions will be discussed with the annotated codes in the following subsection. The Government Printing Office publishes an annual CD-ROM edition, incorporating the supplement and including the popular name table and general index. The code is also available on the Internet from Cornell Law School's Legal Information Institute <www.law.cornell.edu/uscode>, GPO Access <www.gpoaccess.gov/uscode/>, and the House of Representatives Office of the Law Revision Counsel <uscode.house.gov/>. These versions offer flexi-

Blue Star Mothers of America Act
Pub. L. 86-653, July 14, 1960, 74 Stat. 515

Board for International Broadcasting Act of 1973
Pub. L. 93-129, Oct. 19, 1973, 87 Stat. 456 (22 U.S.C. 2871 et seq.)
Short title, see 22 U.S.C. 2871 note

Board for International Broadcasting Authorization Act, Fiscal Years 1980 and 1981
Pub. L. 96-60, title III, Aug. 15, 1979, 93 Stat. 402

Board for International Broadcasting Authorization Act, Fiscal Years 1982 and 1983
Pub. L. 97-241, title IV, Aug. 24, 1982, 96 Stat. 295

Board for International Broadcasting Authorization Act, Fiscal Years 1984 and 1985
Pub. L. 98-164, title III, Nov. 22, 1983, 97 Stat. 1036

Board of Veterans' Appeals Administrative Procedures Improvement Act of 1994
Pub. L. 103-271, July 1, 1994, 108 Stat. 740
Short title, see 38 U.S.C. 301 note

Bodie Protection Act of 1994
Pub. L. 103-433, title X, Oct. 31, 1994, 108 Stat. 4509

Boggs Act
Nov. 2, 1951, ch. 666, 65 Stat. 767 (21 U.S.C. 174)

Boiler Inspection Act of the District of Columbia
July 25, 1936, ch. 802, 49 Stat. 1917

Boise Laboratory Replacement Act of 2000
Pub. L. 106-291, title III, § 351, Oct. 11, 2000, 114 Stat. 1004

Bomb Threats Act
Pub. L. 91-452, title XI, § 1102(a), Oct. 15, 1970, 84 Stat. 956 (18 U.S.C. 844)

Bond Act (Public Officers)
Mar. 2, 1895, ch. 177, § 5, 28 Stat. 807

Bond Limitation Act
See Second Liberty Bond Act

Bond Purchase Clause (Sundry Civil Appropriation Act)
Mar. 3, 1881, ch. 133, § 2, 21 Stat. 457

Bonner Act
See Federal Boating Act of 1958

Bonneville Project Act of 1937
Aug. 20, 1937, ch. 720, 50 Stat. 731 (16 U.S.C. 832 et seq.)
Short title, see 16 U.S.C. 832 note

Bonus Act
See World War Adjusted Compensation Act

Bonus Payment Act, 1936
See Adjusted Compensation Payment Act, 1936

Book Postage Act
June 30, 1942, ch. 459, 56 Stat. 462

Booth Act (California School Lands)
Mar. 1, 1877, ch. 81, 19 Stat. 267

Borah Act
Aug. 25, 1937, ch. 777, 50 Stat. 810

Borah Resolution (Armament Conference)
See Disarmament Conference Resolution

Border Smog Reduction Act of 1998
Pub. L. 105-286, Oct. 27, 1998, 112 Stat. 2773
Short title, see 42 U.S.C. 7401 note

Borland Amendment (District of Columbia Improvements)
July 21, 1914, ch. 181, 38 Stat. 524

Bosque Redondo Memorial Act
Pub. L. 106-511, title II, Nov. 13, 2000, 114 Stat. 2369 (16 U.S.C. 431 note)

Boston National Historical Park Act of 1974
Pub. L. 93-431, Oct. 1, 1974, 88 Stat. 1184 (16 U.S.C. 410z et seq.)
Short title, see 16 U.S.C. 410z note

Boulder Canyon Project Act
Dec. 21, 1928, ch. 42, 45 Stat. 1057 (43 U.S.C 617 et seq.)
Short title, see 43 U.S.C. 617t

Boulder Canyon Project Adjustment Act
July 19, 1940, ch. 643, 54 Stat. 774 (43 U.S.C. 618 et seq.)
Short title, see 43 U.S.C. 618o

Boulder City Act of 1958
Pub. L. 85-900, Sept. 2, 1958, 72 Stat. 1726 (43 U.S.C. 617u note)

Bowman Act (Claims)
Mar. 3, 1883, ch. 116, 22 Stat. 485

Boykin Merchant Marine Act
June 6, 1939, ch. 186, 53 Stat. 810

Brady Handgun Violence Prevention Act
Pub. L. 103-159, title I, Nov. 30, 1993, 107 Stat. 1536
Short title, see 18 U.S.C. 921 note

Breast and Cervical Cancer Mortality Prevention Act of 1990
Pub. L. 101-354, Aug. 10, 1990, 104 Stat. 409 (42 U.S.C. 300k et seq.)
Short title, see 42 U.S.C. 201 note

Breast and Cervical Cancer Prevention and Treatment Act of 2000
Pub. L. 106-354, Oct. 24, 2000, 114 Stat. 1381
Short title, see 42 U.S.C. 1305 note

Bretton Woods Agreements Act
July 31, 1945, ch. 339, 59 Stat. 512 (22 U.S.C. 286 et seq.)
Short title, see 22 U.S.C. 286 note

Bretton Woods Agreements Act Amendments of 1978
Pub. L. 95-435, Oct. 10, 1978, 92 Stat. 1051

Bridge Act of 1906
Also known as the General Bridge Act of 1906
Mar. 23, 1906, ch. 1130, 34 Stat. 84 (33 U.S.C. 491 et seq.)
Short title, see 33 U.S.C. 491 note

Bring Them Home Alive Act of 2000
Pub. L. 106-484, Nov. 9, 2000, 114 Stat. 2195 (8 U.S.C. 1157 note)

Exhibit 42.   Acts Cited by Popular Name, 27 UNITED STATES CODE 669 (2000).

GENERAL INDEX Page 1188

WEAPONS—Continued
Glacier National Park, 16 §171
Grants,
  Bulletproof vests, 42 §3796ll
  Criminal background checks, system improvements, 42 §14601
  Education, 16 §669h-1; 42 §3760
  Safety, 16 §669h-1; 42 §3760
  Training, 16 §669h-1; 42 §3760
Great Smokey Mountains National Park, 16 §403h-4
Gun-free school zones, 18 §922
Handguns, 18 §921 et seq.
Hawaii National Park, 16 §395d
Hearings, 18 §926
  Licenses and permits, applications, importers, manufacturers, dealers, 18 §923
  Rules and regulations, 18 §926
House of Representatives, sergeant-at-arms, 2 §78 note
Identity and identification,
  Criminal background checks, system improvements, 42 §14601
  Importers, manufacturers, 18 §923
  Taxation, post
Imitation, penalties for entering into commerce, exceptions, 15 §5001
Imports, Exports and imports, generally, ante
Indebtedness, promotion of Rifle Practice and Firearms Safety Corporation, 36 §40703
Independent States of the Former Soviet Union, this index
Indictment and information,
  Dealers, license, 18 §925
  Definitions, 18 §921
  Sales, transportation, 18 §922
Information, licenses and permits, disposition in course of criminal investigation, 18 §923
Insignia, civilian marksmanship, 36 §40721 et seq.
Inspection and inspectors, dealers, 18 §923
Instructions, civilian marksmanship, 36 §40721 et seq.
Internal Revenue Service, Taxation, generally, post
Interstate and foreign commerce, 18 §926A
  Definitions, 18 §921
  Gun trafficking, fines, penalties and forfeitures, 18 §924
  Penalties, exceptions, 15 §5001
  Theft, fines, penalties and forfeitures, 18 §924
  Transportation, shipping, 18 §922
Intimate partner, definitions, domestic violence, 18 §921
Inventory, 18 §923
Isle Royale National Park, 16 §408l
Issuance, civilian marksmanship, 36 §40731
Juvenile Delinquents and Dependents, this index
Landmines, Antipersonnel Landmines, generally, this index
Larceny,
  Interstate and foreign commerce, handgun control, 18 §922
  Fines, penalties and forfeitures, 18 §924
  Inventory, collections, reports, 18 §923
Lassen Volcanic National Park, 16 §204d
Leases, promotion of Rifle Practice and Firearms Safety Corporation, 36 §40703
Library of Congress, 2 §167d
Licenses and permits, 18 §923
  Armored car industry, 15 §5901 et seq.
  Collectors, theft, fines, penalties and forfeitures, 18 §924
  Dealers, 18 §923
    Curios, relics, 18 §923
    Definitions,
      Crimes and offenses, 18 §921
      Handgun control, 18 §922 note
    Handgun control, 18 §922
    Indictment and information, 18 §925
    Records and recordation, inspection and inspectors, crimes and offenses, 18 §923
    Theft, fines, penalties and forfeitures, 18 §924
  Definitions, handgun control, 18 §922 note
  Exports and imports, 18 §923
    Definitions,
      Crimes and offenses, 18 §921
      Handgun control, 18 §922 note
    Handgun control, crimes and offenses, 18 §922
    Indictment and information, 18 §925
    Records and recordation, inspection and inspectors, crimes and offenses, 18 §923
    Theft, fines, penalties and forfeitures, 18 §924
  Handgun control, crimes and offenses, 18 §922
  Manufacturers and manufacturing, 18 §923
    Definitions, crimes and offenses, 18 §921
      Handgun control, 18 §922 note
    Handgun control, crimes and offenses, 18 §922
    Indictment and information, 18 §925
    Records and recordation, inspection and inspectors, crimes and offenses, 18 §923
    Theft, fines, penalties and forfeitures, 18 §924
Liquidations, promotion of Rifle Practice and Firearms Safety Corporation, 36 §40706
Loans, civilian marksmanship, 36 §§40721 et seq., 40731
Local law enforcement agency, information, 18 §923
Location specified on license, inspection and inspectors, 18 §923
Look-alike firearms, definitions, penalties for entering into commerce, exceptions, 15 §5001
Loss, inventory, collection, reports, 18 §923
M-1 rifles, demilitarization, 36 §40728
Machine Guns, generally, this index
Mail and mailing, 18 §§921 note, 1715
  Fines, penalties and forfeitures, 18 §1715
  Nonmailable matter, 39 §3001
  Persons eligible to receive, exemptions, 18 §922
Major component, definitions, undetectable firearms, 18 §922
Mammoth Cave National Park, 16 §404c-4
Manufacturers and manufacturing,
  Consumer Product Safety Commission, ruling or order to restrict, prohibition, 15 §2080 note
  Definitions, 18 §921
  Exemptions, 18 §925
  Fees, licenses and permits, 18 §923
  Fines, penalties and forfeitures, 18 §924
  Identity and identification, 18 §923
  Inspection and inspectors, records and recordation, 18 §923
  Licenses and permits, ante
  Mail and mailing, 18 §1715
  Records and recordation, 18 §§922, 923
  Taxation, post
Marking system, imitation firearms, 15 §5001
Mass destruction, 50 §1701 note, Ex. Ord. No 12938
  Assessments, 50 §2301 note

Exhibit 43. General Index, 35 UNITED STATES CODE 1188 (2000).

ble search approaches, but they are no more up-to-date than the most recent printed edition. It is necessary to note the date of either print or electronic sources consulted and then check the session laws or online databases for recent legislation. The House of Representative version includes classification tables <uscode.house.gov/uscct.htm> listing the *U.S. Code* citations of public laws passed since the most recent edition.

c. Annotated Codes

The *United States Code* has the text of federal laws, but two major shortcomings limit its value to legal researchers. It is not updated on a very timely basis, and there is no information about court decisions applying or interpreting code sections. These decisions are so important that most researchers turn instead to one of two commercially published, annotated editions of the code, *United States Code Annotated (USCA)*, published by West Group, or *United States Code Service (USCS)*, published by LexisNexis. Beyond the text of the law and notes of court decisions, they also provide references to legislative history, administrative regulations, and various secondary sources. These features have made the annotated codes the most widely used sources of federal statutes.

Unlike the official *U.S. Code*, which is published in a new edition every six years, *USCA* and *USCS* consist of volumes of varying ages, all updated with annual pocket parts or pamphlet supplements. Replacement volumes are published when supplements get too unwieldy. In the case of the illustrations in Exhibits 44-46, showing firearms sections of Title 18, the *USCA* volume was published in 2000 and the *USCS* volume in 1996. For other provisions, the *USCS* volume may well be the more current of the two.

Exhibit 44 shows the beginning of § 921, the definitions section, in *USCA*. Note that these are the legal definitions for terms "as used in this chapter," one reason it is essential to be aware of context and neighboring sections. These definitions may affect interpretation of other sections in the chapter, but they can't be applied to matters elsewhere in the code.

Exhibit 45 shows a *USCA* page containing annotations for § 925, including references to Am. Jur. 2d, two law review articles (including one on manufacturer liability), and the beginning of the notes of decisions. These notes are preceded by an alphabetical subject index. Exhibit 46 shows a similar page of § 925 annotations in *USCS*, with references to *Am. Jur. 2d*, *ALR* annotations, and case notes arranged by topic.

Either annotated code will serve admirably for most research purposes, but for extensive analysis of a particular statute it may be necessary to check both *USCA* and *USCS*. Each provides selective annotations of court decisions, and some cases may be found in one but not in the other. *USCA's* annotations are generally the more extensive of the two, but numerous cases appear only in *USCS*. The excerpted summaries shown in Exhibits 45 and 46, for example, have only one case in common. These two exhibits cover the same code section, but the annotations are arranged differently and each version cites cases not found in the other.

It is also worth noting that not every code section is followed by notes of decisions. Every single section of the *U.S. Code* has not been the subject of judicial interpretation. Some sections are uncontroversial and have not led to litigation, while others may be too new for any reported cases. The absence of annotations means that a section must be interpreted without the assistance of court decisions directly on point.

For more information on using WESTLAW to supplement your research, see the WESTLAW Electronic Research Guide, which follows the Explanation.

§ 921.   Definitions

(a) As used in this chapter—

(1) The term "person" and the term "whoever" include any individual, corporation, company, association, firm, partnership, society, or joint stock company.

(2) The term "interstate or foreign commerce" includes commerce between any place in a State and any place outside of that State, or within any possession of the United States (not including the Canal Zone) or the District of Columbia, but such term does not include commerce between places within the same State but through any place outside of that State. The term "State" includes the District of Columbia, the Commonwealth of Puerto Rico, and the possessions of the United States (not including the Canal Zone).

(3) The term "firearm" means (A) any weapon (including a starter gun) which will or is designed to or may readily be converted to expel a projectile by the action of an explosive; (B) the frame or receiver of any such weapon; (C) any firearm muffler or firearm silencer; or (D) any destructive device. Such term does not include an antique firearm.

(4) The term "destructive device" means—

(A) any explosive, incendiary, or poison gas—

(i) bomb,

(ii) grenade,

(iii) rocket having a propellant charge of more than four ounces,

(iv) missile having an explosive or incendiary charge of more than one-quarter ounce,

(v) mine, or

(vi) device similar to any of the devices described in the preceding clauses;

(B) any type of weapon (other than a shotgun or a shotgun shell which the Secretary finds is generally recognized as particularly suitable for sporting purposes) by whatever name known which will, or which may be readily converted to, expel a projectile by the action of an explosive or other propellant, and which has any barrel with a bore of more than one-half inch in diameter; and

Exhibit 44.   18 U.S.C.A. § 921 (West 2000).

Ch. 44   FIREARMS

18 § 925
Note 3

Administrative Law, 1 Am Jur 2d § 650.
Weapons and Firearms, 79 Am Jur 2d § 33.

Forms

Weapons and Firearms, 20 Am Jur Legal Forms 2d §§ 262:1–5.

Law Review and Journal Commentaries

Congress paralyzes section 925(c) of the Gun Control Act. 49 Administrative L.Rev. 501 (1997).

Hitting the mark: strict liability for defective handgun design. Michael Dillon, 24 Santa Clara L.Rev. 743 (1984).

WESTLAW ELECTRONIC RESEARCH

See WESTLAW guide following the Explanation pages of this volume.

Notes of Decisions

1.   Constitutionality

Congress acted within its power under the Commerce Clause in enacting statute which barred domestic violence misdemeanants from possessing firearms, including government-issued firearms, given requirement that government satisfy statute's jurisdictional element in prosecuting violation by proving that defendant possessed firearm in or affecting commerce. Fraternal Order of Police v. U.S., C.A.D.C.1999, 173 F.3d 898, 335 U.S.App.D.C. 359, certiorari denied 120 S.Ct. 324.

2.   Construction with other laws

Provision of this section affording a procedure to secure relief from any firearms disability imposed on a convicted felon applies not only to those disabilities imposed by this chapter, but also to disabilities on possession imposed by sections 1201 and 1202 of the Appendix to this title.   U. S. v. Graves, C.A.3 (Pa.) 1977, 554 F.2d 65.

3.   Importation

Secretary of Treasury's temporary suspension on importation of semiautomatic assault weapons was not arbitrary or capricious, notwithstanding firearms dealer's contention that semiautomatic rifle had not physically changed and that suspension was not based on any evidence: Gun Control Act required consideration of rifle's use in addition to its physical structure, and there was sufficient evidence of dramatic proliferation in use of assault-type rifles in criminal activity. Gun South, Inc. v. Brady, C.A.11 (Ala.) 1989, 877 F.2d 858.

Authority of Bureau of Alcohol, Tobacco and Firearms to regulate importation of assault rifles for official use of federal, state and local governmental entities encompasses first domestic sale of rifle to ensure that it is imported for official government use. U.S. v. Nevius, C.D.Ill. 1992, 792 F.Supp. 609.

Statute under which Secretary of Treasury was required to authorize importation of firearms generally recognized as particularly suitable for or readily adaptable to sporting purposes precluded federal officials' interdiction of a gun dealer's imported semiautomatic weapons purchased under permits validly issued and valid when acted upon; weapons were interdicted by Customs Service upon their arrival in the United States pursuant to intervening moratorium on importation of semiautomatic weapons formulated as part of national drug policy. Gun South, Inc. v. Brady, N.D.Ala. 1989, 711 F.Supp. 1054, reversed 877 F.2d 858.

597

Exhibit 45.   18 U.S.C.A. § 925 notes (West 2000).

Am Jur:
2 Am Jur 2d, Administrative Law § 650.
79 Am Jur 2d, Weapons and Firearms § 33.

Forms:
20 Am Jur Legal Forms 2d, Weapons and Firearms, §§ 262:1–5.

Annotations:
Validity, construction and application of provision of Omnibus Crime Control and Safe Streets Act of 1968, 18 USCS Appx § 1202(a)(1) making it federal offense for convicted felon to possess firearm. 13 ALR Fed 103.

Validity, construction and application of provisions of National Firearms Act (26 USCS § 5845(f)) and Omnibus Crime Control and Safe Streets Act (18 USCS § 921) defining "destructive device". 25 ALR Fed 346.

Petition for relief, under 18 USCS § 925(c) and implementing regulations, from disabilities imposed by federal gun control laws upon persons convicted of crime. 66 ALR Fed 351.

Liability of one who provides, by sale or otherwise, firearm or ammunition to adult who shoots another. 39 ALR4th 517.

Validity and construction of gun control laws. 28 ALR3d 845.

INTERPRETIVE NOTES AND DECISIONS

1. Generally
2. Construction
3. Relation to other laws
4. Exemption for government
5. Expiration of license of indictee
6. Relief from disabilities of purchaser
7. Authorization to import particular items
8. Judicial review of administrative proceedings
9. Search and seizure

1. Generally

18 USCS § 925(a) does not exempt any sale or delivery of firearms by its terms; it expressly covers only "transportation, shipment, receipt, or importation". United States v Brooks (1980, CA5 Fla) 611 F2d 614 (ovrld in part on other grounds by United States v Henry (1984, CA5 Tex) 749 F2d 203).

Neither 18 USCS § 925 nor any purported application of state statutes will exempt defendant from application of federal firearms laws where a defendant is convicted felon and seeks to individually purchase and own firearm. United States v Kozerski (1981, DC NH) 518 F Supp 1082, affd without op (1984, CA1 NH) 740 F2d 952, cert den (1984) 469 US 842, 83 L Ed 2d 86, 105 S Ct 147.

2. Construction

Relief provision, 18 USCS § 925, is applicable to 18 USCS Appx § 1202, since first provision speaks broadly, declaring that Secretary of Treasury could grant relief from disabilities imposed "by federal

laws," and since it refers to "possession," activity largely within province of 18 USCS Appx § 1202. United States v Graves (1977, CA3 Pa) 554 F2d 65.

3. Relation to other laws

By means of 18 USCS § 925, person may obtain relief from 18 USCS Appx § 1202(a)(1), which makes it crime for any person who has been convicted of crime punishable by imprisonment for term exceeding one year to ship, transport or receive firearm. United States v Synnes (1971, CA8 Minn) 438 F2d 764, vacated on other grounds (1972) 404 US 1009, 30 L Ed 2d 657, 92 S Ct 687.

Restoration of civil rights to federal felon by state statute operated to exempt felon from 18 USCS § 922(g), even though 18 USCS § 925(c) provides alternative means for exemption, since this is plain meaning of unambiguous 18 USCS § 921(a)(20). United States v Edwards (1991, CA8 Minn) 946 F2d 1347, reh, en banc, den (1992, CA8) 1992 US App LEXIS 1153.

As matter of law, gun dealer who is winding down his operations under 18 USCS § 925(b) pursuant to valid license cannot be convicted of possession of firearms under 18 USCS § 922(g)(1). United States v Douglass (1992, CA9 Nev) 974 F2d 1046, 92 CDOS 7081, 92 Daily Journal DAR 11408, amd, reh den (1992, CA9 Nev) 92 Daily Journal DAR 14059.

Exhibits 46.   18 U.S.C.S. § 925 notes (LexisNexis 1996).

There are small discrepancies in statutory language between the versions of the code. The official *U.S. Code* and *USCA* both make minor technical changes in integrating *Statutes at Large* provisions into the code format, while *USCS* preserves the original language as published in the *Statutes at Large*. In some sections, for example, the *U.S. Code* and *USCA* refer to "this chapter" while *USCS* uses the term "this Act" as it appears in the original public law.

When using a *USCA* or *USCS* volume, *always* check its pocket part for recent amendments and notes of new decisions. Exhibit 47 shows both of these features in a *USCS* pocket part, showing 1996 amendments to § 925 and reference to cases decided since the publication of the 1996 volume.

The annotated codes also include extensive indexes, parallel reference tables, and popular name tables similar to those in the *U.S. Code*. Like the code sections, these features are updated in the annual supplements and interim pamphlets.

Both annotated editions of the code are available in CD-ROM and online (*USCA* on Westlaw and *USCS* on LexisNexis). Exhibits 48 and 49 show § 925 as it appears in its Westlaw and LexisNexis versions. The database systems also provide access to the parallel reference and popular name tables in the annotated codes. Westlaw, which has the *USCA* index as well, has convenient links from the tables and index to the text of listed code sections.

Westlaw has the code in both unannotated (USC) and annotated (USCA) forms, allowing the researcher to decide whether or not to include the extensive case annotations in a search. In some instances searching keywords in the annotations may retrieve far too many documents, but at other times the wording of the annotations may lead to sections that might not appear relevant at first glance.

18 USCS § 925   CRIMES & CRIMINAL PROCEDURE

§ 925. Exceptions: Relief from disabilities

(a)(1) The provisions of this chapter [18 USCS §§ 921 et seq.], except for sections 922(d)(9) and 922(g)(9) and provisions relating to firearms subject to the prohibitions of section 922(p), shall not apply with respect to the transportation, shipment, receipt, possession, or importation of any firearm or ammunition imported for, sold or shipped to, or issued for the use of, the United States or any department or agency thereof or any State or any department, agency, or political subdivision thereof.

(2) The provisions of this chapter [18 USCS §§ 921 et seq.], except for provisions relating to firearms subject to the prohibitions of section 922(p), shall not apply with respect to (A) the shipment or receipt of firearms or ammunition when sold or issued by the Secretary of the Army pursuant to section 4308 of title 10 before the repeal of such section by section 1624(a) of the Corporation for the Promotion of Rifle Practice and Firearms Safety Act, and (B) the transportation of any such firearm or ammunition carried out to enable a person, who lawfully received such firearm or ammunition from the Secretary of the Army, to engage in military training or in competitions.

(3), (4) [Unchanged]

(5) For the purpose of paragraph (3) of this subsection, the term "United States" means each of the several States and the District of Columbia.

(b)–(f) [Unchanged]

(As amended Oct. 11, 1996, P. L. 104-294, Title VI, § 607(c), 110 Stat. 3511; Sept. 30, 1996, P. L. 104-208, Div A, Title I, § 101(f) [Title VI, § 658(c)], 110 Stat. 3009-372.)

HISTORY; ANCILLARY LAWS AND DIRECTIVES

References in text:

"Section 1624(a) of the Corporation for the Promotion of Rifle Practice and Firearms Safety Act", referred to in subsec. (a)(2), is § 1624(a) of Act Feb. 10, 1996, P. L. 104-106.

Prospective amendments:

Amendment of subsec. (a)(1)–(4), effective December 10, 2003. Act Nov. 11, 1988, P. L. 100-649, § 2(f)(2)(E), 102 Stat. 3818 (effective 15 years after the effective date of such Act (effective on the 30th day after enactment), as provided by § 2(f)(2) of such Act, which appears as 18 USCS § 922 note), provides for the amendment of subsec. (a)(1)–(4) by striking ", except for provisions relating to firearms subject to the prohibitions of section 922(p),".

Repeal of subsec. (f), effective December 10, 2003. Act Nov. 11, 1988, P. L. 100-649, § 2(f)(2)(C), 102 Stat. 3818 (effective 15 years after the effective date of such Act (effective on the 30th day after enactment), as provided by § 2(f)(2) of such Act, which appears as 18 USCS § 922 note), provides that subsec. (f) is repealed.

Amendments:

1996. Act Feb. 10, 1996 (effective on the earlier of (1) the date on which the Secretary of the Army submits a certification in accordance with 36 USCS § 5523 or (2) Oct. 1, 1996, as provided by § 1624(c) of such Act, which appears as 10 USCS § 4313 note), in subsec. (a)(2)(A), inserted "before the repeal of such section by section 1624(a) of the Corporation for the Promotion of Rifle Practice and Firearms Safety Act".

Act Sept. 30, 1996, in subsec. (a)(1), inserted "sections 922(d)(9) and 922(g)(9) and".

Act Oct. 11, 1996, in subsec. (a)(5), substituted "For the purpose of paragraph (3)" for "For the purpose of paragraphs (3) and (4)".

INTERPRETIVE NOTES AND DECISIONS

1. Generally

18 USCS § 925 was unconstitutional insofar as it purported to withhold public interest exception from those convicted of domestic violence misdemeanors; government may not bar such people from possessing firearms in public interest while imposing lesser restriction on those convicted of crimes that differ only in being more serious. FOP v United States (1998, App DC) 152 F3d 998.

Fraternal Order of Police failed to prove that 18 USCS § 922(g)(9) impacted militia so as to violate Second Amendment, or that it violated Tenth Amendment or was beyond Congress's powers under Commerce Clause. FOP v United States (1999, App DC) 173 F3d 898.

Reasonable reading of 18 USCS § 925(b) would permit law enforcement officers to conclude that federally licensed firearms dealer must inform Secretary of Treasury of fact of indictment in application, and, thus, such officers would enjoy qualified immunity from liability in civil rights suit, where dealer under indictment for embezzlement filed application for license renewal that falsely noted that he was not under indictment, and when charged with receipt of weapons while under indictment and filing false statement, he claimed exception under statute as having timely filed license renewal and brought action against officers for alleged violation of right to be secure against unreasonable searches and seizures. David v Mosley (1996, ED Va) 915 F Supp 776.

2. Construction

Firearms importer's challenge to ATF's interpretation of sporting purposes standard of 18 USCS § 925(d)(3) is denied summarily, where it complains about disqualification of modified semiautomatic rifles it proposed to import due to detachable large capacity military magazines (LCMM), because decision to consider "particularly suitable for or readily adaptable to" sporting purposes as one standard no longer including LCMM rifles was reasonable and

Exhibit 47.   18 U.S.C.S. § 925 (LexisNexis Supp. 2002).

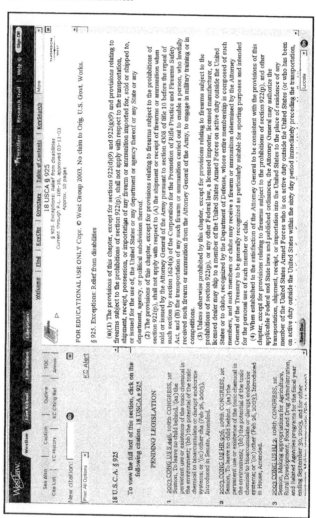

Exhibit 48.   18 U.S.C.S. § 925 (West, Westlaw through
Pub. L. No. 108-10, 2003).

LexisNexis *The Total Research System*

Search Search Advisor ▶ Get a Document ▶ Shepard's ® Check a Citation ▶

Practice Area Pages Change Client Options Feedback Switch Client Sign off Help

ECLIPSE ▾ History ᕤ

View TOC | Cite | Full | Custom

Book Browse | FOCUS™ | More Like This | More Like Selected Text

Print | Download | Fax | Email | Text Only

Pages: 13

Service: Get by LEXSTAT®
TOC: United States Code Service, Court Rules, Constitutions & Public Laws > ... > CHAPTER 44. FIREARMS > § 925. Exceptions: Relief from disabilities
Citation: 18 USC 925

Document 1 of 2 SELECT

18 USCS § 925

☐ Select for FOCUS™ or Delivery

18 USCS § 925

UNITED STATES CODE SERVICE
Copyright © 2003 Matthew Bender & Company, Inc.,
one of the LEXIS Publishing (TM) companies
All rights reserved

*** CURRENT THROUGH P.L. 108-6 APPROVED 2/14/03 ***

TITLE 18. CRIMES AND CRIMINAL PROCEDURE
PART I. CRIMES
CHAPTER 44. FIREARMS

• GO TO CODE ARCHIVE DIRECTORY FOR THIS JURISDICTION

18 USCS § 925 (2003)

§ 925. Exceptions: Relief from disabilities

(a) (1) The provisions of this chapter [18 USCS §§ 921 et seq.], except for sections 922(d)(9) and 922(g)(9) and provisions relating to firearms subject to the prohibitions of section 922(p), shall not apply with respect to the transportation, shipment, receipt, possession, or importation of any firearm or ammunition imported for, sold or shipped to, or issued for the use of, the United States or any department or agency thereof or any State or any department, agency, or political subdivision thereof.

(2) The provisions of this chapter [18 USCS §§ 921 et seq.], except for provisions relating to firearms subject to the prohibitions of section 922(p), shall not apply with respect to
(A) the shipment or receipt of firearms or ammunition when sold or issued by the Secretary of the Army pursuant to section 4308 of title 10 before the repeal of such section by section 1624(a) of the Corporation for the Promotion of Rifle Practice and Firearms Safety Act; and (B) the transportation of any such firearm or ammunition carried out to enable a person, who lawfully received such firearm or ammunition from the Secretary of the Army, to engage in military training or in competitions.

(3) Unless otherwise prohibited by this chapter [18 USCS §§ 921 et seq.], except for provisions relating to firearms subject to the prohibitions of section 922(o), or any other Federal law, a licensed importer, licensed manufacturer, or licensed dealer may ship to a member of the United States Armed Forces on active duty outside the United States or to clubs, recognized by the Department of Defense, whose entire membership is composed of such members, and such members or clubs may receive a firearm or ammunition determined by the Attorney General to be generally recognized as particularly suitable for sporting purposes and intended for the personal use of such member or club.

(4) When established to the satisfaction of the Attorney General to be consistent with the provisions of this chapter [18 USCS §§ 921 et seq.], except for provisions relating to firearms subject to the prohibitions of section 922(o), and other applicable Federal and State laws and published ordinances, the Attorney General may authorize the transportation, shipment, receipt, or importation into the United States to the place of residence of any member of the United States Armed Forces who is on active duty outside the United States (or who has not been on active duty outside the United States within the sixty day period immediately preceding the transportation, shipment, receipt, or importation), of any firearm or ammunition which is (A) determined by the Attorney General to be generally recognized as particularly suitable for sporting purposes, or determined by the Department of Defense to

◀ Explore

Exhibit 49.   18 U.S.C.S. § 925 (LexisNexis, Lexis through Pub. L. No. 108-6, 2003).

LexisNexis does not have a separate unannotated database, but a *text* or *unanno* segment search will limit queries to the statutory language. Because statutory language often includes cross-references and exceptions which may result in retrieval of irrelevant documents, it may help to use fields or segments to limit a search further to words in the title, chapter, and section headings. Westlaw uses the field *prelim* or *pr* for title, subtitle and chapter designations, and *caption* or *ca* for the section number and description. LexisNexis uses the segment *heading* for titles, subtitles and chapters, and *caption* for individual sections.

The online code databases are updated to include laws from the current session of Congress; a note below the section heading indicates the latest public law included in code coverage. If a section has been amended by a public law too recent to be incorporated, both services provide notices to check for more current information.

One advantage of using a code section online is that amendments and new casenotes are incorporated into the main document rather than found in a separate pocket supplement. It may be easier in a printed book to survey neighboring sections to get a sense of a statute's context, but Westlaw and LexisNexis both provide the capacity to scan neighboring sections. Westlaw users can click on the TOC tab at the top left (above "Annos" in Exhibit 48) to see a list of chapter and section headings, or select "Docs in Seq" from the drop-down list in the lower right corner to go from one section to the next. LexisNexis users can either click on the TOC link at the top of the screen or select "Book Browse" to move between sections.

Looseleaf services provide another source for current, annotated statutes in some subject fields. Most services include federal statutes affecting their fields, accompanied by abstracts of judicial and administrative decisions, rele-

vant administrative regulations, and explanatory text. Major tax services such as the *Standard Federal Tax Reporter* (CCH) and *United States Tax Reporter* (RIA) are basically heavily annotated editions of title 26 of the *U.S. Code*, also known as the Internal Revenue Code.

D. KEYCITE AND SHEPARD'S CITATIONS

While *USCA* and *USCS* provide notice of statutory amendments and citing cases, more extensive research leads can be found by using KeyCite or Shepard's Citations. Westlaw's KeyCite is available only electronically, while Shepard's information can be found in the printed *Shepard's Federal Statute Citations* or online through LexisNexis. A major advantage of KeyCite and Shepard's is that they provide much more current information than the annotations in the codes. The latest decisions can be found in the citators months before case annotations are written and published.

KeyCite's coverage of statutes includes the cases summarized in *USCA's* annotations, but it expands on these by listing other citing cases and articles as well as recent and pending legislation. The cases in the annotations are listed under the index headings used in *USCA*, but without the annotation abstracts. For these cases, KeyCite is less useful than the annotations themselves unless a researcher wishes to use KeyCite's "Limit Citing Refs" feature to focus retrieval on particular jurisdictions or dates. Other cases are simply listed by jurisdiction in reverse chronological order as "additional citations," with no indexing, but they represent references that cannot be found through the annotated code. The older "additional citations" cases listed may not be very important, but this is also where the most recent court decisions can be found. KeyCite also provides references to pending legislation and to any law review articles and other secondary sources available through Westlaw.

Westlaw's statutory display includes KeyCite flags similar to those used for cases. A red flag indicates that a section has been amended or repealed, or that it's been ruled unconstitutional or otherwise invalid. A yellow flag indicates that pending legislation affecting the section is available, or that court decisions may have limited its scope or validity. The section in Exhibit 48 has pending legislation and is therefore shown with a yellow flag.

LexisNexis statutory displays do not include a Shepard's link, but clicking on *Shepard's--Check a Citation* while viewing a statute automatically inserts its citation into the search box. A number of separate documents may be retrieved, because Shepard's, online or in print, lists citing sources under the exact provision or provisions cited. A case citing a specific subsection is listed under that subsection, while one citing a range of sections is listed under an entry for the entire range. It may therefore be necessary to scan a number of entries to find relevant citations. Shepard's has separate listings, for example, for "18 U.S.C. § 925" and for subsections such as "18 U.S.C. § 921(a)" and "18 U.S.C. § 921(d) (2)." Still other documents citing the entire chapter are listed under "18 U.S.C. §§ 921 et seq." or "18 U.S.C. 921 to 930." This approach makes it more difficult to get a comprehensive listing of all relevant documents, but it is ideal for research needing to focus in on a very specific subsection. Shepard's coverage of citations in law reviews, both in print and online, is less extensive than KeyCite's.

Shepard's also covers other forms of legislative material besides the current *United States Code.* In print, other sections of *Shepard's Federal Statute Citations* cover citations to the U.S. Constitution and acts in the *Statutes at Large* which have not been incorporated into the code. Finding citations to the Constitution or federal statutes in state cases or law review articles, however, requires checking other publica-

tions. State court decisions citing federal laws are listed in Shepard's individual state citators, and citing articles in several law reviews are listed in *Shepard's Federal Law Citations in Selected Law Reviews.* The electronic version of Shepard's cumulates these various citing sources into one listing.

Both citators provide notice of legislative changes as well as judicial citations. As shown in Exhibit 48, KeyCite lists any newly passed acts that amend a section and pending bills that would affect it, followed by the statutory notes from *USCA.* Shepard's includes *Statutes at Large* references with symbols indicating the nature of the change, but it doesn't cover current legislation.

§5-6. State Statutes

State statutes appear in many of the same forms as their federal counterparts, with slip laws, session laws, codes, and annotated codes. Current session laws and codes are available from government Internet sites, and annotated codes are published both online and on CD-ROM as well as in print.

A. Slip Laws and Session Laws

Slip laws are issued in many of the states, but they are rarely distributed very widely in paper. On the other hand, every state legislature now provides Internet access to recently enacted laws. In most instances, however, these are available as bills, not as session laws, and are mixed in with bills that are still pending or that did not become law. Two easy ways to find legislative websites are to start with the state homepage (<www.state.__.us>, using the state's postal abbreviation), or to check a site with multistate links such as "State and Local Government on the Net" <www.statelocalgov.net>.

Every state has a session law publication similar to the *U.S. Statutes at Large,* containing the laws enacted at each sitting of its legislature, usually with an index for each volume or session. The names of these publications vary from state to state *(e.g., Acts of Alabama, Statutes of California, Laws of Delaware).* In most states the session laws are the authoritative positive law text of the statutes, and they may be needed to examine legislative changes or to reconstruct the language in force at a particular date.

Commercially published session law services for most states contain laws from a current legislative session, very much as *USCCAN* and *USCS Advance* do for congressional enactments, and the online systems provide the texts of new legislation from every state, with retrospective files going back to at least 1991.

B. Codes

All states have subject compilations of their statutes similar to the *U.S. Code.* Some states publish unannotated official codes, but most researchers rely on commercially published collections annotated with summaries of relevant court decisions and other references. The authority of unofficial codes varies from state to state, but they are usually accepted as at least *prima facie* evidence of the statutory law.

Annotated state codes are edited and supplemented in much the same way as federal statutes, although there are variations from state to state. Some codes are more thorough and comprehensive than others. Most codes are published by either West Group or LexisNexis, and some states have competing codes from both publishers. Supplementation is generally by annual pocket parts, updated in many states by quarterly interim pamphlets. A

few state codes are published in binders or in annual soft-cover editions, rather than as bound volumes with pocket parts.

The outline and arrangement of code material vary from state to state. While most codes are divided into titles and sections, in a format similar to the *U.S. Code,* several states have individual codes designated by name rather than title number (e.g., commercial code, penal code, tax code). Exhibit 50 shows a section of the California Penal Code, as published in *West's Annotated California Codes.* Note that it provides not only the text of the statute, but historical notes tracing its development, references to regulations and encyclopedias, and annotations of a court decision and a California Attorney General opinion.

State codes usually provide references to the original session laws in parenthetical notes following each section, as shown in Exhibit 50, but only some include notes indicating the changes made by each amendment. Most also include tables with cross references from session law citations and earlier codifications to the current code. Each state code has a substantial general index of one or more volumes.

At least one annotated code from every state is in each ABA-approved law school library. The *Bluebook* provides a listing by state of the names and citations of current official and commercially published codes. State legal research guides (listed in Appendix B on page 404) provide information about earlier codes and statutory revisions, official and unofficial editions, and statutory indexes for individual states.

Almost every state provides access to its code through a government website. The official status of these codes varies, and the statutes are rarely accompanied by very

174 ■ LEGAL RESEARCH

MACHINE GUNS
Title 2
§ 12200. **Definition**

§ **12200**
Note 1

The term "machinegun" as used in this chapter means any weapon which shoots, or is designed to shoot, automatically, more than one shot, without manual reloading, by a single function of the trigger, and includes any frame or receiver which can only be used with that weapon. The term also includes any part or combination of parts designed and intended for use in converting a weapon into a machinegun. The term also includes any weapon deemed by the federal Bureau of Alcohol, Tobacco, and Firearms as readily convertible to a machinegun under Chapter 53 (commencing with Section 5801) of Title 26 of the United States Code.

(Added by Stats.1953, c. 36, p. 661, § 1. Amended by Stats.1965, c. 33, p. 913, § 1; Stats.1967, c. 1281, p. 3084, § 1; Stats.1969, c. 1003, p. 1974, § 1; Stats.1983, c. 101, § 148; Stats.1986, c. 1423, § 1.)

Historical and Statutory Notes

The 1965 amendment rewrote the section which read:

"The term machine gun as used in this chapter shall apply to and include all firearms known as machine rifles, machine guns, or submachine guns capable of discharging automatically and continuously loaded ammunition of any caliber in which the ammunition is fed to such gun from or by means of clips, disks, drums, belts or other separabl¹ mechanical device and all firearms which are automatically fed after each discharge from or by means of clips, disks, drums, belts or other separable mechanical device having a capacity greater than 10 cartridges."

The 1967 amendment deleted the words "or semiautomatically" following automatically and included frame or receiver.

The 1969 amendment added the last sentence relating to any combination of parts for use in converting a weapon into a machine gun.

The 1983 amendment made nonsubstantive changes.

The 1986 amendment substituted "also includes any part or" for "shall also include any" in the second sentence, and added the third sentence.

Derivation: Stats.1927, c. 552, p. 938, § 2; Stats.1933, c. 450, p. 1170, § 3.

Library References

Firearms control recommendation. Report of Assembly Interim Committee on Criminal Procedure, 1965 to 1967. Vol. 22, No. 12, p.49. Vol. 2 of Appendix to Journal of Assembly, Reg. Sess., 1967.

Regulation and control of firearms. Report of Assembly Interim Committee on Criminal Procedure, 1963 to 1965, Vol. 22, No. 6. Vol. 2 of Appendix to Journal of the Assembly, Reg.Sess., 1965.

Words and Phrases (Perm.Ed.)

Legal Jurisprudences

Cal Jur 3d Crim L § 1600.
Am Jur 2d Weapons and Firearms §§ 1, 2, 4, 32.

Treatises and Practice Aids

Witkin & Epstein, Criminal Law (2d ed) §§ 1090, 1107, 1501.

Notes of Decisions

In general   1

1. In general

In prosecution for possession of a machine gun, evidence supported finding that the part of alleged 50-caliber machine gun found in search was a "frame" or "receiver" which could only be used with machine gun. People v. Tall-

madge (App. 2 Dist. 1980) 163 Cal.Rptr. 372, 103 Cal.App.3d 980.

A U.S. model M1.30 caliber carbine was a machine gun under this section, as it read prior to 1965 amendment, when a clip with a capacity of more than 10 cartridges is attached to the gun or such a clip and gun are within the immediate possession of one person or corporation. 43 Ops.Atty.Gen. 314, 6–19–64.

419

Exhibit 50.   CAL. PENAL CODE § 12200 (West 2000).

extensive notes. Most codes can be accessed through browsing the table of contents or searching by keyword. Several convenient compilations of links are available, including FindLaw's list of state codes <www.findlaw.com/11stategov/indexcode.html> and the simple but well-maintained "Full Text State Statutes and Legislation on the Internet" <www.prairienet.org/~scruffy/f.htm>.

LexisNexis and Westlaw provide access to codes from all fifty states, as well as the District of Columbia, Puerto Rico, and the Virgin Islands. Almost all of the state code databases include the case notes and other references from the annotated codes. As in the federal databases, Westlaw users can choose between annotated and unannotated versions of codes, and LexisNexis users can search in the *text* or *unanno* segment to avoid cases where relevant terms appear only in the annotations. The fields and segments for limiting searches to captions and section headings, discussed in the federal section, are also available. Both systems add notices to recently amended statutes of slip laws that have not yet been incorporated into the code database.

c. KeyCite and Shepard's Citations

State code sections can also be checked in KeyCite or Shepard's Citations, which may retrieve cases and articles not mentioned in the annotated code. KeyCite generally provides more references to secondary sources, but its coverage is limited to current code sections. Shepard's also covers state constitutions and session laws, as well as earlier versions of code provisions. Shepard's generally lists statutes as cited, so it may be necessary to check references under both a current code section and its predecessors to find relevant material.

Printed state Shepard's Citations volumes include a "Table of Acts by Popular Names or Short Titles," providing the code citations of listed acts. Statutes from all jurisdictions are covered, in one alphabetical listing, in *Shepard's Acts and Cases by Popular Names: Federal and State.* This set is most useful when the title of an act is known but not its state, or when similar acts from several states are sought.

d. Multistate Research Sources

Most state statutory research situations require finding the law in one particular state, for which that state's code is the primary research tool. Sometimes, however, it is necessary to compare statutory provisions among states or to survey legislation throughout the country. Multistate surveys of state laws can be frustrating and time-consuming, since different state codes may not use the same terminology for similar issues. It is possible, and sometimes necessary, to begin with each state code's index, but several other resources can assist in this research.

Topical looseleaf services often collect state laws in their subject areas, making it easy to compare state provisions in areas such as taxation or employment law. More general coverage is provided by the *Martindale-Hubbell Law Digest,* a companion publication to the *Martindale-Hubbell Law Directory.* An annual two-volume publication summarizing state law on a variety of subjects, the *Digest* is arranged by state and covers more than a hundred legal topics. It focuses on commercial and procedural information most likely to be needed by lawyers in other states, and provides citations to both code sections and court decisions. The *Digest* isn't included with the free Internet version of Martindale-Hubbell, but it is available through LexisNexis. Exhibit 51 shows the LexisNexis version of the Massachusetts criminal law digest, including a reference to an assault weapons

ban. Note that it includes citations to several Massachusetts statutes, as well as a link in the second paragraph to a court decision.

Another source comparing state laws is Richard A. Leiter, *National Survey of State Laws* (4th ed. 2003). This book is arranged by topic rather than by state, with tables summarizing state laws in 45 areas and providing citations to codes. Its "Gun Control" section, for example, includes information on illegal arms, waiting periods, ownership restrictions, and laws prohibiting firearms on or near school grounds. The *National Survey* focuses more on social and political issues than Martindale-Hubbell, with sections on topics such as capital punishment, prayer in public schools, right to die, and stalking.

Numerous other resources summarize or reprint state laws on specific topics. While many of these omit the code references that are essential for verifying and updating their information, those that do can be invaluable time-savers. State gun laws, for example, are reprinted in the Bureau of Alcohol, Tobacco Firearms, and Explosives website "State Laws and Published Ordinances—Firearms" <www.atf.gov/firearms/statelaws/>, providing a quick head start for anyone doing multistate research in this area.

Collections and lists of state statutes are described in a valuable series of bibliographies called *Subject Compilations of State Laws* (1981-date). This set does not itself summarize or cite the statutes, but it provides annotated descriptions of sources that do so. These include books, compendia, websites, and law review articles, which often have footnotes with extensive listings of state code citations. Exhibit 52 shows a page from this publication, with entries under the heading "Firearms" for a Supreme Court brief and several law review articles.

LexisNexis

Search▸ Search Advisor▸ Get a Document▸ Shepard's®·Check a Citation▸

View: KWIC | Full | Custom

FOCUS™ | Save As ECLIPSE | More Like This | More Like Selected Text

Source: Legal > Entfohren > Martindale-Hubbell(R) > Law Digests > Martindale-Hubbell(R) Law Digest - Massachusetts ①
Terms: "assault weapon" (Edit Search)

Martindale-Hubbell, Massachusetts Law Digest, CRIMINAL LAW

Copyright 2002 by Reed Elsevier Inc.
Martindale-Hubbell Law Digest

MASSACHUSETTS LAW DIGEST

CATEGORY: CRIMINAL LAW

TOPIC: CRIMINAL LAW

TEXT: Crimes are defined by statute (see particularly cc. 264 to 274) and common law. Criminal procedure is governed by statute (see particularly cc. 263, 275-280) and Rules of Criminal Procedure effective July 1, 1979. (Mass. R. Crim. P.).

Access to Records. – Access to certain criminal records is restricted. (c. 6, §§172-175). Provision denying access to indices of criminal records (§172) unconstitutional (310 F. Supp. 95). Legislature enacted sex offender registry to track recidivism rates of sex offenders. (c. 6, §§178 et al.).

Indictment or Information. – Prosecution is by grand jury indictment in Superior Court (absent waiver of indictment) and by complaint in District Court. (Mass. R. Crim. P. 3-5).

Bail. – All crimes, except capital offenses and treason, are bailable on personal recognizance unless person authorized to admit to bail determines in exercise of his discretion that release will endanger safety of other persons or community or that release on personal recognizance will not assure defendant's appearance in court (cc. 276, §§8, c. 264, §1).

Gun Control. – Carrying firearm without license or firearm identification card is punishable by imprisonment for not more than two years, and fire of not more than $ 500. (c. 269, §10(h)); Carrying firearms with or without license onto secondary school, college or university property without written authorization from institution administrators punishable by fine of no more than $ 1,000, prison term of no more than one year or both. (c. 269, §10(j)). Statutes governing licensing of firearms and firearm identification cards is controlled by c. 140, §§121-131C. Ban on sale of assault weapons made after 1994. (c. 140, §131M).

Right to Counsel. – Right to counsel exists at every step of any criminal proceeding, including examination before grand jury. (c. 277, §14A).

Victims of Violent Crimes. – Victims of violent crimes or their dependents may be eligible for compensation by commonwealth for lost earnings, medical, funeral and other expenses up to $ 25,000. (c. 258C, §3[a]). Funeral expenses may not exceed $ 4,000. (c. 258C, §3[b][1]).

REVISER: Revised for 2002 edition by PROFESSOR RICHARD M. PERLMUTTER, assisted by Herbert N. Ramy, Ann T. McGonigle and Elysa Diamond Moskowitz, Suffolk University Law School, Boston.

(Citations, unless otherwise indicated, refer to 1988 Official Edition Massachusetts General Laws, as amd. Session laws as amd. Parallel citations to the North Eastern Reporter begin with 139 Mass. "SJC" is used as abbreviation for Supreme Judicial Court; "BMC" is used as abbreviation for Boston Municipal Court. "Mass. R. Civ. P." refers to Massachusetts Rules of Civil Procedure; "MRAP" refers to Massachusetts Rules of Appellate Procedure; "Mass. R. Dom. Rel. P." refers to Massachusetts Rules of Domestic Relations Procedure; "CMR" refers to Code of Massachusetts Regulations "Unif. Prob. Ct. Prac." refers to Uniform Probate Court Practice.)

Note: This revision covers acts of 1999 and 2000 adopted and approved by Governor through July 19, 2001 up to Chapter 42 of 2001. Legislature convenes annually in Jan. Note: Readers are advised that the full text of every opinion of the Massachusetts Supreme Judicial Court and the Appeals Court is available at the Massachusetts Lawyers Weekly Internet site: http://www.asslaw.com".

Exhibit 51. Massachusetts Law Digest: CRIMINAL LAW, MARTINDALE-HUBBELL LAW DIGEST (LexisNexis 2002).

Firearms

3999.01 *Brief of Petitioner on the Merits. State of Florida v. J.L., No. 98-1993 (Dec. 23, 1999).*

Pp. 17-18, fns. 5 and 6. Citations only. Cites to codes. Covers the forty-three states that have laws on licenses or permits to carry concealed firearms.

Note: Available on the Internet. URL: [supreme.lp.findlaw.com /supreme_court/briefs/98-1993/98-1993mo1/brief.pdf]. Available on LexisNexis (1998 U.S. Briefs 1993) and Westlaw (1999 WL 1259993).

3999.02 Burnett, H. Sterling. "Suing Gun Manufacturers: Hazardous to Our Health." *Texas Review of Law & Politics* 5 (2001):433-94.

P. 489, fn. 269. Citations only. Cites to bills and codes. Covers the twenty-three states that have laws "limiting the liability of gunmakers and distributors for the negligent or criminal misuse of their products or forbidding cities from filing liability suits entirely."

3999.03 Cabana, Andrew S. "Missing the Target: Municipal Litigation Against Handgun Manufacturers: Abuse of the Civil Tort System." *George Mason Law Review* 9 (2001):1127-75.

P. 1172, fns. 409 and 410. Citations only. Cites to session laws and codes. Covers the fifteen states that have laws prohibiting municipalities from suing handgun manufacturers (fn. 409) and the two states that have laws exempting gun manufacturers from lawsuits (fn. 410).

Exhibit 52.   Cheryl Rae Nyberg, SUBJECT COMPILATIONS OF STATE LAWS, 2000-2001: AN ANNOTATED BIBLIOGRAPHY 89 (2002).

Westlaw and LexisNexis offer databases combining the state codes or state session laws from all fifty states. These databases can save considerable time, although it is important to remember that any single search may not retrieve all relevant laws. Different legislatures may use different terminology for similar laws. Some libraries subscribe to LexisNexis State Capital <web.lexis-nexis.com/ stcapuniv/>, which provides a similar service, with multistate access to constitutions, statutes, and other materials.

The Internet provides convenient multistate access to code provisions in some subject areas. One of the most comprehensive sites is Cornell Legal Information Institute's topical index to state statutes on the Internet <www.law.cornell.edu/topics/state_statutes.html>, with links in several dozen broad categories. More specific sites are listed in recent *Subject Compilations of State Laws* volumes; as with printed sources, it is important that these are regularly updated and that they provide the code citations necessary for further research.

E. UNIFORM LAWS

Most multistate research requires finding a wide variety of legislative approaches to a particular topic. In a growing number of areas, however, states have adopted virtually identical acts. This can dramatically reduce the confusion caused by the application of conflicting state statutes. The National Conference of Commissioners on Uniform State Laws (NCCUSL), created in 1892 to prepare legislation which would decrease unnecessary conflicts, has drafted more than two hundred laws. Most of these are in force in at least one state, and some (such as the Uniform Commercial Code or Uniform Child Custody Jurisdiction Act) have been enacted in virtually every jurisdiction.

Uniform Laws Annotated, a multivolume set published by Thomson West (and available online from Westlaw), contains every uniform law approved by the NCCUSL, lists of adopting states, Commissioners' notes, and annotations to court decisions from any adopting jurisdiction. These annotations allow researchers in one state to study the case law developed in other states with the same uniform law. A decision from another state is not binding authority, but its interpretation of similar language may be quite persuasive. The set is supplemented annually by pocket parts and by a pamphlet entitled *Directory of Uniform Acts and Codes;*

Tables—Index, which lists the acts alphabetically and includes a table of jurisdictions indicating the acts adopted in each state.

The text of a uniform law can also be found, of course, in the statutory code of each adopting state, accompanied by annotations from that state's courts. The state code contains the law as actually adopted and in force, rather than the text as proposed by the Commissioners. The NCCUSL version is merely a proposal, but the state code version is the law.

NCCUSL uniform laws, as well as drafts of its current projects, are available on the Internet <www.law.upenn.edu/bll/ulc/ulc_frame.htm>. Cornell's Legal Information Institute provides "Uniform Law Locators" <www.law.cornell.edu/states/>, which list links to official sites where the text as adopted in particular states can be found.

The NCCUSL is not the only organization drafting legislation for consideration by state legislatures. The American Law Institute has produced the Model Penal Code and other model acts; the American Bar Association has promulgated and revised the Model Business Corporation Act; and the Council of State Governments publishes an annual volume of *Suggested State Legislation.*

§5-8. Conclusion

In some ways statutory research is easier than case research, because the major resources are more accessible and more regularly updated. In many situations a good annotated code provides most of the necessary research leads. This convenience is undercut, however, by the opacity of statutory language. Judicial prose can be a model of clarity when compared to the texts of many federal and state statutes.

In researching statutory or constitutional law, the resources discussed in this chapter are only a first step. Besides finding a relevant provision and making sure that it remains in force, it is usually necessary to read judicial decisions applying or construing its language. Administrative regulations may provide more specific requirements, and attorney general opinions on the meaning of the provision may also be available. A further understanding can be gained from treatises or law review articles.

Finally, ambiguities and vagueness in statutes often lead to difficulties in interpretation. Some statutory ambiguities stem from poor draftsmanship, but many are the inevitable result of negotiation and compromise in the legislative process. Lawyers frequently study legislative documents in order to determine the meaning of the statutory text. This research in legislative history is the focus of the next chapter.

CHAPTER 6
LEGISLATIVE INFORMATION

■　■　■　■　■　■　■　■　■　■

§6-1. INTRODUCTION

The ambiguities so common in the language of statutes require lawyers and scholars to locate legislative documents from which they can try to discern the intended purpose of an act or the meaning of particular statutory language. Researchers also need to investigate the current progress of proposed laws under consideration by the legislature. These processes—determining the meaning or intent of an enacted law, and ascertaining the status of a pending bill—comprise legislative history research.

Legislative history is an area in which there is a strong dichotomy between federal and state research. Federal legislative history is thoroughly documented with numerous sources, while state legislative history research can be quite frustrating. On both the federal and state level, however, it is an area in which the Internet has made a significant contribution to the dissemination of information. Government websites make it quite easy to learn about the status of pending legislation and to obtain documents relating to recently passed acts. Research into the background of older laws, however, still requires access to printed sources.

§6-2. FEDERAL LEGISLATIVE HISTORY SOURCES

An understanding of the legislative process is essential for research in legislative history. Numerous background sources are available for understanding Congress and its work. One of the most extensive reference works is Donald C. Bacon, Roger H. Davidson & Morton Keller, eds., *Encyclopedia of the United States Congress* (4 vols. 1995), which provides a broad historical and political science perspective on the institution. *Congressional Quarterly's Guide to Congress* (2 vols., 5th ed. 2000) has a wide range of political, historical, and statistical information; Part III, Congressional Procedures, is particularly useful in under-

standing committee and floor action. Two shorter official documents prepared by the House and Senate parliamentarians, *How Our Laws Are Made* and *Enactment of a Law*, are available from the Library of Congress' THOMAS system <thomas.loc.gov>, under the heading "How Congress Makes Laws."

Each stage in the enactment of a federal law may result in a significant legislative history document. The following are the most important potential steps in the legislative process and their related documents:

ACTION	DOCUMENT
Preliminary inquiry	Transcripts of hearings on the general subject of the proposed legislation
Executive recommendation	Presidential message proposing an administration bill
Introduction of bill and referral to committee	Slip bill as introduced
Hearings on bill	Transcript of testimony and exhibits
Approval by committee	Committee report, including committee's version of bill
Legislative debates	*Congressional Record,* sometimes including texts of bill in amended forms
Passage by first house	Final House or Senate version of the proposed legislation

Other house	Generally same procedure and documents as above
Referral to conference committee (if texts passed by houses differ)	Conference committee version of bill; conference committee report
Passage by one or both houses of revised bill	Enrolled bill sent to President
Approval by President	Presidential signing statement; slip law (also *USCCAN* and *USCS Advance* pamphlets); subsequently published in *Statutes at Large* and classified by subject in the *U.S. Code*

Of the many types of documents issued by Congress, a few are particularly important for legislative history research. *Bills* are the major source for the texts of pending or unenacted legislation. *Committee reports* analyze and describe bills and are usually considered the most authoritative sources of congressional intent. *Floor debates* may contain a sponsor's interpretation of a bill or the only explanation of last-minute amendments. *Hearings* can provide useful background on the purpose of an act.

This section introduces these various documents, with a brief explanation of how they are published and their availability in electronic sources including THOMAS <thomas.loc.gov>, the Library of Congress website for legislative information, and the Government Printing Office's GPO Access <www.gpoaccess.gov> as well as Westlaw and LexisNexis. Section 6-3 then looks in greater depth at these and other resources for legislative history research.

A. BILLS

The texts of bills are needed by researchers interested in pending or failed legislation, and may also help in interpreting enacted laws. Variations among the bills and amendments can aid in determining the intended meaning of an act, as each deletion or addition made during the legislative process implies a deliberate choice of language by the legislators.

Bills are individually numbered in separate series for each house, and retain their identifying numbers through both sessions of a Congress. Pending bills lapse at the end of the two-year term, and they must be reintroduced the following term if they are to be considered.

Some public laws arise from *joint resolutions* rather than bills. These usually, but not always, deal with matters of a limited or temporary nature. Joint resolutions and bills differ in form but have the same legal effect. Two other forms of resolution are less important because they do not have the force of law: *concurrent resolutions* expressing the opinion of both houses of Congress, and *simple resolutions* concerning the procedures or expressions of just one house.

An individual bill or resolution can be obtained from its sponsor, the clerk of the House or Senate, or a congressional committee to which it was referred. Bills are received by many large law libraries on microfiche, and they are available electronically from several sources. THOMAS has the text of bills since 1989, and GPO Access begins coverage in 1993 with PDF files replicating the printed bills. Texts of bills are also available online from commercial electronic services, including LexisNexis (101st Congress-date) and Westlaw (104th Congress-date).

Exhibit 53 shows the bill H.R. 1025 as read for the first time in the Senate, printed from the GPO Access website. This bill, as amended, became the Brady Handgun Violence Prevention Act, Pub. L. 103-159, 107 Stat. 1536 (1993).

B. COMMITTEE REPORTS

Reports are generally considered the most important sources of legislative history. They are issued by the committees of each house on bills they approve and send to the whole house for consideration, and by conference committees of the two houses to reconcile differences between House and Senate versions of a bill. (Committees also issue reports on various investigations, nominations and hearings not related to pending legislation.) Reports usually include the text of the bill, describe its contents and purposes, and give reasons for the committee's recommendations, sometimes with minority views. One of the most informative portions of a committee report is the section-by-section analysis of the bill, explaining the purpose and meaning of each provision.

Committee reports are published in numbered series which indicate house, Congress, and report number, with conference committee reports included in the series of House reports. Exhibit 54 shows the first page of H.R. Rep. No. 103-344 (1993), reporting the House Committee on the Judiciary's views on H.R. 1025. Note at the bottom of the page that the committee is amending the bill by deleting everything after the enacting clause ("Be it enacted . . .") and substituting its own language. This is not an uncommon form of amendment, but it is one that can make it difficult to track changes between versions of a bill.

103d CONGRESS
1st Session

H. R. 1025

IN THE SENATE OF THE UNITED STATES

November 17 (legislative day, November 2), 1993
Received

November 20 (legislative day, November 2), 1993
Read the first time

AN ACT

To provide for a waiting period before the purchase of a handgun, and for the establishment of a national instant criminal background check system to be contacted by firearms dealers before the transfer of any firearm.

1   *Be it enacted by the Senate and House of Representa-*

2   *tives of the United States of America in Congress assembled,*

3   **SECTION 1. SHORT TITLE.**

4   This Act may be cited as the "Brady Handgun Vio-

5   lence Prevention Act".

Exhibit 53.   H.R. 1025 (103d Cong. 1993).

Committee reports are issued by the Government Printing Office, and are sometimes available from the committee or from the House or Senate clerk. All the reports for a session are published, along with House and Senate Documents, in the bound official compilation called the *Serial Set*. (These volumes are not widely distributed after the 104th Congress, but many libraries now bind their own

103D CONGRESS 1st Session	HOUSE OF REPRESENTATIVES	REPORT 103–344

BRADY HANDGUN VIOLENCE PREVENTION ACT

NOVEMBER 10, 1993.—Committed to the Committee of the Whole House on the State of the Union and ordered to be printed

Mr. BROOKS, from the Committee on the Judiciary, submitted the following

REPORT

together with

ADDITIONAL AND DISSENTING VIEWS

[To accompany H.R. 1025]

[Including cost estimate of the Congressional Budget Office]

The Committee on the Judiciary, to whom was referred the bill (H.R. 1025) to provide for a waiting period before the purchase of a handgun, and for the establishment of a national instant criminal background check system to be contacted by firearms dealers before the transfer of any firearm, having considered the same, report favorably thereon with an amendment and recommend that the bill do pass as amended.

The amendment is as follows:

Strike out all after the enacting clause and insert in lieu thereof the following:

SECTION 1. SHORT TITLE.

This Act may be cited as the "Brady Handgun Violence Prevention Act".

SEC. 2. FEDERAL FIREARMS LICENSEE REQUIRED TO CONDUCT CRIMINAL BACKGROUND CHECK BEFORE TRANSFER OF FIREARM TO NONLICENSEE.

(a) INTERIM PROVISION.—

(1) IN GENERAL.—Section 922 of title 18, United States Code, is amended by adding at the end the following:

"(s)(1) Beginning on the date that is 90 days after the date of enactment of this subsection and ending on the day before the date that the Attorney General certifies under section 3(d)(1) of the Brady Handgun Violence Prevention Act that the national instant criminal background check system is established (except as provided in paragraphs (2) and (3) of such section), it shall be unlawful for any licensed importer, licensed manufacturer, or licensed dealer to sell, deliver, or transfer a handgun to an individual who is not licensed under section 923, unless—

79–006

Exhibit 54.   H.R. REP. NO. 103-344 (1993).

sets of individual reports.) GPO Access and THOMAS coverage begins in 1995, and the commercial databases have all committee reports beginning in 1990 as well as selected earlier coverage. Selected reports are also reprinted in *United States Code Congressional and Administrative News* (*USCCAN*).

Reports are the final product of committee deliberation. The process by which committees reach consensus is through *markup sessions*, but the proceedings of these sessions are only rarely published. Newspapers and wire services reporting on Capitol Hill matters, however, frequently publish stories on markup sessions, which are available through online services including LexisNexis and Westlaw.

c. DEBATES

Debates in the House and Senate are generally not as influential as committee reports as sources of legislative intent. While reports represent the considered opinion of those legislators who have studied the bill most closely, floor statements are often political hyperbole and may not even represent the views of legislators supporting the bill. The most influential statements are those from a bill's sponsor or its floor managers (the committee members responsible for steering the bill through consideration). These may even explain aspects of a bill not discussed in a committee report or correct errors in a report.

In a few instances, floor debates are the best available legislative history source. Bills are often amended on the floor, sometimes with language that was not considered in committee and thus was not discussed in a committee report. If so, the record of floor debate may be the only explanation available of the intended purpose of the amendment.

The source for debates is the *Congressional Record*, a near-ly verbatim transcript published each day that either house is in session. It is subject to revision only by members of Congress who wish to amend their own remarks. In addition, the *Record* includes extensions of floor remarks, exhibits from legislators, communications on pending legislation, and other material Senators and Representatives wish to have printed. Each daily issue has separately pagi-nated sections for Senate and House proceedings.

The *Congressional Record* never contains hearings and only rarely includes committee reports—although it does include the text of conference committee reports. Bills are sometimes read into the *Record*, particularly if they have been amended on the floor or in conference committee. The *Congressional Record*'s primary role, however, is as a report of debates and actions taken. An excerpt from the *Record*, showing Senate consideration of H.R. 1025, is shown in Exhibit 55. The illustrated page concludes with the Senate's amendment of the bill to substitute its own text and the results of the roll-call vote in which it passed. (Voting records are not always available, as motions and amendments are often put to a simple voice vote.)

Each *Congressional Record* issue contains a Daily Digest summarizing the day's activities. The Digest lists the bills introduced, reports filed, measures debated or passed, and committee meetings held. *Record* page references for floor activity are included, making the Daily Digest a good start-ing place if only the date of congressional action is known. An index to the *Record*, by subject, name of legislator, and title of legislation, is published every two weeks. The index includes a "History of Bills and Resolutions" table provid-ing index references and status information by bill number.

November 20, 1993 CONGRESSIONAL RECORD—SENATE 31039

Mr. DOLE addressed the Chair.

The PRESIDING OFFICER. The Republican leader.

Mr. DOLE. Mr. President, I will take 1 minute.

I think it is unfortunate that the chairman of the committee announced in advance that he had no confidence in what the Senate might do.

Some of us have been working all day on this in good faith. Maybe we should not have. But we have been trying in good faith to find a compromise, and I think it is most unfortunate the chairman of the committee said that whatever happened it is going to be 5 years. Maybe he can do that. But there will be that in mind as we look down the road.

I think many of our Members who might have been able to support this measure are now put on notice by the chairman that it does not make any difference what you did, it is going to be 5 years.

There are a number of good provisions in this bill that have not been in any Brady bill before. There are about seven or eight provisions on law enforcement, going after the criminals and not after the victims that are in this bill that have not been in the bill before.

So I assume the chairman is going to knock them out in conference too. If we are going to do all that, we might as well vote "no," and then we can filibuster the conference report when it comes back.

Mr. BIDEN. Mr. President, that would be fine with me. But let me make it clear what I meant. The fact of the matter is that on this provision it is not worth much of a distinction in where the House is. The House made it clear. They voted overwhelmingly—5 years. We are at 4 years with the right of the Attorney General to extend it to 5.

I have been to enough conferences to know where it is going to end up. I do not want to mislead anybody. When we come back here, and if it comes back, there is an understanding that somehow I am going to be able to protect 4 years with a 1-year extension by the Attorney General versus what the Mitchell-Dole substitute. But as it relates to this latest change that is bringing about this so-called compromise, I do not want anybody to be misled as to what is likely to happen. But it seems to me that we will go into the conference, we will take the Senate's position into the conference. But I am a realist.

Mr. MITCHELL. Mr. President, 2½ years ago we began the legislative process that culminates in just a few moments. Senator METZENBAUM has for years been advocating the Brady bill. He is joined by others here.

The bill in its initial form, I stated then, I believed would not accomplish the purpose of its supporters, and we then had in 1991 a serious good faith, lengthy negotiation, principally involving Senator DOLE and myself, Senator METZENBAUM, and Senator KOHL. We then came up with the bill which we thought was a good bill, and so did the Senate—67 Senators voted for it.

Mr. President, that bill did not become law because it was included in the larger bill which was not enacted. Now we have come to this year, and we have had another good faith negotiation. It has been as long and tedious as any negotiation I have ever been involved in. We have been 5 days, most nights—not so much as but our poor staffers working through the night—trying to reach agreement.

There are a lot of good provisions in this bill. We had some disagreement. The principal disagreements were over preemption which the Senate rejected. That rejection stands now. There is no preemption in this bill.

The second most difficult agreement was over sunsetting, which the Senate included. The sunsetting was at 5 years. The House did the same thing. It rejected preemption and accepted a 5-year sunset.

Now, over the past days since we were unable to get cloture, we have modified it in the manner that has been stated by the clerk which we have agreed upon. This has been painful and difficult for everybody. But let us not lose sight of the fact that for those who believe this to be an important measure, this is a significant success. Just a few days ago, just a few hours ago, we were in the position of not even being able to vote on this. Now we are going to vote on this.

I fully respect the views of the Senator from Idaho, and those who may vote on this, because on principle they disagree with what this bill will do, and they disagree with the motivation behind it.

Those of us who share an opposite view ought not to let it be obscured by the difficulty and the problems that have developed, particularly in these most recent moments, and statements about the significance of what is occurring. This is a significant action.

The Senate is now going to pass a Brady bill. And I hope and trust that when we come back from conference, whenever and in whatever form that is, we will be in a position to adopt that and have it enacted into law.

Mr. President, I ask unanimous consent that immediately following the vote on the Brady bill, without any intervening action or debate, the Senate vote on the North American Free Trade Agreement.

The PRESIDING OFFICER. Is there objection? Without objection, it is so ordered.

Mr. KERRY. I ask the majority leader if we could be 10 minutes.

Mr. MITCHELL. No. There may be Senators not present.

I would like, if I could. We will try to speed it up.

Mr. President, I inquire of the Republican leader. Is there anything he wishes to say at this time on either subject?

Afterward, there will be time for statements by Senators.

Mr. President, have the yeas and nays been ordered?

The PRESIDING OFFICER. It requires unanimous consent to request the yeas and nays at this point.

Mr. MITCHELL. Mr. President, I ask unanimous consent that it be in order to ask for the yeas and nays.

The PRESIDING OFFICER. Without objection, it is so ordered.

Mr. MITCHELL. Mr. President, I ask for the yeas and nays.

The PRESIDING OFFICER. Is there a sufficient second?

There is a sufficient second.

The yeas and nays were ordered.

The PRESIDING OFFICER. Without objection, the bill is read a second time.

Without objection, the text of S. 414 is substituted.

The clerk will read the bill for the third time.

The bill (H.R. 1025) was read for the third time.

The PRESIDING OFFICER. The bill having been read for the third time, the question is. Shall the bill pass?

On this question, the yeas and nays have been ordered, and the clerk will call the roll.

The assistant legislative clerk proceeded to call the roll.

Mr. FORD. I announce that the Senator from North Dakota [Mr. DORGAN] is necessarily absent.

The PRESIDING OFFICER. Are there any other Senators in the Chamber who desire to vote?

The result was announced—yeas 63, nays 36, as follows:

[Rollcall Vote No. 394 Leg.]

YEAS—63

Akaka	Durenberger	Lautenberg
Baucus	Exon	Levin
Biden	Feingold	Lieberman
Bingaman	Feinstein	Luzar
Boud	Ford	Mathews
Boren	Glenn	Metzenbaum
Bumpers	Gorton	Mikulski
Bradley	Graham	Mitchell
Bumpers	Harkin	Moseley-Braun
Byrd	Hatfield	Moynihan
Chafee	Hutchinson	Murray
Coats	Inouye	Nunn
Cohen	Jeffords	Packwood
Conrad	Kassebaum	Pell
Danforth	Kennedy	Pryor
Daschle	Kerrey	Reid
DeConcini	Kerry	Riegle
Dodd	Kohl	Robb

Exhibit 55. 139 Cong. Rec. 31,039 (1993).

The *Congressional Record* can be searched electronically through several online sources. Coverage begins in 1989 on THOMAS, and in 1994 on GPO Access (which also has the index back to 1983 and "History of Bills and Resolutions" tables with page references beginning in 1993). THOMAS's

version has links from the index and Daily Digest to *Record* pages and to bill texts, while GPO Access offers the *Record* in PDF format replicating the printed version. Westlaw and LexisNexis coverage extends back to 1985.

Several years after the session, a bound edition of more than twenty volumes is published. This edition renumbers the separately paginated Senate and House sections into one sequence, and it includes a cumulative index, a compilation of the Daily Digest, and a cumulative "History of Bills and Resolutions" table listing all bills introduced during the session and summarizing their legislative history.

The predecessors of the *Congressional Record*, which began in 1873, are the *Annals of Congress* (1789-1824); the *Register of Debates* (1824-37); and the *Congressional Globe* (1833-73). *House* and *Senate Journals* are also published, but unlike the *Congressional Record* they do not include the verbatim debates. The journals merely record the proceedings, indicate whether there was debate, and report the resulting action and votes taken. The *House Journal* is more voluminous and includes the texts of bills and amendments considered; both journals also include "History of Bills and Resolutions" tables.

D. HEARINGS AND OTHER CONGRESSIONAL PUBLICATIONS

Senate and House committees hold hearings on proposed legislation and on other subjects under congressional investigation such as nominations or impeachments. Government officials, scholars, and interest group representatives deliver prepared statements and answer questions from committee members. The transcripts of most hearings are published, accompanied by material submitted by interested individuals and groups such as letters and article reprints.

The purpose of a hearing is to determine the need for new legislation or to bring before Congress information relevant to its preparation and enactment. Hearings provide useful background information, but they are not generally considered persuasive sources of legislative history on the meaning of an enacted bill. Their importance as evidence of legislative intent is limited because they focus more on the views of interested parties than those of the lawmakers themselves.

Hearings are generally identified by the title which appears on the cover, the bill number, the name of the subcommittee and committee, the term of Congress, and the year. Exhibit 56 shows the first page of *Brady Handgun Violence Prevention Act: Hearing Before the Subcomm. on Crime and Criminal Justice of the House Comm. on the Judiciary*, 103d Cong. (1993).

A search for relevant hearings should not be limited to the term in which a particular law is enacted, because consideration of an issue may extend over several years. Hearings on earlier versions of the Brady Act, for example, were held in 1989 and 1991. Hearings are not held for every bill, however, and not all hearings are published.

Hearings are available from the issuing committee and are published by the Government Printing Office. Some hearings beginning in 1997 are available through GPO Access, and witnesses' statements are usually available online from Westlaw or LexisNexis well before the full transcripts are published. Most committee websites (linked from the Senate <www.senate.gov> and House <www.house.gov> sites) provide access to material from current hearings, including prepared statements of legislators and witnesses.

BRADY HANDGUN VIOLENCE PREVENTION ACT

THURSDAY, SEPTEMBER 30, 1993

HOUSE OF REPRESENTATIVES,
SUBCOMMITTEE ON CRIME AND CRIMINAL JUSTICE,
COMMITTEE ON THE JUDICIARY,
Washington, DC.

The subcommittee met, pursuant to notice, at 10:08 a.m., in room 2226, Rayburn House Office Building, Hon. Charles E. Schumer (chairman of the subcommittee) presiding.

Present: Representatives Charles E. Schumer, Don Edwards, Romano L. Mazzoli, Dan Glickman, George E. Sangmeister, David Mann, F. James Sensenbrenner, Jr., Lamar S. Smith, Steven Schiff, Jim Ramstad, and George W. Gekas.

Also present: Andrew Fois, counsel; David Yassky, assistant counsel; Tom Diaz, assistant counsel; Steven Goldstein, assistant counsel; Rachel Jacobson, secretary; Aliza Rieger, secretary; and Lyle Nirenberg, minority counsel.

OPENING STATEMENT OF CHAIRMAN SCHUMER

Mr. SCHUMER. The hearing will come to order. The Chair has received a request to cover this hearing in whole or in part by television broadcast, radio broadcast, still photography, or other similar methods.

In accordance with committee rule 5, permission will be granted unless there is objection.

Without objection.

OK. Good morning. We are meeting today to consider a bill whose time has come—the Brady Handgun Violence Prevention Act. The waiting period can wait no longer.

There is nothing complicated about this bill. What it mandates is clear—a simple 5-day waiting period and background check. What it will do is equally clear. It will save lives. The Brady bill will save lives that are being wasted in an epidemic of handgun violence from Brooklyn to Florida and all across America. And that is not theory, that is fact.

After Brady passes, a convicted felon will no longer be able to walk into a gunstore, as thousands have done this year, and walk out 10 minutes later with a murder weapon. State after State has shown that waiting periods and background checks work.

The people who spend every day fighting criminals and seeing the criminals get better and better armed know that waiting periods work. We will hear from some of them today. They will tell us

(1)

Exhibit 56. *Brady Handgun Violence Prevention Act: Hearing Before the Subcomm. on Crime and Criminal Justice of the House Comm. on the Judiciary,* 103d Cong. 1 (1993).

Congress also produces a variety of other publications which are less frequently consulted in legislative history research. These publications can, however, be important sources of related information.

Committee prints contain a variety of material prepared specifically for the use of a committee, ranging from studies by its staff or outside experts to compilations of earlier legislative history documents. Some prints contain statements by committee members on pending bills. Others can be useful analyses of laws under the jurisdiction of a committee, such as the House's biennial *Green Book: Background Material and Data on Major Programs Within the Jurisdiction of the Committee on Ways and Means*. Committee prints are distributed by the Government Printing Office, but they are not as widely available online as reports or hearings. Selective coverage through LexisNexis begins in 1994, and GPO Access has a limited number of prints beginning in 1997.

The two series of *House* and *Senate documents* are only occasionally useful as sources of legislative history. They include material such as the *Budget of the United States Government*, special studies or exhibits prepared for Congress, presidential messages, and communications from executive departments or agencies. They are published in a numbered series for each house, appear in the official *Serial Set*, and are available starting in 1995 on GPO Access and LexisNexis. Presidential messages accompanying proposed legislation and statements issued when signing or vetoing bills are also printed in the *Congressional Record*.

The Senate issues two series of publications in the process of treaty ratification. *Treaty documents* contain the texts of treaties before the Senate for its advice and consent, and *Senate executive reports* from the Foreign Relations

Committee contain its recommendations on pending treaties. These publications are discussed more fully in Chapter 11.

§ 6-3. CONGRESSIONAL RESEARCH RESOURCES

While researchers are interested in Congress for numerous reasons, this discussion focuses on tools useful for two basic legal research tasks: investigating the meaning of an enacted law, and tracking the status of pending legislation. A number of approaches can be used for these purposes. For recently enacted laws and pending legislation, electronic resources provide current and thorough coverage. For older bills, the choices dwindle to a few tools that provide retrospective coverage.

The bill number is usually the key to finding congressional documents or tracing legislative action. It appears on an enacted law both in its slip form and in the *Statutes at Large.* In chapter 5, note in Exhibit 38 on page 150 that the bill number (H.R. 1025) is included in brackets in the left margin. Bill numbers have been included in the *Statutes at Large* since 1903; earlier numbers can be found in Eugene Nabors, *Legislative Reference Checklist* (1982). Bill numbers do not appear, unfortunately, in the *United States Code* or in either of its annotated editions.

Bill numbers lead easily to printed or electronic status tables, which indicate actions taken and provide references to relevant documents. These tables can be used both for pending bill searches and for retrospective research on enacted laws.

A quick head start in legislative history research can come from the public law itself. At the end of each act, in either the slip law or the *Statutes at Large,* there appears a brief legislative history summary with citations of commit-

tee reports, dates of consideration and passage in each house, and references to presidential statements. The summary for the Brady Handgun Violence Prevention Act is shown in Exhibit 57. Note that it provides references to the House report and *Congressional Record* debate shown in earlier exhibits, but no references to hearings. Summaries have appeared at the end of each law passed since 1975, and *Statutes at Large* volumes from 1963 to 1974 include separate "Guide to Legislative History" tables.

Gathering a complete legislative history can be a very time-consuming process, as the necessary documents are scattered among many publications and may be difficult to obtain. For some major enactments, however, convenient access is provided by publications reprinting the important bills, debates, committee reports, and hearings. These compiled histories can save the considerable time and trouble involved in finding relevant references and documents. They are published both by government agencies (particularly the Congressional Research Service of the Library of Congress) and by commercial publishers. Online compiled legislative histories, including bills and committee reports, are available on LexisNexis and Westlaw for several dozen major acts in areas such as bankruptcy, tax, and environmental law.

The basic tool for identifying and locating published compiled legislative histories is Nancy P. Johnson's *Sources of Compiled Legislative Histories* (1979-date). Arranged chronologically by Congress and public law number, it provides a checklist of all available compiled legislative histories for acts as far back as 1789, and includes an index by name of act. It covers not only compilations which reprint the legislative history documents in full, but also law review articles and other sources that list and discuss relevant documents but do not reprint them. Another source listing compilations issued by the government is

LEGISLATIVE HISTORY—H.R. 1025 (S. 414):

HOUSE REPORTS: Nos. 103-344 (Comm. on the Judiciary) and 103-412
(Comm. of Conference).
CONGRESSIONAL RECORD, Vol. 139 (1993):
  Nov. 10, considered and passed House.
  Nov. 19, 20, considered and passed Senate, amended, in lieu of S. 414.
  Nov. 23, House agreed to conference report.
  Nov. 24, Senate agreed to conference report.
WEEKLY COMPILATION OF PRESIDENTIAL DOCUMENTS, Vol. 29 (1993):
  Nov. 30, Presidential remarks.

Exhibit 57.   Legislative History, Pub. L. No. 103-159, 107
Stat. 1536, 1546 (1993).

Bernard D. Reams, Jr., *Federal Legislative Histories: An Annotated Bibliography and Index to Officially Published Sources* (1994).

A. THOMAS AND OTHER CONGRESSIONAL WEBSITES

For current legislation or laws enacted since 1973, one of the easiest places to begin research is with Congress itself. THOMAS <thomas.loc.gov> is the website introduced in 1995 by the Library of Congress to make legislative information freely available to the public. The scope of THOMAS has grown considerably since its debut, and it now provides access to a wide range of information and documents.

THOMAS is arranged by term of Congress, so it is necessary to identify the appropriate Congress before searching either bill text or bill summary and status databases. Several ways to find documents relevant to specific legislation are available, including searches by bill or public law number, keyword, subject, date, or sponsor. Exhibit 58 shows part of the search screen for bill summary and status information in the 108th Congress (2003-04).

Legislative history summaries are available in THOMAS for laws enacted since 1973, but summaries for older laws lack some of the features included for more recent legislation. Links to the text of legislation, for example, are available beginning in 1989, and *Congressional Record* page references and links have been added beginning in 1993. A portion of the THOMAS summary for H.R. 1025 is shown in Exhibit 59. This excerpt is the "Floor Actions" status section, with links to the *Congressional Record* and references to the House report and the conference report.

THOMAS has the text of many congressional documents, and it also includes links to the Government Printing Office's GPO Access <www.gpoaccess.gov/legislative.html>, which provides these documents as PDF files. GPO Access is the more comprehensive source for documents, but it is a less user-friendly and informative site than THOMAS. Its search functions are more limited, and there are no links between its congressional documents.

THOMAS and GPO Access are the major comprehensive websites for congressional information. In addition, each chamber maintains a website (<www.senate.gov> and <www.house.gov>) with information on its procedures as well as links to pages for individual members and committees. Most committee homepages have summaries of major pending legislation, background information, hearing statements, and schedules of upcoming meetings.

Numerous other government, educational, and commercial websites have congressional information. THOMAS's "Information Sources for Legislative Research" page <thomas.loc.gov/home/legbranch/otherleg.html> has links to many of these sites.

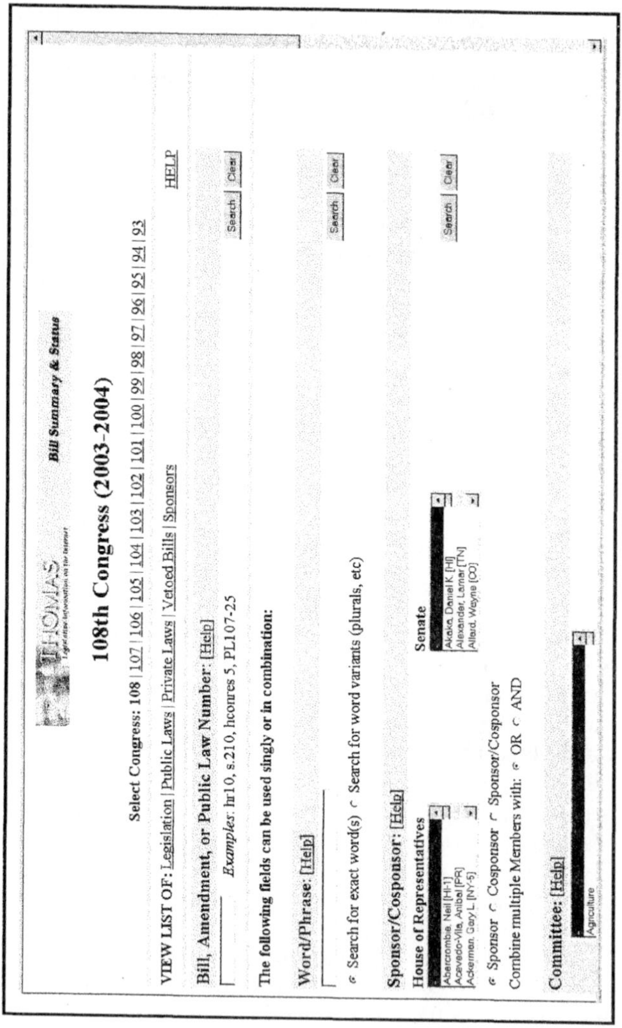

Exhibit 58.   THOMAS Bill Summary & Status search
screen <www.thomas.gov>.

H.R.1025
Sponsor: Rep. Schumer, Charles E. (introduced 2/22/1993)
Related Bills: H.RES.302, H.RES.322, H.R.277, H.R.3268, S.414
Latest Major Action: 11/30/1993 Became Public Law No: 103-159.
Title: To provide for a waiting period before the purchase of a handgun, and for the establishment of a national instant criminal background check system to be contacted by firearms dealers before the transfer of any firearm.

Floor Actions

11/30/1993 Public Law 103-159
11/30/1993 Measure presented to President (1/26/94 CR H79)
11/30/1993 Enrolled Measure signed in Senate (1/25/94 CR S43)
11/29/1993 Enrolled Measure signed in House (1/25/94 CR H15)
11/24/1993 Senate agreed to conference report (CR S17091)
11/23/1993 Unanimous consent agreement in Senate to consider conference report on Dec. 1 (CR S17065-17067)
11/23/1993 Cloture motion on conference report filed in Senate (Second Motion) (CR S17067)
11/23/1993 Unanimous consent agreement in Senate to consider conference report on Nov. 30 (CR S17065-17067)
11/23/1993 Cloture motion on conference report filed in Senate (CR S17067
11/23/1993 House agreed to conference report, roll call #614 (238-187) (11/22/93 CR H10905-10908)
11/22/1993 Conference report filed in House, H. Rept. 103-412 (CR H10983)
11/22/1993 Motion to instruct House conferees passed House (CR H10716-10720)
11/20/1993 Conference scheduled in House (CR H10716-10720)
11/20/1993 Conference scheduled in Senate (CR S16713)
11/20/1993 Measure passed Senate, amended, in lieu of S. 414, roll call #394 (63-36) (CR S16712)
11/20/1993 Measure considered in Senate (CR S16711-16712)
11/20/1993 Measure called up by unanimous consent in Senate (CR S16711)
11/10/1993 Measure passed House, amended, roll call #564 (238-189) (CR H9145)
11/10/1993 Motion to recommit to Committee on the Judiciary rejected in House, roll call #563 (200-229) (CR H9144)
11/10/1993 Measure considered in House (CR H9088-H9145)
11/10/1993 Measure called up by special rule in House (CR H9088)
11/10/1993 Reported to House from the Committee on the Judiciary with amendment, H. Rept. 103-344 (CR H9563)
10/7/1993 Discharge petition 6 filed in House (CR H7671)

Congressional Record Page References

2/22/1993 Introductory remarks on Measure (CR H731)
2/23/1993 Introductory remarks on Measure (CR H755)
3/30/1993 Introductory remarks on Measure (CR H693)
8/3/1993 Introductory remarks on Measure (CR H672)
11/22/1993 Full text of conference report printed (CR H10894-10897)

Exhibit 59. THOMAS Bill Summary & Status, H.R. 1025 (103d Cong. 1993) <www.thomas.gov>.

B. CONGRESSIONAL INFORMATION SERVICE (CIS)

Despite its official-sounding name, Congressional Information Service (CIS) is not an government office but a commercial enterprise (and now a branch of LexisNexis). CIS provides the most extensive indexing available of congressional information, covering virtually all of its publications since 1789 except the *Congressional Record* and its predecessors. CIS publishes its information both in printed indexes and online through LexisNexis Congressional <web.lexis-nexis.com/congcomp/>.

CIS first began indexing congressional materials in 1970, and its coverage is divided into two basic time periods. For the period before 1970, it publishes several retrospective indexes covering the Serial Set, executive documents and reports, hearings, and committee prints. These printed indexes are cumulated online as "Congressional Indexes, 1789-1969." Access is generally by keyword searching, but specific fields such as bill numbers can be searched and retrieval can be limited to designated years in order to focus on particular legislation.

For the period since 1970, CIS coverage is more sophisticated. Extensive abstracts and subject indexes cover all congressional publications except the *Congressional Record*. These abstracts and indexes are available in monthly pamphlets (*CIS Index*) with annual cumulations (*CIS Annual*) or through LexisNexis Congressional.

In the printed *CIS Index*, reports, hearings, prints, and documents are indexed by subject, title, and bill number; the indexes provide references to abstracts summarizing the contents of these documents. Exhibit 60 shows part of the CIS abstract for the hearing shown in Exhibit 56 on page 196, indicating the names and affiliations of the witnesses and the focus of their testimony. The number beginning with "Y4.J89/1" below the title of the hearing is the

Superintendent of Documents classification, which is used in most libraries for locating government publications. The "H521-14" in the heading for the abstract is the CIS accession number for the publication, and is the number used to find this hearing in CIS's microfiche collection of documents. To experienced legislative researchers, both "Y4.J89/1" and "H521" identify this hearing as a publication of the House Committee on the Judiciary.

Since 1984, *CIS Annual* has included *Legislative Histories* volumes providing references for each public law to bills, hearings, reports, debates, presidential documents and any other legislative actions. Rather than limiting coverage to a single term of Congress, these include references to earlier hearings and other documents on related bills from prior congressional sessions. They are generally considered the most complete and descriptive summaries of the legislative history of federal enactments. Exhibit 61 shows a portion of the CIS legislative history of the Brady Act on LexisNexis Congressional. This summary includes not only the report, debate and hearing shown in this chapter's exhibits, but also citations to documents in earlier Congresses that may be quite relevant in interpreting the bill that was eventually passed in 1993.

From 1970 to 1983, CIS included legislative histories of enacted laws in its *Abstracts* volumes. These are nearly as extensive as the later histories, but they are less convenient to use because they simply list the CIS numbers for the reports, hearings and other materials cited. It is necessary to turn to the abstracts for more information. These summaries, nonetheless, are among the most thorough sources available for their period.

The LexisNexis Congressional website provides all the information in *CIS Index*, with several enhancements including keyword searching and links from legislative histories to the documents described. Other features

H521-14 **BRADY HANDGUN VIOLENCE PREVENTION ACT.**
Sept. 30, 1993. 103-1.
iv+276 p. GPO $11.00
S/N 552-070-16277-1.
CIS/MF/5
•Item 1020-A; 1020-B.
°Y4.J89/1:103/26.
MC 94-20913.

Committee Serial No. 26. Hearing before the *Subcom on Crime and Criminal Justice* to consider H.R. 1025 (text, p. 4-27), the Brady Handgun Violence Prevention Act, to amend the Omnibus Crime Control and Safe Streets Act of 1968 to regulate sales and other transfers of handguns.

Includes provisions to:

a. Require prospective handgun buyers to provide certain information to gun dealers, and establish a national five-day waiting period to allow local law enforcement agencies to conduct background investigations on prospective buyers.

b. Direct the Department of Justice to establish a national computerized criminal history information system, incorporating State criminal history records, to enable gun dealers to immediately verify an individual's eligibility to purchase a handgun.

Supplementary material (p. 107-113, 247-276) includes correspondence and submitted statements.

H521-14.1: Sept. 30, 1993. p. 68-74.
Witnesses: **BRADY, Sarah**
BRADY, James S., both representing Handgun Control, Inc.
HILL, Brenda

Exhibit 60.   CIS Annual 1994: Abstracts of Congressional Publications 273 (1995).

include bill-tracking summaries; full-text access to bills, reports, the *Congressional Record,* and other congressional documents beginning in the 1980s; transcripts of hearing testimony; and information on committees and legislators.

c. USCCAN

United States Code Congressional and Administrative News (*USCCAN*) was mentioned in Chapter 5 as a source for the texts of enacted laws. For major acts it also reprints one or more committee reports, making it a convenient compilation for basic legislative research. The scope of coverage varies, but *USCCAN* generally prints either a House or Senate report and the conference committee report, if one was issued. It also provides references to some of the committee reports it does not reprint, and to the dates of consideration in the *Congressional Record.*

The public laws and committee reports are published in separate "Laws" and "Legislative History" sections of *USCCAN*. Each section prints material in order by public law number, and cross-references are provided between the laws and reports. Exhibit 62 shows the beginning of the House report on the Brady Act, as set out in *USCCAN*. Note that the report is preceded by references to steps in the passage of the legislation, including dates of consideration and passage in each house. The report is reprinted in full, except for the portion printing the text of the act.

Both monthly advance sheets and annual bound volumes of *USCCAN* also include tables with basic legislative history information, listing each public law's date of approval, *Statutes at Large* citation, bill and report numbers, committees, and dates of passage in each house. Monthly issues also include a "Major Bills Pending" table, arranged by subject and showing the progress of current legislation.

139 Congressional Record, 103rd Congress, 1st Session - 1993
Nov. 10. House consideration and passage of H.R. 1025, p. H9088.
Nov. 19. Senate consideration of S. 414, p. S16304.
Nov. 20. Senate consideration of S. 414, consideration and passage of H.R. 1025 with an amendment, and indefinite postponement of S. 414. Senate insistence on its amendment to H.R. 1025, request for a conference, and appointment of conferees, p. S16710.
Nov. 22. House disagreement to the Senate amendment to H.R. 1025, agreement to a conference, and appointment of conferees, p. H10716.
Nov. 22. House agreement to the conference report on H.R. 1025, p. H10905.
Nov. 24. Senate agreement to the conference report on H.R. 1025, p. S17090.

REPORTS:

101st Congress

H. Rpt. 101-691 on H.R. 467, "Brady Handgun Violence Prevention Act," Sept. 10, 1990.
CIS NO: 90-H523-25
LENGTH: 23 p.
SUDOC: Y1.1/8:101-691

102nd Congress

H. Rpt. 102-47 on H.R. 7, "Brady Handgun Violence Prevention Act," May 2, 1991.
CIS NO: 91-H523-3
LENGTH: 22 p.
SUDOC: Y1.1/8:102-47

H. Rpt. 102-405, conference report on H.R. 3371, "Violent Crime Control and Law Enforcement Act of 1991," Nov. 27, 1991.
CIS NO: 91-H523-32
LENGTH: 211 p.
SUDOC: Y1.1/8:102-405

103rd Congress

H. Rpt. 103-344 on H.R. 1025, "Brady Handgun Violence Prevention Act," Nov. 10, 1993.
CIS NO: 93-H523-25
LENGTH: 40 p.
SUDOC: Y1.1/8:103-344

Exhibit 61.   Legislative history summary for Pub. L. No. 103-159 (1993), LexisNexis Congrassional

BRADY HANDGUN VIOLENCE PREVENTION ACT

P.L. 103–159, see page 107 Stat. 1536

Dates of Consideration and Passage

House: November 10, 22, 1993
Senate: November 19, 20, 24, 1993

Cong. Record Vol. 139 (1993)

House Report (Judiciary Committee) No. 103–344, Nov. 10, 1993
[To accompany H.R. 1025]

House Conference Report No. 103–412, November 22, 1993
[To accompany H.R. 1025]

No Senate Report was submitted with this legislation. The House Report (this page) is set out below and the House Conference Report (page 2011) follows.

HOUSE REPORT NO. 103–344

[page 1]

The Committee on the Judiciary, to whom was referred the bill (H.R. 1025) to provide for a waiting period before the purchase of a handgun, and for the establishment of a national instant criminal background check system to be contacted by firearms dealers before the transfer of any firearm, having considered the same, report favorably thereon with an amendment and recommend that the bill as amended do pass.

*　　　　*　　　　*　　　　*　　　　*

[page 7]

Explanation of Amendment

Inasmuch as H.R. 1025 was ordered reported with a single amendment in the nature of a substitute, the contents of this report constitute an explanation of that amendment.

Summary and Purpose

The purpose of H.R. 1025 is to prevent convicted felons and other persons who are barred by law from purchasing guns from licensed gun dealers, manufacturers or importers. The bill would establish a national, five-working-day waiting period for the purchase of a handgun. Local law enforcement officials are required to use the waiting period to determine whether a prospective handgun purchaser has a felony conviction or is otherwise prohibited by law from buying a gun. States with their own programs for conducting background checks of handgun purchasers would be exempt from the waiting period, provided they are in compliance with criminal record computerization timetables to be established by the Attorney General. The bill also exempts from the waiting period any individual who obtains from the chief law enforcement officer in his

Exhibit 62.　H.R. Rep. No. 103-344 (1993), *reprinted in* 1993 U.S.C.C.A.N. 1984.

USCCAN provides only selective coverage of committee reports, and further research is often required. But it does provide a handy starting point and is easily accessible in most law libraries. For a researcher looking for general background or a quick section-by-section analysis, *USCCAN* may be all that is needed.

The LH database on Westlaw includes the reports reprinted in USCCAN beginning in 1948, and from 1990 on it contains all congressional committee reports, including reports on bills that did not become law. As noted earlier, Westlaw also has databases with congressional bills, the *Congressional Record*, and hearing testimony.

D. CQ Resources

Congressional Quarterly (CQ) is a news service and publisher of several sources of information on congressional activity. Its most widely read publication is *CQ Weekly* (formerly *Congressional Quarterly Weekly Report*), which provides background information on pending legislation and news of current developments. Exhibit 63 shows a page from a 1993 issue discussing the final passage of the Brady Bill. *CQ Weekly* contains tables of House and Senate votes, a status table for major legislation, and a legislative history table for new public laws. An annual *Congressional Quarterly Almanac* cumulates much of the information in the *Weekly Report* into a useful summary of the congressional session. More frequent publications for current congressional news include *CQDaily* and *CQ Midday Update*, which is available free by e-mail.

CQ publications are available through LexisNexis in the legal, government and business markets. For academic and public libraries, CQ Library <library.cqpress.com> provides a subscription-based Web version of *CQ Weekly* and free access to its index, which is updated weekly. For

LAW/JUDICIARY

Brady Bill Goes to the Brink, But Senate Finally Clears It

Handgun waiting period passes after seven-year battle; opponents win a promise to revisit topic in 1994

After seven years of debate and a harrowing final week of kamikaze political maneuvering, the Brady bill will become law.

The Senate passed the handgun waiting period bill (HR 1025) by voice vote Nov. 24, after pulling back from an escalating standoff between gun control advocates and opponents that had imperiled a planned Thanksgiving departure.

President Clinton, an enthusiastic supporter of the bill, promptly announced plans to sign it.

The Brady bill is the first major gun control legislation to pass Congress since 1968, when lawmakers approved restrictions in response to urban violence and the assassinations of Robert F. Kennedy and the Rev. Dr. Martin Luther King Jr. Passage marks a victory for gun control advocates, although the National Rifle Association (NRA) and other opponents achieved significant changes from the bill first introduced in the late 1980s.

The bill would institute a five-day waiting period for handgun purchases, eventually to be replaced by a nationwide "instant check" system of criminal records to make sure guns are not sold to felons or other unqualified buyers. The bill is named for former White House press secretary James S. Brady, who was wounded in the 1981 assassination attempt on President Ronald Reagan.

Many on both sides describe the bill as a modest measure that at best will make only a small dent in crime.

But the well-publicized legislation has taken on gigantic political dimensions, as evidenced by an exhausting week of brinkmanship in the final days of the session.

Public clamor for the Brady bill

By Holly Idelson

Senate Minority Leader Dole, left, and other congressional leaders met with the president Nov. 23 to seek a compromise on the Brady bill. The breakthrough came the following day.

BOXSCORE

Bill: HR 1025 — H Rept 103-412, the so-called Brady bill.

Latest action: The Senate adopted the conference report by voice vote Nov. 24, thus clearing the bill. The House adopted the conference report, 238-187, on Nov. 23. The Senate passed its version of HR 1025, 63-36, on Nov. 20.

Next likely action: President Clinton is expected to sign the bill. Congress will consider modifying legislation next year.

Background: The bill would impose a five-day waiting period on the purchase of handguns.

Reference: *Weekly Report,* pp. 3199, 3127, 3048.

---

helped dislodge it Nov. 20 from the Senate, where lawmakers abandoned a Republican-led filibuster and passed it, 63-36. *(Vote 394, p. 3294)*

Next, House and Senate negotiators agreed to a compromise bill after a raucous negotiating session Nov. 22. House

leaders rushed the deal to the floor, where it was adopted, 238-187, just after midnight. *(Vote 614, p. 3292)*

Minority Leader Bob Dole, R-Kan., balked in the Senate, saying Democratic negotiators had sold out the Senate position and approved an unacceptable bill.

Majority Leader George J. Mitchell, D-Maine, vowed to force the issue to another vote this year, even if it meant reconvening the Senate after Thanksgiving. With no compromise in hand, Mitchell on Nov. 23 scheduled cloture votes for Nov. 30 and Dec. 1.

But Republicans did not want to be blamed for thwarting the bill, which has overwhelming support in polls and among law enforcement groups. And most senators were loath to return to Washington the week of Nov. 29 to try to break a filibuster.

Mitchell and Dole reached a deal by early afternoon Nov. 24, just in time to pass the bill and call off the post-Thanksgiving session. Opponents agreed to let the bill go through by voice vote on the condition that Congress take up a package of proposed modifications to the law next year.

"The Brady bill is passed," Vice President Al Gore announced from the chair, where he was presiding over Senate action.

"After a long, long, hard fight — Jim Brady has won," said Dole, who in the final days of negotiation had at times appeared to be the bill's ally, at times its nemesis.

Brady appeared at a subsequent Capitol Hill news conference along with his wife, Sarah, Attorney General Janet Reno and others. "How sweet it is," he said "It's an awfully nice Thanksgiving present for the American people."

Both sides must now test their relative political strength on additional

---

Exhibit 63. Holly Idelson, *Brady Bill goes to the Brink, But Senate Finally Clears It,* 51 Cong. Q. Wkly. Rep. 3271 (1993).

---

researchers whose primary focus is legislative research, CQ also has a subscription Internet service, CQ.com <www.cq.com> , which provides customized bill-tracking information including a Bill Comparison feature that

makes it easier to find changes between two versions of proposed legislation. It also has the text of documents, including bills, committee reports, and the *Congressional Record*, as well as extensive information about committee meetings and floor activity.

Numerous other newspapers and magazines also focus on developments in Washington. In addition to general news sources, specialized publications include *National Journal* (weekly) and *Roll Call* (twice weekly). National Journal also publishes a *CongressDaily* newsletter, and all three of these publications are available through both Westlaw and LexisNexis.

E. PRINTED STATUS TABLES

CCH's *Congressional Index* is issued in two looseleaf volumes for each Congress, with weekly updates. Its extensive coverage of pending legislation includes an index of bills by subject and author, a digest of each bill, and a status table of actions taken on each bill (but not the documents themselves). This status table contains references to hearings, a feature lacking in many other legislative research aids. Although similar services are also provided by THOMAS and other electronic sources, *Congressional Index* remains one of the most convenient and current printed sources of congressional information.

Often several bills are introduced on related topics, and it can be difficult to tell from electronic sources which of these bills (if any) is being acted upon. In such cases, using a printed index and status table may be a quicker way to compare bills than a series of electronic queries. Exhibit 64 shows an excerpt from the status table section of *Congressional Index*, with information on the progress of H.R. 1025 from introduction to passage and enactment. The key stages, including hearings, are indicated in a standard,

rather telegraphic format. Unlike the CIS legislative history, there are no references to related bills in earlier terms of Congress.

Congressional Index does not contain the texts of bills or reports, but it does provide a wide range of other information on Congress, including lists of members and committee assignments; an index of enactments and vetoes; lists of pending treaties, reorganization plans, and nominations; a table of voting records; and a weekly newsletter.

Congressional Index began publication in 1938, and the older volumes can be valuable sources of information on bills predating the coverage of electronic bill-tracking services.

As noted earlier, the *Congressional Record* includes status tables which can be useful for both current and retrospective research. A "History of Bills and Resolutions" table is published in the biweekly index and cumulated for each session in the bound index volume. It includes a brief summary of each bill, the committee investigating the proposed legislation, and any actions taken to date, including amendments and passage. This is one of the best sources of page citations for debates within the *Record*. It includes report and public law numbers, but no references to hearings.

The biweekly table lists only those bills and resolutions acted upon within the preceding two week period, so it may be necessary to consult more than one index to find references to a particular bill. If a bill is listed, however, the information is cumulative from date of introduction. (Unlike the printed table, the online version through GPO Access <www.gpoaccess.gov/hob/> includes entries for all bills introduced in the session.)

★ 1025

Introduced	2/22/93
Ref to H Judiciary Com	2/22/93
Hrgs by Crime Subcom	9/30/93
Approved w/amdts by Crime Subcom	10/29/93
Ordered reptd w/amdts by Com	11/4/93
Rule granted allowing limited amdts (H Res 302)	11/9/93
Reptd w/amdts, H Rept 103-344, by Com	11/10/93
Amdts adopted (431 to 2; H Leg 558)	11/10/93
Amdts adopted (236 to 198; H Leg 559)	11/10/93
Amdts rejected (175 to 257; H Leg 560)	11/10/93
Amdts rejected (200 to 229; H Leg 563)	11/10/93
Passed by H (238 to 189; S Leg 564)	11/10/93
Passed by S amended to contain S 414 as amended (63 to 36; S Leg 394)	11/20/93
S insisted on its amdts and requested conf (Voice)	11/20/93
Rule granted allowing no amdts (H Res 322)	11/21/93
H agreed to conf (249 to 178; H Leg 606)	11/22/93
Conf rept filed, H Rept 103-412	11/22/93
H instructed its conferees (Voice)	11/22/93
H agreed to conf rept (238 to 187; H Leg 614)	11/22/93
S agreed to conf rept (Voice)	11/24/93
Signed by President	11/30/93
Public Law 103-159 (107 Stat 1536)	11/30/93

Exhibit 64. Status of House Bills, 1993-1994 Cong. Index (CCH) 53, 016.

The final cumulative table is not issued for several years after the end of a session. It is published after the bound edition of the *Record* and uses the final pagination instead of the separate "S" and "H" pages in the daily edition. Although this table is less complete than commercial

sources such as *CIS/Index* or *Congressional Index*, it remains
one of the best sources available for older laws. These
tables have been published annually since the 1867 volume
of the *Congressional Globe*, long before the earliest coverage
of most commercial publications. An entry for H.R. 1025
from the cumulative table is shown in Exhibit 65. Note that
it provides detailed *Congressional Record* page references
and identifies the House Report and the Conference
Report, but has no mention of the hearing shown in
Exhibit 56 or of actions on any related bills.

Both houses and most committees issue calendars of
pending business for the use of their members. Perhaps the
most valuable of these is *Calendars of the United States House
of Representatives and History of Legislation*, which is issued
daily. Each issue is cumulative and lists all bills in either
House or Senate that have been reported out of committee.
Committee calendars are also excellent sources of information on upcoming hearings. Current House and Senate calendars, and final calendars beginning with the 104th
Congress, are available on the Internet through GPO
Access <www.gpoaccess.gov/calendars/>.

f. Directories

One of the fastest and simplest ways to find out about the
status of pending legislation is to call congressional staff
members responsible for drafting or monitoring the bill.
They may be able to provide information or insights that
would never appear in published status tables or reports.
The best sources for detailed information on staff members
are two competing commercial directories, *Congressional
Staff Directory* (three times per year) and *Congressional
Yellow Book* (quarterly). Internet versions of both directories
(<www.csd.cq.com>, <www.leadershipdirectories.com/
cyb.htm>) are updated weekly but are available to subscribers only.

H.R. 1025—A bill to provide for a waiting period before the purchase of a handgun, and for the establishment of a national instant criminal background check system to be contacted by firearms dealers before the transfer of any firearm; to the Committee on the Judiciary.

By Mr. SCHUMER (for himself, Mr. Sensenbrenner, Mr. Synar, Mr. Mazzoli, Mr. Gibbons, Mr. Glickman, Mr. Bryant, Mr. Sawyer, Mr. Stark, Mr. Fazio, Mr. Studds, Mr. Reynolds, Mr. McDermott, Mr. Jacobs, Mr. Manton, Ms. Pelosi, Mr. Porter, Mr. Towns, Mr. Berman, Mr. Borski, Mr. Bacchus of Florida, Mrs. Schroeder, Mr. Moran, Ms. Slaughter, Mr. Filner, Mr. Boehlert, Mr. Hall of Ohio, Mr. Barrett of Wisconsin, Mr. Shays, Mr. Skaggs, Mrs. Roukema, Mr. Klein, Mr. Evans, Mr. Mineta, Mr. Derrick, Mr Lipinski, Mr. Klug, Mr. Andrews of Maine, Mr. Deutsch, Mr. Edwards of California, Mr. Conyers, Mr. Yates, Mr. Torricelli, Mr. Wheat, Mr. Tucker, Mr. Roemer, Ms. Furse, Ms. Molinari, Ms. Byrne, Mrs Bentley, Ms. Maloney, Mr. Cardin, Mr. Gejdenson, Mr. Meehan, Mr. Fingerhut, Mr. Sangmeister, Mr. Nadler, Mr. Markey, Mr. Hughes, Mr. Dellums, Mr. Owens, Ms. Waters, Mr. de Lugo, Mr. Hyde, Mr. Stokes, Mr. Waxman, Mr. Durbin, Mr. Ackerman, Mr. Bonior, Mr. Serrano, Mr. Coyne, Mr. Lantos, Mr. Mfume, Mrs. Morella, Ms. DeLauro, Mr. Andrews of New Jersey, Ms. Norton, Mr. Faleomavaega, Mr. Hoagland, Mr. Miller of California, Mr. Reed, Mr. Hoyer, Mr. Hochbrueckner, Mr. Johnston of Florida, Mr. Sabo, Mr. Brown of California, Mr. Lewis of Georgia, Mr. Foglietta, Mr. Frank of Massachusetts, Mr. Gutierrez, Mr. Goss, Mrs. Kennelly, Mr. Beilenson, Ms. Kaptur, Mrs. Mink, Mr. Matsui, Mr. Flake, Ms. Velazquez, Ms. Lowey, and Mr. Wynn), 3245—Cosponsors added, 4184, 5707, 7432, 10108, 13094, 20366, 24178, 27323—Reported with amendments (H. Rept. 103–344), 29008—Provided for consideration (H. Res. 302), 28103—Debated, 28538, 31038—Text, 28560—Amendments, 28564, 28565, 28573—Passed House amended, 28586—Passed Senate amended (in lieu of S. 414), 31040—Senate insisted on its amendment and asked for a conference, 31040—House disagreed to Senate amendment and agreed to a conference, 31814—Conferees appointed, 31041, 31814—Change of Conferees, 31630—Conference report (H. Rept. 103–412) submitted in the House, 31992—Explanatory statement, 31995—Conference report agreed to in the House, 32004—Conference report agreed to in the Senate, 32281—Presented to the President (November 30, 1993)—Approved [Public Law 103–159] (signed November 30, 1993)

Exhibit 65. History of Bills and Resolutions, 139 CONG. REC. 2781 (1993).

The *Official Congressional Directory* (biennial) is not as detailed as the commercial directories, but it provides information about individuals, offices and the organizational structure of Congress. This directory is available through GPO Access <www.gpoaccess.gov/cdirectory>; the Internet version, unlike its print counterpart, is modified during the term to reflect changes. Two useful sources for background information on members of Congress, both published biennially, are National Journal's *Almanac of American Politics* and *CQ's Politics in America*.

§ 6-4. STATE LEGISLATIVE INFORMATION

Legislative history on the state level is a research area of sharp contrasts. Information on current legislation is widely available on the Internet, but documents that might aid in the interpretation of enacted laws can be difficult or impossible to find.

First the good news: Most state legislatures do excellent jobs of providing Internet access to current status information and to the text of pending bills. The better websites have several means of searching for bills, and some offer e-mail notification services when particular bills are acted upon.

These legislative websites can be found from state homepages (<www.state.__.us>, using the state's postal abbreviation), or from one of the many general starting points. The National Conference of State Legislatures maintains a convenient "State Legislatures Internet Links" site <www.ncsl.org/public/leglinks.cfm>, which allows the researcher either to go directly to a specific site or to create a customized list of links for specific content (such as bill information or legislator biographies) from all states or a selected list of states.

A valuable feature found on many legislative websites is an introductory guide to the state's lawmaking procedures. State legislatures generally follow the federal paradigm, but there can be significant differences from state to state. An important first step in studying legislative action in a particular state is to learn about its procedures. Guides and other resources, such as charts showing how bills become law, can save considerable time and confusion.

The commercial databases also provide text and status information for pending legislation. Both Westlaw and LexisNexis have databases for each state, as well as multistate databases useful for monitoring developments in legislatures throughout the country. Historical bill text and tracking databases extend on both systems back to the early 1990s. Researchers in university and public libraries may have access to LexisNexis's bill-tracking and other legislative information through its State Capital website <web.lexis-nexis.com/stcapuniv/>.

Researchers needing to interpret enacted statutes face a more difficult task. Bills from older sessions can be hard to locate. Almost every state has a legislative journal, but very few of these actually include transcripts of the debates. Only a few states publish committee reports, and even fewer publish hearings.

The materials that are available vary widely from state to state. Often they are not published in either print or electronic form, but are only available at the state capitol. Some states have "bill jackets" with legislative information, and some have microform records or tape recordings of sessions. In many instances, contemporary newspaper accounts may be the best available source of information about a sponsor's statements or proceedings.

Two useful books identify the resources available for each state. Lynn Hellebust's annual *State Legislative Sourcebook: A Resource Guide to Legislative Information in the Fifty States* provides information on the legislative processes and include references to available published and online sources. References include a "best initial contact" for each state, as well as information on websites, introductory guides, telephone numbers for ascertaining bill status, bill tracking services, and legislative documents such as session laws and summaries of legislation. William H. Manz's biennial *Guide to State Legislative and Administrative Materials* (2000-date) covers a broader range of printed and online sources for bills, legislative history materials, and numerous other sources of state law.

A guide to legislative research processes in a specific state can be invaluable. Most of the state legal research guides listed in Appendix B, on page 404, include discussion of available legislative history resources for their states. Jennifer Bryan's "State Legislative History Research Guides and State Legislatures on the Web" <www.law.indiana.edu/lib/netres/govt/stateurlslist.html> provides links to nearly a hundred online guides, and others are listed in Manz's *Guide to State Legislative and Administrative Materials*.

Many states have official agencies responsible for recommending and drafting new legislation. These groups, including law revision commissions, judicial councils, and legislative councils, often publish annual or topical reports summarizing their work. For recommendations enacted into law, these reports may be valuable legislative history documentation.

Directory information on state legislatures, including organization, members, committees, and staffs, is contained in official state manuals (sometimes called *Bluebooks* or

Redbooks), published annually or biennially by most states. The directory for a specific state is likely to provide the most detailed information, but several multistate directories are also published. General multistate government directories such as *State Yellow Book* and *State Staff Directory* include extensive coverage of the legislative branches, with information on both individual members and committees. The Council of State Governments publishes an annual *CSG State Directory*, which covers legislatures in *Directory I: Elective Officials* and *Directory II: Legislative Leadership, Committees and Staff.*

§6-5. CONCLUSION

Legislative history is sometimes viewed as an arcane and complex field, rather than as a basic legal research process. Every lawyer should have a grasp of the major resources. Legislative materials are essential tools both in interpreting statutes and in monitoring current legal developments.

The electronic resources available from the online databases and from the government itself have made information on pending legislation easily accessible, while research into the history of enacted laws requires more refined skill. For federal statutes, a review of material reprinted in *USCCAN* may be sufficient to determine whether a further inquiry in legislative resources is necessary; from there a fuller picture may be obtained from *CIS Index* or other tools. The materials for state statutes vary dramatically between jurisdictions, but no state has resources comparable to those available for federal statutes.

Legislative history documents can be useful in statutory research, but they are just one of several important resources in understanding statutes. The court decisions found through annotated codes and other means may provide authoritative judicial interpretations. Even secondary

sources may be persuasive in determining the scope and meaning of an act. Many statutes are implemented by more detailed regulations and decisions from administrative agencies, which are essential for fully understanding the underlying statute.

CHAPTER 7
ADMINISTRATIVE LAW

■　■　■　■　■　■　■　■　■　■

§7-1. Introduction

The executive is one of the three coordinate branches of government, but historically its lawmaking role was limited to orders and regulations needed to carry out the legislature's mandates. With the modern growth of government bureaucracy, however, the rules created by executive agencies can be the legal sources with the most immediate and pervasive impact.

Administrative law takes several forms, as agencies can act both somewhat like legislatures and somewhat like courts. They may promulgate binding regulations governing areas of their expertise, or they may decide matters involving particular litigants on a case-by-case basis. Approaches vary from agency to agency.

Although executive agencies have existed in this country since its creation, the real growth of administrative law began in the late nineteenth century as the government sought to deal with the increasingly complex problems of industrialized society. In the 1930s, Congress created new independent regulatory agencies such as the Federal Communications Commission and the Securities and Exchange Commission to administer its New Deal programs. A third boom in administrative law occurred around 1970, as agencies such as the Environmental Protection Agency, the Consumer Product Safety Commission, and the Occupational Safety and Health Administration were created to address growing environmental and health concerns. The regulatory landscape is still evolving, as the Homeland Security Act of 2002 created a new cabinet department and several new agencies. Administrative regulations and decisions continue to proliferate.

Most of this chapter focuses on federal administrative law, but state agencies can play an important a role in many areas of activity. States also delegate lawmaking responsibilities to counties and cities, which enact ordinances and have their own local agencies. While federal administrative law is relatively easy to research, state and local sources may be difficult to locate and even harder to update.

§7-2. BACKGROUND REFERENCE MATERIALS

In researching administrative law, it is important to determine what agency has jurisdiction and to develop a preliminary understanding of its structure and functions. In some situations the relevant agency is obvious, but in others it may require background analysis or a close reading of statutory and judicial sources to determine an agency's role.

A useful source for finding federal agencies is CQ Press's annual *Washington Information Directory,* which is organized by subject and provides descriptions and access information for federal agencies as well as congressional committees and nongovernmental organizations. Exhibit 66 shows an excerpt from this directory for the topic "Gun Control," with information about the Bureau of Alcohol, Tobacco and Firearms (ATF), as well as interest groups such as the Brady Center to Prevent Handgun Violence and the Citizens Committee for the Right to Keep and Bear Arms. (ATF was a division of the Department of the Treasury until January 2003, when the Homeland Security Act split it into two separate bureaus. Firearms regulations are now overseen by a new Bureau of Alcohol, Tobacco, Firearms, and Explosives in the Department of Justice.)

Once a relevant agency has been identified, a valuable next step is to consult the *United States Government Manual.* This annual directory of the federal government,

Gun Control

AGENCIES

Bureau of Alcohol, Tobacco, and Firearms (ATF), *(Treasury Dept.), Field Operations,* 650 Massachusetts Ave. N.W., #8100 20226; (202) 927-7970. Fax, (202) 927-7756. David L. Benton, Deputy Director. Information, (202) 927-7777. Press, (202) 927-9510.
Web, www.atf.treas.gov

Enforces and administers laws to eliminate illegal possession and use of firearms. Investigates criminal violations and regulates legal trade, including imports and exports. To report thefts, losses, or discoveries of explosive materials, call (800) 800-3855.

NONPROFIT

Brady Campaign to Prevent Gun Violence, 1225 Eye St. N.W., #1100 20005; (202) 898-0792. Fax, (202) 371-9615. Sarah Brady, Chair.
Web, www.bradycampaign.org

Public interest organization that works for handgun control legislation and serves as an information clearinghouse.

Brady Center to Prevent Gun Violence, 1225 Eye St. N.W., #1100 20005; (202) 289-7319. Fax, (202) 408-1851. Michael Barnes, President.
Web, www.bradycenter.org

Educational, research, and legal action organization that seeks to allay gun violence, especially among children, through gun control legislation. (Affiliated with Brady Campaign to Prevent Gun Violence.)

Citizens Committee for the Right to Keep and Bear Arms, *Publications and Public Affairs, Washington Office,* 1090 Vermont Ave. N.W., #800 20005; (202) 326-5259. Fax, (202) 898-1939. John M. Snyder, Director. General e-mail, gundean@aol.com
Web, www.ccrkba.org

Concerned with rights of gun owners. Maintains National Advisory Council, comprising members of Congress and other distinguished Americans, which provides advice on issues concerning the right to keep and bear arms. (Headquarters in Bellevue, Wash.)

Coalition to Stop Gun Violence, 1023 15th St. N.W., #600 20005; (202) 408-0061. Fax, (202) 408-0062.

Exhibit 66. WASHINGTON INFORMATION DIRECTORY 2002-2003, at 539 (Talia Greenberg ed., 2002).

available in print and on the Internet
<www.gpoaccess.gov/gmanual/>, provides descriptive
listings of each executive department and more than fifty
independent agencies and commissions. It includes references to statutes under which the agencies operate and
explains their functions and major operating units.
Organizational charts are provided for most major agencies, and sources of information (including publications,
telephone numbers, and websites) are listed. The
Government Manual is one of the most important reference
books of the federal government, and can often save a
researcher considerable time by providing quick answers
to questions which might otherwise require extensive
research. Exhibit 67 shows the first page of its entry for the
ATF, providing a description of the agency's mission and
major activities as well as a list of field operations offices.

The *United States Government Manual* provides an
overview of the entire federal government, focusing on the
executive branch. CQ Press's biennial *Federal Regulatory
Directory* has a more extensive analysis of twelve major
regulatory agencies, with shorter treatment of more than a
hundred other agencies and offices. Historical background
can be found in George T. Kurian, ed., *A Historical Guide to
the U.S. Government* (1998), with alphabetically arranged
entries on departments and agencies, as well as major concepts and issues in administrative law. John J. Patrick et al.,
The Oxford Guide to the United States Government (2001) provides a more cursory look at a wider range of topics.

While the *Government Manual* and the *Federal Regulatory
Directory* provide the names of major agency officials, neither volume is updated very frequently and neither provides an extensive listing of other staffers. Several directories provide more detailed information about specific
personnel, including telephone numbers and e-mail

fraud, waste, and abuse; investigating activities or allegations related to fraud, waste, and abuse by IRS personnel; and

protecting the IRS against attempts to corrupt or threaten its employees.

For further information concerning the Departmental Offices, contact the Public Affairs Office, Department of the Treasury, 1500 Pennsylvania Avenue NW., Washington, DC 20220. Phone, 202–622–2960.

Bureau of Alcohol, Tobacco, and Firearms

The mission of the Bureau of Alcohol, Tobacco, and Firearms (ATF) is to reduce violent crime, collect revenue, and protect the public through criminal law enforcement, regulatory enforcement, and tax collection.

The Bureau was established by Department of Treasury Order No. 221, effective July 1, 1972, which transferred the functions, powers, and duties arising under laws relating to alcohol, tobacco, firearms, and explosives from the Internal Revenue Service to the Bureau. Responsibilities regarding enforcement of interstate trafficking laws in contraband cigarettes, combating commercial arson, and enforcement of laws pertaining to the transfer of handguns have also been assigned to ATF.

The Bureau is responsible for enforcing and administering firearms and explosives laws, as well as those covering the production, taxation, and distribution of alcohol and tobacco products. The Bureau's objectives are to

maximize compliance with and investigate violations of these laws.

In collaborative partnerships with government agencies, industry, academia, and others, ATF works to reduce crime and violence by safeguarding the public from arson and explosives incidents, denying criminals access to firearms, removing violent offenders from communities, and preventing violence through community outreach; and to maintain a sound revenue management and regulatory system which reduces the burden on industry, collects revenues which are rightfully due, and uses electronic commerce. ATF also works to protect the public and prevent consumer deception by assuring the integrity of the products, people, and companies in the marketplace; ensuring compliance with laws and regulations through education, inspection, and investigations; and informing the public about ATF regulations and product safety using various media.

Field Operations Offices—Office of Enforcement

Field Division	Address	Special Agent in Charge	Telephone
Atlanta, GA	Suite 300, 2600 Century Pkwy., 30345–3104	John C. Killorin	404–417–2600
Baltimore, MD	5th Fl., 31 Hopkins Plz., 21201	(Vacancy)	410–779–1700
Boston, MA	Rm. 253, 10 Causeway St., 02222–1047	Dewey Webb	617–557–1200
Brentwood, TN	Suite 200, 5300 Maryland Way, 37027	James M. Cavanaugh	615–565–1400
Charlotte, NC	Suite 200, 6701 Carmel Rd., 28209	Lester D. Martz	704–716–1800
Chicago, IL	Suite 350 S., 300 S. Riverside Plz., 60606	Wilfred L. Ford	312–353–6935
Columbus, OH	Suite 200, 37 W. Broad St., 43215	Christopher P. Sadowski	614–469–5303
Dallas, TX	Suite 303, 1114 Commerce St., 75242	Jimmy Wooten	469–227–4300
Detroit, MI	Suite 300, 1155 Brewery Park Blvd., 48207–2602	Gregory Holley	313–259–8050
Houston, TX	Suite 210, 15355 Vantage Pkwy. W., 77032	Vanessa L. McLemore	281–372–2900
Kansas City, MO	Suite 200, 2600 Grant Ave., 64108	Mark S. James	816–559–0700
Los Angeles, CA	Suite 800, 350 S. Figueroa St., 90071	Donald R. Kincaid	213–534–2450
Louisville, KY	Suite 322, 600 Dr. Martin Luther King Jr. Pl., 40202	Karl Stankovic	502–753–3400
Metairie, LA	Suite 1008, 111 Veterans Blvd., 70005	Jerry W. Taie	504–841–7000
Miami, FL	Suite 300, 5225 NW. 87th Ave., 33178	Hugo J. Barrera	305–597–4800
New York, NY	300 Coffey St., 11231	Edgar A. Domenech	718–254–7883
Philadelphia, PA	Rm. 607, 2d & Chestnut Sts., 19106	Lawrence L. Duchnowski	215–717–4700
Phoenix, AZ	Suite 1010, 3003 N. Central Ave., 85012	Virginia T. O'Brien	602–776–5400
San Francisco, CA	11th Fl., 221 Main St., 94105	John A. Torres	415–947–5100
Seattle, WA	Rm. 790, 915 2d Ave., 98174	Carson Carroll	206–220–6440
St. Paul, MN	1870 World Trade Ctr., 30 E. 7th St., 55101	Richard E. Chase	651–290–3092

Exhibit 67. THE UNITED STATES GOVERNMENT MANUAL 2002/2003, at 339 (2002).

addresses. Three with comparable coverage are *Carroll's Federal Directory* (bimonthly), CQ Press's *Federal Staff Directory* (three times a year), and Leadership Directories' *Federal Yellow Book* (quarterly). Carroll Publishing and Leadership Directories also produce companion volumes covering federal regional offices outside the Washington, D.C. area. All of these directories are also available through their publishers' subscription websites (<www.govsearch.com>, <fsd.cq.com>, and <www.leadershipdirectories.com>).

An agency's website often provides a convenient source of information on its history and current activities. Here, depending on the agency, it is usually possible to find introductory overviews, speeches, policy documents, directories, and other useful resources. The ATF website, for example, includes annual snapshots of the bureau's activity, information on its history, and an overview of its program. Several lists of government websites can be found on the Internet. One of the most thorough and reliable of these lists is Louisiana State University's Federal Agencies Directory <www.lib.lsu.edu/gov/fedgov.html>.

§7-3. Federal Regulations

The basic mechanism by which most agencies govern their areas of expertise is the *regulation*, a detailed administrative order similar in form to a statute. Regulations are also known as *rules*; these terms are used interchangeably in administrative law. The publication of regulations follows a standard procedure: they are first issued chronologically in a daily gazette, the *Federal Register*; and then the rules in force are arranged by subject in the *Code of Federal Regulations*. These two publications are the central official resources in federal administrative law research.

A. Federal Register

As more and more executive and administrative orders and regulations were promulgated in the early New Deal period, locating regulations and determining which were in force became increasingly difficult. There was no requirement that regulations be published or centrally filed, and two cases reached the U.S. Supreme Court before it was discovered that the administrative orders on which they were based were no longer in effect. This embarrassment, and the resulting criticism, led Congress in 1935 to establish a daily publication of executive and administrative promulgations. The *Federal Register* began publication on March 14, 1936 as a chronological source for administrative documents, similar to a session law text.

In 1946 the Administrative Procedure Act expanded the scope of the *Federal Register* considerably by creating a rule-making system requiring the publication of proposed regulations for public comment. Judicial decisions in the 1960s and 1970s, overturning regulations seen as arbitrary or capricious, led agencies to provide fuller explanations of their actions and greater evidence of public involvement in the decisionmaking process. In addition to the text of proposed and final rules, the *Register* now includes extensive preambles describing the need for the regulatory changes and responding to comments on proposed rules.

These preambles make the *Federal Register* much more than a simple "session regulation" text, because the explanatory information never appears in the *Code of Federal Regulations*. Exhibit 68 shows a final rule of the Bureau of Alcohol, Tobacco and Firearms as published in the *Federal Register*, implementing regulations under the Brady Handgun Violence Prevention Act. The page shown contains a summary, contact information, and background on the statutory basis of the new regulations.

DEPARTMENT OF THE TREASURY

Bureau of Alcohol, Tobacco and Firearms

27 CFR Parts 178 and 179

[T.D. ATF–415; Ref: Notice No. 857; 93F–057P]

RIN 1512–AB67

Implementation of Public Law 103–159, Relating to the Permanent Provisions of the Brady Handgun Violence Prevention Act

AGENCY: Bureau of Alcohol, Tobacco and Firearms (ATF), Department of the Treasury

ACTION: Final rule, Treasury decision.

SUMMARY: The Bureau of Alcohol, Tobacco and Firearms (ATF) is amending the regulations to implement the provisions of Public Law 103–159, relating to the permanent provisions of the Brady Handgun Violence Prevention Act. These regulations implement the law by requiring, with some exceptions, a licensed firearms importer, manufacturer, or dealer to contact the national instant criminal background check system (NICS) before transferring any firearm to an unlicensed individual. NICS will advise the licensee whether the system contains any information that the prospective purchaser is prohibited by law from possessing or receiving a firearm.

DATES: This rule is effective November 30, 1998

FOR FURTHER INFORMATION CONTACT: James P. Ficaretta, Regulations Division, Bureau of Alcohol, Tobacco and Firearms, 650 Massachusetts Avenue, NW., Washington, DC 20226 (202–927–8230).

SUPPLEMENTARY INFORMATION:

Background

On November 30, 1993, Public Law 103–159 (107 Stat. 1536) was enacted, amending the Gun Control Act of 1968 (GCA), as amended (18 U.S.C. Chapter 44). Title I of Public Law 103–159, the Brady Handgun Violence Prevention Act (the "Brady law" or "Brady"), imposed as an interim measure a waiting period of 5 days before a licensed importer, manufacturer, or dealer may sell, deliver, or transfer a handgun to an unlicensed individual. The waiting period applies only in States without an acceptable alternate system of conducting background checks on handgun purchasers. The interim provisions of the Brady law, 18 U.S.C. 922(s), became effective on February 28, 1994, and cease to apply on November 30, 1998.

Permanent Provisions of the Brady Law

The permanent provisions of the Brady law provide for the establishment of a national instant criminal background check system ("NICS") that a firearms licensee must contact before transferring any firearm to an unlicensed individual. The law requires that the permanent system be established not later than November 30, 1998. While the interim provisions apply only to handguns, the permanent provisions of the Brady law apply to all firearms. Furthermore, the law provides that the system may take up to three business days to notify the licensee whether receipt of a firearm by the prospective purchaser would be in violation of law.

National Instant Criminal Background Check System

The Brady law requires that the Attorney General establish a permanent national instant criminal background check system that any licensee may contact, by telephone or by other electronic means in addition to the telephone, for information on whether receipt of a firearm by a prospective transferee would violate Federal or State law. The law requires that the permanent system be established not later than November 30, 1998. It is expected that the NICS will be established by October 31, 1998, although licensees will not be required to contact NICS until November 30, 1998.

Upon establishment of the system, the Attorney General is required to notify each firearms licensee and the chief law enforcement officer of each State of the existence and purpose of NICS and the means to be used to contact NICS. Beginning on the date that is 30 days after the Attorney General notifies firearms licensees that NICS is established, the permanent provisions of Brady, 18 U.S.C. 922(t), become effective.

Statutory Requirements

Section 922(t) generally makes it unlawful for any licensed firearms importer, manufacturer, or dealer to sell, deliver, or transfer a firearm to an unlicensed individual (transferee), unless—

1. Before the completion of the transfer, the licensee contacts the national instant background check system;

2. The system provides the licensee with a unique identification number signifying that transfer of the firearm would not be in violation of law OR 3 business days (meaning a day on which

State offices are open) have elapsed from the date the licensee contacted the system and the system has not notified the licensee that receipt of the firearm by the transferee would be in violation of law; and

3. The licensee verifies the identity of the transferee by examining a valid identification document containing a photograph of the transferee.

Exceptions to NICS

The statute provides the following exceptions to the national instant background check system:

1. The transferee presents to the licensee a permit which was issued not more than 5 years earlier by the State in which the transfer is to take place and which allows the transferee to possess or acquire a firearm, and the law of the State provides that such a permit is to be issued only after an authorized government official has verified that available information does not indicate that possession of a firearm by the transferee would be in violation of the law;

2. Purchases of firearms which are subject to the National Firearms Act and which have been approved for transfer under 27 CFR Part 179 (Machine Guns, Destructive Devices, and Certain Other Firearms); or

3. Purchases of firearms for which the Secretary has certified that compliance with NICS is impracticable because the ratio of the number of law enforcement officers of the State in which the transfer is to occur to the number of square miles of land area of the State does not exceed 0.0025 (i.e., 25 officers per 10,000 square miles), the premises of the licensee are remote in relation to the chief law enforcement officer of the area, and there is an absence of telecommunications facilities in the geographical area in which the business premises are located.

Penalties for Noncompliance

Section 922(t) provides that a firearms licensee who transfers a firearm and knowingly fails to comply with the requirements of the law, in a case where compliance would have revealed that the transfer was unlawful, is subject to license suspension or revocation and a civil fine of not more than $5,000.

Notice of Proposed Rulemaking

On February 19, 1998, ATF published in the **Federal Register** a notice proposing regulations to implement the requirements placed on Federal firearms licensees by section 922(t) (Notice No. 857; 63 FR 8379). The comment period for Notice No. 857 closed on May 20, 1998.

Exhibit 68.   Implementation of Public Law 103–159, Relating to the Permanent Provisions of the Brady Handgun Violence Prevention Act, 63 Fed. Reg. 58,272 (1998) (to be codified at 27 C.F.R. pts. 178 and 179).

Each daily *Federal Register* begins with a table of contents and a list of the *Code of Federal Regulations* citations for new or proposed regulations in the issue. The table of contents is organized alphabetically by agency, so researchers can easily monitor a particular agency's activity. A portion of the table of contents for the issue containing the regulation in Exhibit 68 is shown in Exhibit 69, indicating this final rule as well as proposed and finàl rules and notices from several other agencies. Exhibit 70 shows part of the list of *CFR* parts affected in the same *Federal Register* issue, with a reference to the new ATF Brady Act regulations.

Several readers' aids are provided in the back of each issue, including telephone numbers for information and assistance, a list of new public laws, and a listing of *Federal Register* pages and dates for the month (so that someone with a page reference can determine which issue to consult). The most important of these readers' aids is a cumulative list of *CFR* parts affected since the beginning of the month. This list, similar to but longer than the one shown in Exhibit 70, is one of the basic tools for determining the current status of federal regulations.

An index to the *Federal Register* is published monthly. Each index cumulates references since the beginning of the year. The index is arranged like the daily table of contents, with entries by agency rather than by subject.

Recent *Federal Register* issues, back to volume 59 (1994), are available on the Internet from GPO Access <www.gpoaccess.gov/fr/>, with each new issue added the morning of its publication. Regulations can be found by browsing the daily tables of contents or through keyword searches. Retrieval can be limited to particular sections of the *Register* (e.g. final rules and regulations, proposed rules, notices) or specific dates, and results are ranked for relevance. Documents can then be viewed either as simple

iii

Contents

Federal Register

Vol. 63, No. 209

Thursday, October 29, 1998

Agency for Health Care Policy and Research
NOTICES
Meetings:
Health Care Policy, Research, and Evaluation National Advisory Council, 58052–58053

Agricultural Marketing Service
RULES
Dairy promotion and research order, 57893–57895
Peanuts, domestically produced, 57891–57893

Agriculture Department
See Agricultural Marketing Service
See Animal and Plant Health Inspection Service
See Commodity Credit Corporation
See Farm Service Agency
See Food and Nutrition Service
See Forest Service
See Grain Inspection, Packers and Stockyards Administration
See Natural Resources Conservation Service
See Rural Business-Cooperative Service
See Rural Housing Service
See Rural Utilities Service

Alcohol, Tobacco and Firearms Bureau
RULES
Alcohol, tobacco, and other excise taxes:
Brady Handgun Violence Prevention Act; implementation—
National instant criminal background check system; firearms dealer, importer, and manufacturer requirements, 58271–58281

Animal and Plant Health Inspection Service
PROPOSED RULES
Plant-related quarantine, foreign:
Orchids in growing media; importation, 57932

Army Department
NOTICES
Environmental statements; availability, etc.:
Base realignment and closure—
Charles E. Kelly Support Facility, PA, 58017–58018

Arts and Humanities, National Foundation
See National Foundation on the Arts and the Humanities

Children and Families Administration
RULES
Personal Responsibility and Work Opportunity Reconciliation Act of 1996; implementation:
Welfare-to-work grants; data collection and reporting requirements for States and Indian Tribes, 57919–57929

Civil Rights Commission
NOTICES
Meetings; State advisory committees:
West Virginia, 58008

Coast Guard
PROPOSED RULES
Drawbridge operations:
New Jersey, 57963–57964
Waterfront facilities:
Handling of Class 1 (explosive) materials or other dangerous cargoes; improved safety procedures, 57964–57970
NOTICES
Meetings:
Navigation Safety Advisory Council, 58087–58088

Commerce Department
See Economic Development Administration
See International Trade Administration
See National Oceanic and Atmospheric Administration

Committee for the Implementation of Textile Agreements
NOTICES
Cotton, wool, and man-made textiles:
Sri Lanka, 58015
Thailand, 58015–58016

Commodity Credit Corporation
NOTICES
Peanut butter; change in procurement process, 58005

Commodity Futures Trading Commission
NOTICES
Contract market proposals:
Chicago Mercantile Exchange—
Russian rubles, 58016–58017

Defense Department
See Army Department

Economic Development Administration
NOTICES
Trade adjustment assistance eligibility determination petitions:
Samax Precision, Inc., et al., 58008–58009

Employment and Training Administration
NOTICES
Grants and cooperative agreements; availability, etc.:
Welfare-to-work program, 58067–58068

Energy Department
See Federal Energy Regulatory Commission
See Western Area Power Administration

Environmental Protection Agency
RULES
Air pollution control; new motor vehicles and engines:
Nonroad diesel engines; emission standards
Correction, 58101
Hazardous waste program authorizations:
Michigan, 57912–57918
PROPOSED RULES
Hazardous waste program authorizations:
Michigan, 57996

Exhibit 69. Contents, FEDERAL REGISTER, Oct, 29, 1998, at iii.

text or as PDF files replicating the printed page. The *Federal Register* is also available online through several commercial services. Westlaw and LexisNexis coverage begins in the summer of 1980, and CQ.com coverage in 1990. These services also generally have new issues online the day they are published.

VIII   Federal Register / Vol. 63. No. 209 / Thursday, October 29, 1998 / Contents

CFR PARTS AFFECTED IN THIS ISSUE

A cumulative list of the parts affected this month can be found in the
Reader Aids section at the end of this issue.

7 CFR
997.......................57891
998.......................57891
1150.....................57893
Proposed Rules:
319.......................57935
1940.....................57935
1944.....................57935

12 CFR
Proposed Rules:
Ch. VII...................57938
701 (2 documents).........57942,
                57943
711.......................57945
714.......................57950

14 CFR
39 (2 documents).........57895,
                58102
55.......................57899
Proposed Rules:
39 (2 documents).........57953,
                57955

21 CFR
Proposed Rules:
1020.....................57957

23 CFR
1240.....................57904

27 CFR
178.......................58272
179.......................58272

29 CFR
4044.....................58101

30 CFR
Proposed Rules:
57.......................58104

33 CFR
Proposed Rules:
117.......................57963
126.......................57964

39 CFR
6.......................57911

Proposed Rules:
111.......................57970

40 CFR
86.......................58101
271.......................57912
Proposed Rules:
271.......................57996

42 CFR
1001.....................57918

45 CFR
276.......................57919

49 CFR
171.......................57929

50 CFR
648.......................57931
Proposed Rules:
679.......................57996

Exhibit 70.   CFR Parts Affected in This Issue, FEDERAL
REGISTER, Oct, 29, 1998, at viii.

For *Federal Register* issues before Westlaw and LexisNexis
coverage begins, the leading source is HeinOnline
<www.heinonline.org>, which is building a PDF collection
of older issues back to the *Register*'s inception in 1936.
HeinOnline currently provides issues from 1968 to 1980,

fully searchable, as well as the annual indexes for this period. In addition, most large law libraries have complete runs of the *Federal Register* back to 1936 in microform.

The *Register* has permanent reference value because it contains material which never appears in the *Code of Federal Regulations*. Not only does it provide the agency preambles explaining regulatory actions, but it may also be the only available source for temporary changes occurring between annual *CFR* revisions. Researching the histories of administrative agency regulations would be impossible without access to the *Federal Register*.

The Federal Register: What It Is and How to Use It (rev. ed. 1992) provides a detailed explanation of the publication of federal regulations. This pamphlet's discussion of print research methods is still useful, although it lacks coverage of GPO Access and other electronic resources.

B. CODE OF FEDERAL REGULATIONS

As with statutes, chronological publication of regulations is insufficient for most legal research. It is necessary to know what regulations are in force, regardless of when they were first promulgated. In 1937 the Federal Register Act was amended to create the *Code of Federal Regulations*, the first edition of which was published in 1938. The set now consists of more than two hundred paperback volumes, revised on an annual basis.

The regulations in the *CFR* are collected from the *Federal Register* and arranged in a subject scheme of fifty titles, similar to that of the *U.S. Code*. Titles are divided into chapters, each containing the regulations of a specific agency. The back of every *CFR* volume contains an alphabetical list of federal agencies indicating the title and chapter (or chapters) of each agency's regulations.

CFR chapters are divided into parts, each of which covers a particular topic. Finally parts are divided into sections, the basic unit of the *CFR*. Exhibits 71 and 72 show sample pages of the *CFR* from Title 27 (Alcohol, Tobacco Products, and Firearms), Chapter I (Bureau of Alcohol, Tobacco and Firearms), Part 178 (Commerce in Firearms and Ammunition). A citation to the *CFR* provides the title, part, section, and year of publication. The section in Exhibit 72 on armor piercing ammunition intended for sporting purposes, for example, is cited as 27 C.F.R. § 178.148 (2002). (Note that the section is a distinct number, not a decimal; § 178.148 is not between § 178.14 and § 178.15.)

At the beginning of each *CFR* part is an *authority note* showing the statutory authority under which the regulations have been issued. After this note, or at the end of each section, is a *source note* providing the citation and date of the *Federal Register* in which the regulation was last published in full. This reference is the key to finding background information and comments explaining the regulations. In Exhibit 71, note that the regulations are issued under the authority of several sections of the *United States Code*, including the firearms laws shown in Chapter 5 at 18 U.S.C. §§ 921-930; and that the source for Part 178 generally is 33 Fed. Reg. 18,555, Dec. 14, 1968. In Exhibit 72, § 178.150 is followed by a note that its source is the Oct. 29, 1998 *Federal Register* issue shown in Exhibit 68.

CFR volumes are updated and replaced on a rotating cycle throughout the year. The revisions of the various titles are issued on a quarterly basis: Titles 1-16 with regulations in force as of January 1; titles 17-27 as of April 1; titles 28-41 as of July 1; and titles 42-50 as of October 1. The volumes usually come out three or four months after these cutoff dates. The *CFR* pages shown in Exhibits 71 and 72 are current as of April 1, 2002, and appear in a volume published in August 2002.

§ 178.1

Subpart G—Importation

178.111 General.
178.112 Importation by a licensed importer.
178.113 Importation by other licensees.
178.113a Importation of firearm barrels by nonlicensees.
178.114 Importation by members of the U.S. Armed Forces.
178.115 Exempt importation.
178.116 Conditional importation.
178.117 Function outside a customs territory.
178.118 Importation of certain firearms classified as curios and relics.
178.119 Importation of ammunition feeding devices.
178.120 Firearms or ammunition imported by or for a nonimmigrant alien.

Subpart H—Records

178.121 General.
178.122 Records maintained by importers.
178.123 Records maintained by manufacturers.
178.124 Firearms transaction record.
178.124a Firearms transaction record in lieu of record of receipt and disposition.
178.125 Record of receipt and disposition.
178.125a Personal firearms collection.
178.126 Furnishing transaction information.
178.126a Reporting multiple sales or other disposition of pistols and revolvers.
178.127 Discontinuance of business.
178.128 False statement or representation.
178.129 Record retention.
178.131 Firearms transactions not subject to a NICS check.
178.132 Dispositions of semiautomatic assault weapons and large capacity ammunition feeding devices to law enforcement officers for official use and to employees or contractors of nuclear facilities.
178.133 Dispositions of transactions in semiautomatic assault weapons.
178.134 Sale of firearms to law enforcement officers.

Subpart I—Exemptions, Seizures, and Forfeitures

178.141 General.
178.142 Effect of pardons and expunctions of convictions.
178.143 Relief from disabilities incurred by indictment.
178.144 Relief from disabilities under the Act.
178.145 Research organizations.
178.146 Deliveries by mail to certain persons.
178.147 Return of firearm.
178.148 Armor piercing ammunition intended for sporting or industrial purposes.

178.149 Armor piercing ammunition manufactured or imported for the purpose of testing or experimentation.
178.150 Alternative to NICS in certain geographical locations.
178.151 Semiautomatic rifles or shotguns for testing or experimentation.
178.152 Seizure and forfeiture.
178.153 Semiautomatic assault weapons and large capacity ammunition feeding devices manufactured or imported for the purposes of testing or experimentation.

Subpart J [Reserved]

Subpart K—Exportation

178.171 Exportation.

AUTHORITY: 5 U.S.C. 552(a); 18 U.S.C. 847, 921–930; 44 U.S.C. 3504(h).

SOURCE: 33 FR 18555, Dec. 14, 1968, unless otherwise noted. Redesignated at 40 FR 16835, Apr. 15, 1975.

EDITORIAL NOTE: Nomenclature changes to part 178 appear by T.D. ATF–411, 64 FR 17291, Apr. 9, 1999.

Subpart A—Introduction

§ 178.1 Scope of regulations.

(a) *General.* The regulations contained in this part relate to commerce in firearms and ammunition and are promulgated to implement Title I, State Firearms Control Assistance (18 U.S.C. Chapter 44), of the Gun Control Act of 1968 (82 Stat. 1213) as amended by Pub. L. 99–308 (100 Stat. 449), Pub. L. 99–360 (100 Stat. 766), Pub. L. 99–408 (100 Stat. 920), Pub. L. 103–159 (107 Stat. 1536), Pub. L. 103–322 (108 Stat. 1796), Pub. L. 104–208 (110 Stat. 3009), and Pub. L. 105–277 (112 Stat. 2681).

(b) *Procedural and substantive requirements.* This part contains the procedural and substantive requirements relative to:

(1) The interstate or foreign commerce in firearms and ammunition;

(2) The licensing of manufacturers and importers of firearms and ammunition, collectors of firearms, and dealers in firearms;

(3) The conduct of business or activity by licensees;

(4) The importation of firearms and ammunition;

(5) The records and reports required of licensees;

(6) Relief from disabilities under this part;

Exhibit 71.   27 C.F.R. § 178.1 (2002).

§178.148 Armor piercing ammunition intended for sporting or industrial purposes.

The Director may exempt certain armor piercing ammunition from the requirements of this part. A person who desires to obtain an exemption under this section for any such ammunition which is primarily intended for sporting purposes or intended for industrial purposes, including charges used in oil and gas well perforating devices, shall submit a written request to the Director. Each request shall be executed under the penalties of perjury and contain a complete and accurate description of the ammunition, the name and address of the manufacturer or importer, the purpose of and use for which it is designed and intended, and any photographs, diagrams, or drawings as may be necessary to enable the Director to make a determination. The Director may require that a sample of the ammunition be submitted for examination and evaluation.

[T.D. ATF-270, 53 FR 10507, Mar. 31, 1988]

§178.149 Armor piercing ammunition manufactured or imported for the purpose of testing or experimentation.

The provisions of §§178.37 and 178.99(d) with respect to the manufacture or importation of armor piercing ammunition and the sale or delivery of armor piercing ammunition by manufacturers and importers shall not apply to the manufacture, importation, sale or delivery of armor piercing ammunition for the purpose of testing or experimentation as authorized by the Director. A person desiring such authorization to receive armor piercing ammunition shall submit a letter application, in duplicate, to the Director. Such application shall contain the name and addresses of the persons directing or controlling, directly or indirectly, the policies and management of the applicant, the nature or purpose of the testing or experimentation, a description of the armor piercing ammunition to be received, and the identity of the manufacturer or importer from whom such ammunition is to be received. The approved application shall be submitted to the manufacturer or importer who shall retain a copy as

part of the records required by subpart H of this part.

[T.D. ATF-270, 53 FR 10507, Mar. 31, 1988]

§178.150 Alternative to NICS in certain geographical locations.

(a) The provisions of §178.102(d)(3) shall be applicable when the Director has certified that compliance with the provisions of §178.102(a)(1) is impracticable because:

(1) The ratio of the number of law enforcement officers of the State in which the transfer is to occur to the number of square miles of land area of the State does not exceed 0.0025;

(2) The business premises of the licensee at which the transfer is to occur are extremely remote in relation to the chief law enforcement officer; and

(3) There is an absence of telecommunications facilities in the geographical area in which the business premises are located.

(b) A licensee who desires to obtain a certification under this section shall submit a written request to the Director. Each request shall be executed under the penalties of perjury and contain information sufficient for the Director to make such certification. Such information shall include statistical data, official reports, or other statements of government agencies pertaining to the ratio of law enforcement officers to the number of square miles of land area of a State and statements of government agencies and private utility companies regarding the absence of telecommunications facilities in the geographical area in which the licensee's business premises are located.

(c) For purposes of this section and §178.129(c), the "chief law enforcement officer" means the chief of police, the sheriff, or an equivalent officer or the designee of any such individual.

(Approved by the Office of Management and Budget under control number 1512–0544)

[T.D. ATF-415, 63 FR 58280, Oct. 29, 1998]

§178.151 Semiautomatic rifles or shotguns for testing or experimentation.

(a) The provisions of §178.39 shall not apply to the assembly of semiautomatic rifles or shotguns for the purpose

1197

Exhibit 72.   27 C.F.R. §§ 178.148-.150 (2002).

The *CFR* includes an annually revised *Index and Finding Aids* volume providing access by agency name and subject. This index is far less thorough than most statutory indexes, and it lists parts rather than specific sections. It has no entries under "Handguns" or "Machine guns" and only cross-references under "Firearms" and "Weapons," but Exhibit 73 shows a page under "Arms and munitions" with a reference to 27 C.F.R. Part 178. Much more detailed subject access is provided in CIS's annual multivolume *Index to the Code of Federal Regulations*.

The *CFR* is available in several electronic formats. The most widely available is the Internet version at GPO Access <www.gpoaccess.gov/cfr/>. This version replicates the paper edition and is updated on the same basis. Sections can be retrieved by citation, and either individual titles or the entire *CFR* can be searched. As with the *Federal Register*, documents can be viewed and printed as PDF files. Exhibit 74 shows the list of sections in 27 C.F.R. Part 178 as shown in GPO Access, with icons for viewing these as plain text or PDF.

GPO Access also offers a prototype version of a much more current *Electronic Code of Federal Regulations*, or *e-CFR* <www.access.gpo.gov/ecfr/>. This edition incorporates new amendments from the *Federal Register* within days. While this is presently a demonstration project and not an official legal edition of the *CFR*, it represents a significant improvement in the government's timely delivery of regulatory information.

Regularly updated versions of the *CFR* are also available online from Westlaw and LexisNexis. Like the *e-CFR*, these files are updated on an ongoing basis to reflect changes published in the *Federal Register*. Both incorporate amendments two or three weeks after they appear in the *Register*. Westlaw's *CFR* is even more up to date, because it includes

Exhibit 73. CFR Index, CFR INDEX AND FINDING AIDS 75 (2002).

Title 27--Alcohol, Tobacco Products and Firearms

CHAPTER I--BUREAU OF ALCOHOL, TOBACCO AND
FIREARMS, DEPARTMENT OF THE TREASURY

PART 178--COMMERCE IN FIREARMS AND AMMUNITION

178.1   Scope of regulations.
178.2   Relation to other provisions of law.
178.11   Meaning of terms.
178.21   Forms prescribed.
178.22   Alternate methods or procedures; emergency variations from requirements.
178.23   Right of entry and examination.
178.24   Compilation of State laws and published ordinances.
178.25   Disclosure of information.
178.25a Responses to requests for information.
178.26   Curio and relic determination.
178.27   Destructive device determination.
178.28   Transportation of destructive devices and certain firearms.
178.29   Out-of-State acquisition of firearms by nonlicensees.
178.29a Acquisition of firearms by nonresidents.
178.30   Out-of-State disposition of firearms by nonlicensees.
178.31   Delivery by common or contract carrier.
178.32   Prohibited shipment, transportation, possession, or receipt of firearms and ammunition by certain persons.
178.33   Stolen firearms and ammunition.
178.33a Theft of firearms.

Exhibit 74.   List of C.F.R. sections, GPO Access
<www.gpoaccess.gov>.

"This document has been amended" notices linking affected sections to *Federal Register* documents the same day they are published.

To determine what regulations were in force at a particular time, older editions of the *CFR* are sometimes needed. GPO Access retains older editions as new versions are added, with coverage starting with selected 1996 volumes. Westlaw and LexisNexis provide more extensive historical access, with older editions of the *CFR* back to the early 1980s. Most large law libraries have microform collections of older *CFR*s back to the original 1938 edition.

c. FINDING AND UPDATING REGULATIONS

Regulatory research involves several distinct steps. The first is finding regulations, by using an index or through leads in an annotated code or other source. Once a relevant regulation is found, it must be updated to determine whether any changes have occurred since the most recent *CFR* version. Finally, it is necessary to check for any judicial decisions applying the regulation or adjudicating its validity.

Federal regulations can be found through keyword searches in GPO Access or a commercial database, or by agency or subject in the *Federal Register* and *CFR* indexes. Numerous other sources provide references to relevant regulations. Agency websites usually include links to regulations, on their own sites or at GPO Access, and citations are often provided in cases, texts, and articles.

Cross-references from statutes to regulations can be found following code sections in both annotated editions of the United States Code. 18 U.S.C.S. §§ 921 and 925, for example, both provide references to 27 C.F.R. Part 178, while 18 U.S.C.A. § 921 includes a reference to a specific section in Part 178. In addition, the *Index and Finding Aids*

volume of the *Code of Federal Regulations* contains a "Parallel Table of Authorities and Rules," allowing a researcher with a statute or presidential document to find regulations enacted under its authority. 18 U.S.C. §§ 921-928 is listed in this title, with a reference to 27 C.F.R. Part 178.

Administrative regulations on selected subjects, such as taxation, labor relations, and securities, also appear in commercially published looseleaf services in those fields. Most services are thoroughly indexed and frequently supplemented, usually on a weekly or biweekly basis. For that reason and also because regulations are integrated with related primary sources and interpretive material, researchers often turn to looseleaf services, if available, for convenient access to current administrative regulations.

Finding relevant regulations, however, is only the first step of research. Next it is necessary to verify that those regulations remain current. For users of the *e-CFR*, commercial databases, or looseleaf services, this is a relatively simple task because the versions of *CFR* available through these sources are regularly updated. For others, it is necessary to update a regulation from the most recent annual *CFR* edition. The key tool for this purpose is a monthly pamphlet accompanying the *CFR* entitled *LSA: List of CFR Sections Affected* (also available through GPO Access <www.gpoaccess.gov/lsa/>).

LSA lists *Federal Register* pages of any new rules affecting *CFR* sections, and indicates the nature of the change with notes such as "amended," "removed," or "revised." *LSA* also includes references to proposed rules, listed separately by part rather than by specific section. Exhibit 75 shows a page from the October 1998 *LSA*, indicating that several sections of 27 C.F.R. had been revised, removed, or added since the April 1, 1998 revision. This pamphlet includes

several references to the final rule shown in Exhibit 68, providing the specific pages where the revised sections appeared in the *Federal Register*.

Each *LSA* cumulates all changes since the latest *CFR* edition, so it is usually not necessary to examine more than the most recent monthly issue. (The exception is if the latest *CFR* volume is more than a year old.) *LSA* brings a search for current regulations up to date within a month or so. The most recent changes not yet covered in *LSA* can then be found by using the cumulative List of CFR Parts Affected in the latest *Federal Register* issue, as well as in the last issue of any month not yet covered by *LSA*. This updating process is somewhat cumbersome but reasonably straightforward.

Because regulations change so frequently, it is not uncommon to hit a dead end when trying to track down a *CFR* reference from a case or article. The cited regulations may have been repealed or moved to another *CFR* location. Tables to help trace what has happened to regulations are published in the back of each *CFR* volume, indicating all sections that have been repealed, transferred, or otherwise changed since 2001. Earlier changes from 1949 to 2000 are listed in a separate series of *List of CFR Sections Affected* volumes for the entire *CFR*. HeinOnline's *Federal Register* collection includes *LSA* issues for the period it covers, currently 1968-1980.

Whether used online or in print, the *CFR* contains no annotations of court decisions like those in *United States Code Annotated* or *United States Code Service*. Yet a court may invalidate a regulation or provide an important interpretation of key provisions. As they do with cases and statutes, Shepard's Citations and KeyCite provide references to court decisions citing regulations.

70   LSA—LIST OF CFR SECTIONS AFFECTED

CHANGES APRIL 1, 1998 THROUGH OCTOBER 30, 1998

TITLE 27—ALCOHOL, TOBACCO PRODUCTS AND FIREARMS

Chapter I—Bureau of Alcohol, Tobacco and Firearms, Department of the Treasury (Parts 1—299)

4.21 (e)(5) amended...........................44782
4.24 (b)(1) amended..........................44783
9.93 (c)(11), (17) and (18) revised;
  (c)(19) added...............................16904
9.156 Added.....................................33853
9.159 Added.....................................16904
19.11 Amended.................................44783
24.10 Amended.................................44783
24.76 Heading revised.......................44783
24.257 (a)(3)(iii) revised; (a)(3)(iv)
  and (c) added; OMB number
 44783
24.278 (d) revised.............................44783
53.11 Amended.................................52603
53.61 (b) revised..............................52603
55.11 Amended.................................45001
55.30 (a), (b) and (d) introductory
  text amended; (c)(4) and
  (d)(3) revised...............................45002
55.41 (b)(2) revised..........................45002
55.42 Revised...................................45002
55.43 Revised...................................45002
55.45 (b) amended............................45002
55.46 (b) revised..............................45002
55.51 Revised...................................45002
55.63 (d) heading revised.................45002
55.102 Revised.................................45002
55.103 (a)(1) and (2) revised............45003
55.105 (d) revised............................45003
55.122 (b)(4), (5), (c)(4) and (5)
  amended.......................................45003
55.123 (b)(3), (4), (c)(4), (5) and
  (d)(3) amended.............................45003
55.124 (b)(4), (5), (c)(4) and (5)
  amended.......................................45003
55.125 (a) amended; (b) removed;
  (c) through (f) redesignated
  as (b) through (e); heading,
  (a) introductory text, new
  (b)(4) and (5) revised....................45003
55.127 Amended...............................45003
55.141 (a)(7) revised........................45003
55.163 Amended...............................45003
55.201 (d) revised; (f) added; OMB
  number...45003
55.202 (b) revised.............................45003
55.206 (b) amended..........................45003
55.218 Amended...............................45003

55.221 Heading, (a) and (d) revised...45004
55.222 Amended...............................45004
55.223 Table amended......................45004
55.224 Table amended......................45004
178.1 (a) revised...............................35522
178.11 Amended...................35522, 58278
178.32 (a)(7), (8)(iii)(B), (d)(7),
  (8)(ii)(B) amended; (a)(9) and
  (d)(9) added.................................35522
178.50 (b) and (c) amended; (d)
  added...35523
178.73 Revised.................................58278
178.74 Revised.................................58278
178.78 Revised.................................58278
178.96 (b) amended; (c) revised.......58278
178.97 Revised.................................58278
178.99 (c)(7) and (8)(ii)(B) amend-
  ed; (c)(9) added............................35523
178.100 (a) existing text des-
  ignated as (a)(1); (a)(2) added;
  (c) revised....................................35523
178.102 Revised...............................58279
178.103 Added.................................37742
178.124 (c) revised; (d), (e) and (f)
  amended; OMB number.........58279
178.124a (e) introductory text
  amended.......................................58280
178.125a Amended..........................58280
178.129 (b) revised; (c), (d) and (e)
  redesignated as (d), (e) and
  (f); new (c) added..........................58280
178.130 (a)(1) amended...................35523
  Removed..58280
178.131 Revised...............................58280
178.134 Added.................................35523
178.141 Introductory text revised
 35523
178.144 (c)(6) and (7) amended;
  (c)(8) added..................................35523
178.150 Revised...............................58280
179.86 Amended..............................58281
194 Authority citation revised.........44783
194.239—194.241 Undesignated
  center heading and sections
  removed...44784
250.11 Amended...............................44784
251.11 Amended...............................44784

Proposed Rules:

4........................27017, 44819, 49883
9..................................45427, 48658
19...44819
24...44819
178...35551
194...44819

Exhibit 75.   LSA: LIST OF CFR SECIONS AFFECTED, Oct. 1998, at 70.

In print, *Shepard's Code of Federal Regulations Citations* provides references to court decisions and selected law review articles which have cited or discussed *CFR* sections. Shepard's indicates the year of the *CFR* edition cited (with an asterisk), or the year of the citing reference if no *CFR* edition is specified (with a delta). As in Shepard's statutory citators, alphabetical symbols indicate significant impact of court decisions on cited regulations. Exhibit 76 shows a page from this citator, listing decisions under regulations in Titles 27 and 28 of the *CFR*. Note that various sections in Part 178 have been cited in court decisions, while the 1998 version of 27 C.F.R. § 179.111(a) was found valid (Va) in a D.C. Circuit case at 135 F.3d 829.

The electronic versions of Shepard's mirror its printed counterpart, with the same scope of coverage and similar descriptive notes. KeyCite simply provides a list of case citations, without annotations, but its coverage of citations in law reviews and other secondary sources is considerably more extensive than Shepard's.

To summarize research approaches using printed sources, a complete search for a current regulation involves these steps:

(a) Find a relevant *Code of Federal Regulations* section, by consulting the subject index in the *Index and Finding Aids* volume or through references in an annotated code or other source.

(b) Locate the regulation in the current annual edition of its *CFR* title, noting the date of the latest revision.

(c) Check the latest monthly pamphlet of *LSA* to determine if changes in the section have occurred since the last revision.

TITLE 27	CODE OF FEDERAL REGULATIONS		
§ 178.124(c)(1) Cir. 11 71F3d824△1995 889FS1535△1995	Cir. 9 2001USApp LX2341△2001 Cir. 10 173FS2d1292△1999 Cir. 11 57FS2d1363△1999	**§ 179.105(e)** Cir. 11 123F3d1393△1997 **§ 179.111** Cir. DC 135F3d827△1998 923FS245△1996	Cir. 2 −181F3d331△1999 181F3d338△1999 61LCP(1)165*1998 61LCP(2)178*1997 **§ 0.20(a)** 513US91*1993
§ 178.124(f) Cir. 9 109F3d1470△1997 Cir. 11 71F3d824△1995	**§§ 179.31 to 179.52** Cir. 11 123F3d1385△1997	**§ 179.111(a)** Cir. DC Va 135F3d829△1998 923FS243△1996	130LR444*1993 115SC539*1993 82CaL274*1992 **§ 0.20(b)** Cir. 1
§ 178.125 Cir. 9 28F3d942△1994	**§ 179.62** Cir. 9 2001USDist LX1758△2001	**§ 179.111(b)** CIT 880FS862△1995	218F3d22△2000 Cir. 7 130F3d1277△1997 Cir. 9
§ 178.125(e) Cir. 6 113F3d606△1997	**§ 179.65** Cir. 2 167F3d124△1999	**§ 179.141** Cir. 7 1100F3d1383△1996	179F3d788△1999 194F3d1000△1999 **§ 0.22(a)(1)** 75NYL960*1999
§ 178.126 Cir. 4 94F3d696△2000	**§ 179.66** Cir. 7 870FS261△1995	**§ 191.27(c)** Cir. Fed. 194F3d1359△1999	**§ 0.22(b)** Cir. DC
§ 178.142 Cir. 2 220F3d58△2000	**§ 179.82** Cir. 2 61F3d146△1995	**§ 194.226** Cir. 1 158F3d57△1998 999FS151△1998	875FS869△1995 Cir. Fed. 69F3d1139△1995
§ 178.143 Cir. 4 915FS785△1996	**§ 179.84** Cir. 2 61F3d146△1995 167F3d122△1999	**§§ 200.55 to 200.118** Cir. 8 26F3d86△1993	**§ 0.25** Cir. 2 209F3d220△2000 Cir. 9
§ 178.144 Cir. 1 159F3d665△1998 Cir. 2 220F3d56△2000 Cir. 3 68F3d705△1995 850FS308△1994 48FS2d484△1999 Cir. 4 50FS2d513△1999 Cir. 5 74F3d63△1996 89FS2d630△2000 Cir. 6 230F3d217△2000 Cir. 10 122F3d135△1997 936FS1569△1996 Md 671A2d517△1995	Cir. 7 870FS261△1995 **§ 179.85** Cir. 2 2001USDist LX1758△2001 Cir. 4 61F3d146△1995 167F3d122△1999 852FS138△1994 Cir. 5 77F3d870△1996 Cir. 7 870FS262△1995 **§ 179.86** Cir. 2 61F3d146△1995 167F3d122△1999	**§ 240.1051** ClCt 40FedCl 110*1985 **§ 240.1051a** ClCt 40FedCl 110*1985 **§ 275.11** Cir. DC 94FS2d63△2000 **§ 275.83** Cir. DC 94FS2d63△2000 **§ 290.185** Cir. 9 100FS2d1204△2000	856FS1377△1994 61LCP(2)160*1997 **§ 0.25(a)** ClCt 34FedCl 439*1995 86VaL697*1999 **§ 0.35** Cir. 11 957FS1245△1997 **§ 0.36** Cir. 11 957FS1245△1997 **§ 0.37** 62LCP(1)167*1973
§ 178.144(b) Cir. 3 228F3d325△2000 Cir. 9 120F3d1089△1997	**§ 179.89** Cir. 2 61F3d146△1995 **§ 179.90** Cir. 2 61F3d146△1995	**TITLE 28** **§ 0.1** Cir. 3 95FS2d241△2000	**§ 0.39a** Cir. DC 910FS55△1995 Cir. 6 22FS2d676△1998
§ 178.144(d) Cir. 3 228F3d325△2000 Cir. 7 884FS1198△1995 Cir. 9 120F3d1089△1997	**§ 179.103** Cir. DC 111F3d163△1997 Cir. 10 49F3d640△1995	**§ 0.5(a)** Cir. 11 910FS618*1994 **§ 0.13** Cir. 9	**§ 0.39b** Cir. 2 2FS2d403△1998 **§ 0.45** 83MnL1209*1997
Part 179 Cir. 7 149F3d707△1998	**§ 179.105** Cir. 7 91F3d885△1996	35F3d1339△1994 **§ 0.15(a)** Cir. 8	**§ 0.55(f)** Cir. 11 120F3d1423*1995
§ 179.11 304US508*1991 Cir. DC 102F3d594△1996 111F3d163△1997 Cir. 6 2001USApp LX1190△2001	**§ 179.105(a)** Cir. 2 157F3d96*1988 Cir. 11 123F3d1393△1997 **§ 179.105(b)** Cir. 11 123F3d1393△1997	89FS2d1041△2000 **§ 0.15(f)** 98CR1024*1997 **§ 0.20** 513US93*1993 130LR445*1993 115SC540*1993	**§ 0.57** Cir. 3 117F3d740*1996 120F3d459△1997 Cir. 4 86F3d1317△1996 104F3d632*1996 139F3d1000*1997 915FS791△1996

314

(d) Use the cumulative List of CFR Parts Affected in the most recent issue of the *Federal Register*. This list updates the *LSA* pamphlet by indicating any changes made within the current month. Depending on the dates covered in the most recent *LSA*, it may be necessary to check the last *Federal Register* in the preceding month as well.

(e) Locate changes found in steps (c) and (d) by consulting the daily issues of the *Federal Register*.

(f) Check the regulation in *Shepard's Code of Federal Regulations Citations* to obtain citations to decisions interpreting it.

GPO Access users must follow most of these steps, as the official online *CFR* and *Federal Register* mirror their print counterparts. The new *e-CFR* simplifies much of this process, and several of these steps can be avoided by using commercial electronic resources or a looseleaf service, if available. Whatever approach is used, it is necessary to verify that the regulation is current and to find court decisions that may affect its scope or validity.

d. Supplementary Sources of Information

Regulations published in the *Federal Register* and *CFR* are the most authoritative sources of agency law, but they are frequently supplemented with manuals, policy statements, and a variety of other documents that do not appear in either publication. These subsidiary documents are generally for guidance only, without the same force of law as regulations, but they can still provide greater detail or clarify ambiguous regulations with illustrative examples.

Most supplementary materials such as these are not widely published in printed form, but many are available through agency websites. The amount of documentation

online is increasing as agencies come into greater compliance with the Electronic Freedom of Information Act Amendments of 1996 (E-FOIA), which mandated that they make policy statements, manuals, and frequently requested information available to the public electronically.

Website organization and ease of access vary considerably from agency to agency. The ATF website's Electronic Reading Room, for example, includes briefs, orders, and comments received on proposed rulemaking. Elsewhere on its site are rulings, bulletins, forms, statistics, and a variety of other publications. Exhibit 77 shows the ATF page providing links to sources for regulations, including the *e-CFR* and notices of proposed rulemaking. An important first step in working with a particular agency is to survey its website and learn what information it makes available.

§7-4. ADMINISTRATIVE DECISIONS AND RULINGS

Besides promulgating regulations of general application, administrative agencies also have quasi-judicial functions in which they hold hearings and issue decisions involving specific parties. The procedures and precedential value of these decisions vary among agencies, as do means of publication and ease of access.

About fifteen regulatory commissions and other agencies publish their decisions in a form similar to official reports of court decisions. These reports are usually published first in advance sheets or slip decisions and eventually cumulated into bound volumes. Depending on the agency, the volumes may include indexes, digests and tables. Because most of these aids are noncumulative and apply only to the decisions in one volume, however, they are of limited research value.

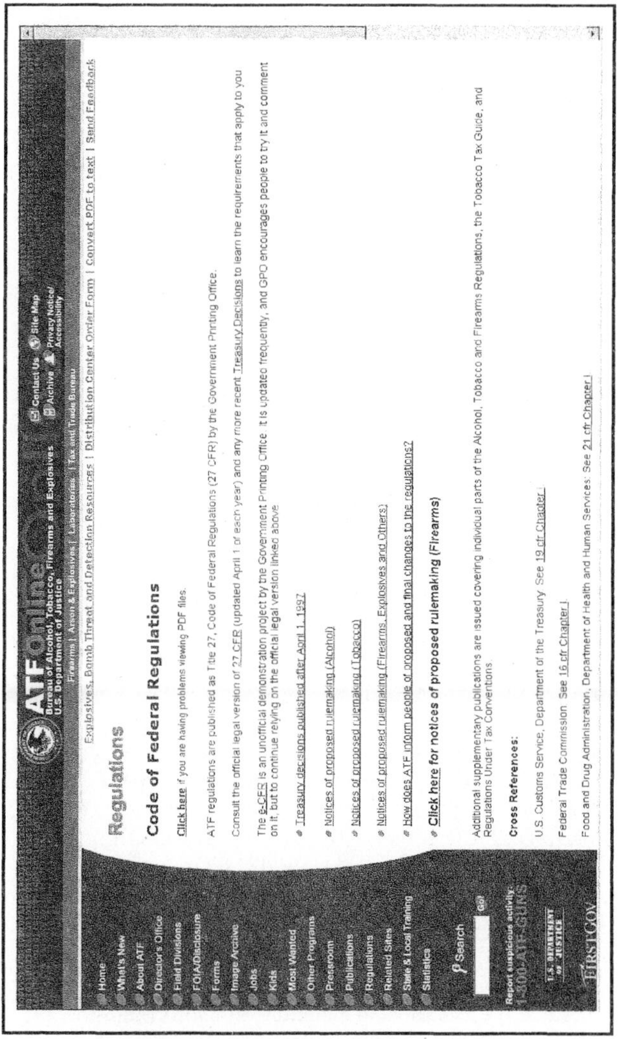

Exhibit 77. Regulations, Bureau of Alcohol, Tobacco, Firearms and Explosives <www.atf.gov>.

Commercial looseleaf services and topical reporters are major sources of administrative decisions in their subject fields. Various Securities and Exchange Commission decisions and releases, for example, are printed in CCH's *Federal Securities Law Reporter*, and National Labor Relations Board decisions appear in BNA's *Labor Relations Reporter*. These services, which will be discussed in Chapter 9, usually appear more promptly and contain better indexing than the official reports, and they combine these administrative decisions with other related sources such as statutes, regulations, and court decisions.

A growing number of administrative decisions are available on the Internet, but there is little consistency in how agencies provide access to these documents. One of the most extensive and current listings of websites with decisions is available from the University of Virginia Law Library <www.law.virginia.edu/admindec>. LexisNexis and Westlaw include decisions of several dozen agencies in topical databases. Online coverage includes many administrative decisions that are not published in either official reports or looseleaf services, and generally extends much earlier than official websites.

Attorney General opinions deserve special mention. As the federal government's law firm, the Department of Justice provides legal advice to the President and to other departments. Traditionally these opinions were signed by the U.S. Attorney General and published in a series entitled *Opinions of the Attorneys General of the United States*; this function is now delegated to the Office of Legal Counsel (OLC), which has published *Opinions of the Office of Legal Counsel* since 1977. Opinions of both the Attorney General and OLC are also available online through the database systems, and OLC opinions are on the Internet <www.usdoj.gov/olc/opinions.htm> from 1992 to date.

A researcher specializing in a particular area must be familiar with decisions of relevant agencies. For nonspecialists, the easiest way to learn of administrative decisions is through the annotations in *United States Code Service*. *USCS* includes notes of decisions from more than fifty commissions and board. The firearms sections at 18 U.S.C.S. §§ 921 and 925, for example, are accompanied by notes of ATF rulings as well as court cases. *United States Code Annotated* does not include references to administrative decisions but does cite opinions of the Attorney General and Office of Legal Counsel.

Shepard's covers the decisions of federal agencies in several of its topical citators and in *Shepard's United States Administrative Citations*, which lists citations to the decisions and orders of more than a dozen major administrative tribunals. These citators provide references to agency decisions cited in court cases and law review articles as well as in later agency decisions. Decisions of the Federal Energy Regulatory Commission, for example, can be Shepardized in *Shepard's Federal Energy Law Citations*. Other topical citators containing coverage of administrative decisions include *Federal Occupational Safety and Health Citations*, *Federal Tax Citator*, *Labor Law Citations*, and *Immigration and Naturalization Citations*. These citators are available both in print and through LexisNexis. On Westlaw, KeyCite provides citing references for selected administrative decisions.

§7-5. Presidential Lawmaking

In addition to supervising the executive departments and agencies, the President of the United States also has several lawmaking roles. He sends legislative proposals to Congress, approves or vetoes bills which have passed both houses, and issues a range of legally binding documents in his own right.

A number of reference sources provide background information on the presidency. These address numerous political and historical aspects of the institution and the men who have been president. The most extensive is Leonard W. Levy & Louis Fisher, eds., *Encyclopedia of the American Presidency* (4 vols., 1994), with more than 1,000 articles, including discussion of presidential powers, relations with Congress, and key legislation. Michael Nelson, ed., *Guide to the Presidency* (2 vols., 3d. ed. 2002) is another major reference work, arranged topically rather than alphabetically. Part III, "Powers of the Presidency," discusses the president's various roles and actions; and Part VI, "Chief Executive and the Federal Government," analyzes relations with Congress, the Supreme Court, and the federal bureaucracy.

The major legal documents issued by the president are *executive orders* and *proclamations*. While the distinction between the two can be blurred, executive orders usually involve an exercise of presidential authority related to government business while proclamations are announcements of policy or of matters requiring public notice. Proclamations are often ceremonial or commemorative, but some have important legal effects such as implementing trade agreements or declaring treaties to be in force.

Executive orders and proclamations are issued in separate numbered series and published in the *Federal Register*. A variety of other presidential documents are also printed in the *Federal Register* but not included in either of these series. Presidential determinations, issued pursuant to particular statutory mandates, are also issued in a numbered series, and unnumbered documents include various memoranda and notices. Many, but not all, of these documents deal with foreign affairs. Exhibit 78 shows a presidential proclamation about young people and gun violence, as printed in the *Federal Register*.

63763

Federal Register

Vol. 65, No. 207

Wednesday, October 25, 2000

Presidential Documents

Title 3—

The President

Proclamation 7368 of October 20, 2000

National Day of Concern About Young People and Gun Violence, 2000

By the President of the United States of America

A Proclamation

Every day in America, approximately 10 children are shot and killed. Children 15 years old and younger are murdered with firearms at a higher rate in this country than in 25 other industrialized countries combined. These tragedies are an urgent reminder that we must not waver in our national commitment to reduce gun violence and to make our society safer for our children.

We are beginning to see some progress in our efforts. Since 1992, the national violent crime rate has dropped by more than 20 percent; violent crimes committed with firearms have dropped by 35 percent; and the firearms homicide rate has fallen over 40 percent. We have achieved much of this progress by embracing a collaborative, community-based approach to gun crime prevention and reduction.

Gun violence issues differ in each community, and no single program or approach works everywhere. In response to a directive I issued last year to help reduce gun violence and save lives, United States Attorneys and the Bureau of Alcohol, Tobacco, and Firearms Field Division Directors for each of our Nation's 94 Federal judicial districts have developed locally coordinated gun violence reduction strategies. Working closely with local law enforcement, elected officials, and other community leaders, they are tailoring plans to local needs and developing strategies to prevent gun crimes from occurring and crack down on gun criminals.

A major goal of our strategy to reduce gun violence and ensure the safety of our children is to keep guns out of the wrong hands. We passed the Brady Act to help accomplish this goal by requiring that every person who purchases a firearm from a federally licensed dealer submit to a background check. To date, Brady background checks have prevented more than 536,000 felons and other prohibited individuals from acquiring firearms. We also succeeded in banning assault weapons, making "zero tolerance" for guns in schools the law of the land, and passing legislation that prohibits juveniles from possessing handguns. However, our determination to reduce gun violence must not stop there. I have called on the Congress to build on these measures by passing legislation that closes the gun show loophole, mandates child safety locks with every handgun sold, and bans large-capacity ammunition clips.

We have also provided funding for more than 100,000 community police officers; for the Safe Schools/Healthy Students initiative to reduce youth violence through collaborative, community-based efforts; and for the 21st Century Community Learning Centers—safe places where students can go after school to participate in constructive activities and avoid the dangers of guns, gangs, and drugs.

But none of these efforts can succeed without the commitment of America's youth. It takes courage to resist negative peer pressure; it takes character to settle disputes without resorting to violence; and it takes a sense of personal responsibility to tell an adult when others fail to live up to these

---

Exhibit 78.   Proclamation No. 7368, 65 Fed. Reg. 63,763 (2000).

Presidential documents in the *Federal Register* are covered in its monthly and annual indexes. Older documents can be found in the *CIS Index to Presidential Executive Orders and Proclamations* (covering 1787-1983) and *CIS Federal Register Index* (1984-98).

Presidential documents from the *Federal Register* are reprinted in a number of locations, including *USCS Advance*, *USCCAN* (in which coverage is generally limited to executive orders and proclamations), and an annual compilation of title 3 of the *Code of Federal Regulations*. This compilation includes a subject index and several tables which list the year's presidential documents, indicate older executive orders and proclamations affected during the year, and list statutes cited as authority for presidential documents. The *CFR* is the preferred *Bluebook* and *ALWD Citation Manual* source for presidential documents it contains.

Proclamations, but not executive orders, are printed in the annual *Statutes at Large* volumes. Major orders and proclamations are also reprinted after relevant statutory provisions in the *U.S. Code*, *USCA*, and *USCS*; tables in each version of the code list presidential documents by number and indicate where they can be found. Reorganization plans, an older form of presidential action no longer in use, were published in the *Federal Register*, *CFR*, and *Statutes at Large*, and many are reprinted in all three versions of the code (in appendices to title 5 in the *U.S. Code* and *USCA*, and following 5 U.S.C.S. § 903).

Several other presidential documents do not appear in the *Federal Register*. Messages to Congress, explaining proposed legislation or vetoes, reporting on the state of the nation, or serving other functions, are published in the *Congressional Record* and as *House Documents*. Signing statements are often issued when approving legislation, and may provide the president's interpretation of a statute. Although their value as legislative history is disputed, since 1986 these statements have been reprinted with the committee reports in *USCCAN*.

Most of these various presidential documents, including those published in the *Federal Register*, appear in the official *Weekly Compilation of Presidential Documents* along with speeches, transcripts of news conferences, and other material. The *Weekly Compilation* is accompanied by quarterly, semiannual and annual indexes.

Public Papers of the Presidents is an official publication cumulating the contents of the *Weekly Compilation of Presidential Documents*. Series of annual volumes have been published for Herbert Hoover and for all presidents after Franklin D. Roosevelt, and cumulated indexes for the papers of each administration have also been published. Papers of Roosevelt and most of the earlier presidents are generally available in commercially published editions.

On the Internet, the *Weekly Compilation of Presidential Documents* since 1993 is available from GPO Access <www.gpoaccess.gov/wcomp/>, as are *Public Papers* volumes beginning with 1992 <www.gpoaccess.gov/pubpaps/>. Westlaw has executive orders since 1936 and other presidential documents since 1984, and LexisNexis has all presidential documents since 1981.

Coverage of proclamations, executive orders, and reorganization plans is included in *Shepard's Code of Federal Regulations Citations*, in print or on LexisNexis. The presidential documents are listed by number, with references to citing court decisions and law review articles. KeyCite does not cover citations to presidential documents.

§7-6. State Administrative Law

Like the federal government, the states have experienced a dramatic increase in the number and activity of their administrative agencies. In most states, however, publication of agency rules and decisions is far less systematic than it is on the federal level.

Nearly all states publish official manuals paralleling the *United States Government Manual* and providing quick access to information about government agencies and officials. These directories vary in depth and quality; some describe state agency functions and publications, while others are simply government phone directories. They're listed and described in the "General State Government Information" sections of the annual *State Legislative Sourcebook*, along with information about Internet sites, general reference works, statistical abstracts, and other sources.

In addition, a number of directories provide multistate access to officials' names and numbers. CQ Press's *State Information Directory* is arranged by state and provides contact information for dozens of agencies in each state, including websites, fax numbers and names and e-mail addresses of directors and commissioners. More extensive listings are provided by *Carroll's State Directory* (three times a year) and Leadership Directories' *State Yellow Book* (quarterly); like the federal directories described on page 226-228, these are also available as subscription-based Internet services. The Council of State Governments' annual *CSG State Directory III: Administrative Officials* lists officials by function, rather than by state, and may be the most convenient source for someone needing to contact similar officials in several states. CSG's biennial *Book of the States* supplements these directories with more than 170 tables presenting a broad range of information on government operations in each of the fifty states.

Of several websites providing links to state government information on the Internet, one of the most thorough is State and Local Government on the Net <www.statelocalgov.net>. It provides extensive listings of general state websites, executive departments and agencies, regional commissions, counties, and cities.

A. REGULATIONS

Almost every state issues a subject compilation of its administrative regulations, and most supplement these with weekly, biweekly or monthly registers. While the states generally follow the paradigm established by the *CFR* and *Federal Register*, few state administrative codes and registers are as organized and accessible as their federal counterparts. Some simply compile a variety of material submitted by individual agencies, and some have incomplete coverage. Indexing is often inadequate, sometimes even nonexistent.

The *Bluebook* identifies administrative codes and registers in its list of basic primary sources for each state. More detailed information is available in William H. Manz's biennial *Guide to State Legislative and Administrative Materials*, which lists print, online, and CD-ROM sources for each state's administrative code. The annual two-volume *CAL INFO Guide to the Administrative Regulations of the States & Territories* provides the tables of contents for each administrative code, making it easier to track down relevant regulations without access to the actual code volumes.

Although fewer states provide Internet access to regulations than to statutes, a majority of administrative codes and a growing number of registers are now available. One of the easiest ways to find available sites is through the National Association of Secretaries of State's list of administrative code and register links <www.nass.org/acr/internet.html>. Westlaw and LexisNexis do not have comprehensive coverage, but each has administrative codes from about forty states.

Some of the administrative codes and registers include executive orders or similar legal pronouncements from governors. Several governors include the text of executive

orders on their websites, which can be accessed through state government homepages or by links from the National Governors Association <www.nga.org>.

B. DECISIONS AND RULINGS

Decisions of some state agencies, especially those dealing with banking, insurance, public utilities, taxation, and workers' compensation, may be published in official form in chronological series. A few looseleaf services and topical reporters also include state administrative decisions, and a growing number of state agency decisions are included in the online databases and on agency websites. Manz's *Guide to State Legislative and Administrative Materials* lists electronic sources for agency rulings, decisions, and order.

The opinions of state attorneys general, issued in response to questions from government officials, can have considerable significance in legal research. Although attorney general opinions are advisory in nature and do not have binding authority, they are given considerable weight by the courts in interpreting statutes and regulations. Most states publish attorney general opinions in slip opinions and bound volumes. Each volume generally has an index, but these rarely cumulate. Many attorney generals have recent opinions on their websites, which can be found through links at the National Association of Attorneys General website <www.naag.org>. State attorney general opinions are also available online in LexisNexis and Westlaw, with coverage in most states beginning in 1977. Some attorney general opinions are included in the annotations in state codes, but this coverage is quite incomplete.

§7-7. LOCAL LAW

Cities and counties are administrative units of the states, with lawmaking powers determined by state constitution or by legislative delegation of authority. They create a vari-

ety of legal documents which can be important in legal research. *Charters* are the basic laws creating the structure of local government, and *ordinances* are local enactments governing specific issues. In addition many localities have administrative agencies which issue rules or decisions.

Local law sources can often be quite difficult to locate. Most large cities and counties publish collections of their charters and ordinances, with some attempt at regular supplementation, and in recent years there has been a significant improvement in the publication of municipal ordinances of smaller jurisdictions. For many cities and counties, however, there is still no accessible, up-to-date compilation, and individual ordinances must be obtained from the local clerk's office.

A growing number of county and city codes are available on the Internet. The Seattle Public Library <www.spl.org/selectedsites/municode.html> and the Municipal Code Corporation <www.municode.com> have the most extensive sets of links to collections of local ordinances. Each provides access to several hundred codes, and together they cover cities from almost every state.

Ordinance Law Annotations (15 vols., 1969-date), a subject digest of judicial decisions involving local ordinances, provides brief abstracts of decisions under alphabetically arranged subject headings divided into specific subtopics. A case table accompanying this set lists court decisions on local law issues, by state and locality.

Because much local law information is not available in print or on the Internet, direct contact by telephone or e-mail may be essential. Directories with information on local governments throughout the country include *Carroll's County Directory*, *Carroll's Municipal Directory*, and *Municipal Yellow Book*. These directories are all updated

twice a year and are available to subscribers through their publishers' websites (<www.govsearch.com> and <www.leadershipdirectories.com>). State and Local Government on the Net <www.statelocalgov.net> has convenient links to county and city homepages, which usually provide background and contact information, as well as the text of ordinances and regulations in some instances.

§7-8. CONCLUSION

From its early days as one of the most bibliographically inaccessible areas of law, federal administrative law has developed a highly sophisticated research framework. This development stemmed from several publishing innovations, including the looseleaf services, the improvements brought by the Federal Register System, and access through the online databases and the Internet. State administrative law resources are generally less widely available, but access is gradually improving.

It is important to remember that administrative agency actions are governed by statutes and reviewable by the courts. Administrative procedure acts and judicial decisions have established many important procedural safeguards of agency rulemaking and adjudication. Administrative law research is rarely limited to the specialized publications discussed in this chapter.

CHAPTER 8
COURT RULES AND PRACTICE

■　　■　　■　　■　　■　　■　　■　　■　　■　　■

§8-1. Introduction

This chapter covers a number of resources dealing with court proceedings. Some, such as the rules governing trial procedures and lawyer conduct, have the force of law. Others, such as briefs and docket sheets, contain background information on decided cases or pending lawsuits. A third group, the directories and formbooks, provide practical assistance for lawyers or anyone else who needs to contact courts, draft documents, or transact other legal business.

These are materials with which any litigator should be familiar, but their value extends to other legal research situations as well. All lawyers, of course, must follow rules of professional conduct, and sources such as briefs and model jury instructions can provide important information about substantive legal issues.

§8-2. Court Rules

Rules for the regulation of court proceedings have the force of law, but they generally cannot supersede or conflict with statutes. Most jurisdictions have sets of rules governing trial and appellate procedure, as well as rules for specialized tribunals or for particular actions such as admiralty or habeas corpus. These rules are created in a variety of ways. Some are enacted by statute, but most are promulgated by the courts themselves or by conferences of judges.

A. Federal Rules

Under the Rules Enabling Act, 28 U.S.C. § 2072, federal courts have the power to adopt rules governing their procedures as long as they do not "abridge, enlarge, or modify any substantive right." Individual federal courts have had rules since the beginning of the judicial system, but the modern era of rules of national scope began with the adoption of the Federal Rules of Civil Procedure in 1938. These

rules were prepared by a judicial advisory committee and approved by the Supreme Court, as were subsequent sets of rules governing criminal procedure (1946) and appellate procedure (1968). The Federal Rules of Evidence were originally drafted by judges, but they were enacted by Congress in 1975 due to their potential impact on substantive rights.

Federal court rules are available in a variety of pamphlets and reference publications, as well as online from both Westlaw and LexisNexis. All of the major sets of rules are printed in the *U.S. Code*, accompanied by the advisory committee's explanatory comments after each section. *USCA* and *USCS* also include annotations of cases in which the rules have been applied or construed, as well as other research aids such as references to treatises, law review articles, and legal encyclopedias. These annotations can be quite extensive; the Federal Rules of Civil Procedure, for example, occupy ten volumes in *USCA*.

A somewhat less overwhelming source of annotated federal rules is the *United States Supreme Court Digest, Lawyers' Edition*. Volumes 17 to 22 of this set include the text of all of the major rules series, as well as rules for specialized federal courts, accompanied by advisory committee comments, scholarly commentaries, and annotations of Supreme Court cases. While this is a less comprehensive source, it may be a useful starting point for someone seeking significant judicial interpretations of the rules.

The most scholarly sources for analysis of the federal rules are the treatises on federal procedure, Wright & Miller's *Federal Practice and Procedure* (64 vols., 1969-date) and *Moore's Federal Practice* (33 vols., 3d ed. 1997-date). These works are organized rule-by-rule, providing the texts and official comments accompanied by historical background and extensive discussion of cases. Both ana-

lyze the civil, criminal, and appellate rules; *Federal Practice and Procedure* also covers the Federal Rules of Evidence. These treatises are among the secondary sources most often cited by the federal courts. *Federal Practice and Procedure* is available on Westlaw, and *Moore's Federal Practice* is on LexisNexis.

Individual courts have rules to supplement the national sets of rules. Supreme Court rules are also included in the *U.S. Code, USCA*, and *USCS*; the annotated codes also have rules of the individual Courts of Appeals. Lower federal court rules from the entire country are published in a seven-volume looseleaf set, *Federal Local Court Rules* (3d ed. 2001-date), and local U.S. District Court rules are usually available in court rules pamphlets published for individual states. Exhibit 79 shows Local Rule 83.5 of the United States District Court for the Northern District of Georgia, on the prohibition of weapons in the courthouse. This is from an annual publication called *Georgia Rules of Court Annotated*, containing both state and federal rules. Note the case note and research references at the top of the page; some, but not all, state pamphlets include such annotations. Local court rules are also available on Westlaw and LexisNexis, although they may be found in databases with state court rules rather than with other federal materials.

Most court rules are available at free Internet sites, but usually without the helpful commentary and annotations found in the treatises or annotated codes. The House Committee on the Judiciary provides PDF copies of the Federal Rules of Appellate Procedure, Civil Procedure, Criminal Procedure, and Evidence <www.house.gov/judiciary/documents.htm>. The Administrative Office of the U.S. Courts website has a section on rules <www.uscourts.gov/rules/>, which includes links to these documents as well as information on proposed amendments and numerous other documents.

825   CIVIL LOCAL RULES   LR 83.7

JUDICIAL DECISIONS

Cited in Hegwood v. United States, 659 F.2d 1078 (5th Cir. 1981).

RESEARCH REFERENCES

Am. Jur. 2d. — 7 Am. Jur. 2d, Attorneys at Law, §§ 41, 119, 75 Am. Jur. 2d, Trial, §§ 196-204. **C.J.S.** — 7 C.J.S., Attorneys at Law, § 52, 16

C.J.S., Constitutional Law, § 213, 23 C.J.S., Criminal Law, § 1134-1141.

LR 83.5. WEAPONS NOT ALLOWED IN COURTHOUSE.

A. *Weapons Not Allowed.* — Firearms or other weapons shall not be worn or brought into the courtrooms of this court or into the buildings in which they are located, except with the specific authorization of the court. The court has excused, to the extent hereinafter stated, the following persons or groups from this rule:

(1) The United States Marshal and his duly assigned deputy marshals, court security officers and other security personnel engaged by the U.S. Marshal.

(2) Federal Protective Service officers on assignment or upon call.

(3) Any federal law enforcement officer presenting a prisoner before a magistrate judge for initial appearance.

(4) Other federal law enforcement officials whose permanent assignment offices are located within the security parameters of the various courthouses; provided, however, that this exclusion does not allow these officials to carry weapons to the facilities of the United States District Court, including, but not limited to judges' chambers, offices and courtrooms.

(5) United States Probation Officers are authorized to wear or carry firearms to and from their offices within the district's courthouses; but probation officers are not authorized to wear firearms inside their offices. Firearms brought to the probation office will be secured in a locked container.

(6) Other officers as designated by court order.

B. *Checking of Weapons.* — Firearms and weapons must be checked with security personnel. If no security officer is on duty or locatable, weapons should be checked with either the clerk or the United States Marshal.

C. *Sanction for Noncompliance.* — Any person or law enforcement officer who fails to comply with this rule shall be guilty of contempt and shall be subject to the appropriate disciplinary action.

Editor's notes. — This rule was amended effective June 1, 2002.

LR 83.6. CERTIFICATE OF INTERESTED PERSONS. (205).

Refer to LR 3.3.

LR 83.7. BANKRUPTCY JUDGES.

A. *Delegated Jurisdiction. (265-1(a))* — Bankruptcy judges are judicial officers of this court serving in the unit of this court known as the United States Bankruptcy Court for the Northern District of Georgia. Each bankruptcy judge shall perform the duties set forth and may exercise the authority conferred in Section 104 of the Bankruptcy Amendments and Federal Judgeship Act of 1984, Pub. L. No. 98-353, 98 Stat. 333 (July 11, 1984) (to be codified as 28 U.S.C. §§ 151-58) with respect to any action, suit, or proceeding and may preside alone and hold a regular or special session of the bankruptcy court, except as otherwise provided by law or by rule or order of this court.

B. *Jury Trials in Bankruptcy Court.* — In accordance with 28 U.S.C. § 157(e), the bankruptcy judges of this court are specially designated to conduct jury trials where the right to a jury trial applies. This jurisdiction is subject to the express consent of all parties pursuant to the procedure set forth in BLR 9015-2, NDGa.

Exhibit 79.   N.D. Ga. R. 83.5, *reprinted in* GEORGIA RULES OF COURT ANNOTATED 825 (LexisNexis 2003).

Local rules are increasingly available on individual courts' websites, and some sites also include answers to frequently asked questions about filing requirements and trial procedures. Links to local pages are also available through the U.S. Courts website <www.uscourts.gov/links.html>, and Law Library Resources Xchange provides a "Court Rules, Forms and Dockets" page <www.llrx.com/courtrules/> listing more than 1,400 federal and state sources for these materials.

Lawyers can learn of changes in procedural rules by monitoring the advance sheets for any of West's federal court reports. *Federal Rules Decisions* provides the most extensive documentation of these changes, reprinting numerous amendments and committee reports in its advance sheets and bound volumes. Amendments to the major federal rules are also printed by Congress as House Documents and are reproduced in the official *U.S. Reports*, *Lawyers' Edition*, *USCCAN* and *USCS Advance*.

KeyCite and Shepard's coverage of federal court rules is similar to that for statutes. KeyCite begins with the annotations from *USCA*, but expands this to include additional cases and secondary sources. Shepard's can be accessed online or in *Shepard's Federal Statute Citations*, and covers local rules as well as the major national sets. The printed version provides references to rule amendments and to citations in federal court decisions and *ALR* annotations. Citing law review articles are listed separately in *Shepard's Federal Law Citations in Selected Law Reviews*, and state cases citing federal rules are listed in the individual Shepard's state citators. These various references are combined in one listing in the online version of Shepard's.

The Federal Sentencing Guidelines are not court rules, but they occupy a similar position in the hierarchy of legal authorities. They were originally promulgated in 1987 by

the U.S. Sentencing Commission, which was created by Congress as an independent agency within the judicial branch. The sentencing guidelines are not published with the official *U.S. Code*, but the commission publishes an annual *Guidelines Manual* in print and on the Internet <www.ussc.gov/guidelin.htm>. Both *USCA* and *USCS* include annotated versions accompanied by notes of court decisions and other references. Like the court rules, the sentencing guidelines are also available from the online databases and are covered by KeyCite and in *Shepard's Federal Statute Citations*.

Federal Practice and Procedure and *Moore's Federal Practice* do not cover sentencing guidelines, but shorter works such as Roger W. Haines, Jr., et al., *Federal Sentencing Guidelines Handbook: Text and Analysis*, and Thomas W. Hutchison et al., *Federal Sentencing Law and Practice*, provide similar treatment, combining the text of the guidelines with commentary and analysis of cases. Both of these are published in annual paperback editions.

B. STATE RULES

There are significant differences in rules and procedures from state to state, although these distinctions are gradually decreasing as more and more states have adopted provisions modeled on the federal rules. A few states, however, have court procedures governed by statutory codes rather than rules.

The rules governing proceedings in state courts are usually included in the annotated state codes, accompanied by notes of relevant cases, as well as on Westlaw and LexisNexis. Most states also have annual paperback volumes providing convenient access to rules and procedural statutes. Many of these publications are unannotated, but some contain useful case notes and comments by scholars or drafting committees.

More elaborate practice sets in many jurisdictions include all of these features, often accompanied by procedural forms. Like *Federal Practice and Procedure* or *Moore's Federal Practice*, the best of these provide a scholarly commentary on the rules and extensive analysis of relevant case law.

Most state court websites provide convenient access to rules and other procedural information. Two leading sources for finding both trial and appellate state courts on the Web are the National Center for State Courts <www.ncsconline.org> and Courts.net <www.courts.net/>.

Coverage of state court rules in KeyCite and Shepard's is similar to that for statutes, with references to citations in federal and state court decisions, law reviews, and other sources. The text of new amendments to rules can be found in the advance sheets to most court reports, including the West regional reporters.

§8-3. LEGAL ETHICS

Courts are responsible in most jurisdictions for governing the professional activities of lawyers, although in some states that power is delegated to bar associations or oversight boards. The materials in this area are found in a distinct body of literature consisting of codified rules of conduct, advisory ethics opinions, and disciplinary decisions.

While rules vary from state to state, most jurisdictions have adopted some form of the Model Rules of Professional Conduct, promulgated by the American Bar Association in 1983. A few states still have rules based on the ABA's older Model Code of Professional Responsibility (1969). The rules in force are usually included in the volumes containing a state's court rules, although in some states they are incorporated into longer sets of rules and

can be a bit difficult to find. Only a few of these sources are annotated with notes of decisions under the rules. The *National Reporter on Legal Ethics and Professional Responsibility* (1982-date), a looseleaf service, reprints the unannotated rules for every state as well as the District of Columbia and Puerto Rico. The American Legal Ethics Library at Cornell's Legal Information Institute <www.law.cornell.edu/ethics/> provides links to websites providing the rules in force in each state.

Annotated Model Rules of Professional Conduct (4th ed. 1999) provides the text of the ABA rules with comments, legal background, and notes of decisions from various jurisdictions. Although it contains the ABA's rules rather than those adopted in any specific state, this is a useful source for comparative analysis and commentary. The annotated rules are available online from Westlaw; LexisNexis has the Model Rules with official comments but no background notes and annotations. The ABA Center for Professional Responsibility <www.abanet.org/cpr/> has the text of both Code and Rules, as well as a directory of lawyer disciplinary agencies and a wide range of other information and documents on legal ethics.

The leading modern treatise on legal ethics is Geoffrey C. Hazard, Jr. & W. William Hodes, *The Law of Lawyering* (2 vols., 3d ed. 2000-date). The American Law Institute's *Restatement of the Law: The Law Governing Lawyers*, adopted in 1998 and published in 2000, has already been cited in several hundred cases.

Ethics opinions, generally prepared in response to inquiries from attorneys, are issued by the American Bar Association and by state and local bar associations. ABA opinions are available in Westlaw and LexisNexis, as are opinions from selected state and local bars. Ethics opinions

can also be found in the *National Reporter on Legal Ethics and Professional Responsibility*, and most state bars have some sort of publication either summarizing their opinions or reprinting them in full text.

State bars and disciplinary agencies generally have websites providing information about procedures for filing complaints and resolving problems with lawyers, and some of these include the text of rules and ethics opinions. The ABA and Cornell sites mentioned above both include links to these sites.

The *ABA/BNA Lawyers' Manual on Professional Conduct* (1984-date) is often a good place to begin research. This looseleaf service includes an extensive commentary with background and practical tips, as well as news of developments and abstracts of new decisions.

Judges are governed by a separate set of rules, in almost every jurisdiction based either on the ABA's 1990 Model Code of Judicial Conduct or its 1972 predecessor. These rules are generally published in state court rules pamphlets with the rules of professional conduct. The Model Code is available on the ABA Center for Professional Responsibility's website, and Cornell's American Legal Ethics Library provides links to state versions. The leading analysis of judicial conduct issues is Jeffrey M. Shaman et al., *Judicial Conduct and Ethics* (3d ed. 2000).

§8-4. RECORDS AND BRIEFS

The materials submitted by the parties in cases before appellate courts are often available for research use. Briefs are the written arguments and authorities cited by the attorneys for the parties on appeal. Records are documents from the lower court proceeding, usually reprinted as an appendix to the briefs and often including pleadings,

motions, trial transcripts, and judgments. These documents enable researchers to study in detail the arguments and facts of significant decisions.

Records and briefs are usually filed by the docket number of the case in which they were submitted. There is rarely subject or keyword access to these documents, except in the case of Supreme Court briefs available online. A researcher interested in a particular decision, however, can pursue these additional sources of background information.

United States Supreme Court records and briefs go to several libraries around the country, while many more libraries subscribe to microform editions. Filings since 1979 are available online through LexisNexis, and Westlaw coverage begins in 1990. Many cases have a substantial number of briefs, often with filings by *amici curiae* supporting one side or the other. For example, in *Muscarello v. United States*, the case shown in Exhibits 9 through 11 in Chapter 3, a brief supporting the petitioner was filed by the National Association of Criminal Defense Lawyers and Families against Mandatory Minimums Foundation.

Transcripts of Supreme Court oral arguments are also available in various formats. Microform collections begin with the 1953 term, and online coverage starts in 1979 (LexisNexis) or 1990 (Westlaw). The Supreme Court website <www.supremecourtus.gov> provides PDF transcripts of arguments beginning with the 2000 term, and Northwestern University's Oyez Project <www.oyez.com> has RealAudio files with recorded arguments in more than eight hundred cases dating back to 1956.

Briefs and argument transcripts for hundreds of major cases, dating back to the 19th century, are reprinted in *Landmark Briefs and Arguments of the Supreme Court of the*

United States: Constitutional Law (1975-date). Cases through the 1973 term are covered in the first eighty volumes of this set, and about a dozen new cases are added each year.

Records and briefs of the U.S. Courts of Appeals and state appellate courts have a more limited distribution, although a few courts are now providing Internet access to these documents. In most instances they can often be found in local law libraries within the circuit or state, and for a few courts they are also available in microform. In many cases, however, it may be necessary to contact the court or a judicial records center to obtain copies. Michael Whiteman & Peter Scott Campbell, *A Union List of Appellate Court Records and Briefs: Federal and State* (1999) provides contact information for court clerks and libraries, with notes indicating the scope and format of each library's holdings and its lending policy.

Some briefs are available on the Internet even if not on court websites. Parties or *amici curiae* may post their briefs in major cases, and high profile documents are often available from sites such as FindLaw <www.findlaw.com> or CNN <www.cnn.com>. The "Legal Documents" link on the U.S. Department of Justice homepage <www.usdoj.gov> provides access to briefs and other materials prepared by the department's divisions and offices, including Solicitor General briefs in the Supreme Court since 1997.

§8-5. OTHER CASE INFORMATION

Appellate cases generally follow a standard path and produce documentation consisting of the parties' briefs, the lower court record, and the court's opinion. Material from trial court litigation, on the other hand, may be harder to identify and find. Some cases result in judges' opinions,

such as a decision granting a motion for summary judgment, but many matters are decided without a written opinion. Cases may be decided by jury verdict, summary disposition, or settlement agreement. Some cases produce dozens of memoranda or briefs submitted to support or oppose motions before, during and after trial, while others go to trial without any written submissions on points of law. It may be possible to examine a trial transcript; this can be an essential but voluminous source of information. News reports may provide some discussion of trial court proceedings, but to obtain a transcript or other documents it is usually necessary to contact the court directly.

Documents submitted in a case are kept on file at the courthouse or a records center. Many courts are developing electronic systems in which pleadings and other documents are submitted and retained online, but paper filings remain common. The first step in obtaining documents is usually to determine the case number, or docket number. This may be mentioned in a published decision or secondary source, but it might be necessary to ask the court clerk to consult an index by party name. Each case has a docket sheet listing the proceedings and documents filed, providing the information needed to obtain documents. Some courts accept requests electronically or by telephone, while for others it is necessary to apply by mail or in person.

In many instances, access to docket sheet information for pending cases is available electronically. The federal courts' fee-based information system is known as PACER (Public Access to Court Electronic Records) <pacer.psc.uscourts.gov>. Each court maintains its own records and database, but the system has a central registration process and a national index of cases by party name. The main PACER site has links to the individual courts' sites.

Commercial subscription services, such as CourtLink <www.courtlink.com> and CourtEXPRESS <www.courtexpress.com>, also monitor activity in federal district courts, and some state courts, and provide more convenient access to this information for a higher fee. CourtLink is a division of LexisNexis, and Westlaw is developing its own WestDocket system for case information. These resources are not available, however, under most academic subscriptions.

While docket information for some state courts is available online, for others it may be more difficult to obtain. Most states have electronic docket systems, but means of access vary. The Center for Democracy & Technology, a Washington-based interest group, has prepared an extensive state-by-state guide <www.cdt.org/publications/020821courtrecords.shtml> indicating the information available and providing links to court sites in each jurisdiction.

Access methods for both federal and state courts are explained in *The Sourcebook to Public Record Information: The Comprehensive Guide to County, State, & Federal Public Records Sources* (4th ed. 2002). This book also explains how to obtain other public records, such as property and licensing information. Much of this data is available through subscription based commercial services, including Westlaw and LexisNexis, although access through academic subscriptions may be limited.

§8-6. DIRECTORIES OF COURTS AND JUDGES

Court directories serve a number of purposes. They provide contact information for clerks' offices, and some include judges' biographical data. This can be useful information for litigants appearing before a particular judge or panel; in law schools, the heaviest use of court directories is by students applying for clerkships after graduation.

Most court websites also provide names and contact information, and sometimes biographies; these are accessible through portals such as the "Court Links" section of the federal judiciary homepage <www.uscourts.gov/links.html>.

Federal courts and judges are covered in a number of directories. *Judicial Staff Directory* and *Judicial Yellow Book* (both semiannual) include basic biographical information for judges, as well as extensive listings of court personnel such as clerks and staff attorneys. Like other volumes in the Staff Directories and Yellow Books series, these are available electronically as well as in print. A two-volume looseleaf publication, *Almanac of the Federal Judiciary*, is the most thorough source for biographical information, including noteworthy rulings, media coverage, and lawyers' evaluations of the judge's ability and temperament. *WANT's Federal-State Court Directory* (annual) provides a concise listing of contact information for federal judges, clerks, and other court personnel.

Several directories cover both federal and state courts. *BNA's Directory of State and Federal Courts, Judges, and Clerks* (biennial) provides addresses and telephone numbers, and includes a list of Internet sites and a personal name index. *The American Bench* (biennial) is the most comprehensive biographical source, covering almost every judge in the United States. It includes a name index indicating the jurisdictions for all judges listed. *Judicial Yellow Book* includes state appellate courts but not trial courts, and *WANT's Federal-State Court Directory* has just one page per state listing a few key officials. WANT provides more thorough coverage in its *Directory of State Court Clerks & County Courthouses* (annual) and through its subscription website <www.courts.com>. As noted in Chapter 3 on page 72, *BNA's Directory* and *WANT's Federal-State Court Directory* both include charts explaining the structure of each court's judicial system.

Sometimes information is needed about a judge involved in an older case or sitting on a particular court. If only the last name at the head of an opinion is known, the first step may be to determine a judge's full name. This can be found in tables in the front of most reporter volumes. For example, since 1882 the *Federal Reporter* has listed the sitting federal judges, with footnotes indicating any changes since the previous volume. Similar listings appear in each of West's regional reporters and in most official state reports. Biographical information on most appellate judges can be found in standard sources such as *American National Biography* (24 vols., 1999) or *Who Was Who in America* (16 vols., 1943-date). The Federal Judicial Center website <www.fjc.gov> has a database providing biographical information about all life-tenured federal judges since 1789. Entries include links to information about manuscript sources and lists of more extensive biographical sources, where available.

§8-7. FORMBOOKS AND JURY INSTRUCTIONS

In the course of legal practice, many basic transactions and court filings occur with regularity. Rather than redraft these documents each time the need arises, attorneys frequently work from sample versions of standard legal documents and instruments. Model forms are available from a variety of sources, in both printed collections and electronic products. Some sets of forms are annotated with discussion of the underlying laws, checklists of steps in completing the forms, and citations to cases in which the forms were in issue.

Several multivolume compilations of forms, with extensive indexing, notes and cross-references, are published. Some of these are comprehensive national works containing both procedural forms, such as complaints and

motions, and transactional forms, such as contracts and wills. Most, however, are limited to particular jurisdictions or particular types of forms.

Two of the major form sets are published as adjuncts to *American Jurisprudence 2d* and are linked to that encyclopedia by frequent cross-references. *American Jurisprudence Legal Forms 2d* (65 vols., 1971-date) provides forms of instruments such as contracts, leases, and wills, and *American Jurisprudence Pleading and Practice Forms* (rev ed., 80 vols., 1966-date) focuses on litigation and other practice before courts and administrative agencies. Both sets are divided into several hundred topical chapters mirroring the organization of *Am. Jur. 2d*. Exhibit 80 shows a page from *Am. Jur. Pleading and Practice Forms*, containing the beginning of a model complaint by a city or county against handgun manufacturers and distributors.

Other comprehensive sets include Jacob Rabkin & Mark H. Johnson, *Current Legal Forms, with Tax Analysis* (34 vols., 1948-date), and *West's Legal Forms* (50 vols., 2d ed. 1981-date). Unlike the *Am. Jur.* sets, these are arranged by broad practice area such as estate planning or real estate. They may be better for understanding a wider range of related issues than for finding forms on very fact-specific topics.

Three major sets devoted to forms used in federal practice are *Bender's Federal Practice Forms* (20 vols., 1951-date), *Federal Procedural Forms, Lawyers' Edition* (40 vols., 1975-date) and *West's Federal Forms* (24 vols., 1952-date). Each of these has a different structure. *Bender's Federal Practice Forms* is arranged by court rule. *Federal Procedural Forms, Lawyers' Edition* is a companion to Thomson West's encyclopedic *Federal Procedure, Lawyers' Edition*, and is organized similarly, with several dozen subject chapters. *West's Federal Forms* is arranged instead by court, with

278 ■ LEGAL RESEARCH

§ 9   Complaint, petition, or declaration—By political subdivision—Against manufacturers and distributors of handguns, and their trade associations— Dangerous instrumentalities; handguns—Products liability; unreasonably dangerous and negligent design; inadequate warning; unjust enrichment; nuisance abatement; negligence

[Title of Court]

The _____ *[City of _____, or County of _____, (State of _____)]*, by the _____ *[City Council or Board of Supervisors]* of the _____ *[county or city]*, consisting of _____ *[list members]*,
         Plaintiff,

v.

_____,
         Defendant.

No. _____
[Designate name of document]

COMPLAINT

I. NATURE OF THE CASE

1. _____ *[Name of mayor]*, the duly elected and present Mayor of the City of _____, brings this action on behalf of _____ *[himself or herself]* and the City of _____ (sometimes here referred to as "the City"), and respectfully represents that under the Charter of the City of _____, the Mayor is charged with the duty to "define, prohibit, abate, suppress, and prevent all things detrimental to the health, morals, conduct, safety, convenience and welfare of the inhabitants of the City, and all nuisances and causes thereof."

2. Pursuant to the Charter of the City of _____ and under the Constitution of the State of _____, the Mayor and the City of _____ are responsible for the general health, safety, and welfare of its citizens. The Mayor has a duty to protect the interests of the general public.

3. As a result of the manufacturing, marketing, promotion, and sale of firearms which, under _____ *[state]* law, are defective in design and fail to incorporate firearm safety features designed to prevent harm caused by foreseeable human error making the firearms unreasonably dangerous, the City and its citizens have suffered harm and have incurred substantial expenses. In addition to the defective designs and failure to incorporate feasible safety features, defendants' guns are unreasonably dangerous as they can be and are fired by unauthorized users, including, but not limited to children, criminals, mentally unstable persons, and others who put themselves and/or others at risk when they possess a firearm.

4. This action is brought to recover damages and other equitable relief as may be obtained, for the harm unjustly, intentionally and wrongfully done and that continues to be done to the City and its citizens by defendants, who have been and continue to be unjustly enriched by such harm at the expense of the City and its residents.

115

Exhibit 80.   25 AM. JUR. PLEADING & PRACTICE FORMS
Weapons and Firearms § 9 (2001).

separate volumes covering forms needed in the Supreme Court, Courts of Appeals, District Courts, Bankruptcy Courts, and specialized national courts such as the Court of Federal Claims.

Sets of forms, varying in complexity and size, are also published for most states and for particular subject areas. Practice-oriented treatises and manuals frequently include appendices of sample forms, and in some states compilations of official forms are issued in conjunction with statutory codes.

Several sets of forms are available online and on CD-ROM, streamlining the drafting process by eliminating the need to retype each new form. LexisNexis provides access to *Bender's Federal Practice Forms*, while Westlaw has both *Am. Jur.* form sets, *Federal Procedural Forms*, and numerous state-specific collections.

A more limited range of forms is available from free Internet sites, but these may be satisfactory for simple transactions or court filings. LexisONE <www.lexisone.com> provides access to more than 6,000 forms, listed topically and by jurisdiction. FindLaw <forms.lp.findlaw.com> has links to official sites for federal circuits and states, as well as a variety of other resources including an extensive list of sites providing free and fee-based legal forms.

Most jurisdictions have published sets of *model* or *pattern jury instructions*, used by judges to explain the applicable law to jurors before they weigh the evidence and reach their decision. Model jury instructions can be useful as forms, and they also provide a concise summary of a jurisdiction's ruling law on the issues covered. Some of these sets of instructions are published by state court systems, and others by bar associations. Still others are unofficial

but highly respected, such as Kevin F. O'Malley et al., *Federal Jury Practice and Instructions* (5th ed., 9 vols. 2000-date). The subject heading used by the Library of Congress and in most online catalogs for these sets is "Instructions to juries—[Jurisdiction]."

Both Westlaw and LexisNexis include jury instructions for federal courts and for selected states. Westlaw has *Federal Jury Practice and Instructions* and publications for about sixteen states, while LexisNexis provides the competing *Modern Federal Jury Instructions* and instructions for about ten states.

§8-8. Conclusion

Court rules have taken a back seat in this text to more substantive sources such as judicial decisions and statutes, but they have the force of law and can be vital in determining procedural rights. Some rules, such as those establishing the principles of legal ethics, must be known and followed by every practicing attorney. Most of the materials discussed in this chapter may primarily be of use in litigation, but a working knowledge is essential in dealing with many other aspects of the legal system as well.

CHAPTER 9
TOPICAL RESEARCH SOURCES

■　　■　　■　　■　　■　　■　　■　　■　　■　　■

§9-1. INTRODUCTION

The resources many lawyers turn to most often are tools narrowly designed for use in specialized areas of law, rather than the general codes, digests, and databases we have discussed thus far. Topical looseleaf and electronic services make lawyers' work easier by compiling related statutes, cases, and regulations in one location, along with explanations, forms, and other research aids. These services also provide the current awareness lawyers need to respond to and anticipate new legal developments, such as recently decided cases or proposed regulations. These are essential tools for specialists, and other researchers can make profitable use of them as well.

A general research guide such as this *Nutshell* cannot examine the idiosyncracies of specialized areas of law, but guides to specific topics are also available. Many guides (sometimes called "pathfinders") have been published in legal bibliography journals such as *Law Library Journal*, *Legal Reference Services Quarterly*, and LLRX.com <www.llrx.com>; and law library websites often provide guidance on legal research issues in their home jurisdictions.

Tax research is the focus of several published works, including Gail Levin Richmond, *Federal Tax Research: Guide to Materials and Techniques* (6th ed. 2002), and Barbara H. Karlin, *Tax Research* (2d ed. 2003). Leah Chanin, ed., *Specialized Legal Research* (1987-date), covers more than a dozen topics, with chapters on admiralty, banking law, copyright, customs, environmental law, government contracts, immigration, income tax, labor and employment law, military and veterans law, patents and trademarks, securities regulation, and the Uniform Commercial Code. The volume also includes a bibliography of other specialized legal research sources.

§9-2. Looseleaf Services

The looseleaf service, one of the unique inventions of legal publishing, is a frequently supplemented tool which focuses on a specific subject area and contains primary legal sources, finding aids, and secondary material. The best looseleaf services provide coordinated access to a diverse collection of documents as well as prompt notice of developments in the courts, legislatures, and agencies.

The first looseleaf services were issued just before World War I to facilitate research in the new federal income tax law. By the 1930s other services had developed in public law areas where government regulation was the central focus of legal development, such as labor law, antitrust, and securities. Services are now also published in such varied areas as criminal law, environmental protection, health care, and products liability.

There are several ways to determine whether a service is published in a particular area of interest. References to looseleaf services may appear in law review articles and cases, and lawyers or professors specializing in a field can provide helpful advice. The annual directory *Legal Looseleafs in Print* includes regularly supplemented services, although it also lists numerous publications that are not updated very frequently. At the end of this volume, Appendix C provides a selected list of looseleaf and electronic services in fields of major interest.

There are two basic types of looseleaf services, *cumulating* and *interfiling*. In a cumulating service, new updating material is usually issued as a newsletter and filed at the end of the set. This material supplements the existing compilation and does not replace pages already filed. Cumulating services are useful in areas where it is necessary to monitor new information from a variety of sources. *The United States Law Week*, published by the Bureau of

National Affairs (BNA), is representative of the genre. Other cumulating BNA services, such as *Antitrust & Trade Regulation Report*, *Criminal Law Reporter*, *Family Law Reporter*, and *Securities Regulation & Law Report*, serve as excellent current awareness tools in their fields.

Interfiling services, on the other hand, are updated by replacing superseded material with revised pages. New pages are inserted where appropriate within the service, rather than simply added at the end. Page numbering is designed to facilitate filing of new material and can be rather convoluted; pages 603-1 to 603-24 may be inserted, for example, between pages 603 and 604. To help researchers find specific references, many interfiling services assign *paragraph numbers* to each section of material. A "paragraph" in this sense can vary in length from a few sentences to several pages. Each code section, for example, may be assigned one paragraph number, regardless of its length. It retains this number no matter how many new pages are added to the service. Paragraph numbers, not page numbers, are generally used in indexes and cross-references.

Interfiling services are well suited to areas in which it is essential to integrate recent legal developments with a large body of primary sources such as statutes or regulations. CCH (formerly Commerce Clearing House) publishes a wide variety of interfiling services, such as *Federal Securities Law Reports*, *Standard Federal Tax Reports*, and *Trade Regulation Reports*.

Some services have the attributes of both cumulating and interfiling services, with current awareness newsletters and regularly updated compilations of primary sources. Whether cumulating or interfiling, or both, a looseleaf service must be frequently supplemented if it is to be a trustworthy resource. Most of the major services are updat-

ed weekly or biweekly. Many treatises are also published in looseleaf binders, but they are not looseleaf *services* if they are only updated once or twice a year.

Looseleaf services cover a wide range of subjects, and no two services are exactly alike. The methods of access and organization vary according to the nature of the primary sources, the characteristics of the legal field, and the editorial approach. In areas where one major statute dominates the legal order, the service may be arranged by statutory sections or divisions. Most federal tax services, for example, are structured according to the sections of the Internal Revenue Code. If several statutes are significant, the service can be divided into areas by the relevant statutes. Labor law services, for example, offer separate treatment of the Labor Management Relations Act, Title VII of the Civil Rights Act of 1964, and the Fair Labor Standards Act. In other fields where common law or judicial rules predominate, or where there is a mixture of case and statutory law (such as family law, trusts and estates, or corporations), the service may be arranged by subject.

Despite differences in organization, looseleaf services share several common features. They present all relevant primary authority in one place, regardless of its original source and form of publication. This may include decisions of federal and state courts; statutes, both federal and state; and regulations, decisions, and other documents from administrative agencies in the field. It could be quite timeconsuming to check all of these various sources when beginning each research project.

Looseleaf services also summarize and analyze these primary sources. Some contain detailed analytical notes by topic, which function like case digests in explaining and providing access to the primary sources. Exhibits 81 and 82 show sample pages from CCH's *Standard Federal Tax*

Reporter, a typical interfiling service. Exhibit 81 provides part of the statute governing IRS enforcement of liquor, tobacco and firearms law, followed by excerpts from legislative history materials and the beginning of the publisher's explanation of this code section. Exhibit 82 contains the end of this explanation, followed by annotations of court decisions. Much of this material is available elsewhere in the law library, but the looseleaf service brings it together along with an explanatory overview and news of developments.

Looseleaf and topical reporters often contain cases that are not published in West's National Reporter System, such as trial court decisions and rulings of state and federal administrative agencies. These decisions and rulings are generally published first in weekly looseleaf inserts. Some services then publish permanent bound volumes of decisions, while others issue transfer binders for storage of older material.

In addition to publishing court and administrative decisions, looseleaf services also provide systems for digesting and indexing these decisions. This coverage is similar to West's key-number digest system, but a specialized system can respond more quickly to developments in a particular area and may offer a more sophisticated analysis of topics within its expertise. The West system, for example, has just one key number for sexual harassment, but BNA's digests for *Fair Employment Practices* have more than twenty distinct subdivisions, including classifications for specific issues such as union liability, constructive discharge, and same-sex harassment.

The cases in most topical reporters can be updated using KeyCite or Shepard's Citations. In print, several specialized citators include coverage of these reporters. *Shepard's Environmental Law Citations*, for example, covers decisions

INTERNAL REVENUE OFFICERS—§7608 [¶42,880]   72,001

'86 Code

(IV) the results of the operation including the results of criminal proceedings.

(5) DEFINITIONS.—For purposes of paragraph (4)—

(A) CLOSED.—The term "closed" means the date on which the later of the following occurs;

(i) all criminal proceedings (other than appeals) are concluded, or

(ii) covert activities are concluded, whichever occurs later.

(B) EMPLOYEES.—The term "employees" has the meaning given such term by section 2105 of title 5, United States Code.

(C) UNDERCOVER INVESTIGATIVE OPERATION.—The term "undercover investigative operation" means any undercover investigative operation of the Service; except that, for purposes of subparagraphs (A) and (C) of paragraph (4), such term only includes an operation which is exempt from section 3302 or 9102 of title 31, United States Code.

(6) APPLICATION OF SECTION.—The provisions of this subsection—

(A) shall apply after November 17, 1988, and before January 1, 1990, and

(B) shall apply after the date of the enactment of this paragraph and before January 1, 2006.

All amounts expended pursuant to this subsection during the period described in subparagraph (B) shall be recovered to the extent possible, and deposited in the Treasury of the United States as miscellaneous receipts, before January 1, 2006.

.01 Added by P.L. 85-859. Amended by P.L. 107-217 (conforming amendment), P.L. 106-554, P.L. 105-206, P.L. 104-316, P.L. 104-168, P.L. 100-690, P.L. 94-455 (Deadwood Act) and P.L. 87-863. For details, see the Code Volumes.

Committee Report on P.L. 106-554 (Community Renewal Tax Relief Act of 2000)

.75 Extension of authority for undercover operations—

House Bill.—No provision. However, H.R. 5542 extends the authority of the IRS to "churn" the income earned from undercover operations for an additional five years, through 2005.

Effective Date.—The provision is effective on the date of enactment.

Senate Amendment.—No provision.

Conference Agreement.—The conference agreement follows H.R. 5542.—Conference Committee Report (H.R. CONF. REP. NO. 106-1033).

.79 Committee Reports on P.L. 105-206 (IRS Restructuring and Reform Act of 1998) appear at ¶43,258.19.

Committee Report on P.L. 104-168 (Taxpayer Bill of Rights 2 (1996))

.80 Five-year extension of authority for undercover operations.—The bill reinstates the IRS's offset authority under section 7608(c) from the date of enactment until January 1, 2001. The bill amends the IRS annual reporting requirement under section 7608(c)(4)(B) to require the provision of the following data: (1) the date the operation was initiated; (2) the date offsetting was approved; (3) the total current expenditures and the amount and use of proceeds of the operation; (4) a detailed description of the undercover operation projected to generate proceeds, including the potential violation being investigated, and whether the operation is being conducted under grand jury auspices; and (5) the results of the operation to date, including the results of criminal proceedings.

Effective Date.—The provision would be effective on the date of enactment.—House Committee Report.

[¶42,885] Enforcement of Internal Revenue Laws by Enforcement Officers

• • *CCH Explanation*

.01 Synopsis - Subtitle E and other laws pertaining to liquor, tobacco and firearms.—Investigators, agents or other internal revenue officers whom the Secretary of the Treasury has charged with the duty of enforcing any of the criminal, seizure or forfeiture provisions of subtitle E or any other law of the

Exhibit 81. I.R.C. § 7608, [2003] 18 Stand. Fed. Tax Rep. (CCH) ¶ 42,880.

INTERNAL REVENUE OFFICERS—§ 7608 [¶ 42,880]   **72,003**

Enforcement of Internal Revenue Laws by Enforcement Officers

• • *CCH Explanation*

(1) the date the operation began and the date it was certified for offsetting;

(2) the total expenditures under the operation and the amount and use of the proceeds of the operation;

(3) a detailed description of the operation, including the potential violation being investigated and whether the operation is being conducted under grand jury auspices; and

(4) the results of the operation, including the result of criminal proceedings (Code Sec. 7608(c)(4)).

The IRS must conduct a detailed financial audit of every undercover operation closed in each fiscal year, regardless of the amount of receipts or expenditures. The audit requirement was previously subject to floors on receipts and expenditures.—CCH.

.25 **Legal basis for power to execute warrants.**—Failure of Congress to re-enact special authorization to execute warrants under the 1954 Code in respect to authority generally provided for under the Federal Rules of Criminal Procedure is not to be interpreted as an implied repeal of such authority. Furthermore, the subsequent re-enactment of express authorization to execute and serve search warrants by amendment of Code Sec. 7608(b), effective after the date of the search and seizure in issue, is not to be construed as establishing lack of prior authority under the criminal rules as recognized by the courts.

J. Aliota, DC, 63-2 USTC ¶ 9552, 216 FSupp 48.

A taxpayer's petition to quash four third-party recordkeeper summonses issued by the IRS to two financial institutions was denied. The taxpayer's argument that the IRS agent was authorized under Code Sec. 7608 only to issue summonses in cases pertaining to the taxation of alcohol, tobacco, and firearms was rejected. The agent was a civil investigator and his authority was derived from Code Sec. 7602 and, thus, was not limited to the investigation of any particular type of tax.

D. Runkle, DC Ind., 95-2 USTC ¶ 50,343.

A taxpayer's petition to quash third-party recordkeeper summonses issued by the IRS was denied. Code Sec. 7608(b) confers specific authority on particular IRS agents; it does not limit the authority of agents to issue or serve third-party summonses.

J.R. Gaunt, DC Pa., 96-1 USTC ¶ 50,291.

A taxpayer who marketed a book promoting strategies to avoid federal income taxes failed to state a *Bivens* -type claim against IRS agents for violations of his constitutional rights arising out of the search of his home and business. The reference in Code Sec. 7608 to "Intelligence Division" did not limit the authority of an IRS Criminal Investigation Division (CID) agent to present an affidavit of probable cause for the search warrants.

D.L. Leveto, DC Pa., 2000-1 USTC ¶ 50,278. Aff'd. on other issues, CA-3, 2001-2 USTC ¶ 50,536.

A taxpayer's contention that searches and seizures executed by an IRS Criminal Investigation Division agent pursuant to an investigation for tax evasion were void because the agent lacked authority to present the application and affidavit of probable cause and execute the search warrant was rejected. The special agent's primary responsibilities included the investigation of alleged criminal violations under the federal tax law, and Code Sec. 7608(b)(2)(A) authorized him to execute search warrants and seize property. Since the warrant was valid and lawfully executed, the taxpayers were not entitled to compensation for the items seized during the execution of the lawfully executed warrants.

D.L. Tatacher, DC Pa., 2000-1 USTC ¶ 50,346. Aff'd, *per curiam,* CA-3 (unpublished opinion), 2001-1 USTC ¶ 50,139.

2003(18) CCH—Standard Federal Tax Reports   **Reg. § 7608(c)(6)(B)   ¶ 42,885.25**

Exhibit 82.   Enforcement of Internal Revenue Laws by Enforcement Officers: CCH Explanation, [2003] 18 Stand. Fed. Tax Rep. (CCH) ¶ 42,885.

published in BNA's *Environment Cases* and the
Environmental Law Institute's *Environmental Law Reporter*,
and *Shepard's Labor Law Citations* provides coverage of several reporters including CCH's *Employment Practices
Decisions* and BNA's *Fair Employment Practice Cases*.

One of the most valuable features of looseleaf services is
coverage of proposed legislation, pending litigation, and
other legal developments. Approaches vary from service to
service. *Fair Employment Practices* includes a biweekly
Summary of Latest Developments newsletter. *Standard Federal
Tax Reporter* has several current awareness approaches,
including weekly "CCH Comments" articles, a *Taxes on
Parade* newsletter, and extra issues providing the text of
important new documents such as tax reform bills and
congressional committee reports.

Detailed, regularly updated indexes provide fast and convenient access to looseleaf services. A typical service
includes several types of indexes. The general or *topical
index* provides detailed subject access. In many services, an
additional index known as a "Current Topical Index" or
"Latest Additions to Topical Index" covers new material
between the periodic recompilations of the main index.
Cumulating services such as BNA's *Antitrust & Trade
Regulation Report* or *Family Law Reporter* generally have just
one index, which is updated every two or three months.
Exhibit 83 shows a page from the topical index for the
Standard Federal Tax Reporter, with a reference under
"Firearms" to the material shown in Exhibits 81 and 82.
Note that the index includes very detailed references to
annotations of court decisions and administrative rulings.

Finding lists provide direct references to particular
statutes, regulations, or cases by their citations. These can
be particularly useful in searching for numerically

10,532 **Topical Index**
References are to paragraph (¶) numbers.

FINANCIAL INSTITUTIONS—continued
. 100% penalty for failure to withhold or pay over withheld tax
. . lender or surety relationship establishing liability 39,780.723
. real property acquired by exempt organizations from troubled financial institutions 22,830; 22,837.035
. retirement plan fundholders
. . prohibited transactions, exemption from excise taxes on 34,410.03
. S corporations 32,026.032
. tax-exempt 23,607.045
. tax-exempt obligations
. . interest paid to carry . . 15,190; 15,191.035; 15,191.18
. tax preference items
. . interest expense 15,191.035; 15,191.18
. . reduction 15,190; 15,191.01; 15,191.035

Financial security program, regulated investment company status 26,408.19

Financial services organization, advertising expenses 8851.1342

Financial statements—see Books and records

Financing corporations, notes sold to 21,471.45

FINANCING COSTS—see also Carrying charges 29,225.044
. oil and gas wells 23,950.021

FINDERS' FEES 8636.1763
. tax-free exchange arranged 29,615A.049

Finding lists of sections of regulations and law—see Finding Lists, Citator Vol. N-Z

Findings of fact—see Tax Court

FINES—see also Penalties, civil
. automobile law violations 8954.322
. contempt of court 8954.323
. deductibility . . . 8500; 8953; 8954.01—8525.33
. food law violations 8954.326
. slot machine owner sharing profits with owner of location 8954.3293
. truckers 8954.322
. union members paying, deductibility 8853.205

FINLAND
. tax treaty . . . . 26,885.01—26,885.80
. . fellowships 26,885.35
. . nondiscrimination clause 26,885.40
. . royalties 26,885.50
. . teachers and researchers 26,885.65
. . withholding of tax on wages 26,885.80

Finnish Relief Fund, Inc., exemption 22,609.26

Fire box relining, capital expenditures 13,709.547

Fire clay, percentage depletion . 23,960; 23,964

FIRE DEPARTMENTS
. employees of, withholding of tax on wages 33,538.474
. volunteer
. . contributions 11,620.162
. . exempt status 22,609.55; 22,611.86
. . unrelated business income 22,846.73

Fire escape costs 13,709.345

Fire escapes and exits, repairs 8630.37

Fire insurance companies—see Insurance companies

Fire losses—see Casualty losses

Fire patrols and salvage corps, gross income 5504.207

Fire protection equipment, investment tax credit 4580.246; 4580.853

Firearms, enforcement of law by revenue agents and officers . . . . 42,880—42,885.03

FIREFIGHTERS
. compensation for injuries
. . exclusion from income 5504.028
. compensation received 5507.0178
. educational expenses 8632.186
. length-of-service awards, deferred compensation 21,536.033
. retirement benefits
. . early retirement 19,218.031
. . inflation adjustment 1201.49
. survivors' annuities 5504.028; 5507.0178
. uniform expenses 8524.265

Firm sales contracts, inventories . . . 22,210.42

FIRST AMENDMENT
. freedom of association 2900.15
. freedom of religion
. . programs funded by taxes 2900.113
. . qualified organizations 2900.114
. . religious education expenses 2900.115
. . secular purpose 2900.119
. . substantial burden 2900.118
. . summonses 2900.117
. . testimony without oath 2900.116
. freedom of speech
. . protest speech on returns 2900.133
. . tax avoidance speech 2900.135

FIRST-IN, FIRST-OUT RULE
. bond transactions 29,336.365
. inventories 22,206.01; 22,210.40
. short sales 29,336.475
. stock rights exercised 29,336.46
. stock transactions—see also Stock: first-in first-out, rule . . . . 29,336.01—29,336.49
. transfer of stock 29,336.481
. Treasury securities 29,336.483

First-tier taxes, abatement of . . . . 34,280—34,302.40

FIRST-TIME HOMEBUYERS
. credits against tax
. . District of Columbia enterprise zone . . . . 32,428—32,429.05
. District of Columbia enterprise zone
. . first-time homebuyer defined . . 32,429.021
. . information reporting 32,429.05
. . principal residence 32,429.035

First-year rentals in acquisition of noncompetitive government oil and gas leases 8754.43

Fiscal Management Division, Internal Revenue Service delegation of authority . . 43,266.307

FISCAL-YEAR TAXPAYERS
. alien's first return 20,502.15
. basis, change to or from 20,400
. . return for short period 20,500
. calendar of due dates 105
. definitions 20,303; 20,307.70
. due date of returns 36,723.01
. extensions to include later income 20,307.40
. first return 20,307.68
. fiscal year defined 20,307.027
. inventories
. . extensions to include later income 20,307.40

FIN ©2002, CCH INCORPORATED

Exhibit 83. Topical Index, [2003 Index] Stand. Fed. Tax Rep. (CCH) 10,532.

designated agency materials, such as IRS rulings or SEC releases. Some of these lists also serve as citator services, providing information on the current validity of materials listed.

Note that Exhibits 81 and 82 have both page numbers at the top (72,001 and 72,003) and paragraph numbers at the bottom (¶42,885.01 and ¶42,885.25). It is easy to be misled by the page numbers, but remember that they are used only for filing purposes and that the paragraph numbers are the points of reference used in indexes and finding lists.

Another device used in some services is the *cumulative index*. This is not a subject index but a tool providing cross-references from the main body of the service to current material. Under listings by paragraph number, cumulative indexes update each topic with leads to new materials which have not yet been incorporated into the main discussion.

Detailed instructions, often entitled "How to Use This Reporter" or "About This Publication," are frequently provided at the beginning of the first volume of a looseleaf service. A particular service may include features that appear confusing at first but are very useful to the experienced researcher. These instructions are often neglected by new users, but a few moments of orientation can save considerable time and frustration.

Because looseleaf services differ depending on the subject matter and the publisher's approach, it is difficult to generalize about the best research procedures. The following steps, however, are applicable in most instances:

1. Determine whether a looseleaf service is available for the subject.

2. Obtain an adequate working orientation by perusing the instructions at the front of the service.

3. Use the service's finding aids to locate the specific material needed for the problem. Most often this means beginning in the topical index by subject. A finding list can be used if you already have a reference to a specific document (such as an order, regulation, or ruling).

4. Study the texts of the relevant primary sources, as well as the service's editorial explanations and commentary.

5. Follow research leads suggested by cross-references to cases and other documents.

6. Update your research results by checking the cumulative or "latest additions" indexes for recent materials, and by using a citator if available.

§9-3. TOPICAL ELECTRONIC RESOURCES

Looseleaf services remain the preferred research tools of many specialists, and they are the topical resources most likely to be available to public law library patrons. An increasing number of lawyers and other researchers, however, rely on electronic services to perform similar functions. Like looseleaf services, topical CD or Internet resources provide both the texts of primary sources and explanatory or analytical material. Keyword searching provides more flexibility than looseleaf indexes, and hypertext links allow researchers to move conveniently back and forth between various documents. Some of the information available through these services is only issued electronically, but many online services have counterparts in print.

The *Standard Federal Tax Reporter* discussed in the preceding section, for example, is also available in both CD and Internet versions.

CD services eliminate the need for laborious filing of replacement pages, but new discs are generally not issued as frequently as looseleaf supplements. CD users must usually finish updating their research through an online system or by other means. Internet-based services, on the other hand, can be constantly updated without need for new discs or other supplementation.

The annual *Directory of Law-Related CD-ROMs* provides an extensive listing of more than 1,600 electronic services. The directory's primary focus is CDs, but it also indicates which services are available on the Internet. Appendix C in this volume, listing major services, includes coverage of both CD and Internet services.

LexisNexis and Westlaw have numerous topical electronic libraries with cases, statutes, regulations, and other sources in specialized areas. Both systems, for example, have files combining federal tax cases, legislation, regulations, and administrative rulings. Their tax libraries also provide access to treatises, newsletters, and other secondary sources. These libraries do not, however, integrate the primary sources and commentary in the same way that the major looseleaf services do.

§9-4. CURRENT AWARENESS SOURCES

It is essential that lawyers be aware of activity in their areas of expertise, not just new court decisions but also legislative and regulatory changes. Several approaches are available to keep on top of current activities, recent scholarly literature, and new developments in the law.

A. Legal Newsletters and Newspapers

Looseleaf services are often excellent sources of current information in particular fields. Many include newsletters summarizing developments; the *Fair Employment Practices* and *Standard Federal Tax Reporter* newsletters noted in § 9-2 are just two examples. A large number of separate current awareness newsletters are also published for this express purpose, in some instances delivered by fax or e-mail instead of in print. Some are available free, but many are quite expensive. Weekly newsletters may cost $1,000 or more per year. Specialized newsletters often have a limited circulation and may not be found in academic or public law libraries. Nevertheless, they may be the best available sources for learning about newly developing areas of law. Newsletters are often the forum through which practitioners in a very specialized area share information and documents. A newsletter may, for example, include photocopies of pleadings or of trial court decisions that will never be published in the regular court reports.

Among the leading newsletter publishers are several companies that make their products available through Westlaw and LexisNexis. These include, for example, several Andrews Publications newsletters on areas of current interest such as class actions, hazardous waste, and repetitive stress injury. Other newsletters are available through one system or the other. LexisNexis, for example, has dozens of specialized newsletters from Mealey Publications.

In addition to its looseleaf services, BNA publishes about two dozen daily newsletters in areas such as environmental law, labor law, and taxation. Some of these are available in print versions, but others are published only electronically. Exhibit 84 shows a screen from the online BNA newsletter *Product Liability Daily*, featuring a report on an Illinois decision on firearms industry litigation.

A BNA Monitoring Service

Product Liability Daily

Wednesday, November 6, 2002
ISSN 1535-1629

Firearms
**Illinois Appellate Court OK's Chicago's Claim
Of Public Nuisance Against Firearms Industry**

News

CHICAGO—The City of Chicago's campaign against the gun industry won an important victory Nov. 4, when the Illinois Appellate Court reversed an earlier trial court decision, which dismissed the city's unique public nuisance lawsuit (*Chicago v. Beretta U.S.A. Corp.*, Ill. App. Ct, No. 1-00-3541, 11/4/2).

The decision, rendered by a three-judge panel from the First Division of the Illinois Appellate Court, finds a Cook County trial court judge erred when he sided with manufacturers, distributors and dealers of firearms and dismissed the city's suit. Instead, the appellate court panel found the city had stated a legitimate cause of action for public nuisance under Illinois law. In so ruling, Schiller's decision was reversed and remanded for further proceedings.

Chicago officials applauded the ruling, saying it validates the city's long-held contention that the firearms industry should be held accountable for implementing reckless design, marketing and distribution strategies that essentially appeal to criminals.

"The court has ruled that this industry can be held liable if it fails to take reasonable precautions to keep guns out of the hands of criminals," said Mara Georges, Chicago's corporation counsel. "We expect this case ultimately to revolutionize the way firearms are sold."

Attorneys for the defendants said the outcome was not necessarily surprising. The same appellate court panel, including Judges William Cousins Jr., Jill McNulty and John Tully, affirmed a series of similar public nuisance claims against the firearms industry in a ruling issued late last year. That ruling found that three separate suits filed on behalf of five victims of handgun violence could proceed to trial under the public nuisance theory (*Young v. Bryco Arms Inc.*, Ill. App. Ct. No. 1-01-0739, 12/31/01).

High Court to Review Similar Ruling

Exhibit 84. *Product Liability Daily* (BNA), Nov. 6, 2002
<www.bna.com>.

Numerous law firms produce newsletters for their clients and other readers. These may serve primarily as marketing tools for their firms, but many also provide useful information about developing areas of law. They are generally available through law firm websites, and may be identified through leads in resources such as FindLaw's guide to websites by legal subject <www.findlaw.com/01topics/>.

The leading source for identifying available newsletters is the annual *Legal Newsletters in Print*. This directory describes more than 2,200 newsletters, with information about subscription prices and Internet access. A subject index provides topical access to its listings. This publication is available to online subscribers, along with *Legal Looseleafs in Print* and *Directory of Law-Related CD-ROMs*, as part of the LawTRIO database <www.infosourcespub.com>.

News on developments in the law is also available from a number of daily and weekly legal newspapers. These vary considerably in coverage. Some serve primarily as vehicles for local court calendars and legal announcements, but others include new court decisions and articles on developing legal topics. Westlaw and LexisNexis provide access to several daily newspapers, including the *Chicago Daily Law Bulletin* and the *New York Law Journal*. They also include two national weekly newspapers, the *National Law Journal* and *Legal Times*, as well as numerous other local and regional legal newspapers.

One of the leading Internet sources for legal news is law.com <www.law.com>, with stories from *American Lawyer*, *National Law Journal*, and regional newspapers. Many legal newspapers, including the *National Law Journal* <www.nlj.com>, have their own websites, and FindLaw Legal News <news.findlaw.com> provides law-related stories from the AP and Reuters wire services.

b. Tables of Contents Services

Specialists need to know about scholarly as well as legal developments. A new article directly on a topic of concern may appear in any of the hundreds of law reviews and other legal journals published in this country. Some lawyers scan new issues of journals in their area of expertise, but more systematic ways of surveying journal literature are also available.

The principal resource providing information about new journal issues is *Current Index to Legal Periodicals*, published weekly by the University of Washington's Marian Gould Gallagher Law Library. This index covers more than 500 law reviews, indexing articles under about a hundred subject headings and listing each issue's table of contents. The index can be searched online through Westlaw, and subscribers can receive customized weekly e-mail limited to particular subjects and journal titles. Further information is available on the Web <lib.law.washington.edu/cilp/cilp.html>.

The Tarlton Law Library at the University of Texas also provides table of contents access to more than 750 law-related journals, free on the Web and updated daily <tarlton.law.utexas.edu/tallons/content_search.html>. The Texas site does not index articles by subject, but keyword searching is available.

Some specialists rely on services such as the Social Science Research Network (SSRN) <www.ssrn.com> to learn of new scholarly work in their area. This network serves as a forum for scholars in various disciplines, including law, to share recent articles and works in progress. New abstracts are delivered to subscribers by e-mail, and a searchable Internet archive includes free access to several thousand downloadable full-text documents.

c. Listservs

One of the most effective ways to keep on top of developments in a particular area, or to seek assistance with difficult research issues, is to subscribe to an e-mail listserv in the area. Some listservs disseminate information by organizations or government agencies, while others are designed for specialists, professors, and others interested in an area to share news and ideas. Posing questions to a list often yields results that would otherwise elude most researchers. Chances are that some list subscriber may be able to help with a thorny legal issue or can identify a source for an obscure document. Older messages to a list, if available in a searchable Internet archive, may form a valuable repository of information in the area.

Hundreds of listservs on legal topics are maintained. The most extensive guide to these sources, covering more than 1,200 law-related lists, is Lyonette Louis-Jacques's Law Lists <www.lib.uchicago.edu/cgi-bin/law-lists>. This searchable database provides information about the scope of each list, instructions for subscribing, and links to archives on the Web. Nonlegal listservs can also provide relevant information, of course, so more general directories such as CataList <www.lsoft.com/lists/listref.html> may also be useful.

A number of courts and state legislatures now provide automatic e-mail notification when a particular case or bill is acted upon, and several government agencies have mailing lists summarizing new developments. These include several dozen EPA lists <www.epa.gov/epahome/listserv.htm>, the FCC Daily Digest <www.fcc.gov/updates.html>, and more than twenty FDA mailing lists <www.fda.gov/emaillist.html>. Other agency websites may provide information about similar listservs in their fields.

§9-5. SPECIALIZED INDEXES

Law journals were introduced in Chapter 2, but that discussion focused on academic law reviews and the general *Index to Legal Periodicals and Books* and *Legal Resource Index*. More specialized publications and indexes are also available.

Besides the numerous topical law reviews edited by students at almost every law school, specialized journals are issued by bar associations and commercial publishers. Articles in these journals tend to be shorter and more practical than those found in academic law reviews, often focusing on current developments of interest to practicing lawyers. Among the most respected of the specialized bar journals are several published by sections of the American Bar Association, although journals published by state and local bar associations may provide the best insights into practice concerns in specific jurisdictions.

A useful source for identifying publications in a particular specialty is *Anderson's Directory of Law Reviews and Scholarly Legal Publications* <www.andersonpublishing.com/lawschool/directory/>, which lists more than 600 journals by subject. It provides separate listing of student-edited journals and non-student-edited peer review and trade journals.

While the major periodical indexes provide extensive coverage, several specialized indexes are also available. Taxation has two major indexes: CCH's *Federal Tax Articles* (1969-date, monthly), with abstracts of journal articles arranged by Internal Revenue Code section; and *Index to Federal Tax Articles* (1975-date, quarterly), a subject/author index with retrospective coverage back to 1913. *Environmental Law Reporter* includes a monthly "Journal Literature" feature listing new law review articles by sub-

ject. *Criminal Justice Periodicals Index* was published in print form from 1975 to 1998, but is now available only online through such suppliers as Dialog, ProQuest, and Westlaw.

For research in legal history, the predecessor to the *Index to Legal Periodicals*, entitled *Index to Legal Periodical Literature* (6 vols., 1888-1939), may be of use. This index covers articles as far back as 1770, and is sometimes called the Jones-Chipman index after the names of its editors. Another useful source for legal historians is Kermit Hall, *A Comprehensive Bibliography of American Constitutional and Legal History* (7 vols., 1984-91), which lists books and articles published between 1896 and 1987 dealing with legal history.

§9-6. CONCLUSION

Looseleaf and electronic services, current awareness tools, and other specialized materials are some of the most important resources in the arsenal of practicing lawyers. Unlike more general sources such as court reports and codes, these materials are not published in one standard-ized format. Learning what resources are available in a particular area may require preliminary research into indexes and directories. Although it may take some time to use these specialized resources effectively, they can lead directly to more productive research and to a better under-standing and anticipation of legal developments.

CHAPTER 10
REFERENCE RESOURCES

■　■　■　■　■　■　■　■　■　■

§10-1. INTRODUCTION

This brief chapter serves two purposes. First, it looks at legal resources designed to provide answers to relatively simple questions. These are not sources for lengthy legal analysis but for telephone numbers, addresses, facts, and statistics. Knowing how to find this information quickly can save valuable time for other pursuits.

Some reference resources have been discussed in earlier chapters. Dictionaries and related research aids were covered in Chapter 1, at pages 10-11, and multistate surveys and almanacs such as the *Martindale-Hubbell Law Digest* were discussed in Chapter 5, at pages 176-180. There remain, however, other reference materials with which lawyers need to be familiar.

The chapter also introduces more general reference sources for interdisciplinary research. Many law students focus so intently on legal literature that they neglect information from other disciplines. General sources, however, can provide essential background information, and scholarship in the sciences and social sciences may add valuable perspectives and insights in analyzing legal issues.

§10-2. LEGAL DIRECTORIES

Chapters 6 through 8 discussed directories covering federal and state governments, including legislatures, administrative agencies, and courts. The law does not live by government alone, however, and directories of lawyers and legal organizations can also be valuable sources of information. Legal directories provide background information on other lawyers and can help in establishing contacts within the profession. Organizations interested in particular issues may provide networking opportunities or insights unavailable in any printed or electronic sources.

Numerous directories provide contact and biographical information for lawyers. Most focus on individual states or particular specialties, but two comprehensive directories of the legal profession are available. These are published by divisions of the parent companies of LexisNexis and Westlaw, and each covers close to a million lawyers. Neither, however, includes every single lawyer in the country.

The more established source, and the only one available in print format, is the *Martindale-Hubbell Law Directory*. Fifteen volumes of this annual publication contain listings of lawyers and law firms, arranged by state and city. At the beginning of each volume are blue pages containing "Practice Profiles," with a one-line entry for each lawyer indicating date of birth, date of admission to practice, college, law school, and address or affiliation. "Professional Biographies" provide fuller descriptions of those lawyers and firms who purchase space beyond the simple alpha-betical listings. Lawyers in corporate law departments are listed geographically and have fuller listings in a separate *Martindale-Hubbell Corporate Law Directory*; selected lawyers in other countries are covered by *Martindale-Hubbell International Law Directory*.

One useful feature of *Martindale-Hubbell* is its rating system, which evaluates U.S. lawyers based on interviews with their peers. Legal ability ratings range from A (Very High to Preeminent) to C (Good to High), and these are published only if accompanied by an ethical standards rat-ing of V (Very High). Ratings are not provided for all lawyers listed in the directory.

The *Martindale-Hubbell Law Directory* is available on CD-ROM, online through LexisNexis, and on the Internet as the Martindale-Hubbell Lawyer Locator <www.martindale.com>. A related site designed for clients

and the public, lawyers.com <www.lawyers.com>, is limited to lawyers and firms with paid listings and does not include *Martindale-Hubbell*'s lawyer ratings.

The other comprehensive directory of attorneys, *West Legal Directory* (WLD), is published only electronically on CD-ROM, through Westlaw, and on the Internet <lawyers.findlaw.com>. Like *Martindale-Hubbell*, WLD has both simple free listings and more extensive paid entries. Coverage in the two sources is comparable, although only WLD includes telephone numbers in its basic listings. Westlaw's new Profiler database links WLD information with a listing of links to relevant cases, articles, and other documents.

Several other national directories of lawyers and law firms are available, although none is as comprehensive as *Martindale-Hubbell* or WLD. *Who's Who in American Law* (biennial) is a useful source of biographical information on prominent attorneys and legal scholars, and the *Law Firms Yellow Book* (semiannual) provides information on the management and recruiting personnel of major law firms. The National Association for Law Placement's annual *Directory of Legal Employers* is designed primarily for job-seeking law students and has basic data on firms and their attorneys. In addition, law firm websites usually include information about the attorneys and their practices.

Other directories focus on attorneys working outside law firms. *Directory of Corporate Counsel* (2 vols., annual) is similar in scope to the *Martindale-Hubbell Corporate Law Directory*, with biographical information on lawyers working for corporations and nonprofit organizations. Directories of public interest and government law offices include *Directory of Legal Aid and Defender Offices in the United States* and *National Directory of Prosecuting Attorneys* (both updated irregularly).

Interest groups, professional organizations, and trade associations can be invaluable sources of information in their areas of concern. Links to legal organization websites, including state bar associations, are available from several websites including FindLaw <www.findlaw.com/06associations/> and WashLaw Web <www.washlaw.edu/bar.html>. Broader coverage of legal and nonlegal organizations is provided by the *Encyclopedia of Associations* (4 vols., annual), with contact information for more than 22,000 national organizations. Exhibit 85 shows its entry for the International Handgun Metallic Silhouette Association (IHMSA). Note that entries include website addresses, if available, and information on organizations' publications and meetings. The *Encyclopedia of Associations* is also available through Westlaw and as part of InfoTrac's *Associations Unlimited* online system <infotrac.galegroup.com>. Another directory, *National Trade and Professional Associations of the United States* (annual), is less extensive than the *Encyclopedia of Associations* but just as useful for finding addresses and telephone numbers of business-related organizations.

While most directories are somewhat specialized, a few try to provide answers to a wider range of inquiries. *Law and Legal Information Directory* (biennial) is a large volume covering legal organizations and bar associations as well as other resources such as law libraries, lawyer referral services, and a variety of federal and state government agencies. A handier desktop work by Arlene L. Eis, *The Legal Researcher's Desk Reference* (biennial), has an impressive array of directory information including government offices, courts, and bar associations, and also includes other resources such as state court organization charts and lists of Internet sites.

★20884★   INTERNATIONAL HANDGUN
METALLIC SILHOUETTE ASSOCIATION
(IHMSA)
PO Box 9
Anoka, MN 55303 .
Steve Riddle, Pres.
PH: (763)323-3359
FX: (763)422-1910
E-mail: sriddle22@home.com
Website: http://www.ihmsa.org
Founded: 1976. **Members:** 55,000. **Membership Dues:**
$30 (annual) ● life, $420. **Staff:** 2. **Regional Groups:** 8.
State Groups: 52. **Local Groups:** 300. **National Groups:**
4. **Languages:** English. **Description:** Handgun enthusi-
asts who shoot at metallic silhouettes of chickens, pigs,
turkeys, and rams at ranges of 50, 100, 150, and 200
meters, respectively. Sanctions tournaments. **Awards:**
Outstanding Service. Frequency: annual. Type: recognition. Recipient: for sportsmanship, volunteerism. **Computer Services:** database ● mailing lists. **Committees:**
Evaluations; Physically Challenged; Rules; Safety; Technical.
Publications: *IHMSANews* (in English), 10/year. Newspaper. Price: $2.00/per issue; free, for members only.
Advertising: accepted ● Brochures.
Conventions/Meetings: annual International Champion-
ship - competition and meeting, handgun tournament
(exhibits) - last week in July or 1st week in August.

Exhibit 85.   1 (pt. 2) ENCYCLOPEDIA OF ASSOCIATIONS 2400
    (39th ed. 2003).

§ 10-3. STATISTICS

Lawyers need demographic and statistical information
for many purposes, from preparing for cross-examination
of an expert witness to supporting a discrimination claim.
Statistics are published in a variety of sources, some
focused on legal matters and some more general.

Statistics on the legal system include data on courts, lawyers, and the criminal justice system. Information on court caseloads can be found in the Administrative Office of the U.S. Courts' annual *Judicial Business of the United States Courts* (also available online <www.uscourts.gov/judbususc/judbus.html>), and the National Center for State Courts' annual *State Court Caseload Statistics* <www.ncsconline.org/D_Research/csp/CSP_Main_Page.html>. The composition of the U.S. legal profession is analyzed in *The Lawyer Statistical Report*, published periodically by the American Bar Foundation; the most recent report, published in 1999, provides data as of 1995.

Criminal statistics are widely available from both federal and state governments. Each year the U.S. Department of Justice publishes two major sources in print and on the Internet. The Federal Bureau of Investigation issues *Uniform Crime Reports* (also known as *Crime in the United States*) <www.fbi.gov/ucr/ucr.htm>, focusing on criminal activities, and the Bureau of Justice Statistics issues *Sourcebook of Criminal Justice Statistics* <www.albany.edu/sourcebook/>, providing a broader survey of the social and economic impacts of crime. The National Criminal Justice Reference Center provides links to dozens of federal, state, and other statistics-related sites <www.ncjrs.org/statwww.html>.

The *Statistical Abstract of the United States*, published annually by the Bureau of the Census in print, on CD-ROM, and on the Internet <www.census.gov/statab/www/>, is a general reference source with which any legal researcher should be familiar. It covers a wide range of economic and demographic statistics, and is particularly useful because it gives source information for each table. It thus serves as a convenient lead to agencies and publications with more extensive coverage of specific areas.

Exhibit 86 shows a table from the *Statistical Abstract*, providing information about firearm manufacturing. Note that the table includes a source reference to the ATF publication *Commerce in Firearms in the United States*, where more detailed information may be available. Another source for statistics from government agencies is the FedStats website <www.fedstats.gov>, with links to numerous federal statistical sources.

Annual reports and other publications of trade associations, labor unions, financial institutions, public interest groups, and government agencies generally contain statistical data relating to their work and interests. Much of this material is now available on organizations' websites, but a subject index can provide helpful guidance in knowing where to look. *American Statistics Index* (1973-date, covering U.S. government sources) and *Statistical Reference Index* (1980-date, covering state government and private sources) are available in print and online as part of LexisNexis Statistical <web.lexis-nexis.com/statuniv/>.

§10-4. News and Business Information

Every practicing lawyer must keep abreast of developments in business, politics, and society. Legal newspapers, discussed in Chapter 9, focus on law-related activity, but for a broader picture it is necessary to monitor more general sources such as the major newspapers or news websites. In addition to providing current awareness, news stories can also be rich sources for factual research or background information.

Two of the most convenient news sources for law students are Westlaw and LexisNexis. Westlaw provides access to hundreds of newspapers, as well as wire services and business publications; and LexisNexis's news library has the text of newspapers, magazines, trade journals, newsletters, and wire services. The two systems have

No. 1015. Firearms Manufacturers—Shipments, Exports, and Imports: 1980 to 1998

[In thousands of units (5,645 represents 5,645,000)]

Year	Shipments				Exports				Imports [1]			
	Total	Hand-guns	Rifles	Shot-guns	Total	Hand-guns	Rifles	Shot-guns	Total	Hand-guns	Rifles	Shot-guns
1980	5,645	2,370	1,936	1,339	517	220	171	127	754	299	182	273
1985	3,460	1,550	1,141	770	183	95	44	45	697	229	271	197
1986	3,040	1,428	971	641	217	121	37	59	701	231	269	201
1987	3,523	1,659	1,006	858	242	159	42	41	1,064	342	414	308
1988	3,818	1,746	1,145	928	254	132	54	69	1,276	622	283	372
1989	4,374	2,031	1,407	936	259	118	73	68	1,008	440	293	274
1990	3,844	1,839	1,156	849	354	178	72	104	844	449	204	192
1991	3,550	1,838	883	828	398	190	91	118	721	293	311	116
1992	4,030	2,010	1,002	1,018	398	189	90	119	2,847	982	1,423	442
1993	5,130	2,825	1,160	1,145	414	149	94	171	1,205	1,205	1,593	246
1994	5,161	2,582	1,324	1,255	401	173	82	147	1,881	915	848	118
1995	4,228	1,723	1,332	1,174	420	230	89	101	1,103	706	261	136
1996	3,835	1,484	1,424	926	326	154	75	97	882	491	263	128
1997	3,574	1,407	1,251	916	271	108	77	86	939	474	359	106
1998	3,645	1,240	1,536	869	200	45	66	90	1,000	532	249	219

[1] 1980-1991, imports are on fiscal year basis; thereafter, calendar year.
Source: U.S. Department of Treasury, Bureau of Alcohol, Tobacco, and Firearms. *Commerce in Firearms in the United States.* February 2000.

Exhibit 86.   U.S. BUREAU OF THE CENSUS, STATISTICAL ABSTRACT OF THE UNITED STATES 638 tbl. 1015 (121st ed. 2001).

considerable overlap in coverage, with the major exceptions being the *Wall Street Journal* (Westlaw only) and the *New York Times* (retrospective coverage on LexisNexis only). Back issues of these and other major newspapers are usually available in large libraries on microfilm, and ProQuest Historical Newspapers <www.proquest.com> provides subscription-based web access to PDF images of issues as far back as 1851.

Other electronic sources of news abound, including websites for newspapers (such as <www.wsj.com> and <www.nytimes.com>) and multisource subscription databases such as Factiva <www.factiva.com>. Websites for newspapers and other news sources can be found through sites such as NewsLink <newslink.org> or Newspaper Links <www.newspaperlinks.com>.

Business developments are a major focus of research in news sources. Company information is also available through a number of other print and electronic directories and databases. The leading provider of data on both public

and private businesses is Dun & Bradstreet, which publishes several directories as well as in-depth profiles of individual companies. D&B material is available through Westlaw and as a subscription website <www.dnb.com>. LexisNexis and Westlaw provide access to numerous other directories. Both have *Standard & Poor's Register of Corporations, Directors & Executives*, which provides basic data and biographical information, and S&P's more extensive *Corporate Descriptions Plus News* database with more extensive background and financial information. Other Internet sources for basic information include Corporate Information <www.corporateinformation.com> and Hoover's Online <www.hoovers.com>.

Publicly traded companies must submit a wide range of financial information to the Securities and Exchange Commission, much of which is available through the SEC's EDGAR (Electronic Data Gathering Analysis and Retrieval) system. EDGAR resources are available directly from the SEC <www.sec.gov/edgar.shtml> and through several commercial services including Westlaw and LexisNexis. Disclosure, the company that processes SEC filings, provides extensive financial information through the Global Access subscription website <www.primark.com>, and can also provide copies of materials not available online.

§10-5. Interdisciplinary Research

Legal research is rarely confined to the insular world of cases, statutes, and law review articles. It is important for researchers to be able to find information in a wide variety of disciplines.

Periodical indexes. Several indexes to nonlegal periodical literature can provide valuable leads. Some of these are specialized indexes in particular disciplines, while others provide comprehensive coverage of a wide range of sources (including legal journals).

One of the simplest places to begin looking for material in nonlegal sources is *Index to Periodical Articles Related to Law* (1958-date, 6 vols. with quarterly updates). This index focuses on articles with legal content but excludes those covered in the standard legal periodical indexes. It covers popular magazines as well as scholarly journals.

Indexes from other disciplines such as *ABI/INFORM* (business and economics), *PAIS International* (public policy), or *PsycINFO* (psychology and related disciplines) may provide background information or interdisciplinary perspectives. A few indexes are available free on the Internet, such as the National Library of Medicine's *PubMed* version of *MEDLINE*, the comprehensive index of biomedical journals <www.ncbi.nlm.nih.gov/entrez/query>. Most, however, are accessible by subscription only. A number of indexes are available through Westlaw, and researchers in university libraries usually have access to many more through subscription websites.

The Institute for Scientific Information (ISI) publishes several citation indexes which function like Shepard's in other academic disciplines. They can be used to find articles citing a particular author or source, or to search for articles by author or keyword. The most useful in legal research is *Social Sciences Citation Index* (covering 1966-date), which includes extensive coverage of law journals. The others are *Science Citation Index* (1955-date) and *Arts & Humanities Citation Index* (1976-date). These are available on CD and online as Web of Knowledge <www.isiwebofknowledge.com>. They are also available through other database systems, including Westlaw, where they are known as *Social Scisearch*, *Scisearch*, and *Arts & Humanities Search*. ISI also publishes several subject-based editions of *Current Contents*, weekly services providing the tables of contents of new scholarly journal issues, available in print or electronically; the *Social & Behavioral Sciences* edition includes numerous law-related titles.

One of the most extensive indexing services is ProQuest <www.proquest.com>, which covers thousands of periodicals and newspapers. Some articles are represented only by citations or abstracts, but many are available in full text or as scanned images of the original printed versions. Ingenta <www.ingenta.com> also provides comprehensive coverage of current journal literature, with tables of contents information from more than 27,000 publications. Searching is free, and articles are available for electronic or fax delivery for a fee. Two subscription web services providing access to older journal articles are *Periodical Contents Index* (PCI) <pci.chadwyck.com>, covering several thousand journals back as far as 1770 and providing the full text of more than 200 titles, and JSTOR <www.jstor.org>, with full-text retrospective coverage of more than three hundred major scholarly journals. JSTOR provides access to dozens of leading economics and history journals, and is in the process of expanding its coverage to major law reviews as well.

Online catalogs. No law library has every possible text, so research limited to one library's holdings may miss important works. FindLaw's list of law schools by state <stu.findlaw.com/schools/usaschools/> includes direct links to library websites. Even more catalogs are accessible through resources such as lib-web-cats <www.librarytechnology.org/libwebcats/>, which lists links to libraries worldwide, geographically or by type (including law and other specialties). One of the most extensive of individual library catalogs is that of the Library of Congress <catalog.loc.gov>, with access to LC's 12 million records as well as a gateway for searching more than 400 other online catalogs.

Two of the most comprehensive resources for bibliographic information are the vast union catalogs of the Online Computer Library Center (OCLC) <www.oclc.org>

and the Research Libraries Group (RLG) <www.rlg.org>. For researchers at member institutions, these databases are available on the Internet as WorldCat and RLIN, respectively. OCLC's FirstSearch and RLG's Eureka websites provide access to this information and other sources such as periodical indexes and current awareness tools.

Other reference sources. Most disciplines have an extensive literature of encyclopedias, dictionaries, bibliographies, research guides, directories, indexes, and other sources that can be of value in a research project. The standard, comprehensive source for identifying available reference materials is the American Library Association's *Guide to Reference Books* (11th ed. 1996). The *Guide* describes basic resources in hundreds of disciplines, providing just enough background to help the legal researcher know where to look.

§10-6. CONCLUSION

This chapter's introductory survey has presented just a small sampling of the many resources available for answering reference questions and for expanding research into other disciplines. Bibliographies such as the *Guide to Reference Books* can provide further leads, and reference librarians can suggest other sources and research approaches.

CHAPTER 11
INTERNATIONAL LAW

■　■　■　■　■　■　■　■　■　■

§11-1. INTRODUCTION

Public international law is the body of law which governs relations among nations. Although its primary historical functions have been the preservation of peace and regulation of war, international law now governs an ever broader range of transnational activities. It regulates matters from copyright protection to the rights of refugees, and agreements such as the Convention on Contracts for the International Sale of Goods (CISG) have made international law an inherent aspect of commercial activity. *Private* international law (or conflict of laws) determines where, and by whose law, controversies involving more than one jurisdiction are resolved, as well as how foreign judgments are enforced.

A modern legal practice often requires knowledge of international law. Lawyers representing an American firm investing in another country, for example, must be aware of treaties between the two nations as well as the investment and trade laws of both the United States and the other country. They may also need to examine jurisdictional issues in resolving disputes or in determining the application of one country's rules in the other's courts. This chapter focuses on international law, while research in the law of foreign countries is the subject of Chapter 12.

The classic statement of the sources of international law doctrine is found in Article 38 of the Statute of the International Court of Justice. *Treaties* and *international custom* are generally considered the two most important sources. If a treaty is relevant to a problem involving its signatories, it is the primary legal authority. International custom consists of the actual conduct of nations, when that conduct is consistent with the rule of law. Custom is not found in a clearly defined collection of sources, but is established instead by evidence of state practices. Other

sources include *judicial decisions* and *scholarly writings*, although these are subsidiary to treaties and international custom. Judicial decisions are not considered binding precedents in subsequent disputes, but they are evidence of international practice and can aid in treaty interpretation and in the definition of customary law.

The Internet has had a dramatic impact on international legal research. International law sources have traditionally been difficult to identify and locate, but many are now widely available through the websites of the United Nations and other international organizations. This chapter discusses some specific resources available electronically and also provides general Internet addresses that can serve as useful starting points for further research.

International law has its own terminology, and a dictionary may be an essential research tool. Two leading works are Clive Parry et al., *Parry and Grant Encyclopaedic Dictionary of International Law* (1986), and James R. Fox, *Dictionary of International and Comparative Law* (2d ed. 1997). More specialized works, such as H. Victor Condé, *A Handbook of International Human Rights Terminology* (1999), are also available.

§11-2. INTERNATIONAL ORGANIZATIONS

While national governments are the major parties in international law, the field cannot be studied without understanding the vital role of intergovernmental organizations. Worldwide and regional organizations establish norms, promote multilateral conventions, and provide mechanisms for the peaceful resolution of conflicts. Several have established adjudicatory bodies by whose decisions nations agree to be bound. Even when not acting as law-making bodies, international organizations compile and publish many of the most important research sources in international law.

A. UNITED NATIONS

The United Nations has greatly influenced the development of international law, by providing an organizational forum and a center for the preparation and promotion of legislation and conventions. Its six principal organs are the General Assembly, Security Council, Economic and Social Council, Trusteeship Council, Secretariat, and International Court of Justice (ICJ). This section provides a general introduction to the UN; its treaty work and the ICJ will be discussed in greater detail in §§ 11-3 and 11-4.

The United Nations website <www.un.org> provides a wealth of information on the organization, including news, descriptive overviews of its activities, and access to numerous documents. The best printed source for basic information on the UN's structure and membership is *United Nations Handbook*, published annually by the New Zealand Ministry of External Relations and Trade. More in-depth reference works include Rüdiger Wolfrum, ed., *United Nations: Law, Policies, and Practice* (2 vols., 1995), with alphabetically arranged chapters on specific issues and entities; and Oscar Schachter & Christopher C. Joyner, eds., *United Nations Legal Order* (2 vols., 1995), an American Society of International Law work providing U.S. perspectives of UN activities in areas such as human rights and environmental law.

The *Yearbook of the United Nations* is one of the best starting points for historical research on UN activities. Although coverage is delayed three or four years, this publication summarizes major developments, reprints major documents, and provides references to other sources for the year covered. Each volume includes a thorough index.

Among the most important documents for UN research are the *General Assembly Official Records* (GAOR). The records of the meetings of the assembly and its committees

are accompanied by *Annexes* containing the more important documents produced during the session, and by *Supplements* containing annual reports submitted by the Secretary-General, the Security Council, the International Court of Justice, and various committees. The final supplement each year compiles all the resolutions passed by the General Assembly during the session.

Resolutions are also reprinted in the *Yearbook of the United Nations* and are available on the Internet. The United Nations Optical Disk System <www.ods.un.org> is a subscription website with the full text of resolutions from the General Assembly, Security Council, and Economic and Social Council since 1946, as well as other documents beginning in 1993. The UN Documentation Centre <www.un.org/documents/> provides free access to a more limited range of material, including General Assembly resolutions since 1976 and Security Council resolutions since 1946.

Early General Assembly and Security Council resolutions were reprinted in separate series of *United Nations Resolutions* (35 vols., 1973-92), edited by Dusan J. Djonovich, but these only cover through 1986 and 1979 respectively. For subject access and more current coverage, Dietrich Rauschning et al., eds., *Key Resolutions of the United Nations General Assembly, 1946-1996* (1997), and Karel C. Wellens, ed., *Resolutions and Statements of the United Nations Security Council (1946-2000): A Thematic Guide* (2001), are helpful.

The UN produces a broad range of other publications, including several specialized yearbooks, statistical compilations, and conference proceedings. Despite the importance of these publications, identifying and finding them is not always easy. The United Nations has successively used

a number of different indexing systems. The current system, *United Nations Documents Index*, began publication in 1998, but it has several predecessors: *UNDOC* (1979-96), *UNDEX* (1974-78), and an earlier *United Nations Documents Index* (1950-73). Two commercial electronic services provide broader and more convenient access. *UNBIS Plus on CD-ROM*, updated quarterly, combines print indexes in a keyword-searchable format, as well as the full text of resolutions; and *Access UN: Index to United Nations Documents and Publications* <www.readex.com/doccoll/accessun.html> has comprehensive retrospective coverage.

Much of the work of the United Nations in particular subject fields is conducted by related international organizations, such as the Food and Agriculture Organization, the World Health Organization, and UNESCO. These organizations are referred to by the UN Charter as "specialized agencies" and submit their reports to the Economic and Social Council, which forwards them to the General Assembly. Several of these agencies have extensive law-related activities which produce documentation useful to the legal researcher. The United Nations System website locator <www.unsystem.org> provides access to sites for more than eighty specialized organizations.

Hans von Mangoldt & Volker Rittberger, eds., *The United Nations System and Its Predecessors* (2 vols., 1997), contains numerous documents on the UN and related agencies, including charters, constitutions, and selected resolutions. *United Nations Documentation: Research Guide* <www.un.org/Depts/dhl/resguide/> provides a concise introduction to UN resources, including an explanation of its document symbols, discussion of the major organizational units, and more in-depth coverage of some topics such as human rights and international law. Several more extensive guides are published, including Peter I.

Hajnal, ed., *International Information: Documents, Publications, and Electronic Information of International Governmental Organizations* (2 vols., 2d ed. 1997-2001).

B. WORLD TRADE ORGANIZATION

The World Trade Organization <www.wto.org>, the successor to the General Agreement on Tariffs and Trade (GATT), was established in 1995 as the principal international body administering trade agreements among member states. The WTO acts as a forum for negotiations, seeks to resolve disputes, and oversees national trade policies. It is governed by a Ministerial Conference, which meets every two years, while most operations are handled by its General Council.

The basic documents governing WTO operations are reprinted in *The Results of the Uruguay Round of Multilateral Trade Negotiations: The Legal Texts* (1994) and are available on the organization's website. The WTO's *Annual Report* (1996-date) provides trade statistics and a commentary on the organization's work every year. The WTO Secretariat has published *Guide to the Uruguay Round Agreements* (1999), designed to make the WTO rules easier to understand; and Joseph F. Dennin, ed., *Law and Practice of the World Trade Organization* (5 vols., 1995-date) is a major collection of treaties, dispute resolution decisions, and commentary.

WTO panel decisions and appellate body reports are available in several commercial series, including the looseleaf *International Trade Law Reports* (1996-date), the bound *WTO Dispute Settlement Decisions: Bernan's Annotated Reporter* (1998-date), and Westlaw and LexisNexis. Dispute resolution pages on the WTO website include these deci-

sions as well as information about rules and procedures. The subscription website WorldTradeLaw.net <www.worldtradelaw.net> provides summaries and text of decisions as well as various other WTO documents.

c. European Union and Other Regional Organizations

For American lawyers, the European Union <europa.eu.int> is probably the most frequently encountered of the world's many regional organizations. The EU was established in 1993 by the Maastricht Treaty, as the more ambitious successor to the European Communities (European Atomic Energy Community, European Coal and Steel Community, and European Economic Community). As economic and social developments lead to increasing European integration, the EU can be seen more as a supranational government than as a regional organization.

The major institutions of the EU are the European Parliament, a large elected body exercising mostly advisory powers; the Council, the major decision-making body consisting of one minister from each member country; the Commission, a permanent executive body responsible for implementing the organizing treaties and managing the Union; and the European Court of Justice (which will be discussed in § 11-3 with other regional courts).

The *Official Journal of the European Union* consists of two series, *Legislation* (L) and *Information and Notices* (C), with European Parliament debates published as an annex. Indexes are issued monthly, and the semiannual *Directory of Community Legislation in Force* provides subject access to treaties, regulations, directives and other legislative actions. The monthly *Bulletin of the European Union* reviews activities and reprints selected documents, and the annual *General Report on the Activities of the European Union* provides an overview of developments.

Several introductory reference works are available. Desmond Dinan, ed., *Encyclopedia of the European Union* (updated ed. 2000) is an alphabetically arranged overview of major topics and institutions, with bibliographies after most articles providing further leads. Other useful one-volume works include K.P.E. Lasok & Dominik Lasok, *Law and Institutions of the European Union* (7th ed. 2001), and P.S.R.F. Mathijsen, *A Guide to European Union Law* (7th ed. 1999). *European Current Law* (1992-date, monthly) provides information on legal developments in the EU and throughout Europe, and *European Access* (1980-date, bimonthly) is a current awareness guide to new publications by and about the EU.

CCH's *European Union Law Reporter* (4 vols., 1962-date) is one of the most useful starting points for American lawyers, because of its familiar looseleaf format, broad scope, and frequent supplementation. In addition to its primary emphasis on the European Union, it also provides limited coverage of other regional organizations and summarizes the domestic legislation of European countries on a variety of subjects.

Two works providing detailed analysis of the treaties creating the European Union are Dennis Campbell, ed., *The Law of the European Community* (6 vols., 1976-date), and Neville March Hunnings, ed., *Encyclopedia of European Union Law: Constitutional Texts* (6 vols., 1996-date). An older companion to the latter work, *Encyclopedia of European Community Law: Secondary Legislation* (11 vols., 1973-date) includes coverage of such matters as employment law, intellectual property, and competition law.

Eur-Lex <europa.eu.int/eur-lex/> is a free website with access to basic EU treaties, the *Directory of Community Legislation in Force*, and recent legislation and cases. A more

extensive legal site, CELEX, is available on a subscription basis <europa.eu.int/celex> and through LexisNexis or Westlaw. Coverage includes treaties, secondary legislation, preparatory documents, and national provisions implementing EU directives. An extensive set of links to numerous other EU Internet resources is maintained by the University of California Library <www.lib.berkeley.edu/doemoff/gov_eu.html>.

Other important regional organizations include the Organization of American States (OAS) <www.oas.org>, often considered the oldest regional organization; and the Council of Europe <www.coe.int>, the major advocate of democracy and the rule of law in Europe. Both of these organizations draft and promote multilateral treaties among their member states, and work to protect human rights in their regions. Their activities in these areas will be discussed in the following sections. G. Pope Atkins, *Encyclopedia of the Inter-American System* (1997) provides a one-volume overview of the OAS and other Western Hemisphere organizations.

Information on major intergovernmental organizations is included as Part One of the *Europa World Year Book* (2 vols., annual), which also provides extensive background information and statistics on the nations of the world. The *Yearbook of International Organizations* (5 vols., biennial; also available on CD and online <www.uia.org/organizations/>) contains descriptions and directory information for thousands of international groups and associations, with indexes by name, country and subject; and U.S.-based organizations interested in international issues are listed by subject in Congressional Quarterly's *International Information Directory* (1999).

§11-3. TREATIES

Treaties are formal agreements between countries, and have legal significance for both domestic and international purposes. Treaties between two governments are called *bilateral*; those entered into by more than two governments are called *multilateral*. The initial signatures to a treaty establish the parties' agreement that its text is authentic and definitive, but nations are not bound until they approve the treaty through ratification, accession, or some other procedure. Parties may add reservations excluding certain provisions, or declarations providing their own interpretations of treaty terms. The texts of treaties usually identify the point at which they enter into force, often (in the case of multilateral conventions) when a specified number of nations have indicated their ratification or accession.

Under Article VI of the U.S. Constitution providing that treaties are part of the supreme law of the land, they have the same legal effect and status as federal statutes. Treaties and statutes can supersede each other as the controlling law within the United States, but a treaty no longer valid as the law of the land may still be binding between the U.S. and another country. Treaties of the United States are negotiated and drafted by the executive branch but require approval by two-thirds of the Senate. Most treaty sources also cover executive agreements, which are made with other countries by the President without Senate consent.

Treaty research generally involves several aspects: (1) finding its text in an authoritative source; (2) determining whether it is in force and with what parties and reservations; and (3) interpreting its provisions, with the aid of commentaries, judicial decisions, and legislative history. The resources available may depend in large part on

whether the United States is a party to a treaty or convention, so answering that question is an important first step in treaty research.

A. SOURCES

Treaties are published in a variety of forms—official and unofficial, national and international, current and retrospective. The *Bluebook* generally specifies citation of bilateral treaties to an official U.S. source (usually *United States Treaties and Other International Agreements*, or *UST*), and of multilateral treaties to an official international source as well (usually the *United Nations Treaty Series*). Not all treaties, however, appear in these standard sources, and it may be necessary to check journals, commercially published compilations, and electronic sources for the texts of some agreements.

U.S. sources. Until 1949, treaties were published in the *Statutes at Large* for each session of Congress. These have been reprinted in a definitive, official compilation, *Bevans' Treaties and Other International Agreements of the United States of America 1776-1949* (13 vols., 1968-75). This set contains four volumes of multilateral treaties (arranged chronologically), eight volumes of bilateral treaties (arranged alphabetically by country), and indexes by country and subject.

Beginning in 1950, *UST* has been the official, permanent form of publication for all treaties and executive agreements to which the United States is a party. *UST* volumes are published after a long delay, currently almost twenty years. Exhibit 87 shows the first page of a treaty between the United States and Iraq, as published in *UST*.

Treaties and agreements are issued first in a slip format in the preliminary series, *Treaties and Other International Acts Series* (*TIAS*). Slip treaties are consecutively numbered and issued in separately paginated pamphlets, containing the

IRAQ

Cultural Relations

Agreement signed at Baghdad January 23, 1961;
Entered into force August 13, 1963.

CULTURAL AGREEMENT BETWEEN THE UNITED STATES OF AMERICA AND THE REPUBLIC OF IRAQ

The Government of the United States of America and the Government of the Republic of Iraq:

In consideration of the bonds of friendship and understanding existing between the peoples of the United States of America and of the Republic of Iraq;

In view of the expressed desire of both Governments for an agreement which would encourage and further stimulate the present cultural exchange between the two countries;

Inspired by the determination to increase mutual understanding between the peoples of the United States of America and the Republic of Iraq;

Agree as follows:

Article I

Each Government shall encourage the extension within its own territory of a better knowledge of the history, civilization, institutions, literature and other cultural accomplishments of the people of the other country by such means as promoting and facilitating the exchange of books, periodicals and other publications; the exchange of musical, dramatic, dance and athletic groups and performers; the exchange of fine art and other exhibitions; the exchange of radio and television programs, films, phonograph records and tapes; and by the establishment of university courses and chairs and language instruction.

Article II

The two Governments shall promote and facilitate the interchange between the United States of America and the Republic of Iraq of prominent citizens, professors, teachers, technicians, students and other qualified individuals from all walks of life.

TIAS 5411   (1168)

Exhibit 87.   Cultural Agreement between the United States of America and the Republic of Iraq, Jan. 23, 1961, U.S.-Iraq, 14 U.S.T. 1168.

treaty text in English and in the languages of the other parties. *TIAS* publication is more current than *UST*, but still involves a time lag of several years.

Because of the long delays in the publication of *TIAS* and *UST*, several commercial services are important sources for current access to treaties. *Hein's UST Current Service* (1990-date), on microfiche, and *Consolidated Treaties & International Agreements* (1990-date), in print, both provide copies of new treaties and agreements, with indexing by country and subject. The American Society of International Law's bimonthly *International Legal Materials* (1962-date) contains the texts of treaties of major significance and sometimes provides drafts before final agreement.

Treaties in *ILM* are available on both Westlaw and LexisNexis, and both systems also have comprehensive databases with treaties back to the 1770s. Another extensive online source, *U.S. Treaties Researcher*, is available as a subscription website from Oceana Publications <www.oceanalaw.com>.

General sources. The most comprehensive source for modern treaties is the *United Nations Treaty Series* (*UNTS*), containing more than 2,000 volumes. Since 1946 this series has published all treaties registered with the United Nations by member nations (including the U.S.) in their original languages, as well as in English and French translations. Exhibit 88 shows the first page of the 1980 Convention on Prohibitions or Restrictions on the Use of Certain Conventional Weapons Which May be Deemed to be Excessively Injurious or to Have Indiscriminate Effects, as published in *UNTS*. Note that footnote 1 identifies the twenty ratifications that caused the convention to enter into force in 1983.

CONVENTION[1] ON PROHIBITIONS OR RESTRICTIONS ON THE USE OF CERTAIN CONVENTIONAL WEAPONS WHICH MAY BE DEEMED TO BE EXCESSIVELY INJURIOUS OR TO HAVE INDISCRIMINATE EFFECTS

The High Contracting Parties,

Recalling that every State has the duty, in conformity with the Charter of the United Nations, to refrain in its international relations from the threat or use of force against the sovereignty, territorial integrity or political independence of any State, or in any other manner inconsistent with the purposes of the United Nations,

Further recalling the general principle of the protection of the civilian population against the effects of hostilities,

Basing themselves on the principle of international law that the right of the parties to an armed conflict to choose methods or means of warfare is not unlimited, and on the principle that prohibits the employment in armed conflicts of weapons, projectiles and material and methods of warfare of a nature to cause superfluous injury or unnecessary suffering,

Also recalling that it is prohibited to employ methods or means of warfare which are intended, or may be expected, to cause widespread, long-term and severe damage to the natural environment,

[1] The Convention, including the three Protocols, came into force on 2 December 1983 in respect of the following States, i.e., six months after the date of deposit of the twentieth instrument of ratification, acceptance, approval or accession with the Secretary-General of the United Nations, in accordance with article 5 (1) and (3):

State	Date of deposit of the instrument of ratification, acceptance (A) or accession (a) and of acceptance of Protocols I, II and III	State	Date of deposit of the instrument of ratification, acceptance (A) or accession (a) and of acceptance of Protocols I, II and III
Austria	14 March 1983	Japan	9 June 1982 A
Bulgaria	15 October 1982	Lao People's Democratic Republic	3 January 1983 a
Byelorussian Soviet Socialist Republic	23 June 1982	Mexico	11 February 1982
China	7 April 1982	Mongolia	8 June 1982
Czechoslovakia	31 August 1982	Poland	2 June 1983
Denmark	7 July 1982	Sweden	7 July 1982
Ecuador	4 May 1982	Switzerland	20 August 1982
Finland	8 April 1982	Ukrainian Soviet Socialist Republic	23 June 1982
German Democratic Republic	20 July 1982	Union of Soviet Socialist Republics	10 June 1982
Hungary	14 June 1982	Yugoslavia	24 May 1983

Subsequently, the Convention came into force for the following State six months after the date on which it deposited its instrument of ratification, acceptance, approval or accession with the Secretary-General of the United Nations, in accordance with article 5 (2):

State	Date of deposit of the instrument of ratification and of acceptance of Protocols I, II and III
Norway	7 June 1983
(With effect from 7 December 1983.)	

Exhibit 88.   Convention on Prohibitions or Restrictions on the Use of Certain Conventional Weapons Which May be Deemed to be Excessively Injurious or to Have Indiscriminate Effects, Oct. 10, 1980, 1342 U.N.T.S. 163.

On the Internet, the United Nations Treaty Collection <treaty.un.org> has the text of more than 30,000 treaties, searchable by name, subject, date, or parties, available on asubscription basis. Free sources for the texts of major multilateral treaties and conventions include the Multilaterals Project at the Fletcher School of Law and Diplomacy <www.fletcher.tufts.edu/multilaterals.html> and the University of Minnesota Human Rights Library <www1.umn.edu/humanrts/>.

Treaties predating the creation of the United Nations can be found in two older series. The *League of Nations Treaty Series (LNTS)* (205 vols., 1920-46) is similar in scope to the *UNTS,* and a retrospective collection, *Consolidated Treaty Series (CTS)* (243 vols., 1969-86) contains all treaties between nation states from 1648 to 1918. *CTS* prints treaties in the language of one of the signatories, usually accompanied by an English or French translation. Although there is no subject index, the set includes a chronological list and an index to parties.

Regional organizations also publish compilations of treaties among their members. The *Organization of American States Treaty Series* (1957-date) and its predecessor, the *Pan American Union Treaty Series* (1934-56), contain multilateral treaties of Western Hemisphere countries, including the United States. Treaties among European states are published individually in the *European Treaty Series* (1950-date) and cumulated in the bound volumes of *European Conventions and Agreements* (1971-date). New European agreements often appear in the annual *European Yearbook,* which also reports on the activities of more than a dozen regional organizations.

Both the OAS <www.oas.org/juridico/english/treaties.html> and the Council of Europe <conventions.coe.int> provide Internet access to major

treaties. The Hague Conference on Private International Law <www.hcch.net/e/conventions/> has the text of several dozen conventions it has drafted on issues such as international civil procedure and recognition of judgments.

National treaty series include *United Kingdom Treaty Series* (1892-date); *Canada Treaty Series/Recueil des Traités* (1928-date); and *Recueil des Traités et Accords de la France* (1958-date). Many foreign countries publish current treaties in their official gazettes and on government websites, and new treaties are often printed in international law yearbooks and journals.

B. INDEXES AND GUIDES

Treaties are generally published chronologically rather than by subject, so finding tools or indexes are needed to identify agreements on a particular topic. Many of these same resources also provide information on treaty status.

Treaties in Force, an annual publication of the Department of State, is the official index to current United States treaties and agreements. It provides citations to all of the major treaty publications, including *Bevans*, *UST*, and the *League of Nations* and *United Nations Treaty Series*. The first section of *Treaties in Force* lists bilateral treaties by country and, under each country, by subject; and the second section lists multilateral treaties by subject. Exhibit 89 shows portions of each section, covering the bilateral and multilateral agreements seen in Exhibits 87 and 88.

A commercially published *Guide to the United States Treaties in Force* is also issued annually and provides several additional means of access to current treaties, including subject and country indexes to both bilateral and multilateral treaties. This can be a valuable resource, particularly because the official *Treaties in Force* provides just lists of treaties with no indexing by subject.

IRAQ

CLAIMS

Agreement concerning claims resulting from attack on the U.S.S. *Stark*. Exchange of notes at Baghdad March 27 and 28, 1989; entered into force March 28, 1989.
TIAS 12030.

COMMERCE (See also ECONOMIC AND TECHNICAL COOPERATION)

Treaty of commerce and navigation. Signed at Baghdad December 3, 1938; entered into force June 19, 1940.
54 Stat. 1790; TS 960; 9 Bevans 7; 203 LNTS 107.

CULTURAL RELATIONS

Cultural agreement. Signed at Baghdad January 23, 1961; entered into force August 13, 1963.
14 UST 1168; TIAS 5411; 488 UNTS 163.

CUSTOMS

Agreement relating to the privilege, on a reciprocal basis, of free entry to all articles imported for the personal use of consular officers. Exchange of notes at Washington March 14, May 15, June 19, and August 8, 1951; entered into force August 8, 1951.
5 UST 657; TIAS 2956; 229 UNTS 185.

WEAPONS

Convention on prohibitions or restrictions on the use of certain conventional weapons which may be deemed to be excessively injurious or to have indiscriminate effects. Adopted at Geneva October 10, 1980; entered into force December 2, 1983; for the United States September 24, 1995.
TIAS

Protocol on non-detectable fragments (Protocol I). Adopted at Geneva October 10, 1980; entered into force December 2, 1983; for the United States December 24, 1995.
TIAS

Protocol on prohibitions or restrictions on the use of mines, booby-traps and other devices (Protocol II). Adopted at Geneva October 10, 1980; entered into force December 2, 1983; for the United States September 24, 1995.[1]
TIAS
Parties:
Argentina
Australia
Austria
Bangladesh
Belarus
Belgium
Benin[2]
Bolivia
Bosnia-Herzegovina
Brazil
Bulgaria
Cambodia
Canada[3]
Cape Verde
China[4]
Colombia
Costa Rica
Croatia
Cuba
Cyprus
Czech Rep
Denmark
Djibouti

Exhibit 89. U.S. DEP'T OF STATE, TREATIES IN FORCE: A LIST OF TREATIES AND OTHER INTERNATIONAL AGREEMENTS OF THE UNITED STATES IN FORCE ON JANUARY 1, 2002, at 141, 480 (2002).

The 2000 edition of *Treaties in Force* is available on the Web <www.state.gov/www/global/legal_affairs/tifindex.html>, but the only treaty information online thus far under the Bush administration is an annual compilation of new treaty actions. These are provided with other international law materials on the Department of State website <www.state.gov/interntl/>. This information was previ-

ously found in the publications *US Department of State Dispatch* (weekly, 1990-99) and *Department of State Bulletin* (monthly, 1939-89).

The major collections and series of U.S. treaties and international agreements are indexed in Igor I. Kavass, ed., *United States Treaty Index: 1776-2000 Consolidation* (13 vols., 1991-2002). This work includes a numerical guide to treaties and agreements, and indexes by subject, date, and country. The consolidated index is updated semiannually by the *Current Treaty Index*, and cumulative electronic access to both publications is available through *Hein's United States Treaty Index on CD-ROM*.

The *United Nations Treaty Series*, the major international source for treaties, has no cumulative official index. Initially, indexes were published for every 100 volumes of *UNTS*; more recent indexes cover 50 volumes apiece and are published after a time lag of several years. A commercial publication, *United Nations Treaty Indexing Service*, consists of a paper *Current United Nations Treaty Index* covering recently published treaties, a *United Nations Cumulative Treaty Index* (15 vols., 1999), and an electronic *United Nations Master Treaty Index on CD-ROM*, with complete retrospective coverage back to 1946.

The leading index for finding multilateral conventions is Christian L. Wiktor, *Multilateral Treaty Calendar, 1648-1995* (1998). This lists more than 6,000 agreements chronologically, identifies sources in more than 100 publications, and provides information on treaty status. The *Multilateral Treaty Calendar* entry for the Conventional Weapons Convention in Exhibit 88 is shown in Exhibit 90. Note that it lists more than a dozen sources for the text of the treaty, including the *UNTS* and several national treaty series and journals, but that it does not list the nations that are parties to the agreement.

October 10, 1980   **Rules of Warfare**

Convention on prohibitions or restrictions on the use of certain conventional weapons which may be deemed to be excessively injurious or to have indiscriminate effects, with protocols (I to IV). *Convention sur l'interdiction ou la limitation de l'emploi de certaines armes classiques qui peuvent être considérées comme produisant des effets traumatiques excessifs ou comme frappant sans discrimination, avec protocoles (I à IV).*

   Concluded at Geneva (U.N.) October 10, 1980

   Printed text: 1342 UNTS 137, 163 (E), 173 (F), US Treaty Doc. 103-25, p. 6; US Treaty Doc. 105-1, pp. 37, and subs. (protocols II to IV); BTS 105(1996). Cm. 3497; CTS 1994/19; ATS 1984/6; SDIA 28:124 (1980); JORF 1988:13843; RTAF 1988/62; 73 VBD A904; UNJY 1980:113; 19 ILM 1523, 1524 (text)

   Depository: United Nations

   Entered into force: December 2, 1983

   Status: 57 parties (UN Status, Dec. 1995, p. 865; 19 UNDY 286)

   Note: Adopted by the United Nations Conference on Prohibitions or Restrictions of Use of Certain Conventional Weapons Which May be Deemed to be Excessively Injurious or to Have Indiscriminate Effects on October 10, 1980, and annexed to the final act as annexes A to D; opened for signature at New York (U.N.) April 10, 1981; refers to U.N. Charter of JUNE 26, 1945, and Geneva conventions of AUGUST 12, 1949; protocol I concerns nondetectable fragments, protocol II the prohibitions or restrictions on the use of mines, boobytraps and other devices, and protocol III the prohibitions or restrictions on the use of incendiary weapons; protocol II was amended on MAY 3, 1996 (see text in US Treaty Doc. 105-1, p. 37; BPP Misc. 2(1997), Cm. 3507; 35 ILM 1206, 1209; 100 RGDIP 1138); see also protocol IV on blinding laser weapons of OCTOBER 13, 1995.

Exhibit 90. CHRISTIAN L. WIKTOR, MULTILATERAL TREATY CALENDAR, 1648-1995, at 1192 (1998).

The source for determining the status of, and identifying the parties to, major conventions is the annual *Multilateral Treaties Deposited with the Secretary-General*, published by the United Nations. This listing of nearly 500 treaties is arranged by subject, and provides citations, information on status, a list of parties with dates of signature and ratification, and the text of any reservations imposed by individual parties. Coverage is limited to treaties concluded under UN auspices or for which the Secretary-General acts as depository, so it excludes such major agreements as the Geneva Conventions of 1949 or the Convention on International Trade in Endangered Species (CITES). Exhibit 91 shows the first page of the entry for the Conventional Weapons Convention as of December 31, 2001, with nearly ninety countries now parties to the convention. Individual countries' declarations, reservations, and objections are noted on following pages after the list of parties.

Subscribers to the United Nations Treaty Collection <untreaty.un.org> have access to an online version that is updated more frequently than the print version.

M.J. Bowman & D.J. Harris, *Multilateral Treaties: Index and Current Status* (1984, with 11th cum. supp. 1995), also provides information on sources and lists parties, although it has not been updated in several years. It covers more than 1,000 agreements, including some predating or not deposited with the UN. The *World Treaty Index*, compiled by Peter H. Rohn (5 vols., 2d ed. 1983-84) is growing increasingly dated, but it provides comprehensive coverage of some 44,000 bilateral and multilateral treaties from 1900 to 1980, indexing *UNTS*, *LNTS*, and numerous other sources by country, subject, date, and international organization.

The status of Inter-American and European treaties can be determined through the OAS and Council of Europe websites, listed above on page 335, and from the periodically revised guides *Inter-American Treaties and Conventions: Signatures, Ratifications, and Deposits with Explanatory Notes* and *Chart Showing Signatures and Ratifications of Council of Europe Conventions and Agreements.*

c. INTERPRETATION

Most treaties contain ambiguities which may lead to controversies in interpretation and application. Several resources can assist in understanding the terms of a treaty. Among the most important are court decisions and documents produced during a treaty's drafting and consideration.

Court decisions interpreting a treaty can provide important information for a researcher seeking to determine its meaning or effect. The best approach is probably a full-text online search for a treaty name, because neither KeyCite

CONVENTIONAL WEAPONS WHICH MAY BE DEEMED TO BE EXCESSIVELY INJURIOUS OR TO HAVE INDISCRIMINATE EFFECTS (WITH PROTOCOLS I, II AND III)

Geneva, 10 October 1980

ENTRY INTO FORCE: 2 December 1983 in accordance with article 5 (1) and (3).
REGISTRATION: 2 December 1983, No. 22495.
STATUS: Signatories: 50. Parties: 88.
TEXT: United Nations, Treaty Series, vol. 1342, p. 137; depositary notifications C.N.356.1981. TREATIES-7 of 14 January 1982 (procès-verbal of rectification of the Chinese authentic text) and C.N.320.1982, TREATIES-11 of 21 January 1983 (procès-verbal of rectification of the Final Act).

Note: The Convention and its annexed Protocols were adopted by the United Nations Conference on Prohibitions or Restrictions of the Use of Certain Conventional Weapons Which May Be Deemed Excessively Injurious or to Have Indiscriminate Effects, held in Geneva from 10 to 28 September 1979 and from 15 September to 10 October 1980. The Conference was convened pursuant to General Assembly resolutions 32/152 of 19 December 1977 and 33/70 of 14 December 1978. The original of the Convention with the annexed Protocols, of which the Arabic, Chinese, English, French, Russian and Spanish texts are equally authentic, is deposited with the Secretary-General of the United Nations. The Convention was open for signature by all States at United Nations Headquarters in New York for a period of twelve months from 10 April 1981.

Participant	Signature	Ratification, Acceptance (A), Approval (AA), Accession (a), Succession (d)	Participant	Signature	Ratification, Acceptance (A), Approval (AA), Accession (a), Succession (d)
Afghanistan	10 Apr 1981		Iceland	10 Apr 1981	
Argentina	2 Dec 1981	2 Oct 1995	India	15 May 1981	
Australia	8 Apr 1982	29 Sep 1983	Ireland	10 Apr 1981	13 Mar 1995
Austria	10 Apr 1981	14 Mar 1983	Israel		22 Mar 1995 a
Bangladesh		6 Sep 2000 a	Italy	10 Apr 19..	20 Jan 1995
Belarus	10 Apr 1981	23 Jun 1982	Japan	22 Sep 1981	9 Jun 1982 A
Belgium	10 Apr 1981	7 Feb 1995	Jordan		19 Oct 1995 a
Benin		27 Mar 1989 a	Lao People's Democratic Republic		3 Jan 1983 a
Bolivia		21 Sep 2001 a	Latvia		4 Jan 1993 a
Bosnia and Herzegovina[1]		1 Sep 1993 d	Lesotho		6 Sep 2000 a
Brazil		3 Oct 1995 a	Liechtenstein	11 Feb 1982	16 Aug 1989
Bulgaria	10 Apr 1981	15 Oct 1982	Lithuania		3 Jun 1998 a
Cambodia		25 Mar 1997 a	Luxembourg	10 Apr 1981	21 May 1996
Canada	10 Apr 1981	24 Jun 1994	Maldives		7 Sep 2000 a
Cape Verde		16 Sep 1997 a	Mali		24 Oct 2001 a
China	14 Sep 1981	7 Apr 1982	Malta		26 Jun 1995 a
Colombia		6 Mar 2000 a	Mauritius		6 May 1996 a
Costa Rica		17 Dec 1998 a	Mexico	10 Apr 1981	11 Feb 1982
Croatia[1]		2 Dec 1993 d	Monaco		12 Aug 1997 a
Cuba	10 Apr 1981	2 Mar 1987	Mongolia	10 Apr 1981	8 Jun 1982
Cyprus		12 Dec 1988 a	Morocco	10 Apr 1981	
Czech Republic[2]		22 Feb 1993 d	Nauru		12 Nov 2001 a
Denmark	10 Apr 1981	7 Jul 1982	Netherlands[3]	10 Apr 1981	18 Jun 1987 A
Djibouti		29 Jul 1996 a	New Zealand	10 Apr 1981	18 Oct 1993
Ecuador	9 Sep 1981	4 May 1982	Nicaragua	20 May 1981	5 Dec 2000
Egypt	10 Apr 1981		Niger		10 Nov 1992 a
El Salvador		26 Jan 2000 a	Nigeria	26 Jan 1982	
Estonia		20 Apr 2000 a	Norway	10 Apr 1981	7 Jun 1983
Finland	10 Apr 1981	8 Apr 1982	Pakistan	26 Jan 1982	1 Apr 1985
France	10 Apr 1981	4 Mar 1988	Panama		26 Mar 1997 a
Georgia		29 Apr 1996 a	Peru		3 Jul 1997 a
Germany[3]	10 Apr 1981	25 Nov 1992	Philippines	15 May 1981	15 Jul 1996
Greece	10 Apr 1981	28 Jan 1992	Poland	10 Apr 1981	2 Jun 1983
Guatemala		21 Jul 1983 a	Portugal	10 Apr 1981	4 Apr 1997
Holy See		22 Jul 1997 a	Republic of Korea		9 May 2001 a
Hungary	10 Apr 1981	14 Jun 1982	Republic of Moldova		8 Sep 2000 a
			Romania	8 Apr 1982	26 Jul 1995

Exhibit 91. 2 UNITED NATIONS, MULTILATERAL TREATIES DEPOSITED WITH THE SECRETARY-GENERAL; STATUS AS AT 31 DECEMBER 2001, at 315 (2002).

nor Shepard's covers citations to treaties. (*Shepard's Federal Statute Citations* includes coverage of treaties in its 1996 volumes, but not in more recent supplements.) *United States Code Service* includes two useful volumes:

International Agreements, containing the texts of about two dozen major conventions and treaties, accompanied by research references and case annotations; and *Annotations to Uncodified Laws and Treaties*, which has no treaty texts but provides broader coverage of decisions interpreting U.S. treaties, including sections for treaties with Native American nations, multilateral treaties (listed by date), and bilateral treaties (listed by country).

For United States treaties, Senate deliberation provides another valuable source of documentation on an agreement's terms and meaning. *Treaty Documents* (until 1980, called *Senate Executive Documents*) contain the text of treaties as they are transmitted to the Senate for its consideration. These documents usually contain messages from the President and the Secretary of State, and also provide an early source for access to the treaty text. The Senate Foreign Relations Committee analyzes treaties, may hold hearings, and issues *Senate Executive Reports* containing its recommendations. Both Treaty Documents and Senate Executive Reports are issued in numbered series which identify the Congress and sequence in which they were issued. Note in Exhibit 90 that two of the sources the *Multilateral Treaty Calendar* lists for the text of the Conventional Weapons Convention are Treaty Docs. No. 103-25 and 105-1.

The *Legislative Calendar* of the Senate Foreign Relations Committee, the official status table of business before the committee, is perhaps the best list of pending treaties with actions taken thereon. The treaties portion of this calendar is available on the committee's website <foreign.senate.gov/treaties.pdf>. *Congressional Index*, CCH's weekly looseleaf service, also includes a table of treaties pending before the Senate, with references to Treaty Documents, Executive Reports, hearings, and ratifications.

Another source available for the interpretation of some multilateral conventions is the *travaux preparatoires* (documents created during the drafting process such as reports and debates). These are recognized under the 1969 Vienna Convention on Treaties as a source for clarifying ambiguous treaty terms, and U.S. courts frequently rely on such sources. *Travaux* for some conventions have been published, e.g. Marc J. Bossuyt, *Guide to the "Travaux Preparatoires" of the International Covenant on Civil and Political Rights* (1987), or Paul Weis, *The Refugee Convention, 1951: The Travaux Preparatoires Analysed with a Commentary* (1995); but for most treaties they may not be as readily available.

§11-4. DISPUTE RESOLUTION

Although most disputes between nations are resolved by direct negotiation between the parties, some are submitted to international tribunals, arbitral bodies, or temporary commissions convened for particular disputes. Adjudications by international courts are generally recognized as authoritative, even if they lack effective enforcement procedures.

Nations are not the only parties to significant international law cases. Courts established by regional organizations resolve disputes between nations and their citizens, and are developing a growing body of international human rights law. Decisions of domestic courts on matters of international law can also be important sources, particularly as evidence of international legal custom. Commercial arbitration is increasingly prevalent in international business, and many of the awards can be located and studied.

A. INTERNATIONAL COURTS

The preeminent international tribunal is the International Court of Justice (also known as the World Court), which

succeeded the Permanent Court of International Justice of the League of Nations. The ICJ, which meets at the Hague, settles legal controversies between countries and resolves a limited number of other cases involving serious questions of international law.

ICJ decisions are published initially in individual slip opinions and later in the bound volumes of *Reports of Judgments, Advisory Opinions and Orders*. Because the Court's own publication system is rather slow, the best printed source for recent decisions is the American Society of International Law's bimonthly *International Legal Materials*. Exhibit 92 shows the first page of a recent order in a case involving the United States, as published officially by the Court.

The ICJ website <www.icj-cij.org> has recent decisions, basic documents, and information on its current docket; a mirror site at Cornell's Legal Information Institute <www.lawschool.cornell.edu/library/cijwww/> may provide quicker access for U.S. researchers. Decisions are also available online through Westlaw.

The most extensive commentary on the work of the ICJ is Shabtai Rosenne, *The Law and Practice of the International Court, 1920-1996* (4 vols., 3d ed. 1997). Rosenne is also the author of a shorter analysis, *The World Court: What It Is and How It Works* (5th ed. 1995), and editor of a useful compilation of source material, *Documents on the International Court of Justice* (3d ed. 1991). Arthur Eyffinger, *The International Court of Justice 1946-1996* (1996) is an extensively illustrated overview of the ICJ's procedures and history, with biographies of every judge during its first fifty years.

The annual *Yearbook of the International Court of Justice* contains a summary of the Court's work since 1946, basic information about the Court, and summaries of judgments

INTERNATIONAL COURT OF JUSTICE

YEAR 1999

2 June 1999

1999
2 June
General List
No. 114

CASE CONCERNING
LEGALITY OF USE OF FORCE

(YUGOSLAVIA *v.* UNITED STATES OF AMERICA)

REQUEST FOR THE INDICATION OF PROVISIONAL
MEASURES

ORDER

Present: *Vice-President* WEERAMANTRY, *Acting President*; *President*
SCHWEBEL; *Judges* ODA, BEDJAOUI, GUILLAUME, RANJEVA,
HERCZEGH, SHI, FLEISCHHAUER, KOROMA, VERESHCHETIN,
HIGGINS, PARRA-ARANGUREN, KOOIJMANS; *Judge* ad hoc KREĆA;
Registrar VALENCIA-OSPINA.

The International Court of Justice,

Composed as above,

After deliberation,

Having regard to Articles 41 and 48 of the Statute of the Court and to
Articles 73 and 74 of the Rules of Court,

Having regard to the Application by the Federal Republic of Yugoslavia (hereinafter "Yugoslavia") filed in the Registry of the Court
on 29 April 1999, instituting proceedings against the United States of
America (hereinafter "the United States") "for violation of the obligation
not to use force",

4

Exhibit 92. Case Concerning Legality of Use of Force
(Yugo. v. U.S.), 1999 I.C.J. 916 (June 2).

and opinions issued during the year. Other Court publications include *Summaries of Judgments, Advisory Opinions and Orders of the International Court of Justice: 1948-1991* (1992, with a 1997 supplement covering 1992-96); *Pleadings, Oral Arguments and Documents*, containing the briefs and documents submitted by the parties; and an annual *Bibliography of the ICJ* listing books and articles written about the Court.

Similar publications were issued by the Permanent Court of International Justice (PCIJ), the ICJ's predecessor as World Court. An unofficial compilation of PCIJ decisions was published as *World Court Reports*, edited by Manley O. Hudson (4 vols., 1934-43). *International Law Reports* (1956-date), succeeding *Annual Digest and Reports of Public International Law Cases* (1932-55), is a widely used reporter of international decisions, including all PCIJ and ICJ decisions. It also prints selected decisions of regional and national courts on international law issues.

The ICJ is not the only court of global scope. The United Nations Convention on the Law of the Sea established an International Tribunal for the Law of the Sea (ITLOS), which is based in Hamburg and issued its first judgment in July 1999. Information on ITLOS procedures and cases are available on its website <www.itlos.org>, and the Tribunal's rules and other documents are published in *Basic Texts 1998* (1999).

An International Criminal Court <www.icc-cpi.int> with jurisdiction over war crimes, genocide, and crimes against humanity also sits in the Hague and had its first session in March 2003, without United States participation. Background information and documents are available on the court's website and in works such as Antonio Cassese et al., eds., *The Rome Statute of the International Criminal Court: A Commentary* (3 vols., 2002).

Two more focused international criminal courts are currently in operation for violations of international humanitarian law in the former Yugoslavia and in Rwanda. The International Criminal Tribunal for the former Yugoslavia (ICTY) <www.un.org/icty/> was established in 1993 and meets in the Hague. ICTY has published a *Basic Documents* compilation (1995) as well as *Yearbook* and *Judicial Reports* series; these materials are also available on its website. The International Criminal Tribunal for Rwanda (ICTR) <www.ictr.org> was established in 1994 and sits in Arusha, Tanzania. Documents and judgments are available on the ICTR homepage.

Documents and analysis of the criminal courts are also available in secondary sources such as two works by Virginia Morris and Michael P. Scharf, *An Insider's Guide to the International Criminal Tribunal for the Former Yugoslavia: A Documentary History & Analysis* (2 vols., 1995) and *The International Criminal Tribunal for Rwanda* (2 vols., 1998); and their developing case law is summarized in John R.W.D. Jones, *The Practice of the International Criminal Tribunals for the Former Yugoslavia and Rwanda* (2d ed. 2000).

B. Regional and National Courts

The decisions of the courts of regional organizations have assumed growing importance in international law, as the range of disputes over which they exercise jurisdiction grows. Among the most important of these regional courts are the European Court of Justice, the European Court of Human Rights, and the Inter-American Court of Human Rights.

The European Court of Justice, an organ of the European Union, is based in Luxembourg and resolves disputes between EU institutions and member states over the interpretation and application of EU treaties and legislation. A

subordinate Court of First Instance was established in 1988 to handle certain classes of cases and reduce the Court of Justice's workload. The official *Reports of Cases Before the Court of Justice and the Court of First Instance* includes decisions from both courts. Commercial publications of these decisions include the CCH *European Union Law Reporter*, described above, and *Common Market Law Reports* (1962-date). All decisions since 1954 are also available online from both Westlaw and LexisNexis, and the ECJ's website <europa.eu.int/cj/> has recent judgments and other information.

The European Court of Human Rights <www.echr.coe.int> was created under the European Convention of Human Rights of 1950, which established a system for the international protection of the rights of individuals, and sits in Strasbourg. The Court's decisions are published officially in *Reports of Judgments and Decisions*, and are also reported commercially in *European Human Rights Reports* (1979-date, available online from Westlaw and LexisNexis). Cases are summarized in *Human Rights Case Digest* (1990-date, bimonthly), published by the British Institute of Human Rights, and major decisions have been compiled by R.A. Lawson & H.G. Schermers in *Leading Cases of the European Court of Human Rights* (1997). A variety of documents and decisions appear in the annual *Yearbook of the European Convention on Human Rights* (1958-date).

The Inter-American Commission on Human Rights <www.cidh.oas.org> was created in 1959 and hears complaints of individuals and institutions alleging violations of human rights in the American countries. The Commission, or a member state, can refer matters to the Inter-American Court of Human Rights <www.corteidh.or.cr>, created in 1978 and based in San José, Costa Rica. At least twenty-two countries (not including the United States) have accepted its jurisdiction. The Court's decisions are reported in two

series of judgments (advisory opinions in Series A, *Judgments and Opinions*; and contentious cases in Series C, *Decisions and Judgments*), in its annual report, and on its website. The *Inter-American Yearbook on Human Rights* (1985-date) covers the work of both the Commission and the Court and includes selected decisions and other documents. Major texts are published in *Basic Documents Pertaining to Human Rights in the Inter-American System* (2001) and are available on the Internet <www.cidh.oas.org/basic.htm>.

Judicial decisions of national courts on matters of international law are also valuable sources of information. While any U.S. court may be faced with international legal issues, one with a particular expertise is the U.S. Court of International Trade (CIT). Its decisions are reported officially in the *U.S. Court of International Trade Reports*, as well as in the *Federal Supplement* and in BNA's *International Trade Reporter* (1980-date), which also includes cases from other courts (including the Court of Appeals for the Federal Circuit reviewing CIT decisions), administrative agencies, and binational panels under the North American Free Trade Agreement. CIT decisions are also available from LexisNexis and Westlaw, and the court's website <www.cit.uscourts.gov> provides copies of slip opinions since 1999.

Cases from the U.S. and other countries under the Convention on Contracts for the International Sale of Goods are published in a looseleaf reporter, *UNILEX* (1996-date), and are available on the Internet through Pace University's Institute of International Commercial Law <www.cisg.law.pace.edu>. International law cases from some countries are published or summarized in national yearbooks, periodicals, and digests of international law, as well as a few specialized case reporters (such as *British International Law Cases* and *Commonwealth International Law*

Cases). As noted earlier, *International Law Reports* includes selected decisions of domestic courts as well as those of international tribunals.

C. Arbitrations

An increasing number of disputes, between nations and between commercial partners, are settled by arbitration. The Hague Peace Conferences of 1899 and 1907 regularized international arbitration and created the Permanent Court of Arbitration and the International Commission of Inquiry. Their decisions were published in the *Hague Court Reports*, edited by James B. Scott (2 vols., 1916-32). This set was continued by the United Nations series, *Reports of International Arbitral Awards* (1948-date), with retrospective coverage back to the end of Scott's reports. The awards now appear in English or French with bilingual headnotes. The UN series includes agreements reached by mediation or conciliation, as well as awards resulting from contested arbitrations, but it is limited to disputes in which states are the parties.

Repertory of International Arbitral Jurisprudence (3 vols., 1989-91) collects arbitral decisions from 1794 to 1987 and arranges them by subject, and A.M. Stuyt, ed., *Survey of International Arbitrations, 1794-1989* (3d ed. 1990) provides an extensive digest of decisions.

Several sources cover international arbitrations between private parties, including *Yearbook: Commercial Arbitration* (1975-date) and Hans Smit & Vratislav Pechota, eds., *World Arbitration Reporter* (1986-date). Some coverage is provided in *International Legal Materials*, and selected decisions appear in the *American Review of International Arbitration* (1990-date). Two major current awareness services in this area are BNA's *World Arbitration &*

Mediation Report (1990-date, monthly) and *Mealey's International Arbitration Report* (1986-date, monthly, available through LexisNexis).

Other major publications on commercial arbitration include Pieter Sanders, ed., *International Handbook on Commercial Arbitration* (4 vols., 1984-date) and Clive M. Schmitthoff, ed., *International Commercial Arbitration* (5 vols., 1979-date). The leading one-volume treatise in the area is Alan Redfern & Martin Hunter, *Law and Practice of International Commercial Arbitration* (3d ed. 1999); Jack J. Coe, Jr., *International Commercial Arbitration: American Principles and Practice in a Global Context* (1997) provides a U.S. perspective as well as numerous appendices containing the major arbitration treaties and rules. Further research leads are available in H. Smit & V. Pechota, *Commercial Arbitration: An International Bibliography* (2d ed. 1998).

§11-5. Secondary Sources and Document Collections

As in other areas of law, it is often best to begin international law research with a reference work or law review article for background information and for help in analyzing the issues involved. A general treatise, such as Peter Malanczuk, *Akehurst's Modern Introduction to International Law* (8th ed. 2002) or Ian Brownlie, *Principles of Public International Law* (5th ed. 1998), can provide an overview of international law doctrine.

The *Encyclopedia of Public International Law,* edited by Rudolf Bernhardt and published under the auspices of the Max Planck Institute for Comparative Public Law and International Law, provides a comprehensive view of international law issues. Its articles are written by respected authorities, are short but informative, and provide brief

bibliographies for further research. The set was originally published in 12 volumes (1981-90), with each volume devoted to one or more specific subjects, and has been reissued in one alphabetical sequence (4 vols., 1992-2000), with some additional articles and addenda.

To study state practice in international law, it is best to turn to sources summarizing or explaining how a particular nation has acted in the past. Reference works such as Bruce W. Jentleson & Thomas G. Paterson, eds., *Encyclopedia of U.S. Foreign Relations* (4 vols., 1997), can provide a background understanding. More detailed discussion of United States practice can be found in a series of encyclopedic digests of international law published by the Department of State. These digests are based on treaties, decisions, statutes and other documents reflecting the U.S. position on major issues of international law, and are essentially official restatements of American international law.

The most current U.S. digest (although long outdated) is Marjorie M. Whiteman's *Digest of International Law* (15 vols., 1963-73), focusing largely on the period from the 1940s to the 1960s. The Whiteman *Digest* is supplemented by a Department of State series called *Digest of United States Practice in International Law*. Annual volumes were issued 1973-80 and three cumulative volumes cover 1981-88; publication was then suspended until annual volumes resumed in 2000. Current materials are digested in "Contemporary Practice of the United States Relating to International Law," a feature in each quarterly issue of the *American Journal of International Law*.

The earlier digests of international law published by the Department of State, with slight variations in title, were by the following compilers: Francis Wharton (3 vols., 1886; 2d

ed. 1887); John Bassett Moore (8 vols., 1906), covering the period 1776 to 1906 and effectively superseding Wharton; and G.H. Hackworth (8 vols., 1940-44), covering the period 1906 to 1939. Since material in Moore and Hackworth is not reprinted in later digests, they retain their research value for the period covered.

More extensive documentation of U.S. practice can be found in *Foreign Relations of the United States* (1861-date), a series prepared by the Historical Office of the Department of State to provide a comprehensive record of material relating to such issues as treaty negotiation and international conflicts. Unfortunately, there is a time lag of more than thirty years between the original (often confidential) issuance of these documents and their publication in this series. Some volumes, particularly from the Kennedy and Johnson administrations, are available online <www.state.gov/r/pa/ho/frus/>. A selected series, *American Foreign Policy: Current Documents*, appeared after a much shorter delay but ceased publication in 1991.

The American Law Institute's *Restatement (Third) of the Foreign Relations Law of the United States* (2 vols., 1987) is an unofficial but respected summary of American law and practice in international law and foreign relations. The *Restatement (Second) of Conflict of Laws* (4 vols., 1971-80) covers private international law from an American perspective. Appendices to both Restatements include abstracts of citing court decisions.

The practices of other nations can often be found in annual publications such as the *British Yearbook of International Law* or the *Annuaire Français de Droit International*. Most of these yearbooks also include scholarly articles on international law and reprint selected major documents. Several countries also publish documentary compilations similar to

the U.S. foreign relations collections, some as large retrospective collections primarily useful for historical research and others providing continuing series of contemporary materials.

Several collections reprint a variety of important international law documents, usually in specific areas. These include Ian Brownlie, ed., *Basic Documents in International Law* (5th ed. 2002); Ian Brownlie & Guy S. Goodwin-Gill, eds., *Basic Documents on Human Rights* (4th ed. 2002); P.W. Birnie & A.E. Boyle, eds., *Basic Documents on International Law and the Environment* (1995); Richard Plender, ed., *Basic Documents on International Migration Law* (2d ed. 1997); and Chia-Jui Cheng, ed., *Basic Documents on International Trade Law* (3d ed. 1999). Online versions of Stephen Zamora & Ronald A. Brand, eds., *Basic Documents of International Economic Law* (2 vols., 1990) are available from both Westlaw and LexisNexis, updated with more recent documents.

§11-6. Sources For Further Information

Materials involved in international law issues are often published in diverse, elusive sources, and specialized bibliographies and research guides can be valuable finding aids. One of the most useful of these, and most frequently updated, is the American Society of International Law's *ASIL Guide to Electronic Resources for International Law*, available in print and online <www.asil.org/resource/home.htm>, with sections on the United Nations, treaties, and several topical areas. In total it provides links to about 2,000 Internet resources in international law.

Another major Internet source for international law information is Law Library Resource Xchange, or LLRX, which publishes heavily linked research guides on specific topics. Its International Law Guides page <www.llrx.com/

international_law.html> provides an annotated list of more than three dozen guides in the area. Many law school library websites also have links to materials in international law; one of the most thorough is New York University's Guide to Foreign and International Legal Databases <www.law.nyu.edu/library/foreign_intl/>.

A number of published guides to specific areas have appeared in recent years, including several prepared under the auspices of the American Association of Law Libraries: Marylin J. Raisch & Roberta I. Shaffer, eds., *Introduction to Transnational Legal Transactions* (1995); Lyonette Louis-Jacques & Jeanne S. Korman, eds., *Introduction to International Organizations* (1996); Gitelle Seer & Maria I. Smolka-Day, eds., *Introduction to International Business Law: Legal Transactions in the Global Economy* (1996); and Ellen G. Schaffer & Randall J. Snyder, eds., *Contemporary Practice of Public International Law* (1997). Other recent works include Jeanne Rehberg & Radu D. Popa, eds., *Accidental Tourist on the New Frontier: An Introductory Guide to Global Legal Research* (1998), and the George Washington University Journal of International Law and Economics, *Guide to International Legal Research* (4th ed. 2002). Jack Tobin & Jennifer Green, *Guide to Human Rights Research* (1994) is a bit more dated, but it is available on the Internet <www.law.harvard.edu/Programs/HRP/guide/rgtoc.html> where it is supplemented by a more current "Getting Started in Human Rights Research" <www.law.harvard.edu/programs/HRP/Publications/research.html>.

Several publications focus on new scholarship in international law. The *Index to Foreign Legal Periodicals* (1960-date, quarterly, available through Westlaw and other database systems) is principally an index of journals published in countries outside the common law system, but it also indexes articles on international law in selected American

law reviews on international law. An Internet-based German index, RAVE (Rechtsprechung und Aufsätze zum Völker- und Europarecht) (Decisions and Articles in Public International Law and European law) <www.jura.uni-duesseldorf.de/rave/> covers recent court decisions and articles in more than 180 legal journals, with links to the full text of articles available on the Internet.

Public International Law: A Current Bibliography of Books and Articles (1975-date, semiannual) is a comprehensive index of the literature in the field. Each issue of the *American Journal of International Law* contains an extensive section reviewing or noting new works in the field, and the *International Journal of Legal Information* regularly publishes bibliographies devoted to specific areas of foreign and international law.

§11-7. Conclusion

This brief survey of international law highlights the extent and variety of available sources. With the increasingly global nature of business and legal relationships, and the frequent treatment of transnational legal issues by American courts, international law research is no longer an exotic specialty known only to a few practitioners.

In researching international law, it is important for American lawyers *not* to limit their inquiry to U.S. sources. Materials from international organizations and other countries can provide new perspectives and present solutions that may not be readily apparent from within the U.S. legal tradition. A facility with other languages assists greatly in broadening the scope of research, but as this chapter has shown there are a large number of English-language resources available for serious international law study.

CHAPTER 12
THE LAW OF OTHER COUNTRIES

■ ■ ■ ■ ■ ■ ■ ■ ■ ■

§12-1. Introduction

Expanded foreign communication, travel, and trade have made the law of other countries increasingly significant to American social and economic life. The law of a foreign country may be relevant in American court proceedings involving international transactions, and scholars and lawmakers can study other legal systems to better understand and improve our own. Foreign law sources are also essential to the study of comparative law, in which differences among national legal systems are analyzed.

The legal systems of most foreign countries can be described as either *common law* or *civil law*. Each system has its own history, its own fundamental principles and procedures, and its own forms of publication for legal sources. Under the common law, as explained in Chapter 1, legal doctrine is derived from specific cases decided by judges rather than from broad, abstractly articulated codifications. Judicial decisions are traditionally the most important and vital source of new legal rules in a common law system.

The civil law system refers to the legal tradition, arising out of Roman law and the European codes, which characterizes the countries of continental Europe, Latin America, and parts of Africa and Asia. There are several distinctive characteristics of the civil law system: the predominance of comprehensive and systematic codes governing large fields of law (civil, criminal, commercial, civil procedure, and criminal procedure); the strong influence of concepts, terms and principles from Roman law; little weight for judicial decisions as legal authority; and great influence of legal scholars who interpret, criticize and develop the law in their writings, particularly through commentaries on the codes.

There are also countries which do not fit clearly into either the civil law or common law systems, but are strongly influenced by customary law or traditional religious systems, particularly Hindu or Islamic law. The law of these countries (e.g. India, Israel, Pakistan and Saudi Arabia) may be a mixture of civil *or* common law and the religious legal system.

The differences between the common law and civil law systems have become less marked in recent years, as each system adopts features of the other. Codes have been enacted in some American jurisdictions, for example, while judicial decisions are being given greater weight in some civil law countries. Nonetheless, basic differences remain in how legal issues are perceived and in how research is conducted.

§12-2. ENGLISH AND COMMONWEALTH LAW

The common law system originated in England and spread to its colonies around the world. Most of these nations, now known as the Commonwealth, still have legal systems modeled on the English common law. This chapter looks at three major common law jurisdictions: England (which is part of the United Kingdom but has a separate body of law from Northern Ireland and Scotland), Canada, and Australia.

While related, the legal systems of these countries are quite distinct. The United Kingdom has an "unwritten constitution," meaning that its basic constitutional principles are not found in one specific document. The U.K. has been part of the European Community (now the European Union) since 1973 and is increasingly governed by EU treaties and legislation. The Canadian and Australian systems have federal governments and written constitutions. Canada's Constitution, dating back to 1867, was dramati-

cally changed when the Constitution Act 1982 added an
extensive new Charter of Rights and Freedoms. The
Australian Constitution has been in effect, with relatively
few amendments, since 1901. Further information is available in overviews such as Stephen Bailey et al., *Smith,
Bailey and Gunn on the Modern English Legal System* (4th ed.
2002); Richard Ward, *Walker & Walker's English Legal System*
(8th ed. 1998); Gerald L. Gall, *The Canadian Legal System*
(4th ed. 1995); or Gerard B. Carter, *Australian Legal System*
(1995).

Although the laws of England and its former colonies
have developed separately in recent years, common law
countries share a heritage which gives their decisions more
persuasive value in each other's courts than that generally
afforded to the law of other countries. English cases have
continued to influence American law on issues such as tort
causation and contract formation. Similarities in publication and research procedures make information about
English legal doctrine easily accessible to researchers in the
United States and other common law countries.

A. CASE LAW

Court reports are central to legal research in England and
other common law countries, and research is simplified by
the relatively small number of published decisions compared to the fifty state jurisdictions and federal system in
the United States. England has one straightforward structure of trial and appellate courts, with the House of Lords
as the court of last resort. The Canadian and Australian
federal court systems are more like that of the United
States, although fundamental differences exist. In the U.S.,
for example, state supreme courts are the final arbiters on
issues of state law, while any decision from a Canadian
provincial court or an Australian state court is generally
subject to review by the highest federal court in its country.

Publication of cases. As in the United States, new decisions in most other common law countries are published first in weekly or monthly advance sheets and later in permanent bound volumes. Both advance sheets and volumes usually include case tables and indexes. Official or authorized series of reports are published, but unofficial commercial reporters often provide quicker access to new cases and may contain more useful headnotes and digests.

English law reporting has had a long and varied history. The recording of cases began with fragmentary reports in the *Plea Rolls*, dating from the reign of Richard I in 1189. The *Year Books*, covering the long period from 1285 to 1537, include both reports of proceedings and brief summaries of decisions. Following the *Year Books* came the *nominate* or *nominative* reports, that is, court reports named for the person who recorded or edited them. The earliest known reporter was probably James Dyer, whose reports were published around 1550. *Plowden's Reports*, first published in 1571, are considered among the finest and most accurate, while the reports of Sir Edward Coke were probably the most influential of the period.

Most nominative reports were cumulated into *The English Reports*, covering cases from 1220 to 1865 in 176 volumes. This invaluable set contains about 100,000 decisions originally published in some 275 series of nominative reporters. The volumes are arranged by court, star-paged to the original reporter, and accessible by a two-volume alphabetical table of cases. There is no subject index, but CD-ROM and Internet versions from Jutastat <www.jutatstat.com> now provide keyword access to the entire set. Another compilation of older cases, the *Revised Reports*, covers 1785 to 1866 in 149 volumes and includes some decisions not found in *The English Reports*.

For decisions since 1865, the standard source is the semi-official *Law Reports*, which now consists of four series: *Appeal Cases* (House of Lords and the Judicial Committee of the Privy Council); *Queen's Bench Division*; *Chancery Division*; and *Family Division*. Before appearing in these four separate series, new cases are published in *Weekly Law Reports*, which also includes some decisions unreported in the four *Law Reports* series.

All England Law Reports (1936-date) is a commercially published reporter which often issues new cases sooner than the *Weekly Law Reports* and contains some decisions which are not published elsewhere. As in the United States, numerous specialized subject reporters are also published.

Exhibit 93 shows a decision of the Court of Exchequer (which was abolished in 1875) in *Fletcher v. Rylands*, the case famous for establishing the ultrahazardous activity doctrine, as published in *The English Reports*. Note the bracketed star paging reference to page 774 of the original nominative reporter, Hurlstone & Coltman's *Exchequer Reports* (cited as H. &. C.).

Canada and Australia both have authorized reports for their federal court of last resort (*Canada Supreme Court Reports*, and *Commonwealth Law Reports* for the High Court of Australia). Both nations also have lower federal courts with trial and appellate jurisdiction, and courts in each province or state. In Canada, the commercially published *National Reporter* contains decisions of the Supreme Court and the Federal Court of Appeal, and *Dominion Law Reports* contains decisions from both federal and provincial courts. The High Court of Australia's decisions are also published in the *Australian Law Reports*, along with lower federal court cases and state court cases on federal issues; *Federal Law Reports* duplicates some of this coverage of lower court

any part of the journey.   That principle was recognized and adopted in *Scothorn* v. *The South Staffordshire Railway Company* (8 Exch. 341). [Martin, B. The decision of the House of Lords in *The Bristol and Exeter Railway Company v. Collins* (7 H. L. Cas. 194) is conclusive of this case.]

Grove (Horatio Lloyd with him), in support of the rule. Pickford & Co. were the agents not of the defendants, but of the London and North Western Railway Company, and had a direct interest in sending goods by that Company.   The contract of the defendants was to carry the clock to Stafford and there deliver it to the London and North Western Railway Company. [Bramwell, B. Suppose a parcel was delivered to the South Western Railway at Reading addressed to a person at Dover, " per London, Chatham and Dover Railway," which Company would have been liable if it was lost?]   The South Western Railway Company would have performed their contract when they delivered the goods to the London, Chatham and Dover Railway.   There was no proof of a contract by the plaintiff with the defendants. The plaintiff's contract **[774]** was with Pickford & Co., who contracted with the defendants. *Muschamp* v. *The Lancaster, &c., Railway Company* (8 M. & W. 421) only decided that where nothing is said about the route, there is primâ facie one contract to carry the whole distance.

Cur. adv. vult.

POLLOCK, C. B., now said,—The question in this case was, whether the Great Western Railway Company were liable to the plaintiff for damage done to his clock during the transit om Worcester to Chester.   I am of opinion v 'h the rest of the Court that there was evidence for the jury of one contract only and not two contracts. The jury have so found, and we think there was evidence to warrant their finding. The rule must therefore be discharged.

Rule discharged.

FLETCHER *v.* RYLANDS AND HORROCKS.   May 3, 4, 5, 1865.—The defendant made a reservoir for water on his land, and in the selection of the site and the planning and construction of the reservoir employed a competent engineer and competent contractors.   In excavating the bed of the reservoir five old shafts were met with, running vertically downwards to old coal workings under the site of the reservoir, and communicating with the plaintiff's colliery by means of other old coal workings under intervening lands.   These shafts were filled with soil of the same kind as that which immediately surrounded them, and it was not known to or suspected by the defendant, or the persons employed by him in planning or constructing the reservoir, that they were shafts which had been made for the purpose of getting coal under the land beneath the reservoir, or that they led down to coal workings under its site.   When the reservoir was completed, and partially filled with water, one of these shafts burst downwards, in consequence of which the water flowed into the old workings underneath the reservoir, and by means of the underground communications, into the plaintiff's colliery, and flooded it.   There was no personal negligence or default on the part of the defendant, but reasonable and proper care and skill were not exercised by the persons employed, with reference to the shafts, to provide for the sufficiency of the reservoir to bear the pressure of water which, when filled, it would have to bear.—Held, that under these circumstances, the defendant was not responsible for the damage done to the plaintiff by the water from the reservoir flooding his colliery : per Pollock, C. B., and Martin, B.   Dissentiente Bramwell, B.—Per Bramwell, B.   That the defendant was responsible, on the ground that he had caused water to flow into the plaintiff's colliery which but for the defendants' act would not have gone there.

[S. C. 34 L. J. Ex. 177 ; 11 Jur. (N. S.) 714 ; 13 W. R. 992 : reversed 1866, 4 H. & C. 263 ; L. R. 1 Ex. 265 ; 35 L. J. Ex. 154 ; 12 Jur. (N. S.) 603 ; 14 W. R. 799 : the latter decision affirmed 1868, L. R. 3 H. L. 330 ; 37 L. J. Ex. 161 ; 19 L. T. 220 : referred to in numerous cases. Applied, *Jones* v. *Festiniog Railway*, 1868, L. R. 3 Q. B. 736.   Not applied, *The Thetis*, 1869, L. R. 2 Adm. & Ec. 369. Distinguished, *Carstairs* v. *Taylor*, 1871, L. R. 6 Ex. 221 ; *Wilson* v. *Newberry*, 1871, L. R. 7 Q. B. 33 ; *Boughton* v. *Midland Great Western*

EX. DIV. XV.—24

Exhibit 93.   Fletcher v. Rylands, 159 Eng. Rep. 737 (Ex. 1865).

decisions. In addition, each country has reporters for the supreme courts of its provinces or states, as well as topical reporters in specialized subject areas.

Extensive coverage of judicial decisions from the United Kingdom, Canada, and Australia is available from LexisNexis and Westlaw, as well as from other commercial systems based in those countries. Free Internet access to decisions is provided by the British and Irish Legal Information Institute <www.bailii.org>, the Canadian Legal Information Institute <www.canlii.org>, and the Australasian Legal Information Institute <www.austlii.edu.au>.

Case research tools. Many of the same types of tools are available for case research in these other common law countries as are found in the United States. Digests and encyclopedias are frequently used. *Shepard's Citations* and KeyCite have no direct counterparts in other countries, but there are tools for finding later cases that have considered an earlier decision.

Each country has a major national digest, somewhat similar to the West digest system: *The Digest: Annotated British, Commonwealth and European Cases* (109 vols., 3d ed. 1971-date); the *Canadian Abridgment* (110 vols., 2d ed. 1966-date); and the *Australian Digest* (60 vols., 3d ed. 1988-date). All three sets include consolidated indexes and tables of cases, and each is updated regularly by bound or looseleaf supplements. The Canadian and Australian digests are further updated in the monthly issues of *Canadian Current Law Case Law Digests* and the *Australian Legal Monthly Digest*.

Another English service useful for both finding and updating cases is *Current Law*. Its *Monthly Digest* contains summaries of new court decisions arranged by subject and a table of cases which have been judicially considered. The

case summaries cumulate at the end of the year into the *Current Law Year Book*, and the case tables into the *Current Law Case Citator*. The *Case Citator*, which consists of two volumes and an annual paperback supplement, lists, by name, cases decided or cited since 1947. For those cases which have been judicially considered, the effect of each later case is indicated with notes such as "Overruled," "Applied," or "Considered."

Updating Canadian and Australian cases is possible through *Canadian Case Citations* and the *Australian Case Citator*. Like their English counterpart, tables in these works are arranged alphabetically by case name and are useful for finding citations as well as for determining later treatment of cited decisions. *Canadian Current Law* and *Australian Current Law Reporter* update these citators and provide information on recent cases.

B. STATUTES AND REGULATIONS

Statutes in other common law jurisdictions are published both in session laws and in compilations of statutes in force. The compilations, however, generally reprint acts alphabetically by name or chronologically, rather than by subject. There is no official counterpart to the *United States Code*, in which each part of an act is systematically assigned to a title and given a section number as part of a general subject compilation of statutes. Instead, acts are usually identified by their original name and date of enactment.

The current national session law publications are *Public General Acts* (for Britain), *Statutes of Canada*, and *Acts of the Parliament of the Commonwealth of Australia*; each is published in annual volumes with subject indexes or tables of acts for each year. Statutes of the individual Canadian provinces and Australian states are published in similar annual volumes.

The standard historical collection of English statutes is the *Statutes of the Realm* (11 vols., 1810-22), covering 1235 to 1713. Several other chronological collections were published during the 19th century under the title *Statutes at Large*, extending coverage to the beginning of the modern *Public General Acts* in 1866.

The source most frequently used for English statutory research is *Halsbury's Statutes of England and Wales* (54 vols., 4th ed. 1985-date), an unofficial compilation similar to U.S. annotated codes, with footnote annotations to judicial decisions. *Halsbury's* is a well-indexed encyclopedic arrangement of acts in force, updated with annual bound supplements and looseleaf volumes (*Current Statutes Service*, containing annotated versions of new statutes, and *Noter-Up Service*, providing references to developments since the latest annual supplement). A consolidated *Table of Statutes and General Index* is published annually. Exhibit 94 shows a page from *Halsbury's Statutes* containing the beginning of an 1883 act still in force as amended; notes provide explanations and cross-references to related acts.

Current English statutes are also available on LexisNexis and Westlaw, and recent acts beginning in 1988 are available on the Internet <www.hmso.gov.uk/acts.htm>. The Parliament website <www.parliament.uk> provides information about procedures, debates, and pending legislation.

Current Law Legislation Citators, published as part of the *Current Law* service, contains a chronological list of British statutes, with each followed by references to later statutes and cases which affect it. Coverage includes any statutes amended, repealed, or considered in judicial decisions since 1947. Four volumes cover 1947 to 1999, with updating provided by annual supplements and monthly coverage in *Current Law Monthly Digest*.

EXPLOSIVE SUBSTANCES ACT 1883

(46 & 47 Vict c 3)

ARRANGEMENT OF SECTIONS

An Act to amend the Law relating to Explosive Substances   [10 April 1883]

Northern Ireland This Act applies As respects Northern Ireland, s 3 was amended as noted thereto; s 4 was amended by the Criminal Justice Act (Northern Ireland) 1953, s 1(2), the Treatment of Offenders (Northern Ireland) Order 1989, SI 1989/1344, Sch 1, para 1, and the Police and Criminal Evidence (Northern Ireland) Order 1989, SI 1989/1341, art 90(2), (3), Sch 7, Pt III; and s 7 was partly repealed by the Indictments Act (Northern Ireland) 1945, s 9(3), Sch 2, the Criminal Law Act (Northern Ireland) 1967, s 15(2), Sch 2, Pt II, and the Criminal Jurisdiction Act 1975, s 14(5), Sch 6, Pt I.

1 Short title

This Act may be cited as the Explosive Substances Act 1883.

[2 Causing explosion likely to endanger life or property

A person who in the United Kingdom or (being a citizen of the United Kingdom and Colonies) in the Republic of Ireland unlawfully and maliciously causes by any explosive substance an explosion of a nature likely to endanger life or to cause serious injury to property shall, whether any injury to person or property has been actually caused or not, be guilty of an offence and on conviction on indictment shall be liable to imprisonment for life.]

NOTES

Amendments Substituted by Criminal Jurisdiction Act 1975, s 7(1), (3).

United Kingdom Ie Great Britain and Northern Ireland; see the Interpretation Act 1978, s 5, Sch 1, **Vol 41**, title Statutes "Great Britain" means England, Scotland and Wales by virtue of the Union with Scotland Act 1706, preamble, Art 1, Vol 10, title Constitutional Law (Pt 1), as read with s 22(1) of, and Sch 2, para 5(a) to, the 1978 Act. Neither the Channel Islands nor the Isle of Man is within the United Kingdom.

Citizen of the United Kingdom and Colonies This expression is defined, for the purposes of enactments passed before 1983, by the British Nationality Act 1981, s 51(3)(a), Vol 31, title Nationality and Immigration. As to references to ceasing to be such a citizen, see s 51(3)(b) of that Act.

Republic of Ireland Ie that part of Ireland previously officially known in this country as Eire and originally called the Irish Free State; see the Ireland Act 1949, s 1(1), (3), Vol 7, title Commonwealth and Other Territories, in conjunction with the Eire (Confirmation of Agreements) Act 1938, s 1 (repealed).

Conviction on indictment All proceedings on indictment are to be brought before the Crown Court; see the Supreme Court Act 1981, s 46(1), Vol 11, title Courts and Legal Services

Visiting forces and international headquarters A member of a visiting force or of a civilian component of such a force and a member of a designated international headquarters or defence organisation is not, in certain cases, liable to be tried by a United Kingdom court for an offence punishable under this section; see the Visiting Forces Act 1952, s 3, Schedule, para 1, Vol 3, title Armed Forces (Pt 4), and the International Headquarters and Defence Organisations Act 1964, s 1, Schedule, para 4, Vol 10, title Constitutional Law (Pt 5).

Exhibit 94.   Explosive Substances Act 1883, 46 & 47 Vict., ch. 70 (Eng.), *reprinted in* 12 HALSBURY'S STATUTES OF ENGLAND AND WALES 12 (4th ed. 2002 reissue).

Canadian and Australian statutes are available online, but neither country has an annotated, regularly updated publication similar to *Halsbury's Statutes*. The Consolidated Statutes of Canada are available from the Department of Justice Canada <laws.justice.gc.ca/en/index.html>, and links to provincial sources can be found through the Canadian Legal Information Institute <www.canlii.org>. The Australasian Legal Information Institute <www.austlii.edu.au> has a wealth of legislative information, including Commonwealth Consolidated Acts and state statutes. Coverage of much of this material is also available from LexisNexis, Westlaw, and other commercial databases.

Recent legislative activity by Canadian federal and provincial governments is noted in *Canadian Current Law Legislation*, and references to citing cases can be found by using *Canadian Statute Citations*. In Australia, *Commonwealth Statutes Annotations* and *Federal Statutes Annotations* both provide references to amendments and to cases citing federal statutes. Similar works are available for some Australian states, and information on federal and state legislative developments is available in such publications as the *Australian Legal Monthly Digest* and *Australian Current Law Legislation*.

While parliamentary debates and other legislative documents are also published in each of these countries, legislative history materials are generally considered less persuasive than in the United States for purposes of statutory interpretation. Some use of parliamentary materials, however, has now been accepted by courts in most countries. Parliamentary websites (<www.parliament.uk>, <www.parl.gc.ca>, <www.aph.gov.au>) provide information on available sources.

As in the United States, delegated legislation such as administrative or local law plays a vital role in the legal system of Commonwealth nations. Regulations, the most common form of delegated legislation, are known in Britain as *statutory instruments* and in Australia as *statutory rules*. The most useful printed source for research in English statutory instruments is the unofficial *Halsbury's Statutory Instruments* (25 vols., 4th ed. 1978-date). The texts of all statutory instruments of general effect currently in force, including many not printed in *Halsbury's*, are available online from Westlaw and LexisNexis, and instruments since 1987 are on the Web <www.hmso.gov.uk/stat.htm>. *Current Law* lists new instruments and includes them in its subject digests, and the *Current Law Legislation Citators* covers statutory instruments, noting amendments or revocations as well as other references. Access to Canadian regulations and Australian statutory rules is similar to that for statutes, with the most current resources available electronically from the websites noted above.

c. SECONDARY SOURCES

The secondary literature of other common law countries parallels that of the United States, with a variety of treatises, practitioners' handbooks, looseleaf services, and other materials. This section examines only a few basic resources.

Encyclopedias. Like *Am. Jur. 2d* and *C.J.S.*, legal encyclopedias in other nations contain concise statements of ruling law and extensive footnote references to primary sources. Foreign legal encyclopedias may be even more useful than those from one's own country, since they summarize unfamiliar legal doctrines and provide convenient references to materials that might otherwise be difficult to find.

Halsbury's Laws of England (84 vols., 4th ed. 1973-date) is more comprehensive than the American legal encyclopedias, because it covers just one jurisdiction and

can encompass statutes and administrative sources as well
as case law. Access to the set is provided by a subject index
and by tables of cases and statutes cited. The encyclopedia
is updated by cumulative annual supplements and *Current
Service* looseleaf volumes, which include a "Monthly
Review" summarizing new developments.

While there is no general legal encyclopedia for all of
Canada, two regional encyclopedias include coverage of
Canadian federal law: *Canadian Encyclopedic Digest
(Ontario)* (40 vols., 3d ed. 1973-date), and *Canadian
Encyclopedic Digest (Western)* (43 vols., 3d ed. 1979-date).
There are two competing comprehensive Australian legal
encyclopedias, *Halsbury's Laws of Australia* (33 vols., 1991-
date) and *The Laws of Australia* (55 vols., 1993-date).

Martindale-Hubbell International Law Digest is hardly a
substitute for an encyclopedic treatment and original
sources, but it provides convenient summaries of major
legal principles and references to primary sources for
England, Canada, and Australia, as well as each Canadian
province, Northern Ireland, Scotland, and several other
common law countries.

Periodicals and treatises. No other country has a profu-
sion of legal periodicals to match that in the United States,
but the forms of publication are similar. Each nation has a
variety of academic law reviews and professional journals.
The major American indexes (*Index to Legal Periodicals* and
Current Law Index/Legal Resource Index) include coverage of
most of the world's major English-language journals, but
indexes published in other countries may provide more
specific coverage of local legal issues. *Legal Journals Index*,
covering more than 400 British publications, is available
through Westlaw (a print version began publication in 1986
but ceased in 1999), and references to recent English books

and articles appear in *Current Law*. The most comprehensive Canadian index is *Canadian Legal Literature* (1981-date), supplemented by listings in *Canadian Current Law*; and recent Australian material can be found using the *Australian Legal Monthly Digest* or *Australian Current Law Reporter*.

Dictionaries and research guides. Reference works can help considerably in researching another country's laws. Legal dictionaries ensure that words are understood in their proper context, and foreign research guides contain more detailed and precise discussion than is possible in an American treatment.

The major English legal dictionary is *Jowitt's Dictionary of English Law* (2 vols., 2d ed. 1977, with 1985 supp.); two shorter, more current works are Elizabeth A. Martin, ed., *A Dictionary of Law* (5th ed. 2002), and *Osborn's Concise Law Dictionary* (9th ed. 2001). Daphne A. Dukelow & Betsy Nuse, *The Dictionary of Canadian Law* (2d ed. 1995) is the most substantial treatment of Canadian legal definitions, and Australian legal terms are defined in *Butterworths Australian Legal Dictionary* (1997). David M. Walker's *Oxford Companion to Law* (1980) is a cross between a dictionary and an encyclopedia, providing concise explanations of basic common and civil law concepts, documents, events, and institutions.

English legal research materials are discussed in Guy Holborn, *Butterworths Legal Research Guide* (2d ed. 2001), and Philip A. Thomas & John Knowles, *Dane & Thomas: How to Use a Law Library* (4th ed. 2001). Similar treatment for Canada is offered by Margaret A. Banks & Karen E.H. Foti, *Banks on Using a Law Library* (6th ed. 1994), and Douglass T. MacEllven & Michael J. McGuire, *Legal Research Handbook* (4th ed. 1998). Texts for Australia include

Enid Campbell et al., *Legal Research: Materials and Methods* (4th ed. 1996), and Richard A. Haigh & Poh York Lee, *Researching Australian Law* (1997).

§12-3. CIVIL LAW

An American lawyer or law student researching the law of a civil law country must be cognizant of the major differences between the civil and common law systems, and the effect of these differences on how legal problems are viewed and how research is conducted. Instead of searching for precedents in factually similar judicial decisions, a civil lawyer looks first to the abstract provisions of the code for a logical and appropriate legal principle. Among the most important sources are extensive article-by-article commentaries on the major codes; the most scholarly and reputable of these commentaries are themselves sources of the law. Other laws, such as legislation, regulations, and decrees, are most often found in official gazettes, which are comparable to but usually broader in scope than the *Federal Register*. Court decisions are published, but they are generally of secondary importance.

Research approaches in civil law vary by country and by topic, and no single procedure will work for all purposes. Because of the difficulty of covering the great variety of sources and procedures in foreign languages and the relative inaccessibility of such sources to most American lawyers, we will focus first on introductory research in English and then briefly treat research in original sources.

A. RESEARCH IN ENGLISH

While thorough research on a foreign law issue can only be undertaken in the language of the jurisdiction, English-language materials can provide a working knowledge of the major legal issues. It is usually best to begin with an encyclopedia or treatise for a general introduction to a

national legal system, or, if possible, to the specific legal subject in question. A bibliographic guide for the jurisdiction or subject, listing and describing available primary and secondary sources, can help clarify the range of research options. With some understanding of the basic concepts and terminology of the subject matter and a general sense of the publications available in English, one can then begin research in translations and summaries.

Encyclopedias and legal guides. Several encyclopedic works provide coverage of legal topics in various nations. The most comprehensive work in English, the *International Encyclopedia of Comparative Law* (17 vols., 1971-date), is still incomplete after more than thirty years. Most of the encyclopedia covers specific legal topics such as contracts or civil procedure, but volume 1 contains a series of "National Reports" on individual countries, with references to the main sources of law and topical bibliographies for each country. Most of these reports, however, were published in pamphlets in the 1970s and have never been updated. Depending on the jurisdiction, much of their information may be of historical value only.

Another series of comparative law works, *International Encyclopaedia of Laws*, consists of several sets focusing on specific subjects with separate monographic pamphlets for individual countries. The oldest and most extensive of these works, *International Encyclopaedia for Labour Law and Industrial Relations* (30 vols., 1977-date), covers more than fifty countries. Newer sets covering fewer countries are available in nearly twenty other areas. These sets currently consist of one to six volumes each, but they are growing steadily. Their areas of focus, and the year each began publication, are: civil procedure (1994), commercial and economic law (1993), constitutional law (1992), contracts (1993), corporations and partnerships (1991), criminal law (1993), energy law (2001), environmental law (1991), family

and succession law (1997), insurance law (1992), intellectual property (1997), intergovernmental organizations (1996), medical law (1993), private international law (2000), property and trust law (2000), social security law (1994), subnational constitutional law (1999), tort law (2002), and transport law (1994). These can be excellent scholarly resources, although the chances of finding a specific country covered in a specific subject area are not yet very promising.

Surveys of the legal systems of more than 170 jurisdictions are included in Kenneth R. Redden & Linda L. Schlueter, eds., *Modern Legal Systems Cyclopedia* (21 vols., 1984-date). These vary considerably in length, from three to more than a hundred pages, and in quality. The dates of chapters are not indicated, but some are now clearly obsolete. This set includes a few chapters on legal research methods as well.

A much more current but less extensive publication, Herbert M. Kritzer, ed., *Legal Systems of the World: A Political, Social, and Cultural Encyclopedia* (4 vols., 2002), provides an introductory overview by subject and by jurisdiction. Articles on countries discuss history, major legal concepts, and the current structure of the legal system. Most also include charts showing the structure of court systems, and each article provides references for further reading.

A number of guides in English to the legal systems of specific countries or regions are published. These generally explain legal institutions and summarize major doctrines. A sample of recently published titles includes Francisco Avalos, *The Mexican Legal System* (2d ed. 2000); Gennady M. Danilenko & William Burnham, *Law and Legal System of the Russian Federation* (2d ed. 2000); Catherine Elliott &

Catherine Vernon, *French Legal System* (2000); Nigel G. Foster & Satish Sule, *German Legal System & Laws* (3d ed. 2002); Herbert Hausmaninger, *The Austrian Legal System* (2d ed. 2000); and Charlotte Villiers, *The Spanish Legal Tradition: An Introduction to the Spanish Law and Legal System* (1999).

The United States government publishes several useful guides to the legal and business environments in foreign countries. *Country Reports on Economic Policy and Trade Practices*, a biennial report from the Department of State to Congress, summarizes basic trade, investment, and employment laws. Internet resources include the Central Intelligence Agency's *World Factbook* <www.odci.gov/cia/publications/factbook/>, which has basic demographic and economic information about the countries of the world. More extensive *Country Commercial Guides* are prepared by the embassy staff in each country. Chapters in these guides cover topics such as economic trends, marketing, investment climate, and project financing; and appendices include addresses and telephone numbers for government and business contacts in the country, as well as statistics and lists of published sources on the country's commercial and economic conditions. These guides and other sources of information are available from the International Trade Administration website <www.export.gov/marketresearch.html>.

Several websites provide links to legal resources by country. One of the most extensive of these is Hieros Gamos <www.hg.org>, a website sponsored by an international association of law firms. Its "Law and Government Resources" section contains links to information for 230 countries. Other thorough listings of links to sites by country are the Law Library of Congress's "Nations of the World" <www.loc.gov/law/guide/nations.html> and

Cornell University's "Law by Source: Global"
<www.law.cornell.edu/world/>. Each of these provides
access to constitutions, government websites, and other
resources.

Bibliographies and research guides. When starting
research in the law of a country other than one's own, it is
essential to have some sense of what publications are available and in what sources research is best conducted. A
wide variety of bibliographic guides to foreign law are
published. Some cover several subjects and many jurisdictions, while others are specialized bibliographic surveys of
particular countries, regions, or subjects.

One of the best starting points is Thomas H. Reynolds &
Arturo A. Flores, *Foreign Law: Current Sources of Codes and
Basic Legislation in Jurisdictions of the World* (7 vols., 1989-
date), covering almost every country in the world.
A separate section for each country contains a description
of its legal system; notes on the major codifications,
gazettes, and sources for legislation and court decisions
(including those available in English or on the Internet);
and a detailed listing of codes and laws covering specific
subject areas. Exhibit 95 shows a page from the Colombia
section of *Foreign Law*, with information about basic primary sources. Note that the Commercial Code entry at the
top of the page includes references to English translations
and online sources.

Law Library Resource Xchange (LLRX) has published
guides to researching the legal systems of more than fifty
countries. Its Comparative & Foreign Law Guides page
<www.llrx.com/comparative_and_foreign_law.html> pro-
vides an annotated list of these sources, which generally
summarize the legal system, describe available documentation, and provide extensive links to electronic resources.

3. Commercial Code

Código de comercio. Decreto 471 of 27 Mar 1971 in *Diario oficial* 16 Jun 1971. Implemented by Decreto 410 of 1 Jan 1972. Translated in consolidated text, as amended through Ley 27 of 1997, in *Commercial laws of the world: Colombia,* * *Foreign tax and commercial laws* and as *New code of commerce, decree 410 of 1971.* Bogotá, Atempi Ltda., 1971– (looseleaf) (no more published?). Spanish text consolidated to Ley 27 of 1997 available on the Internet at <http://www.natlaw.com/>.‡ Full current official text was available via Viajuridica at <http://viajuridica.com>. More than half the Commercial Code translated to date in *Doing business in Colombia.* *

4. Criminal Code

Ley 599 of 24 Jul 2000 in *Diario oficial* 24 Jul 2000. In force 24 Jul 2001 at which time Ley 5 of 7 Dec 1978 and Decreto 100 of 1980 will cease to be in force. English summary and full Spanish text available at <http://www.loc.gov/law/glin/>.‡

Colombian penal code. Translated by P. Eder, South Hackensack, F.B. Rothman, 1967. Note: This is a translation of the 1936 penal code, much changed by the 1980 code, and only of historical interest.

5. Code of Criminal Procedure

Ley 600 of 24 Jul 2000 in *Diario oficial* 24 Jul 2000. In force 24 Jul 2001 at which time Decreto 2,700 of 30 Nov 1991 ceased to be in force. English summary and full Spanish text available at <http://www.loc.gov/law/glin/>.‡

OFFICIAL GAZETTE

Diario oficial. No. 1– , 1821– . Bogotá, etc. [s.n.] 1821– (title varies: *Gaceta de Colombia,* 1821–1831; *Gaceta de Nueva Granada,* 1832–1847; *Gaceta oficial,* 1848–1861; *Registro oficial,* 1862–1863; *Diario oficial,* 1864–).

COMPILATIONS OR OFFICIAL CODIFICATIONS

Exhibit 95. 1 Thomas H. Reynolds & Arturo A. Flores, Foreign Law: Current Sources of Codes and Legislation in Jurisdictions of the World *Colombia* 9 (2003).

One of the most thorough lists of both printed and electronic guides is maintained by the Columbia Law School Library <library.law.columbia.edu/foreignguide.html>.

Germain's Transnational Law Research: A Guide for Attorneys (1991-date) describes sources in international and foreign law, including translations, digests, and current awareness materials. Chapters introducing major procedural and substantive issues are followed by more detailed treatment of sources in more than three dozen subject areas and in seventeen European countries. Most chapters include helpful "where to start" sections listing key resources.

Another source for information on European legal systems is Jules Winterton & Elizabeth M. Moys, eds., *Information Sources in Law* (2d ed. 1997). Its chapters cover more than thirty countries, providing an overview of each legal system and explaining sources for legislation, codes, commentaries, court decisions, secondary sources, and current information sources. More extensive guides for individual countries include Charles Szladits & Claire M. Germain, *Guide to Foreign Legal Materials: French* (2d ed. 1985), and Timothy Kearley & Wolfram Fischer, *Charles Szladits' Guide to Foreign Legal Materials: German* (2d ed. 1990).

Richard A. Danner & Marie-Louise H. Bernal, eds., *Introduction to Foreign Legal Systems* (1994) provides a general introduction to civil law systems and more detailed coverage of the Chinese, French, Ghanaian, Japanese, Mexican, and Taiwanese systems. A chapter by Amber Lee Smith, "Foreign Law in Translation: Problems and Sources," includes an extensive annotated bibliography by jurisdiction of English translations of foreign laws.

One of the most comprehensive sources is the American Library Association's *Guide to Official Publications of Foreign Countries* (2d ed. 1997), which provides an annotated listing of gazettes, statistical yearbooks, court reports, and other publications for more than 170 countries. Commercially published guides, bibliographies, and directories are included as well as official sources.

The most thorough guide to the vast body of English-language secondary literature on foreign legal systems is *Szladits' A Bibliography on Foreign and Comparative Law: Books and Articles in English* (1955-date), now edited by Daniel L. Wade, S. Blair Kauffman, and Tracy L. Thompson. It is arranged by subject with geographical and author indexes. The bibliography is updated periodically by bound supplements, although there is a time lag of three or four years between coverage dates and publication. More current coverage of journal articles is available from the standard legal periodical indexes.

Translations and summaries of foreign law. The growing literature on foreign law includes many translations of actual laws, as well as multinational summaries and digests of laws on specific subjects. While translations and summaries cannot substitute for the original sources, they can provide some familiarity with the basic concepts and issues of a foreign law problem.

The simplest and most convenient starting point may be the annual *Martindale-Hubbell International Law Digest*, which has summaries of basic laws and procedures for more than sixty civil law countries. Topics covered include business regulation, foreign trade, family law, property, and taxation. Most national digests are prepared by lawyers in that nation, and include references to codes, laws, and other sources. The *International Law Digest* is available online through LexisNexis.

While civil codes determine private rights and obligations, the basic laws of government structure and individual liberties are found in national constitutions. The most current comprehensive collection of constitutions in English translation is the looseleaf set edited by Gisbert H. Flanz, *Constitutions of the Countries of the World* (20 vols., 1971-date). For some foreign-language countries, the original text of the constitution is included as well. Robert L. Maddex, *Constitutions of the World* (2d ed. 2001) provides summaries of constitutions and brief constitutional histories for 100 countries. International Constitutional Law at the University of Bern <www.oefre.unibe.ch/law/icl/> has more than eighty constitutions in English, with introductory pages providing constitutional background and history. The Constitution Finder at the University of Richmond <confinder.richmond.edu> is even more extensive, with links to constitutions from more than 180 nations and territories, some in more than one language.

Laws affecting international business are the most likely sources to be available in English. Several collections covering specific topics are published, including *Digest of Commercial Laws of the World* (5 vols., rev ed. 1998-date), *Investment Laws of the World* (10 vols., 1973-date), and *International Securities Regulation* (6 vols., 1986-date). Foreign Tax Law, Inc. publishes two extensive series, *Commercial Laws of the World* (32 vols., 1976-date) and *Tax Laws of the World* (47 vols., 1964-date), each covering more than 100 countries. The International Bureau of Fiscal Documentation publishes several series covering taxation laws throughout the world, including *African Tax Systems* (6 vols., 1970-date), *Guides to European Taxation* (15 vols., 1963-date), *Taxation in Latin America* (4 vols., 1970-date), *Taxes and Investment in Asia and the Pacific* (15 vols., 1978-date), and *Taxes and Investment in the Middle East* (4 vols., 1977-date).

Online access to foreign laws in English is not very extensive, although commercial laws of some countries are available through LexisNexis, Westlaw, and other databases. The Institute of Global Law at the University of London provides English translations of several hundred decisions from French and German courts <www.ucl.ac.uk/laws/global_law/cases/>, and the German Law Archive <iecl.iuscomp.org/gla/> has numerous sources in English including statutes, court decisions, secondary sources, and bibliographies. Several law school libraries provide links to sites for laws in other countries, in translation and in their original languages. The University of Houston's "Foreign Primary Law on the Web" <www.law.uh.edu/libraries/fi/foreignlaw.html> lists sites for almost 100 countries.

B. Research in Original Sources

Translations and summaries of foreign law in English may be quite helpful, but translated texts of legal materials are no substitute for the original documents. The most effective research in any legal system is conducted in the language of the country being studied.

Introductory study in an encyclopedia, treatise, or journal article may provide leads to original sources. The next step is to consult the relevant code (preferably in an edition accompanied by extensive commentary) or other statutes applicable to the problem. One should then find administrative orders and judicial decisions implementing or interpreting the legislative norms. It bears repeating that research usually begins with the code itself, and almost never, as in the United States, with a review of judicial decisions.

Basic legal sources. Most countries in the civil law system have several separately published codes. These include the basic general codes (civil, criminal, commercial, civil procedure and criminal procedure), and minor codes

which are often simply statutory compilations on specific subjects (such as taxation, labor law, and family law). The codes are usually published in frequent unannotated editions, and also in larger editions with scholarly commentary, annotations, and other aids.

In many countries, daily or weekly official gazettes contain the texts of new laws, decrees and administrative orders. These comprehensive gazettes are the official sources for new legislation, but in many countries they are poorly or infrequently indexed. Research is conducted instead in commercially published periodicals which have more thorough and timely indexing.

Because judicial decisions carry less weight in civil law countries, most jurisdictions have fewer official reports of such decisions and less developed means for finding cases by subject. In many countries, legal periodicals publish court decisions in addition to articles and other legal news. Tracking down these decisions can be difficult, but leads are provided by code commentaries and other sources.

Most larger civil law countries have both free and subscription-based legal databases similar to those available in the United States. Among the leading free sites are Legifrance <www.legifrance.gouv.fr>, with codes, the *Journal Officiel*, and cases from several French courts; and DFR (Deutschsprachiges Fallrecht) <www.oefre.unibe.ch/law/dfr/> for German materials. Other sites can be found through portals such as those offered by Hieros Gamos, the Law Library of Congress, and Cornell Law School discussed above on page 369-370.

Secondary materials. Under the civil law system, scholarly commentaries and treatises by recognized experts have considerable weight as persuasive authority. They are

discussed as "secondary materials" here in keeping with our own notion of authority, but in many instances they have greater weight than judicial decisions. The range of available texts, as in common law countries, is quite broad in both subject and quality. There are comprehensive scholarly treatises, highly specialized monographs on narrow topics, pragmatic manuals and guides for the practitioner, and simplified texts for students and popular use. For those with the necessary language skills, these works offer considerable help in legal research. Information about the literature available on specific topics can be found in legal bibliographies and guides published for particular countries, or in the general bibliographies discussed above on pages 370-373.

Foreign legal encyclopedias, particularly the French *répertoires* published by Dalloz, are often of higher quality and reputation than those in this country. Their articles are frequently written by leading legal scholars. Except for major publications such as these, however, many foreign legal sources are difficult to find outside their home countries. The American Association of Law Libraries' *Directory of Foreign Law Collections in Selected Law Libraries* (1991) may be of assistance in identifying possible holding libraries.

Civil law countries have a multitude of legal periodicals covering legal developments and often printing primary sources. In France, for example, the leading legal periodicals, *Recueil Dalloz* (1808-date) and *La Semaine Juridique* (1927-date), provide both legislative texts and judicial decisions, as well as scholarly articles. The *Index to Foreign Legal Periodicals* (1960-date, quarterly; available through various database systems including Westlaw commercial subscriptions) covers nearly 500 journals from more than 70 countries, as well as *festschriften* and other collections of essays. There are also periodical indexes published in some for-

eign countries, limited to the literature of these countries. Like foreign encyclopedias, however, these indexes — and the journals they cover — may be hard to obtain in this country.

Reference aids. Part of the difficulty of doing legal research in the civil law system stems from differences in language. Legal dictionaries can help somewhat, although a dictionary alone can provide only a superficial sense of the differences in meaning and usage.

Numerous bilingual dictionaries are available for assistance in translating foreign terms into English. Two of these, *Dahl's Law Dictionary: Spanish to English/English to Spanish* (3d ed. 1999) and *Dahl's Law Dictionary: French to English/English to French* (2d ed. 2001) are also available through LexisNexis. Several multilingual law dictionaries are also published. The standard work in English, French, and German is Robert Herbst & Alan G. Readett, *Dictionary of Commercial, Financial and Legal Terms* (3 vols., 4th & 5th eds. 1985-date). *West's Law and Commercial Dictionary in Five Languages* (2 vols., 1985) adds Italian and Spanish as well.

Citation forms for foreign legal materials can be very confusing for American lawyers. The *Bluebook* includes citation information for fifteen civil law countries, providing coverage of the most frequently cited sources. More in-depth coverage is available from *World Dictionary of Legal Abbreviations* (4 vols., 1991-date), which has separate sections for abbreviations in French, German, Hebrew, Italian, Japanese, Korean, Portuguese, and Spanish.

§12-4. CONCLUSION

Any serious legal problem involving another jurisdiction will require consultation with a lawyer trained and licensed in that jurisdiction. The resources discussed in this chapter, however, can provide a solid starting point for the American researcher.

Other than availability of materials, there is little hindrance to research in English, Canadian, or Australian law. These countries have legal research resources that are quite similar to our own and are easily accessible to American legal researchers, either for comparative study or for analysis of legal problems arising in those nations.

In researching the law of civil law countries, lawyers limited to English-language materials will be seriously handicapped. However, the increasing availability of secondary sources in English and translations now allows preliminary study of most foreign legal problems. Such study may help the American lawyer to determine the general nature of a problem, and can facilitate communication with the foreign law specialist who may be called in to assist.

APPENDIX A
SOURCES FOR STATE APPELLATE COURT CASES

■　　■　　■　　■　　■　　■　　■　　■　　■　　■

Most state appellate court cases are published in both official reports and the National Reporter System, but there are significant exceptions. Regional reporters did not begin publication until 1879 or later, and several states have discontinued official reports in recent decades and now rely on regional reporter coverage of their courts. The inclusion of volume numbers in this table indicates a reporter series that is no longer published.

This table shows major published and electronic sources for the decisions of state courts of last resort and intermediate appellate courts. Electronic coverage, which of course is subject to change, is current as of May 2003. Internet sites are listed if they provide free access to cases and maintain archives for more than just a few weeks or months. Most of the sites listed are official state sites, but commercial sites are included if they provide coverage or features unavailable from the official site. Those free sites that permit keyword searching are indicated.

Another source for recent decisions, not listed here, is lexisONE <www.lexisone.com>, which provides free access to the most recent five years of cases from all state appellate courts. These can be retrieved using LexisNexis search techniques.

In some instances, entries include earlier courts with similar functions to the current courts listed. Some court systems have changed dramatically under new state constitutions, e.g., New York in 1846 and South Carolina in 1868, but the earlier courts are not listed separately. For more precise information it may be necessary to turn to a state legal research guide (see Appendix B).

The Bluebook: A Uniform System of Citation (17th ed. 2000, pp. 188-241) has listings of state nominative reports (with abbreviations); and Cohen, Berring & Olson, *How to Find the Law* (9th ed. 1989, pages 614-662) includes more extensive coverage of nominative reports, miscellaneous reports, and sources for state trial court cases.

ALABAMA
Supreme Court
> Nominative reports, 1820-39
> 1-295 *Alabama Reports*, 1840-1976
> *Southern Reporter*, 1887 [80 Ala.]-date
> LexisNexis and Westlaw, 1820-date
> Loislaw, 1916-date
> <www.wallacejordan.com/decisions/>,
> > 1998-date [searchable]

Court of Civil Appeals
> 1-57 *Alabama Appellate Court Reports*,
> > 1911-76
> Southern Reporter, 1911 [1 Ala. App.]-date
> LexisNexis and Westlaw, 1911-date
> Loislaw, 1916-date

Court of Criminal Appeals
> 1-57 *Alabama Appellate Court Reports*, 1911-76
> Southern Reporter, 1911 [1 Ala. App.]-date
> LexisNexis and Westlaw, 1911-date
> Loislaw, 1916-date

ALASKA
Supreme Court
Pacific Reporter, 1959-date
LexisNexis, Loislaw, and Westlaw, 1959-date
<www.touchngo.com/sp/sp.htm>,
1991-date [searchable]
Court of Appeals
Pacific Reporter, 1980-date
LexisNexis, Loislaw, and Westlaw, 1980-date
<www.touchngo.com/ap/ap.htm>, 1991-date
[searchable]

ARIZONA
Supreme Court
Arizona Reports, 1866-date
Pacific Reporter, 1866 [1 Ariz.]-date
LexisNexis and Westlaw, 1866-date
Loislaw, 1925-date
<www.supreme.state.az.us/opin/>, 1998-date
Court of Appeals
1-27 *Arizona Appeals Reports*, 1965-76
Arizona Reports, 1976-date
Pacific Reporter, 1965 [1 Ariz. App.]-date
LexisNexis, Loislaw, and Westlaw, 1965-date
Division One <www.cofad1.state.az.us/
opinionfiles/opidx.htm>, 2000-date
Division Two <www.apltwo.ct.state.az.us/
ODSPlus/RecentDecisions.cfm>, 2002-date

ARKANSAS
Supreme Court
Arkansas Reports, 1837-date
South Western Reporter, 1887 [47 Ark.]-date
LexisNexis and Westlaw, 1837-date
Loislaw, 1924-date
<courts.state.ar.us/opinions/opinions.html>,
1994-date [searchable]

Court of Appeals
Arkansas Appellate Reports, 1979-date (bound with
    Arkansas Reports)
South Western Reporter, 1979 [1 Ark. App.]-date
LexisNexis, Loislaw, and Westlaw, 1979-date
<courts.state.ar.us/opinions/opinions.html>,
    1994-date [searchable]

CALIFORNIA
Supreme Court
California Reports, 1850-date
Pacific Reporter, 1883 [64 Cal.]-date
California Reporter, 1960 [53 Cal. 2d]-date
LexisNexis and Westlaw, 1850-date
Loislaw, 1899-date
<www.findlaw.com/cacases/>, 1934-date
    [searchable; registration required]

Courts of Appeal
California Appellate Reports, 1905-date
Pacific Reporter, 1905 [1 Cal. App.]-1959 [175 Cal.
    App. 2d]
California Reporter, 1960 [176 Cal. App. 2d]-date
LexisNexis, Loislaw, and Westlaw, 1905-date
<www.findlaw.com/cacases/>, 1934-date
    [searchable; registration required]

COLORADO
Supreme Court
1-200 *Colorado Reports*, 1864-1980
Pacific Reporter, 1884 [7 Colo.]-date
LexisNexis and Westlaw, 1864-date
Loislaw, 1924-date
<www.findlaw.com/11stategov/co/coca.html>,
    1998-date

Court of Appeals

1-44 *Colorado Court of Appeals Reports*, 1891-1915, 1970-80

Pacific Reporter, 1891 [1 Colo. App.]-1915, 1970-date

LexisNexis and Westlaw, 1891-1915, 1970-date

Loislaw, 1970-date

<www.findlaw.com/11stategov/co/coca.html>, 1998-date

CONNECTICUT
Supreme Court

Nominative reports, 1786-1813

Connecticut Reports, 1814-date

Atlantic Reporter, 1886 [53 Conn.]-date

LexisNexis and Westlaw, 1786-date

Loislaw, 1899-date

<www.jud.state.ct.us/external/supapp/ archiveAROsup.htm>, 2000-date [searchable]

Appellate Court

Connecticut Appellate Reports, 1983-date

Atlantic Reporter, 1983 [1 Conn. App.]-date

LexisNexis, Loislaw, and Westlaw, 1983-date

<www.jud.state.ct.us/external/supapp/ archiveAROap.htm>, 2000-date [searchable]

DELAWARE
Supreme Court

1-3 *Delaware Cases*, 1795-1830

1-59 *Delaware Reports*, 1832-1966

Atlantic Reporter, 1886 [12 Del.]-date

LexisNexis and Westlaw, 1795-date

Loislaw, 1949-date

<courts.state.de.us/supreme/opinions.htm>, 1998-date

DISTRICT OF COLUMBIA
Court of Appeals
Atlantic Reporter, 1942-date
LexisNexis, Loislaw, and Westlaw, 1942-date
<www.dcbar.org/for_lawyers/courts/court_
of_appeals/opinions.cfm>, 1998-date
[searchable]

FLORIDA
Supreme Court
1-160 *Florida Reports*, 1846-1948
Southern Reporter, 1887 [22 Fla.]-date
LexisNexis and Westlaw, 1846-date
Loislaw, 1925-date
<www.flcourts.org/sct/sctdocs/>, 1999-date
<www.findlaw.com/11stategov/fl/flca.html>,
1995-date
District Courts of Appeal
Southern Reporter, 1957-date
LexisNexis, Loislaw, and Westlaw, 1957-date
<www.flcourts.org/sct/sctdocs/>, 2000-date

GEORGIA
Supreme Court
Georgia Reports, 1846-date
South Eastern Reporter, 1887 [77 Ga.]-date
LexisNexis and Westlaw, 1846-date
Loislaw, 1939-date
<www.ganet.org/appeals/opinions/>,
1999-date [searchable]
Court of Appeals
Georgia Appeals Reports, 1907-date
South Eastern Reporter, 1907 [1 Ga. App.]-date
LexisNexis and Westlaw, 1907-date
Loislaw, 1939-date
<www.ganet.org/appeals/opinions/>, 1999-date
[searchable]

HAWAII
Supreme Court
Hawaii Reports, 1847-date
Pacific Reporter, 1884 [43 Haw.]-date
LexisNexis and Westlaw, 1847-date
Loislaw, 1924-date
<64.29.92.28/RW/Legal_Research/Hawaii/
    cases.htm>, 1989-date
<www.hawaii.gov/jud/ctops.htm>, 1998-date
Intermediate Court of Appeals
1-10 *Hawaii Appellate Reports*, 1980-94
Hawaii Reports, 1994-date
Pacific Reporter, 1980 [1 Haw. App.]-date
LexisNexis, Loislaw, and Westlaw, 1980-date
<64.29.92.28/RW/Legal_Research/Hawaii/
    cases.htm>, 1989-date
<www.hawaii.gov/jud/ctops.htm>, 1998-date

IDAHO
Supreme Court
Idaho Reports, 1866-date
Pacific Reporter, 1881 [2 Idaho]-date
LexisNexis and Westlaw, 1866-date
Loislaw, 1922-date
<www.findlaw.com/11stategov/id/idca.html>,
    1998-date
Court of Appeals
Idaho Reports, 1982-date
Pacific Reporter, 1982 [102 Idaho]-date
LexisNexis, Loislaw, and Westlaw, 1982-date
<www.findlaw.com/11stategov/id/idca.html>,
    1998-date

ILLINOIS
Supreme Court
Illinois Reports, 1819-date
North Eastern Reporter, 1884 [112 Ill.]-date

LexisNexis and Westlaw, 1819-date

Loislaw, 1925-date

<www.state.il.us/court/Opinions/Search.htm>,
1996-date [searchable]

Appellate Court

Illinois Appellate Reports, 1877-date

North Eastern Reporter, 1936 [284 Ill. App.]-date

LexisNexis and Westlaw, 1877-date

Loislaw, 1925-date

<www.state.il.us/court/Opinions/Search.htm>,
1996-date [searchable]

INDIANA

Supreme Court

Nominative reports, 1817-47

1-275 *Indiana Reports*, 1848-1981

North Eastern Reporter, 1885 [102 Ind.]-date

LexisNexis and Westlaw, 1817-date

Loislaw, 1923-date

<www.findlaw.com/11stategov/in/inca.html>,
1998-date

<www.ai.org/judiciary/opinions/>, 1999-date
[searchable]

Court of Appeals

1-182 *Indiana Court of Appeals Reports*, 1891-1979

North Eastern Reporter, 1891 [1 Ind. App.]-date

LexisNexis and Westlaw, 1891-date

Loislaw, 1921-date

<www.findlaw.com/11stategov/in/inca.html>,
1998-date

<www.ai.org/judiciary/opinions/>, 1999-date

IOWA

Supreme Court

Nominative reports, 1839-54

1-261 *Iowa Reports*, 1855-1968

North Western Reporter, 1879 [51 Iowa]-date

LexisNexis and Westlaw, 1839-date
Loislaw, 1923-date
<www.judicial.state.ia.us/supreme/>, 1998-date
Court of Appeals
North Western Reporter, 1977-date
LexisNexis, Loislaw, and Westlaw, 1977-date
<www.judicial.state.ia.us/appeals/>, 1998-date

KANSAS
Supreme Court
Nominative reports, 1858-61
Kansas Reports, 1862-date
Pacific Reporter, 1883 [30 Kan.]-date
LexisNexis and Westlaw, 1858-date
Loislaw, 1949-date
<www.kscourts.org/kscases/>, 1996-date
[searchable]
Court of Appeals
Kansas Court of Appeals Reports, 1895-1901, 1977-date
Pacific Reporter, 1895 [1 Kan. App.]-1901, 1977-date
LexisNexis and Westlaw, 1895-1901, 1977-date
Loislaw, 1977-date
<www.kscourts.org/kscases/>,
1996-date [searchable]

KENTUCKY
Supreme Court
1-314 *Kentucky Reports*, 1785-1951
South Western Reporter, 1886 [84 Ky.]-date
LexisNexis and Westlaw, 1785-date
Loislaw, 1924-date
<www.kycourts.net/Supreme/SC_
Opinions.shtm>, 1999-date [searchable]
Court of Appeals
South Western Reporter, 1976-date
LexisNexis, Loislaw, and Westlaw, 1976-date

LOUISIANA
Supreme Court
Nominative reports, 1813-30, 1841-46

1-19 *Louisiana Reports*, 1830-41

1-52 *Louisiana Annual Reports*, 1846-1900

104-263 *Louisiana Reports*, 1900-72

Southern Reporter, 1887 [39 La. Ann.]-date

LexisNexis and Westlaw, 1813-date

Loislaw, 1921-date

<www.lasc.org/opinion_search.asp>,
    1996-date [searchable]

Courts of Appeal
Nominative reports, 1881-85, 1903-23

1-19 *Louisiana Courts of Appeals Reports*, 1924-32

Southern Reporter, 1928 [9 La. App.]-date

LexisNexis and Westlaw, 1881-date

Loislaw, 1972-date

First Circuit <www.la-fcca.org/published_
    opinions.htm>, 2000-date [searchable]

Second Circuit <www.lacoa2.org/opinions.htm>,
    2001-date [searchable]

Fifth Circuit <www.fifthcircuit.org/
    published_opinions.htm>, 2001-date

MAINE
Supreme Judicial Court
1-161 *Maine Reports*, 1820-1965

Atlantic Reporter, 1886 [77 Me.]-date

LexisNexis and Westlaw, 1820-date

Loislaw, 1923-date

<www.courts.state.me.us/opinions/supreme/>,
    1997-date [searchable]

MARYLAND
Court of Appeals
Nominative reports, 1787-1851

Maryland Reports, 1851-date

Atlantic Reporter, 1886 [63 Md.]-date
LexisNexis and Westlaw, 1787-date
Loislaw, 1899-date
<www.courts.state.md.us/opinions.html>,
    1995- date [searchable]

Court of Special Appeals

Maryland Appellate Reports, 1967-date
Atlantic Reporter, 1967 [1 Md. App.]-date
LexisNexis, Loislaw, and Westlaw, 1967-date
<www.courts.state.md.us/opinions.html>,
    1995-date [searchable]

MASSACHUSETTS

Supreme Judicial Court

Massachusetts Reports, 1804-date
North Eastern Reporter, 1885 [139 Mass.]-date
LexisNexis and Westlaw, 1804-date
Loislaw, 1899-date
<www.malawyersweekly.com/sjc.cfm>, 1997-date
    [searchable]

Appeals Court

Massachusetts Appeals Court Reports, 1972-date
North Eastern Reporter, 1972 [1 Mass. App.]-date
LexisNexis, Loislaw, and Westlaw, 1972-date
<www.malawyersweekly.com/mapps.cfm>,
    1997-date [searchable]

MICHIGAN

Supreme Court

Nominative reports, 1838-47
Michigan Reports, 1847-date
North Western Reporter, 1879 [41 Mich.]-date
Westlaw, 1838-date
LexisNexis, 1843-date
Loislaw, 1923-date
<www.icle.org/michlaw/>, 1995-date
    [searchable]

Court of Appeals
Michigan Appeals Reports, 1965-date
North Western Reporter, 1965 [1 Mich. App.]-date
LexisNexis, Loislaw, and Westlaw, 1965-date
<www.icle.org/michlaw/>,
   1996-date [searchable]

MINNESOTA
Supreme Court
1-312 *Minnesota Reports*, 1851-1977
North Western Reporter, 1879 [26 Minn.]-date
LexisNexis and Westlaw, 1851-date
Loislaw, 1924-date
<www.lawlibrary.state.mn.us/archive/>,
   1996-date [searchable]
Court of Appeals
North Western Reporter, 1983-date
LexisNexis, Loislaw, and Westlaw, 1983-date
<www.lawlibrary.state.mn.us/archive/>,
   1996-date [searchable]

MISSISSIPPI
Supreme Court
1-254 *Mississippi Reports*, 1818-1966
Southern Reporter, 1887 [64 Miss.]-date
LexisNexis and Westlaw, 1818-date
Loislaw, 1924-date
<www.mssc.state.ms.us/decisions/search/
   default.asp>, 1996-date [searchable]
Court of Appeals
Southern Reporter, 1995-date
LexisNexis, Loislaw, and Westlaw, 1995-date
<www.mssc.state.ms.us/decisions/search/
   default.asp>, 1996-date [searchable]

MISSOURI
Supreme Court
1-365 *Missouri Reports*, 1821-1956
South Western Reporter, 1886 [89 Mo.]-date
LexisNexis and Westlaw, 1821-date
Loislaw, 1919-date
<www.osca.state.mo.us/courts/
pubopinions.nsf>, 1997-date [searchable]
Courts of Appeals
1-241 *Missouri Appeal Reports*, 1876-1952
South Western Reporter, 1902 [93 Mo. App.]-date
LexisNexis and Westlaw, 1876-date
Loislaw, 1919-date
<www.osca.state.mo.us/courts/
pubopinions.nsf>, 1997-date [searchable]

MONTANA
Supreme Court
Montana Reports, 1868-date
Pacific Reporter, 1884 [4 Mont.]-date
LexisNexis and Westlaw, 1868-date
Loislaw, 1924-date
<www.lawlibrary.state.mt.us>, 1997-date
[searchable]

NEBRASKA
Supreme Court
Nebraska Reports, 1860s-date
North Western Reporter, 1879 [8 Neb.]-date
LexisNexis and Westlaw, 1860s-date
Loislaw, 1949-date
<www.findlaw.com/11stategov/ne/neca.html>,
1997-date
Court of Appeals
Nebraska Appellate Reports, 1992-date
North Western Reporter, 1992 [1 Neb. App.]-date

LexisNexis, Loislaw, and Westlaw, 1992-date
<www.findlaw.com/11stategov/ne/neca.html>,
1997-date

NEVADA
Supreme Court
Nevada Reports, 1865-date
Pacific Reporter, 1884 [17 Nev.]-date
LexisNexis and Westlaw, 1865-date
Loislaw, 1924-date
<www.findlaw.com/11stategov/nv/nvca.html>,
1998-date

NEW HAMPSHIRE
Supreme Court
Nominative reports, 1803-16
New Hampshire Reports, 1816-date
Atlantic Reporter, 1886 [63 N.H.]-date
LexisNexis and Westlaw, 1816-date
Loislaw, 1874-date
<www.courts.state.nh.us/supreme/opinions/>,
1995-date

NEW JERSEY
Supreme Court
1-137 *New Jersey Law Reports*, 1789-1948
1-142 *New Jersey Equity Reports*, 1830-1948
New Jersey Reports, 1948-date
Atlantic Reporter, 1885 [47 N.J. Law,
40 N.J. Eq.]-date
LexisNexis and Westlaw, 1789-date
Loislaw, 1923-date
<lawlibrary.rutgers.edu/search.shtml>, 1994-date
[searchable]
Superior Court, Appellate Division
New Jersey Superior Court Reports, 1948-date
Atlantic Reporter, 1948 [1 N.J. Super.]-date

LexisNexis, Loislaw, and Westlaw, 1948-date
<lawlibrary.rutgers.edu/search.shtml>, 1995-date
[searchable]

NEW MEXICO
Supreme Court
New Mexico Reports, 1852-date
Pacific Reporter, 1883 [3 N.M.]-date
LexisNexis and Westlaw, 1852-date
Loislaw, 1921-date
<www.supremecourt.nm.org>, 1998-date
<www.oscn.net/applications/oscn/index.asp>,
2000-date [searchable]
Court of Appeals
New Mexico Reports, 1966-date
Pacific Reporter, 1966 [78 N.M.]-date
LexisNexis, Loislaw, and Westlaw, 1966-date
<www.supremecourt.nm.org>, 1998-date
<www.oscn.net/applications/oscn/index.asp>,
2000-date [searchable]

NEW YORK
Court of Appeals
Nominative reports, 1791-1847
New York Reports, 1847-date
North Eastern Reporter, 1885 [99 N.Y.]-date
New York Supplement, 1956 [1 N.Y.2d]-date
LexisNexis and Westlaw, 1791-date
Loislaw, 1924-date
<www.law.cornell.edu/ny/ctap/>, 1992-date
[searchable]
Supreme Court, Appellate Division
Appellate Division Reports, 1896-date
New York Supplement, 1896 [1 App. Div.]-date
LexisNexis and Westlaw, 1896-date
Loislaw, 1924-date

Third Department
<decisions.courts.state.ny.us/ad3/Search/
AppDiv3Intro.htm>, 2001-date [searchable]
Fourth Department
<www.courts.state.ny.us/ad4/court/
decision.htm>, 2000-date

NORTH CAROLINA
Supreme Court
North Carolina Reports, 1778-date
South Eastern Reporter, 1884 [96 N.C.]-date
LexisNexis, Loislaw, and Westlaw, 1778-date
<www.aoc.state.nc.us/www/public/html/
opinions.htm>, 1997-date [searchable]
<www.findlaw.com/11stategov/nc/ncca.html>,
1994-date

Court of Appeals
North Carolina Court of Appeals Reports, 1968-date
South Eastern Reporter, 1968 [1 N.C. App.]-date
LexisNexis, Loislaw, and Westlaw, 1968-date
<www.aoc.state.nc.us/www/public/html/
opinions.htm>, 1996-date [searchable]
<www.findlaw.com/11stategov/nc/ncca.html>,
1994-date

NORTH DAKOTA
Supreme Court
1-6 *Dakota Reports*, 1867-89
1-79 *North Dakota Reports*, 1890-1953
North Western Reporter, 1867 [1 Dak.]-date
LexisNexis and Westlaw, 1867-date
Loislaw, 1924-date
<www.court.state.nd.us/court/opinions.htm>,
1982-date [searchable]

Court of Appeals
North Western Reporter, 1987-date
LexisNexis, Loislaw, and Westlaw, 1987-date
<www.court.state.nd.us/Opinions/cite/
NDApp.htm>, 1998-date

OHIO
Supreme Court
1-20 *Ohio Reports*, 1821-52
Ohio State Reports, 1852-date
North Eastern Reporter, 1885 [43 Ohio St.]-date
LexisNexis and Westlaw, 1821-date
Loislaw, 1923-date
<www.sconet.state.oh.us/rod/documents/>,
1992-date [searchable]
<www.ohlawyersweekly.com/ohsc.htm>,
1997-date [searchable]
Courts of Appeals
Ohio Appellate Reports, 1913-date
North Eastern Reporter, 1923 [20 Ohio App.]-date
LexisNexis and Westlaw, 1913-date
Loislaw, 1921-date
<www.sconet.state.oh.us/rod/documents/>,
2001-date [searchable]

OKLAHOMA
Supreme Court
1-208 *Oklahoma Reports*, 1890-1953
Pacific Reporter, 1890 [1 Okla.]-date
LexisNexis and Westlaw, 1890-date
Loislaw, 1934-date
<www.oscn.net>, 1890-date [searchable]
<www.onenet.net/oklegal/sample.basic.html>,
1922-date [searchable]
Court of Criminal Appeals
1-97 *Oklahoma Criminal Reports*, 1908-53
Pacific Reporter, 1980 [1 Okla. Crim.]-date
LexisNexis, Loislaw, and Westlaw, 1908-date

<www.oscn.net>, 1908-date [searchable]
<www.onenet.net/oklegal/sample.basic.html>,
  1995-date [searchable]
Court of Civil Appeals
Pacific Reporter, 1968-date
LexisNexis, Loislaw, and Westlaw, 1968-date
<www.oscn.net>, 1968-date [searchable]
<www.onenet.net/oklegal/sample.basic.html>,
  1968-date [searchable]

OREGON
Supreme Court
Oregon Reports, 1853-date
Pacific Reporter, 1884 [11 Or.]-date
LexisNexis and Westlaw, 1853-date
Loislaw, 1924-date
<www.publications.ojd.state.or.us/supreme.htm>,
  1998-date
Court of Appeals
Oregon Reports, Court of Appeal, 1969-date
Pacific Reporter, 1969 [1 Or. App.]-date
LexisNexis, Loislaw, and Westlaw, 1969-date
<www.publications.ojd.state.or.us/appeals.htm>,
  1998-date

PENNSYLVANIA
Supreme Court
Nominative reports, 1754-1845
Pennsylvania State Reports, 1845-date
Atlantic Reporter, 1886 [108 Pa. St.]-date
LexisNexis and Westlaw, 1754-date
Loislaw, 1924-date
<www.courts.state.pa.us/Index/Opinions/
  IndexOpinions.asp>, 1996-date [searchable]
Superior Court
Pennsylvania Superior Court Reports, 1895-date
Atlantic Reporter, 1930 [102 Pa. Super.]-date

LexisNexis and Westlaw, 1895-date
Loislaw, 1923-date
<www.courts.state.pa.us/Index/Opinions/
IndexOpinions.asp>, 1997-date [searchable]
Commonwealth Court
1-168 *Pennsylvania Commonwealth Court Reports,*
1970-94
Atlantic Reporter, 1970 [1 Pa. Commw.]-date
LexisNexis, Loislaw, and Westlaw, 1970-date
<www.courts.state.pa.us/Index/Opinions/
IndexOpinions.asp>, 1997-date [searchable]

PUERTO RICO
Tribunal Supremo
1-100 *Puerto Rico Reports,* 1899-1972
Decisiones de Puerto Rico, 1899-date
LexisNexis and Westlaw, 1899-date
<www.tribunalpr.org/opiniones/>, 1998-date
Tribunal de Circuito de Apelaciones
LexisNexis, 1995-date
Westlaw, 2001-date

RHODE ISLAND
Supreme Court
1-122 *Rhode Island Reports,* 1828-1980
Atlantic Reporter, 1886 [15 R.I.]-date
LexisNexis, Loislaw, and Westlaw, 1828-date
<www.courts.state.ri.us/supreme/
publishedopinions.htm>, 1999-date
<www.findlaw.com/11stategov/ri/rica.html>,
1997-date

SOUTH CAROLINA
Supreme Court
Nominative reports, 1783-1868
South Carolina Reports, 1868-date
South Eastern Reporter, 1886 [25 S.C.]-date

Westlaw, 1783-date
LexisNexis, 1868-date
Loislaw, 1900-date
<www.law.sc.edu/opinions/opinions.htm>,
  1996-date

Court of Appeals

South Carolina Reports, 1983 [279 S.C.]-date
South Eastern Reporter, 1983-date
LexisNexis, Loislaw, and Westlaw, 1983-date
<www.law.sc.edu/ctapp/scctapp.htm>, 1999-date

SOUTH DAKOTA
Supreme Court

1-6 *Dakota Reports*, 1867-89
1-90 *South Dakota Reports*, 1890-1976
North Western Reporter, 1867 [1 Dak.]-date
LexisNexis and Westlaw, 1867-date
Loislaw, 1949-date
<www.sdbar.org/opinions/default.htm>,
  1996-date
<www.sdjudicial.com>, 1996-date [searchable]

TENNESSEE
Supreme Court

1-225 *Tennessee Reports*, 1791-1971
South Western Reporter, 1886 [85 Tenn.]-date
LexisNexis and Westlaw, 1791-date
Loislaw, 1925-date
<www.tsc.state.tn.us/opinions/tsc/oplsttsc.htm>,
  1995-date

Court of Appeals

1-63 *Tennessee Appeals Reports*, 1925-71
South Western Reporter, 1932 [16 Tenn. App.]-date
LexisNexis, Loislaw, and Westlaw, 1925-date
<www.tsc.state.tn.us/opinions/tca/
  oplsttca.htm>, 1995-date

Court of Criminal Appeals
1-4 *Tennessee Criminal Appeals Reports*, 1967-71
South Western Reporter, 1967 [1 Tenn. Crim.
   App.]-date
LexisNexis and Westlaw, 1967-date
Loislaw, 1977-date
<www.tsc.state.tn.us/opinions/tcca/
   oplstcca.htm>, 1995-date

TEXAS
Supreme Court
Nominative reports, 1840-45
1-163 *Texas Reports*, 1846-1963
South Western Reporter, 1886 [66 Tex.]-date
LexisNexis and Westlaw, 1840-date
Loislaw, 1890-date
<courtstuff.com/sct/search_o.html>, 1997-date
   [searchable]
Court of Criminal Appeals
1-30 *Texas Court of Appeals Cases*, 1876-92
31-172 *Texas Criminal Reports*, 1892-1963
South Western Reporter, 1886 [21 Tex. App.]-date
LexisNexis and Westlaw, 1876-date
Loislaw, 1892-date
<www.cca.courts.state.tx.us>, 1998-date
Courts of Appeals
1-63 *Texas Civil Appeals Reports*, 1892-1911
South Western Reporter, 1892 [1 Tex. Civ.
   App.]-date
LexisNexis and Westlaw, 1892-date
Loislaw, 1892-1911 and 1949-date
First District <www.1stcoa.courts.state.tx.us>,
   1999-date [searchable]
Second District <www.2ndcoa.courts.state.tx.us>,
   2000-date [searchable]
Fourth District <www.4thcoa.courts.state.tx.us>,
   1998-date [searchable]

Thirteenth District
    <www.13thcoa.courts.state.tx.us>,
    2000-date [searchable]
Fourteenth District
    <www.14thcoa.courts.state.tx.us>,
    1999-date [searchable]

UTAH
Supreme Court
1-123, 1-30 2d *Utah Reports*, 1861-1974
Pacific Reporter, 1884 [3 Utah]-date
LexisNexis and Westlaw, 1861-date
Loislaw, 1923-date
<www.utcourts.gov/opinions/>, 1996-date
<www.oscn.net/applications/oscn/index.asp>,
    1861-date [searchable]
Court of Appeals
Pacific Reporter, 1987-date
LexisNexis, Loislaw, and Westlaw, 1987-date
<www.utcourts.gov/opinions/>, 1997-date
<www.oscn.net/applications/oscn/index.asp>,
    1987-date [searchable]

VERMONT
Supreme Court
Nominative reports, 1789-1826
Vermont Reports, 1826-date
Atlantic Reporter, 1885 [58 Vt.]-date
Westlaw, 1789-date
LexisNexis, 1826-date
Loislaw, 1924-date
<dol.state.vt.us/www_root/000000/html/
    supct.html>, 1993-date

VIRGINIA
Supreme Court
Virginia Reports, 1790-date
South Eastern Reporter, 1887 [82 Va.]-date
LexisNexis and Westlaw, 1790-date
Loislaw, 1931-date
<www.courts.state.va.us/opin.htm>, 1995-date
<www.valawyersweekly.com/vasc.cfm>,
     1998-date [searchable]

Court of Appeals
Virginia Court of Appeals Reports, 1985-date
South Eastern Reporter, 1985 [1 Va. App.]-date
LexisNexis, Loislaw, and Westlaw, 1985-date
<www.courts.state.va.us/opin.htm>, 1995-date
<www.valawyersweekly.com/vacoa.cfm>,
     1997-date [searchable]

WASHINGTON
Supreme Court
1-3 *Washington Territory Reports*, 1854-89
Washington Reports, 1889-date
Pacific Reports, 1884 [2 Wash. Terr.]-date
LexisNexis and Westlaw, 1854-date
Loislaw, 1925-date
<www.mrsc.org>, 1939-date [searchable]
<www.findlaw.com/11stategov/wa/waca.html>,
     1998-date

Court of Appeals
Washington Appellate Reports, 1969-date
Pacific Reporter, 1969 [1 Wash. App.]-date
LexisNexis, Loislaw, and Westlaw, 1969-date
<www.mrsc.org>, 1969-date [searchable]
<www.findlaw.com/11stategov/wa/waca.html>,
     1998-date

WEST VIRGINIA
Supreme Court of Appeals
West Virginia Reports, 1864-date
South Eastern Reporter, 1884 [29 W. Va.]-date
LexisNexis and Westlaw, 1864-date
Loislaw, 1923-date
<www.state.wv.us/wvsca/opinions.htm>,
    1991-date [searchable]

WISCONSIN
Supreme Court
Nominative reports, 1839-53
Wisconsin Reports, 1853-date
North Western Reporter, 1879 [46 Wis.]-date
LexisNexis and Westlaw, 1839-date
Loislaw, 1939-date
<www.wicourts.gov/supreme/submenu/
    opinions.htm>, 1995-date [searchable]
<www.wisbar.org/Wis/>, 1995-date [searchable]
Court of Appeals
Wisconsin Reports, 1978-date
North Western Reporter, 1978 [85 Wis. 2d]-date
LexisNexis, Loislaw, and Westlaw, 1978-date
<www.wicourts.gov/appeals/sub_web/
    opinions.htm>, 1995-date [searchable]
<www.wisbar.org/WisCtApp/>, 1995-date
    [searchable]

WYOMING
Supreme Court
1-80 *Wyoming Reports*, 1870-1959
Pacific Reporter, 1884 [3 Wyo.]-date
LexisNexis and Westlaw, 1870-date
Loislaw, 1924-date
<wyomcases.courts.state.wy.us/applications/
    oscn/index.asp>, 1996-date [searchable]

APPENDIX B
STATE RESEARCH GUIDES

■　　■　　■　　■　　■　　■　　■　　■　　■　　■

Because of variations in legal materials from state to state, a general research guide like this *Nutshell* cannot provide the necessary detail for specific state sources. These guides are therefore suggested for further information on the materials of individual states. The list includes several journal articles discussing state practice materials and research methods, and a few chapters in a new looseleaf volume edited by Frank G. Houdek, *State Practice Materials: Annotated Bibliographies* (2002-date). So far this collection only has chapters for four states and the District of Columbia, but its value will increase with its coverage. The American Association of Law Libraries has issued a series of short but useful guides to state materials or government documents, but these titles are generally listed here only if no other recent guide is available for that state.

Other works listing research guides and other basic resources for each state include William H. Manz, *Guide to State Legislative and Administrative Materials* (biennial), and "State Legal Publications and Information Sources," in Kendall F. Svengalis, *Legal Information Buyer's Guide & Reference Manual* (annual).

Alabama	Gary Orlando Lewis, *Legal Research in Alabama: How to Find and Understand the Law in Alabama* (2001).
	Lynne B. Kitchens & Timothy A. Lewis, "Alabama Practice Materials: A Selected Annotated Bibliography," 82 Law Libr. J. 703 (1990).
Alaska	Aimee Ruzicka, *Alaska Legal and Law-Related Publications: A Guide for Law Librarians* (1984).
Arizona	Kathy Shimpock-Vieweg & Marianne Sidorski Alcorn, *Arizona Legal Research Guide* (1992).
Arkansas	Kathryn C. Fitzhugh, "Arkansas Practice Materials II: A Selective Annotated Bibliography," 21 U. Ark. Little Rock L.J. 363 (1999).
California	Larry D. Dershem, *California Legal Research Handbook* (1997).
	John K. Hanft, *Legal Research in California* (4th ed. 2001).
	Daniel W. Martin, *Henke's California Law Guide* (6th ed. 2002).
Colorado	Mitch Fontenot, "Colorado Practice Materials: A Selective Annotated Bibliography," 88 Law Libr. J. 427 (1996).

Connecticut   Shirley Bysiewicz, *Sources of Connecticut Law* (1987).

Lawrence G. Cheeseman & Arlene C. Bielefeld, *The Connecticut Legal Research Handbook* (1992).

Jonathan Saxon, "Connecticut Practice Materials: A Selective Annotated Bibliography," 91 Law Libr. J. 139 (1999).

Delaware   Patrick J. Charles & David K. King, "Delaware Practice Materials: A Selective Annotated Bibliography," 89 Law Libr. J. 349 (1997).

District of   Leah F. Chanin, "Legal Research in the
Columbia   District of Columbia," in *Legal Research in the District of Columbia, Maryland and Virginia* (2d ed. 2000).

Michelle Wu, "District of Columbia Practice Materials: A Selective Annotated Bibliography," in *State Practice Materials: Annotated Bibliographies* (Frank G. Houdek ed., 2002).

Florida   Barbara J. Busharis & Suzanne E. Rowe, *Florida Legal Research: Sources, Process, and Analysis* (2d ed. 2002).

Betsy L. Stupski, *Guide to Florida Legal Research* (6th ed. 2001).

Georgia   Leah F. Chanin & Suzanne L. Cassidy, *Guide to Georgia Legal Research and Legal History* (1990).

Nancy P. Johnson & Nancy Adams
Deel, "Researching Georgia Law
(1998 Edition)," 14 Ga. St. U. L.
Rev. 545 (1998).

Hawaii
Richard F. Kahle, Jr., *How to Research
Constitutional, Legislative, and Statutory
History in Hawaii* (rev. ed. 1997).

Idaho
Leinaala R. Seeger, "Idaho Practice
Materials: A Selective Annotated
Bibliography," 87 Law Libr. J. 534
(1995).

Illinois
Frank G. Houdek & Jean McKnight,
"An Annotated Bibliography of Legal
Research Tools," 16 S. Ill. U. L.J. 767
(1992).

Laurel Wendt, *Illinois Legal Research
Manual* (1988).

Mark E. Wojcik, *Illinois Legal Research*
(forthcoming 2003).

Indiana
Linda K. Fariss & Keith A. Buckley,
*An Introduction to Indiana State
Publications for the Law Librarian* (1982).

Iowa
John D. Edwards, *Iowa Legal Research
Guide* (2003).

Kansas
Joseph A. Custer, ed., *Kansas Legal
Research and Reference Guide* (2d ed. 1997).

Joseph A. Custer, "Kansas Practice
Materials: A Selective Annotated

Bibliography," in *State Practice Materials: Annotated Bibliographies* (Frank G. Houdek ed., 2002).

Kentucky   Kurt X. Metzmeier et al., *Kentucky Legal Research Manual* (2d ed. 2002).

Louisiana   Win-Shin S. Chiang, *Louisiana Legal Research* (2d ed. 1990).

Maine   William W. Wells, *Maine Legal Research Guide* (1989).

Maryland   Pamela J. Gregory, "Legal Research in Maryland," in *Legal Research in the District of Columbia, Maryland and Virginia* (2d ed. 2000).

Massachusetts   Mary Ann Neary, ed., *Handbook of Legal Research in Massachusetts* (rev ed. 2002).

Michigan   Richard L. Beer & Judith J. Field, *Michigan Legal Literature: An Annotated Guide* (2d ed. 1991).

                Nancy L. Bosh, *The Research Edge: Finding Law and Facts Fast* (1993).

Minnesota   Vicente E. Garces, "Minnesota Practice Materials: A Selective Annotated Bibliography," in *State Practice Materials: Annotated Bibliographies* (Frank G. Houdek ed., 2002).

                John Tessner et al., *Minnesota Legal Research Guide* (2d ed. 2002).

Mississippi   Scott D. DeLeve & Anne M. Klingen,
               "Mississippi Practice Materials: A
               Selective Annotated Bibliography," in
               *State Practice Materials: Annotated
               Bibliographies* (Frank G. Houdek ed.,
               2002).

Missouri   Mary Ann Nelson, *Guide to Missouri
               State Documents and Selected Law-Related
               Materials* (1991).

Montana   Stephen R. Jordan, *A Guide to Montana
               Legal Research* (6th ed. 1999).

Nebraska   Patrick J. Charles et al., *Lexis Publishing's
               Research Guide to Nebraska Law* (2001 ed.).

               Beth Smith, "Nebraska Practice
               Materials: A Selective Annotated
               Bibliography," 79 Neb. L. Rev. 118
               (2000).

Nevada   G. LeGrande Fletcher, "Nevada Practice
               Materials: A Selective Annotated
               Bibliography," 91 Law Libr. J. 313 (1999).

New Jersey   Cameron Allen, *A Guide to New Jersey
               Legal Bibliography and Legal History* (1984).

               Paul Axel-Lute, *New Jersey Legal Research
               Handbook* (4th ed. 1998), with Web
               supplement <www.rci.rutgers.edu/
               ~axellute/njlrsupp.html>.

New Mexico   Patricia Wagner & Mary Woodward,
               Guide to New Mexico State Publications
               (2d ed. 1991).

Mary A. Woodward, "New Mexico Practice Materials: A Selective Annotated Bibliography," 84 Law Libr. J. 93 (1992).

New York   Ellen M. Gibson, *New York Legal Research Guide* (2d ed. 1998).

North Carolina Jean Sinclair McKnight, *North Carolina Legal Research Guide* (1994).

Ohio   James Leonard, "A Select, Annotated Bibliography of Ohio Practice Materials," 17 Ohio N.U. L. Rev. 265 (1990).

Melanie K. Putnam & Susan Schaefgen, *Ohio Legal Research Guide* (1997).

Oklahoma   Marilyn K. Nicely, *Oklahoma Legal and Law-Related Documents and Publications: A Selected Bibliography* (2d ed. 1997).

Oregon   Karen S. Beck, "Oregon Practice Materials: A Selective Annotated Bibliography," 88 Law Libr. J. 288 (1996).

Pennsylvania   Frank Y. Liu et al., *Pennsylvania Legal Research Handbook* (2001).

Puerto Rico   Carlos I. Gorrín Peralta, *Fuentes y Proceso de Investigación Jurídica* (1991).

Luis Muñiz Argüelles & Migdalia Fraticelli Torres, *La Investigación Jurídica: Fuentes Puertorriqueñas, Norteamericanas y Españolas* (3d ed. 2000).

Rhode Island Colleen McConaghy, *Selective Bibliography for the State of Rhode Island: State Documents and Law-Related Materials* (1993).

South Carolina Paula Gail Benson & Deborah Ann Davis, *A Guide to South Carolina Legal Research and Citation* (1991).

Duncan E. Alford, "South Carolina Practice Materials: A Selective, Annotated Bibliography," Legal Reference Services Q., Winter 1999, at 23.

South Dakota Delores A. Jorgensen, *South Dakota Legal Research Guide* (2d ed. 1999).

Tennessee Lewis L. Laska, *Tennessee Legal Research Handbook* (1977).

D. Cheryn Picquet & Reba A. Best, *Law and Government Publications of the State of Tennessee: A Bibliographic Guide* (1988).

Texas Lydia M.V. Brandt, *Texas Legal Research: An Essential Lawyering Skill* (1995).

Karl T. Gruben & James E. Hambleton, eds., *A Reference Guide to Texas Law and Legal History: Sources and Documentation* (2d ed. 1987).

Brandon D. Quarles & Matthew C. Cordon, *Legal Research for the Texas Practitioner* (2003).

Pamela R. Tepper & Peggy N. Kerley, *Texas Legal Research* (2d ed. 1997).

Utah	Kory D. Staheli, "Utah Practice Materials: A Selective Annotated Bibliography," 87 Law Libr. J. 28 (1995).
Vermont	Virginia Wise, *A Bibliographical Guide to the Vermont Legal System* (2d ed. 1991).
Virginia	John D. Eure & Robert D. Murphy, Jr., eds., *A Guide to Legal Research in Virginia* (4th ed. 2002).
	Leslie A. Lee, "Virginia Practice Materials: A Selective Annotated Bibliography," in *State Practice Materials: Annotated Bibliographies* (Frank G. Houdek ed., 2002).
	Sarah K. Wiant, "Legal Research in Virginia," in *Legal Research in the District of Columbia, Maryland and Virginia* (2d ed. 2000).
Washington	Penny A. Hazelton et al., *Washington Legal Researcher's Deskbook 3d* (2002).
West Virginia	Sandra Stemple et al., *West Virginia Legal Bibliography* (1990).
Wisconsin	Ellen J. Platt & Mary J. Koshollek, "Wisconsin Practice Materials: A Selective, Annotated Bibliography," 90 Law Libr. J. 219 (1998).
	Ellen J. Platt & Mary J. Koshollek, *Wisconsin Practice Materials: A Selective, Annotated Bibliography* (1999).

Wyoming

Nancy S. Greene, *Wyoming State Legal Documents: An Annotated Bibliography* (1985).

APPENDIX C
TOPICAL LOOSELEAF AND ELECTRONIC SERVICES

■　■　■　■　■　■　■　■　■　■

This is a selective list of topical services useful in legal research. Most services are available in numerous formats, including print, CD-ROM, and online versions, sometimes with slight variations in name. Electronic options are indicated in brackets, and italic type indicates services available only electronically. Basic criteria for inclusion are frequent supplementation (at least bimonthly) and publication of primary documents (either abstracts or full texts). For regularly updated and more comprehensive listings, see publisher websites or the annual *Legal Looseleafs in Print*.

Abbreviation	Publisher
BNA	Bureau of National Affairs <www.bna.com>
CCH	CCH Inc. <www.cch.com>
LRP	LRP Publications <www.lrp.com>
RIA	Thomson RIA <www.riahome.com>
Thompson	Thompson Publishing Group, Inc. <www.thompson.com>

Advertising

Advertising Law Guide (CCH), monthly
[CD, Internet]
Financial Institutions Advertising Law—Federal
(CCH), monthly
Financial Institutions Advertising Law—State (CCH),
monthly

Alcoholic Beverages

Liquor Control Law Reports (CCH), biweekly

Banking

Bank Compliance Guide (CCH), monthly
[CD, Internet]
Banking Compliance Library (CCH), monthly
[CD, Internet]
Banking Report (BNA), weekly *[Internet]*
Federal Banking Law Reporter (CCH), weekly
[CD, Internet]
Financial Privacy Law Guide (CCH), monthly
State Banking Law Reporter (CCH), monthly
[CD, Internet]

Bankruptcy

Bankruptcy Law Reporter (BNA), weekly *[Internet]*
Bankruptcy Law Reports (CCH), biweekly

Commercial Law

Consumer Credit Guide (CCH), biweekly
[CD, Internet]
Mortgage Compliance Guide (CCH) [CD, Internet]
Personal Loan Compliance Guide (CCH), monthly
[CD, Internet]
RICO Business Disputes Guide (CCH), monthly
[CD, Internet]
Secured Transactions Guide (CCH), biweekly
[CD, Internet]

Communications

Communications Regulation (Pike & Fischer),
weekly *[CD, Internet, LexisNexis]*
Media Law Reporter (BNA), weekly

Computers and Internet

Electronic Commerce & Law Report (BNA),
weekly *[Internet]*
Guide to Computer Law (CCH), monthly
[CD, Internet]
Internet Law & Regulation (Pike & Fischer)
[CD, Internet]

Corporations

Business Strategies (CCH), monthly
Corporate Practice Series (BNA), weekly *[Internet]*
Corporate Secretary's Guide (CCH), monthl
[CD, Internet]
Corporation (Aspen Law & Business), biweekly
[CD, Internet]
Mergers & Acquisitions Law Report (BNA), weekly

Criminal Law

Criminal Law Reporter (BNA), weekly *[Internet]*

Disabilities

ADA Compliance Guide (Thompson), monthly
[Internet]
Accommodating Disabilities: Business Management
Guide (CCH), monthly *[CD, Internet]*
National Disability Law Reporter (LRP), biweekly
[CD, Westlaw]

Education Law

Early Childhood Law and Policy Reporter (LRP),
monthly *[CD]*
Individuals with Disabilities Education Law
Reporter (LRP), biweekly *[CD, Westlaw]*

Election Law

Federal Election Campaign Financing Guide (CCH), monthly

Employment and Labor Law

Collective Bargaining Negotiations and Contracts (BNA), biweekly

Employment and Training Reporter (MII Publications), weekly

Employee Relations (CCH), monthly *[CD, Internet]*

Employment Coordinator (West), monthly *[CD]*

Employment Guide (BNA), monthly *[CD, Internet]*

Family and Medical Leave Handbook (Thompson), monthly *[Internet]*

Government Employee Relations Report (BNA), weekly *[Internet]*

Labor Arbitration Information System (LRP), monthly *[CD]*

Labor Relations (CCH), biweekly *[CD, Internet]*

Labor Relations Reporter (BNA), weekly *[CD, Internet]*

Wages / Hours Reporter (CCH), biweekly *[CD, Internet]*

Employment Discrimination

Employment Discrimination Coordinator (West), biweekly *[CD]*

Employment Practices Guide (CCH), biweekly *[CD, Internet]*

Fair Employment Practices (BNA), weekly *[CD, Internet]*

Energy Law

Energy Management and Federal Energy Guidelines (CCH), monthly

Nuclear Regulation Reporter (CCH), bimonthly

Utilities Law Reporter (CCH), bimonthly

Environmental Law

  Chemical Regulation Reporter (BNA), weekly
    [CD, Internet]

  Environment Reporter (BNA), weekly
    [CD, Internet]

  Environmental Due Diligence Guide (BNA),
    monthly

  Environmental Law Reporter (Environmental Law
    Institute), monthly *[CD, Internet, LexisNexis,
    Westlaw]*

  International Environment Reporter (BNA), biweekly
    [Internet]

  Right-to-Know Planning Guide (BNA), biweekly
    [Internet]

  Toxics Law Reporter (BNA), weekly *[Internet]*

  Underground Storage Tank Guide (Thompson),
    monthly

Estate Planning and Taxation

  CCH Financial and Estate Planning, monthly
    [CD, Internet]

  Estate Planning & Taxation Coordinator (RIA),
    biweekly *[CD]*

  Federal Estate and Gift Tax Reports (CCH), weekly
    [CD, Internet]

  Inheritance, Estate and Gift Tax Reports: State
    (CCH), monthly

  United States Tax Reporter: Estate and Gift Taxes
    (RIA), biweekly *[CD, Internet, Westlaw]*

Excise Taxation

  Federal Excise Tax Reports (CCH), monthly
    [CD, Internet]

  United States Tax Reporter: Excise Taxes (RIA),
    monthly *[CD, Internet, Westlaw]*

Family Law
    Family Law Reporter (BNA), weekly *[Internet]*
    Family Law Tax Guide (CCH), monthly

Federal Taxation (General and Income)
    CCH Internet Tax Research Network [Internet only]
    CCH Federal Tax Service (CCH), monthly
        [CD, Internet]
    Federal Tax Coordinator 2d (RIA), weekly
        [CD, Internet, Westlaw]
    Federal Tax Guide (CCH), bimonthly *[Internet]*
    Federal Tax Research Library / OneDisc (Tax Analysts,
        Inc.) [CD, Internet]
    Kleinrock's TaxExpert Online (Kleinrock Publishing)
        [Internet]
    Standard Federal Tax Reporter *(CCH), weekly [CD,*
        Internet]
    United States Tax Reporter (RIA), weekly *[CD,*
        Internet, Westlaw]

Food and Drug
    Food, Drug and Cosmetic Law Reporter (CCH),
        weekly *[CD, Internet]*
    Guide to U.S. Food Labeling Law (Thompson),
        monthly
    Medical Devices Reporter (CCH), monthly
        [CD, Internet]

Foundations and Charities
    Charitable Giving and Solicitation (RIA), monthly
    Exempt Organizations Reports (CCH), monthly
        [CD, Internet]

Franchises
    Business Franchise Guide (CCH), monthly
        [CD, Internet]

Government Contracts

Cost Accounting Standards Guide (CCH), monthly
[CD, Internet]

Federal Contracts Report (BNA), weekly [Internet]

Federal Grants Management Handbook (Thompson),
monthly [Internet]

Government Contracts Reporter (CCH) [CD, Internet]

Health Care

Health Care Policy Report (BNA), weekly [Internet]

Health Law Reporter (BNA), weekly [Internet]

Healthcare Compliance Reporter (CCH) [CD, Internet]

Medicare and Medicaid Guide (CCH), weekly
[CD, Internet]

Medicare Report (BNA), weekly [CD, Internet]

Housing and Real Estate

Fair Housing / Fair Lending (Aspen Publishers,
Inc.), monthly [Internet]

Housing and Development Reporter (West),
bimonthly [CD]

Intellectual Property

Patent, Trademark & Copyright Journal (BNA),
weekly [Internet]

Copyright Law Reporter (CCH), monthly

United States Patents Quarterly (BNA), weekly
[CD, Internet]

International Business and Taxation

International Trade Reporter (BNA), weekly [Internet]

U.S. Taxation of International Operations (RIA),
semimonthly

Lawyers and Legal Ethics

ABA/BNA Lawyer's Manual on Professional
Conduct, biweekly [Internet]

Ethics in Government Reporter (CCH), monthly

National Reporter on Legal Ethics and Professional
Responsibility (LexisNexis), monthly *[Lexis]*

Legislation
Congressional Index (CCH), weekly

Native Americans
Indian Law Reporter (American Indian Lawyer
Training Program), monthly

Occupational Safety and Health
Employment Safety and Health Guide (CCH),
monthly *[CD, Internet]*
Occupational Safety & Health Reporter (BNA),
weekly *[CD, Internet]*

Partnerships and S Corporations
Partnership Tax Planning and Practice (CCH),
monthly
S Corporations Guide (CCH), monthly

Pensions and Compensation
COBRA Guide (CCH), monthly *[CD, Internet]*
Compliance Guide for Plan Administrators (CCH),
monthly *[CD, Internet]*
Employee Benefits Compliance Coordinator (RIA),
monthly
Employee Benefits Management (CCH), biweekly
[CD, Internet]
Executive Compensation and Taxation Coordinator
(RIA), monthly
Fringe Benefits Tax Guide (CCH), monthly
[CD, Internet]
Individual Retirement Plans Guide (CCH), monthly
[CD, Internet]
Payroll Management Guide (CCH), weekly
[CD, Internet]

Pension & Benefits Reporter (BNA), weekly *[Internet]*
Pension and Profit Sharing (RIA), weekly *[CD]*
Pension Coordinator (RIA), weekly *[CD]*
Pension Plan Guide (CCH), weekly *[CD, Internet]*

Products Liability and Consumer Safety

Consumer Product Safety Guide (CCH), biweekly
[CD, Internet]
Product Safety & Liability Reporter (BNA), weekly
[Internet]
Products Liability Reporter (CCH), biweekly
[CD, Internet]

Securities and Commodities

Blue Sky Law Reporter (CCH), bimonthly
[CD, Internet]
Commodity Futures Law Reporter (CCH), bimonthly
[CD, Internet]
Derivatives Regulation Law Reporter (CCH),
bimonthly
Federal Securities Law Reports (CCH), weekly
[CD, Internet]
Global Capital Markets Internet Library (CCH) [Internet]
Insurance Securities Law Reporter (CCH), monthly
[CD, Internet]
Mutual Funds Guide (CCH), monthly
SEC Compliance: Financial Reporting and Forms
(RIA), monthly *[Internet]*
Securities Regulation & Law Report (BNA), weekly
[Internet]
Securities Regulation (RIA), monthly *[Internet]*

State and Local Taxation

All States Tax Guide (RIA), biweekly *[CD, Internet]*
State and Local Taxes (RIA), weekly *[CD]*

State Tax Guide (CCH), biweekly *[CD, Internet]*
State Tax Reporters (CCH) (for each state), monthly
[CD, Internet]

Supreme Court
United States Law Week (BNA), weekly *[Internet]*

Taxation
See Federal Taxation (General and Income) and
specific headings

Trade Regulation
Antitrust & Trade Regulation Report (BNA), weekly
[Internet]
State Unfair Trade Practice Law (CCH), monthly
Trade Regulation Reporter (CCH), weekly
[CD, Internet]

Transportation
Aviation Law Reporter (CCH), biweekly
[CD, Internet]
Federal Carriers Reporter (CCH), biweekly
Motor Carrier — Freight Forwarder Service
(Hawkins Publishing), monthly
Rail Carrier Service (Hawkins Publishing), monthly
Shipping Regulation (Pike & Fischer), biweekly

Unemployment Insurance / Social Security
Social Security Reporter (CCH) *[CD, Internet]*
Unemployment Insurance Reporter (CCH)
[CD, Internet]

Workers' Compensation
Workers' Compensation: Business Management
Guide (CCH), monthly *[CD, Internet]*

WEBSITE INDEX

■　　■　　■　　■　　■　　■　　■　　■　　■　　■

References are to pages

Boldface reference are to exhibits

See also title and subject indexes

Note: This index does not include websites cited in the appendices. A regularly updated set of links to all websites mentioned in the book, listed by page and including the appendices, is available online <www.law.virginia.edu/nutshell>.

TITLE INDEX

■ ■ ■ ■ ■ ■ ■ ■ ■

References are to pages

Boldface reference are to exhibits

See also website and subject indexes

SUBJECT INDEX

■　■　■　■　■　■　■　■　■

References are to pages

Boldface references are to exhibits

See also website and title indexes